The Unruly Life of

WOODY ALLEN

A BIOGRAPHY

Marion Meade

SCRIBNER

SCRIBNER
1230 Avenue of the Americas
New York, NY 10020

SCRIBNER and design are trademarks of Macmillan Library Reference USA, Inc.,
used under license by Simon & Schuster, the publisher of this work.

DESIGNED BY ERICH HOBBING

Set in Adobe Garamond

Manufactured in the United States of America

1   3   5   7   9   10   8   6   4   2

Library of Congress Cataloging-in-Publication Data

Meade, Marion.
The unruly life of Woody Allen: a biography/Marion Meade.
p. cm.
Includes bibliographical references and index.
1. Allen, Woody.
2. Motion picture producers and directors—United States—Biography.
I. Title.
PN1998.3.A45 M43 2000
791.43'092—dc21
[B]   99-045482

ISBN 0-684-83374-3

For Katharine Rose Sprague

CONTENTS

Contents

AUTHOR'S NOTE

Sources for Woody Allen's quotations are cited in the Notes.

PROLOGUE

Grapes of Wrath

It was crazy weather for January. A sudden balmy spell swept a froth of showers and the fresh breezes of April into the city in the dead of winter. On Fifth Avenue, tangled morning traffic inched south toward the crosstown intersection at Seventy-second Street. Under a mottled gray sky, packs of MTA buses, white-and-blue, bunched in twos and threes, crept like a rare breed of tiger down the puddled asphalt of the Upper East Side, swerving royally past fortresses guarded by chandeliered lobbies and spiked gates (where you could buy a full-floor cooperative of eighteen rooms for $14 million); double-parked limousines studded with diplomatic license plates; and imperial-guard doormen all armed with glistening black umbrellas and silver whistles. On the side of every building was clearly posted the constitutional law of the land: ALL DELIVERIES MUST GO THROUGH SERVICE ENTRANCE.

Number 930 Fifth Avenue is a creamy-colored chunk of limestone and brick, its shiny steel-trimmed Art Deco canopy not facing Central Park but located around the corner on narrow East Seventy-fourth Street. The building's shareholders live in big apartments with servants' quarters behind the kitchen and wood-burning fireplaces. More often than not, they own country houses. While 930 does not happen to be among the Avenue's elite *Social Register* addresses—those dozen or so buildings considered white-glove—it is definitely blue-chip, and folks feel particular about their neighbors. They are partial to prospective buyers who maintain a modest profile, which is why entertainers with squealing fans never manage to make it past the co-op board.

Their most famous tenant is a man living in the duplex penthouse, whose double terraces afford a sweeping view of the park—the Bethesda Fountain, the lake, and Strawberry Fields to the west. (The penthouse had been written up in *Architectural Digest.*) He had purchased the eight-room apartment twenty-two years earlier, just as he was achieving fame and fortune in films, after being hailed by one and all as a brilliant young stand-up comedian, the

11

comic's comic, and he had lived there in comfort for most of his adult life. In December he turned fifty-six. He still weighed 128 pounds, but his boyish physique had begun to show signs of wear, and he looked like a smaller, frailer version of himself. Even though he scorned face-lifts, as well as nip-and-tucks, his raggedy reddish hair was stabilized with transplants and dye and combed forward to make himself look youthful. He continued to sport the uniform of a sixties college student: cotton sport shirts, cashmere sweaters, khakis, and tweed jackets. To those who crossed his path in the lobby, he seemed uncommonly reserved. Some of his neighbors judged him a sweetheart who could always be counted on for generous donations to the block association. But to others he was a bit of a sourpuss.

The trouble was that he did not, on the whole, enjoy people very much. There were plenty of things he did appreciate—the New York Knicks, Groucho's gags, Mahler's Fourth Symphony—but he had never felt at ease around people (with some exceptions) or pets and animals (no exceptions). Riding the elevator up to his penthouse, he was known to face the wall like Greta Garbo or stick his nose in a paper to avoid conversation.

On this second Monday of January, after sleeping his usual seven hours, he woke up in his king-size, four-poster, canopy bed with a blue-calico spread. Outside his window, the skies were overcast and it was sprinkling. When the weather was gray and drizzly, he felt reassured that life would go on forever. Sunny days made him want to hide under the covers and think of dying.

A creature of habit, he seldom varied his early-morning routine of treadmill and shower, followed by having his regular breakfast of prune juice and Cheerios with raisins and sliced bananas as he read the *New York Times*. An article reported that he had attended a cocktail party on Friday night, after a private screening of a picture produced by his best friend, and that he sipped a lovely Pavillon Blanc du Château Margaux 1986. After finishing the *Times,* he practiced his clarinet for an hour and then departed for his editing office. Ordinarily, he breezed around the city in his black Mercedes sedan, or a rattling old station wagon, with his driver Don Harris behind the wheel. However, he preferred walking the thirteen blocks to his office at 575 Park Avenue, usually following the same route. At the intersection of Seventy-fourth Street and Madison Avenue, he headed south past Clyde Chemists, which delivers prescriptions to the luxury buildings on Fifth Avenue; past Ralph Lauren's flagship store where he had shot scenes for *Alice,* notably the one in which an invisible Joe Mantegna sneaks into a changing booth with supermodel Elle Macpherson; past the plush Polo restaurant in the Westbury Hotel—a block of cherry-red awnings, where you could spend sixteen dollars on a half portion of fettuccine with fresh crepes, Swiss chard, and mushroom cream; and finally into the valley of the couture ghetto—the houses of Gianni Versace, Giorgio Armani, Valentino—before turning east to Park Avenue.

This morning, he was working on a new picture with his editor, Sandy Morse, who had been with him for fourteen movies. At present, the movie's working title was "Woody Allen Fall Project '91," but eventually it would be called *Husbands and Wives*. Over the years constant experimentation had enabled him to devise an efficient method of working. He shot scenes in one or two setups; dispensed with close-ups and worked only in master shots; eliminated actors' rehearsals and allowed them to change dialogue; and seldom offered direction—all shortcuts allowing him to finish a picture before he got sick to death of it. This time, the use of handheld-camera techniques and long takes running up to nine minutes permitted an even hastier shoot than usual. It was crude, off-the-cuff filmmaking that, in the hands of a less-confident artist, could have spelled amateur, but for him it meant principal photography could be completed ahead of schedule. With every picture, he started out with a strong idea. Unfortunately, however hard he tried, the original idea, gradually diluted along the way, never made it to the screen exactly as planned. Personally, he often said, he didn't care one way or the other what people thought of his films, just as he never saw his pictures after release and never read reviews. More and more, as he grew older, he thought of his work as self-therapy, a means, he said, of keeping busy "so I don't get depressed." But even before the reshoots, he felt good about "Woody Allen Fall Project '91," which was coming in under budget. Already in the pipeline was his next project—his twenty-third film—a murder mystery in which he would play an amateur detective. Shooting would begin in September.

Midway through the day, an assistant ordered takeout for him. It was his regular lunch, the same type of sandwich that he had eaten for the last forty-five years—tuna salad (or occasionally turkey for a change), no lettuce, no tomato, on healthful white bread, followed by a Nestlé Crunch bar or chocolate cake and coffee. On a typical winter evening, after leaving his office, he could be found at Madison Square Garden, watching the New York Knicks from his courtside seats behind the scorer's table. On Monday nights, he would head to his weekly concert at Michael's Pub on East Fifty-fifth Street, where he had been playing New Orleans jazz for more than two decades. Afterward, he would go home, get a bite to eat, usually chocolate-chip cookies washed down with two glasses of milk, and go to bed.

All things considered, there was much for Woody Allen to feel pleased about. In recent months, he had earned $2 million for a series of TV commercials promoting Italy's biggest supermarket chain. And in the bookstores, an adoring new biography solidified the popular myths about himself and his beloved leading lady, the golden-haired waif with the Dresden complexion and chiseled cheekbones.

Midafternoon, Mia Farrow and her four-year-old son, Satchel, who is also Woody's son, stepped off the elevator into the foyer of Woody's penthouse. The actress reached under the umbrella stand for the key.

In backgrounds, Maria de Lourdes Villiers Farrow and Allan Stewart Konigsberg could not have been more dissimilar—a Hollywood blue blood and a Flatbush frog turned movie prince—but they had been together for a dozen years, working side by side in thirteen films. As the quintessential Hollywood couple of the eighties, the new Tracy and Hepburn, Woody and Mia were truly an unusual pair—even for movie stars. They were not married. They did not even live together.

Mia had nine children, three biological with her former husband, the prominent conductor Andre Previn, five adopted, and one, Satchel, whom Woody and Mia had together. Because the commotion made by so many youngsters jangled Woody's nerves, Mia had remained on the opposite side of the park in her eight-room home at 135 Central Park West, the apartment in the Langham where Woody had filmed the Thanksgiving scenes in *Hannah and Her Sisters.* On a clear day, according to local Mia-Woody folklore, the lovers could gaze at each other across the expanse of Central Park through binoculars and wave towels. Several weeks earlier, Woody had co-adopted two of Mia's five adopted children—Korean-born Moses, thirteen, and six-year-old Dylan. While he doted on Dylan, Woody never managed to form a strong bond with his own little boy. Whether for this reason or not, Satchel O'Sullivan Farrow had begun experiencing emotional difficulties. When playing dress-up, for example, he didn't care to act the Prince, and instead always pleaded for the part of Cinderella. His father considered his son wanting to play Cinderella a problem, and so Satchel began therapy with a clinical psychologist in June of 1990, at which time he was only two years and seven months old. Instead of consulting Dr. Susan Coates at her office, Satch had his sessions at his father's apartment. It would not do for word to leak out that Woody's little boy, hardly more than a baby, who was until recently breastfeeding, was so screwed up that he required a shrink.

For the hour Satch was closeted with the gender specialist, his mother waited in the den. In the room where she settled into a chair, there were floor-to-ceiling bookshelves and a comfortable desk, although Woody did his writing with pencil and legal pad upstairs on his bed. The coffee table was always cluttered: He subscribed to *National Geographic, The New York Review of Books, The New Republic,* and there were piles of books, as well as bowls of nuts and fancy candies. To pass the time, Mia thumbed through *The Crooked*

Timber of Humanity by Isaiah Berlin, the philosopher who is Woody's favored essayist. When the telephone rang, she answered knowing that it would be Woody. The previous evening, as on other Sunday nights, they had spent together in her kitchen eating a meal of take-out Chinese with the kids, but there was always news to exchange, and so they spoke on the telephone four or five times a day. After hanging up, she stepped over to the fireplace, where she reached for a box of tissues on the mantel. Under the box, a stack of Polaroid photos caught her eye. They showed a naked woman draped across a sofa, posing suggestively with her legs spread apart, and Mia stared at the pictures in shock and horror. As she wrote in her autobiography, *What Falls Away,* "It took me a moment to realize that it was Soon-Yi," her nineteen-year-old daughter, who to her knowledge lacked any sexual experience, who had never had a date, not so much as a phone call from a boy.

Within minutes she was dialing Woody's office. "I found the pictures!" she screamed. "Get away from us!" Then she phoned her daughter, who hung up on her. "Totally traumatized," she felt as if a stake had been hammered through her heart.

Shortly thereafter, she was seen tearing through the lobby with her son in tow. Her flushed face and rumpled clothing did not seem extraordinary to Woody's neighbors at 930 Fifth. Accustomed to the sight of her yanking around a crew of kids, her tousled hair looking like a hayloft, one occupant recalled, "She always looked like she had just left a mental hospital or was on her way to one."

In the dusky air, the lamps along the footpaths were flickering on automatically as Mia bundled Satchel into a cab and crossed the park with the photographs tucked in her bag. In the hallway of her apartment, she met one of her twin sons. "Woody's been fucking Soon-Yi," she announced to twenty-one-year-old Sascha. "Call Andre." Then she raced into Soon-Yi's room with the pictures. Her voice rose to a screech. "What have you done?"

"Twenty minutes after she found the Polaroids," remembered one of Mia's intimates, "everyone in the family knew about it."

Soon afterward, the glass-and-wrought-iron door of the Farrow apartment burst open. Using his personal key, Woody let himself in and headed down the hall toward Mia's bedroom. Behind the closed door, he admitted to an affair that he said had started a few weeks earlier at Christmas. The Polaroids were shot only the previous night, after dinner, upon their return to his apartment. While sitting around talking, Soon-Yi spoke of wanting a modeling career and suggested he take pictures of her. He found a camera, she undressed, they embarked on an impromptu photo shoot. He recalled having posed her on the sofa, telling her to "lay back and give me your most erotic poses. Let yourself go."

These explanations, however, sounded preposterous to Mia. The photographs did not appear to be posed because Soon-Yi was laughing. They had an eerily spontaneous quality. Horrified that he had dared to seduce her daughter, Mia also felt disgusted about the pictures, which looked pornographic and were left in plain view on the mantel for anyone to see. Astonished by her references to pornography, Woody replied that no sexual acts were shown and would later describe the snapshots as nothing but "graphic, erotic pictures taken between two consenting adults."

That night, he failed to show up at Michael's Pub for his weekly performance. For several hours, he remained in Mia's room. Although he was not quite sure what to tell her, he continued to assure her of his love, she would later recall. The escapade with her daughter, he said, was an insignificant flirtation, "a tepid little affair" that had run its course anyway. He told her that they would get through this bad time and hopefully build a stronger relationship. It might even turn out to be a positive experience for Soon-Yi in the long run. Certainly the girl had not been exploited. She was, after all, an adult who had not been forced to do anything against her will. As he reminded Mia, he was not Soon-Yi's father or stepfather, not even a father figure. Throughout his explanations, Mia barely listened. She was unable to stop crying. Afterward, reporting to a friend, she described her humiliation as "a meltdown of my very core." Woody, too, would remember that she sounded incoherent, "beside herself in rage and anger." Unprepared to play this sort of richly emotional scene, he fled from the apartment when it became more than he could bear.

An hour later, as Mia and the children were having supper, he reappeared. In the kitchen, he stood silently behind the table at first and watched them eating. Nobody spoke to him. Stone-faced, they stared into their plates. In desperation, he sat down at the table and started "chatting with the two little ones, said hi to everybody" as if nothing had happened, Mia would remember. But one by one the older children picked up their plates and left the room.

Almost anywhere in the world, Woody Allen was a household name. With a face as familiar as that of Elvis or Marilyn, he was famous enough to be known by his first name. Everyone recognized the sober demeanor, the trademark black-rimmed glasses, the floppy tan hat that he adopted as a public disguise but which seldom fooled anyone. After thirty years in the spotlight—as comic actor, movie star, author, serious director, amateur musician, maverick filmmaker, and professional neurotic—he was a living legend considered by many to be America's most brilliant humorist, an artist of indisputable originality, a master of irony, the darling of the intelligentsia. Incredibly, he had turned out no fewer than twenty-one features, some classics of the screen and a number of clinkers, but still a formidable record matched by few contemporary filmmakers.

Numbers, however, did not begin to convey his universal appeal. Between 1968 and 1977, he had done nothing less than make the whole world love him and his movies. How could anyone forget *Take the Money and Run* and the most hilarious bank holdup ever filmed, the obvious absurdity of an incompetent crook with crummy penmanship hoping to succeed with a handwritten note? He had us roaring in *Everything You Always Wanted to Know About Sex (But Were Afraid to Ask),* when his frantic medieval court jester tries to pick the lock of the queen's chastity belt. "I must think of something quickly," he murmurs to himself, "because before you know it the Renaissance will be here, and we'll all be painting." And who else but Woody could create the sheer fun of *Bananas,* when his character feeds the rebel troops by ordering takeout from a local greasy spoon: "A thousand grilled cheese sandwiches, three hundred tuna fish, two hundred b.l.t.'s (one on a roll), and coleslaw for a thousand, mayo on the side."

Beyond the laughter, Woody set himself apart by playing the game on his own terms. A nonconformist off the screen, he wore his independence as a kind of badge and lived as he pleased. He hated to compromise but when he did, it was dramatic. In his younger days, he once escorted First Lady Betty Ford to a black-tie gala benefit for Martha Graham's dance company. At the Uris Theater, he made his entrance with the president's wife, and, in the manner of a movie star caught in flagrante delicto, announced to reporters that "we're just good friends." Mrs. Ford wore a purple chiffon dress; he was clad in a tuxedo and black tie, and his feet were encased in white sneakers, an outfit that demanded immediate attention.

Likewise, he bravely thumbed his nose at the Hollywood establishment and created his idiosyncratic pictures on the fringes of the system. From sketch comedies, he progressed to subtle, sophisticated romances such as *Annie Hall,* and crashed the ranks of Chaplin, Keaton, Welles, and Bergman (whom he unashamedly confessed was his idol) as an auteur, who wrote, directed, produced, acted in, and otherwise controlled every aspect of his own work. Even though he had spent only four or five days in the movie capital in the last twenty years, his place in the Hollywood pantheon of superstars could not have been more solid. Hardly an actor alive, offered a chance to work in a Woody Allen film, would not happily accept the sort of walk-on roles normally reserved for unknowns and cut his price to work for union scale. Some accepted roles without asking to see the script.

Besides considerable gifts as an artist, he excelled at confecting his own personal mythology. His most marvelous accomplishment was "Woody Allen," an extremely intricate, layered work composed of autobiography, masterful marketing, and good old-fashioned show business. On stage and screen, he always played the same lovable, self-mocking character, exactly as Chaplin kept portraying his mischievous Little Tramp throughout much of his career. And while Chaplin fans knew better than to confuse the performer with his performance, there was a blurring of the line between Woody and his fictional character, an ageless Peter Pan, endlessly self-deprecating and over-analyzing.

By January 13, 1992, the fictionalized Woody Allen had been enshrined as America's comic sweetheart for as long as most people could remember. As the Ingrid Bergman of film comedians, he was a moral paragon, sanctified beyond all common sense as America's favorite comedy saint by adoring fans who believed he could do no wrong. "Woody Allen, *c'est moi*," argued the critic Richard Schickel, one of his earliest supporters, who claimed to know instinctively "where he's coming from and, equally instinctively, I have some sense of where he's going."

While professionals such as Schickel continued to analyze Woody's comic experiments, we simple fans loved his films wholeheartedly. We knew that each year he would turn out some utterly fresh delight, and we rushed to see his latest creation as soon as it opened. In our excitement, we thought nothing of waiting in lines that snaked around the block; indeed, this ritual was apparently part of the price of admission. Afterward, we emerged smiling and feeling good, eager to pass along the most delicious bits to our friends. Usually we went back to see his films a second and third time because they were truly worth viewing again. If we were lucky, an art house might run a Woody film festival, or a film society screen a retrospective. With the coming of VCRs, when all the old favorites could be enjoyed again at home, we took the opportunity to introduce our children to movies such as *Sleeper.*

As to his feelings about us, the question appeared to be curiously answered in *Stardust Memories,* in which he painted his affectionate fans as ghouls. That didn't mean we abandoned him. Instead, we automatically struggled to understand the wretchedness that drove him. When in that film some-body accuses his character of being an atheist, he retorted, "To you, I'm an atheist. To God, I'm the loyal opposition." That grouchy response seemed to explain everything, more or less. Still, baffling or not, he was our national treasure, not because he always made great films but because he was invariably fascinating, even when he failed. So we paid no attention to what reviewers wrote. Whether Vincent Canby composed a love letter or a truculent Pauline Kael tore a movie to bits did not seem to matter. The important question was: What would he think of next? Would he skid ahead to 2173 and become a household robot? Could he top his chase of an immense terrorist breast over hill and dale before capturing it with an equally immense bra? Get himself executed in Czarist Russia and return to life with a report that death isn't so horrible, at least no worse than an evening with an insurance salesman? Who else but Woody could possibly have imagined diving into a male body during intercourse, as a timid sperm nervously awaiting ejaculation?

Throughout his nearly three decades of celebrity, no scandal ever smudged his golden reputation, almost an impossibility in the entertainment industry, where the road between fame and the dead end of a career is pocked with land mines. Indeed, if any show business figure seemed blessed with a healthy bank account of public affection, it was Woody. The notion that he might be capable of committing a dishonorable act was hard to imagine. We had no doubts that the real Woody was somewhat, but not very, different from the autobiographical character on screen; and while he seemed just like us, we also conjectured that he had to be different, more sensitive, more of a perfection- ist and a depressive, and probably a lot nuttier than we were. In *Annie Hall,* young Alvy Singer's fear that the universe is expanding causes his mother to yell in exasperation, "What is that your business?!" Like the baffled Mrs. Singer, we didn't understand what made him tick either—but we accepted him on faith because we liked and trusted him. The obvious integrity of his conduct made him "one of the good guys," said his friend Walter Bernstein. Certainly we had no doubt about his worth as an artist. He was what the political writer Arthur Schlesinger Jr. referred to as "the most original comic genius in American films since Chaplin and Keaton." To which we said amen.

On that warm rainy night in January 1992, it must have been pretty hard to appreciate the significance of what had just happened. That Mia would be deeply hurt was to be expected. He knew that whenever they fought, calls immediately went forth to the telephone company and a locksmith. He knew it never took more than a few days before she forgave him and turned over the new number and key. This crisis over Soon-Yi was different, of course. Mia would put him through hell for a while. Even so, past experience suggested that it, too, would blow over eventually.

God and Carpeting

Chapter One. He was as tough and romantic as the city he loved.
Behind his black-rimmed glasses was the coiled sexual power of a
jungle cat. . . . New York was his town. And it always would be.

So go the opening lines of *Manhattan,* one of the twenty-nine pictures that, all together, form a cumulative portrait of Woody Allen's life—documents comparable in obsession if not in depth to the seven volumes of Marcel Proust's *Remembrance of Things Past.* His most hugely popular film, as well as his biggest commercial success, *Manhattan* is Woody's anthem to the island, not the whole of it but a particular slice that he likes to call "the Zone." The exclusive Silk Stocking District of New York's Upper East Side runs north-south from Ninety-sixth Street to Fifty-ninth, and from Fifth Avenue to the East River. In the 10021 ZIP code area, there is a little swath of real estate—perhaps a half-dozen blocks below Seventy-second Street—where the median family income of homeowners is more than $700,000 a year. This is Woody Allen country, where there is no squalor or deprivation, no immigrants, virtually no blacks or Latinos in view except those wearing uniforms, and little crime that doesn't involve property. The typical criminal is a snatcher of gold chains.

The very first time Woody Allen set foot in the Upper East Side he was a small boy, trailing saucer-eyed behind his father, up and down leafy boulevards where middle-aged English nannies wheeled brand-new English baby carriages and great swatches of scarlet and gold spring tulips floated up the middle of Park Avenue. In this place that seemed to be his spiritual home, the adult Woody later recalled thinking that there was "something wonderful about the way the streets feel here," and those feelings have stayed with him throughout the years.

Whenever he leaves his home, in his rumpled khaki chinos and pullover sweater, he is able to curl back into his dreams of yesteryear and surround himself with the remembered tableaux of those nannies trudging past the uniformed doormen and chauffeurs. In sixty years, the streets have changed very little. It is he who has traversed far beyond his romantic fantasies to become the district's very own poet laureate.

Deep in the heart of Brooklyn, south of Flatbush, is the neighborhood of Midwood. The distance between the buildings along upper Fifth Avenue and the candy stores of Avenue J, Midwood's major thoroughfare, is barely more than twelve miles. Measured by subway stops, Midwood is twenty stations away on the D train that rumbles across the Manhattan Bridge. By car, the trip is an easy thirty-two minutes. But the two areas might as well be a thousand miles apart. Midwood in the 1930s was a comfortably middle-class, upwardly mobile, heterogenous neighborhood of mostly Jews and a few Italians. On the quiet, tree-lined blocks were small semidetached houses; on the cross streets, the typical sturdy six-floor apartment buildings; and to the east between Coney Island Avenue and Ocean Parkway, the expensive homes. From the raucous markets of Avenue J wafted the dizzying smells of buttery dough: crunchy, dense rye breads, gooey *rugelach* oozing raspberry jam, as well as delicious cinnamon-laced *babkas*. To their oilcloth-covered tables in freshly mopped linoleum kitchens, all the Jewish Midwood housewives carted ingredients to make matzo ball soup and brisket swimming in gravy.

The Konigsbergs lived only a few doors away from the hum of traffic on Avenue J, at 968 East Fourteenth Street, on the upper floor of a redbrick house they had occupied since the birth of their son. Still standing today, it is an imposing example of hybrid Brooklyn architecture, part Tudor cottage and part Italian villa, bristling with a fussy balustrade, a windowed turret, and ornamental brick doodads. The family—father, mother, and son, Allan—were mashed into the apartment with Nettie Konigsberg's sister Ceil and her husband, Abe Cohen. Too many people in too few rooms made daily living somewhat volatile. Most of the time the child was surrounded by people who spoke to one another in loud voices and waved their hands, all of which made quite a powerful impression. As an adult, detesting family turmoil and the forced intimacy of overcrowded households, Woody would be obsessive about solitude.

■ ■ ■ ■ ■ ■ ■

Snapshots: *She is standing next to her bridegroom on her wedding day, wrapped in silk crepe with a fussy double corsage pinned to her waist. Her eyes are shiny. Her hair, chin-length, is set in a softly waved permanent. Nice new accessories have been meticulously chosen: pearl drop earrings, smart elbow-length gloves, tiny dangling evening purse. Judging by her finery, she looks less like a bride than a vamp done up for a* *night of ballroom dancing. She is twenty-one years old, a bookkeeper, the youngest daughter of an immigrant Austrian Jew.*

By her side, facing the camera, is the bridegroom, a short man of twenty-eight. Quite dapper in an expensive tuxedo, he has a long, rubbery face, a crown of dark hair pomaded into a pompadour, and lips that seem to curl into an almost mocking expression. He is the pampered son of a fairly well-off family but is not going to live or die rich.

They are wedded by Rabbi Jacob Katz on Sunday, June 22, 1930, in the Crotona Park section of the Bronx, where the bride lives with her family at 1541 Hoe Avenue. It is a flawless summer afternoon, all golden sunshine and brittle-blue skies. At Coney Island, three hundred thousand bathers cover the beaches. Eight months earlier the stock market collapsed. Variety *headlined the bloodbath,* WALL STREET LAYS AN EGG, *and soon four million people were out of work. Nevertheless, that summer's songs—"I Got Rhythm," "Get Happy"—reflect a peculiar optimism. So does the bride. To look at her on this day when her new life is rolling into focus, she gives the impression of someone expecting a white picket fence in her future.*

■ ■ ■ ■ ■ ■

One of a half-dozen children, Nettie Cherry was born in New York City in 1908. Her father, Leon, at age twenty-six, left Austria and came to America in 1891, a decade after an older brother, Joseph, had made the trip. Four years later, Leon married Sarah Hoff, another Austrian immigrant. Citizenship applications classify the Cherry brothers as skilled workers—Joseph, a bricklayer, and Leon, a polisher of metalware: gold, silver, copper, brass. At the turn of the century, Leon Cherry lived in the Lower East Side, a ghetto that no amount of nostalgia can glamorize. In foul-smelling rows of tenements with jutting iron fire escapes, where families lived ten to a room, ill-lit hallways were untouched by disinfectants. In the streets, curbs were obscured by uncollected garbage alongside an armada of pushcarts vending chickens and vegetables. Men in black hats, with matted beards and side curls, shouldered their way through crowds of swarthy women who covered their heads with shawls and knew only a few words of English.

It took Leon Cherry seventeen years before he could open his own luncheonette, described in the city directory as an "eatinghouse," the first of a succession of food, candy, and variety stores that he would own. Then in 1920, leaving behind the decayed tenements, he took advantage of the newly built subway lines running northward and moved to the rural Bronx, where he rented an apartment near his brother on Freeman Street. The 1920 Census records him as a fifty-five-year-old day laborer employed at the Bronx Borough

Hall in Crotona Park. The Cherrys, like other pious Jews, spoke in Yiddish at home, their adopted English only out on the street, and lit the Sabbath candles on Friday sundowns. None of them seemed to show interest in higher education. There was no time for books, music, or art. Just reaching the shores of the new land, followed by years of backbreaking toil, had exhausted them.

Nettie's sister Molly was regarded by her sisters as painfully timid. Uncommunicative, she may actually have been drowned out by the ruckus of a family that never stopped yapping and complaining. Young Nettie, who was anything but meek, would be, as an adult, famously excitable. In the 1989 film *New York Stories,* she would be memorialized by her son in his vignette "Oedipus Wrecks" as a harpy mother who disappears, only to hang in the sky above New York City like a Bullwinkle balloon in the Macy's Thanksgiving Day parade, from which vantage point she leans down and continues to berate her bad boy. Woody would come to describe his mother as a shallow, narrow-minded woman whose interests tended to be commonplace. He ticked off the highlights of her day: "She gets up in the morning, as she has for years, she works in a little flower shop downtown, she rides the subway home, and she makes dinner. Beyond that she is not too interested in too many things." Apart from his resentment that he had been forced to drink from the same well, the point about his mother's limited world contains a kernel of truth. "She's preoccupied with fundamentals," he remarked. But not entirely so. As a young woman, it was fantasy, not fundamentals, that initially drew her to her future husband.

Growing up, Nettie followed the example of four older sisters who were obliged to work for a living: Sadie was employed as a stencil cutter at *Pictorial Review,* while the other three girls got jobs in the garment business as stenographers and clerks. Their brother became a jeweler's apprentice.

Nettie, like her sisters, studied bookkeeping, and she landed a job with a Brooklyn wholesale business: prime butter, fancy poultry, eggs received daily from the best henneries. Each morning she rode the train from the Bronx to Wallabout Market by the Williamsburg docks, where one day she caught the eye of fifty-six-year-old Isaac Konigsberg, a middle-aged, mustachioed butter-and-egg salesman. Isaac was a Brooklyn bon vivant with hand-tailored suits and worldly tastes, a lover of classical music who listened to *Pagliacci* and *Rigoletto* from his own box at the Metropolitan Opera. To sheltered Nettie, his sophistication made her own family look like country bumpkins.

It is clear that Isaac liked Nettie because he lost no time introducing her to his younger son Martin, his favorite and a boy he had coddled for as long as anybody could remember. A sharp dresser, Marty, however, was not blessed with good looks. He grew up to have a long, gargoylish face and a goofy grin. Nettie, while no great beauty, had blossomed into an attractive young woman, a spunky, tart-tongued redhead. At once she took a shine to Marty, an amusing, amiable young fellow who knew how to have a good time, a "high-stepper," she later called him. At the time they met it was the twenties, and he squired her to Tavern on the Green, an expensive new restaurant in Central Park. Nettie was thrilled. With little to look forward to except marriage to some Bronx palooka, she suddenly was offered unexpected promise.

Isaac had three children but made no secret of his preference for Marty. When Marty was a schoolchild, he pulled strings to get him chosen team mascot for the Brooklyn Dodgers. Not surprisingly, Marty grew up with a sense of entitlement, faithfully nourished by his father. During World War I, Marty joined the Navy. After the Armistice, the nineteen-year-old enjoyed being stationed in England but felt unhappy without a car, a situation Isaac promptly remedied with an expensive Kissel roadster to drive abroad.

Although the Konigsbergs and the Cherrys were first-generation Jewish immigrants, a friend of Woody's observed, "they came from different worlds." The Russian-born Isaac, who was far more successful than Leon, managed to make a good living from several business enterprises. His first port of call, with his wife, Janette, had been England, where he learned to speak the King's English and where his daughter Sadie was born, before making the journey to New York in 1899. In Trow's City Directory for 1901, he is listed as a peddler living on Henry Street on the Lower East Side, but he soon distinguished himself in the wholesale coffee business, traveling abroad on behalf of his employer, sometimes romping off to Europe for the pleasure of attending the horse races. Later, he progressed from salesman to entrepreneur and bought a fleet of taxicabs, then several movie theaters, but these businesses failed. He was reduced to selling butter and eggs when Nettie was introduced to him in the late twenties. To the impressionable Nettie, Isaac appeared to be a prosperous, cultivated gentleman.

■ ■ ■ ■ ■ ■ ■

Commentary:
"My mother is an orthodox paranoid and, while she doesn't believe in an afterlife, she doesn't believe in a present one either."
—WOODY ALLEN, 1967

■ ■ ■ ■ ■ ■ ■

By 1935, after two years of FDR's New Deal, the newspapers were predicting a stronger economy and happier times. Out west there was drought and soil depletion—the talk was of Okies and dust bowl farmers who didn't have a penny—but in New York City, fewer businesses were failing and fewer numbers of people had to go on the dole. Statistics like these were meaningless to the Konigsbergs, who were having trouble putting food on the table. Nettie, like most women of that period, stayed home and kept the house. She cooked, swept, and ironed, but, whether by accident or design, she bore no children. To save on rent, the couple often doubled up with Ceil and Abe Cohen, or sister Sadie and her husband, Joe Wishnick.

Hard times and strong family ties would account for their domestic arrangements, but there may have been another explanation. Husbands, in Nettie's book, were supposed to earn money and pay bills. But Marty, who told everyone that he was a butter-and-egg salesman, moseyed from job to job. He plotted fantastic schemes to get rich fast. Not that he thought of himself as a failure. He changed his clothes three or more times each day. He idled away afternoons at Ebbets Field whenever he got the chance, frequented his favorite pool halls, or slipped into a haberdashery to order a new suit he couldn't afford. If Nettie was always belittling her husband, Marty, too, must have been disappointed to realize his bride could work herself into a temper over practically anything. Unable to enjoy each other's company, gradually having less and less to say to each other, the pair of antagonists still remained together, warily eyeing each other over a Maginot Line. At least that was the way Woody depicted them in his work.

In a comedy routine, "Mechanical Objects," Woody told the audience how his father lost his job after being replaced by a tiny gadget that was able to do everything Marty did—only more efficiently. "The depressing thing is that my mother ran out and bought one," he wisecracked. No row ever put an end to their marriage. However much Nettie may have wished to replace Marty, however loudly she screamed, she never could bring herself to divorce him. Marty drifted from one line of work to another: salesman, pool hustler, bookmaker, bartender, egg candler, jewelry engraver, and cabdriver. He seemed incapable of sticking to one thing for long, subject to a restlessness that would be inherited by his son.

After five years of marriage, Nettie became pregnant. Even though they were residents of Brooklyn, living then at 1010 Avenue K, she decided to deliver the baby in the Bronx, at Mt. Eden Hospital. Allan Stewart Konigsberg was born on a Sunday evening, at 10:55 P.M. on December 1, 1935, which gave him a sun in Sagittarius and a moon in Aquarius. With his carroty hair, big ears, and milky skin, he looked just like his mother.

Parenthood did nothing to improve the relationship between the Konigsbergs, but now there was a witness to the rancor. By this time, daily warfare had become practically a way of life. The household pathology was, as Woody remarked years later, "there all the time as soon as I could understand anything."

Shortly after the baby's first birthday, Nettie found work as a bookkeeper for a Manhattan florist and began traveling back and forth to the city every day. Her son was tended by a succession of caretakers, mostly ill-educated young women who desperately needed the money and were not terribly interested in the fine points of early childhood development. As Woody later recollected, they invited friends to the house and sat around gossiping all day while he played by himself. Although crib memories tend to be suspect, he claimed to distinctly remember that once, as he was lying in his bed, one of these women shoved a blanket over his face and almost suffocated him.

In the evenings when his mother returned from work, she had little time for reciting bedtime stories. When he got on her nerves, which was frequently, she wound up spanking him. As a result, he grew up believing that from the cradle he had been unwanted. Nothing would ever convince him otherwise.

■ ■ ■ ■ ■ ■ ■

On the Couch:
"His one regret in life is that he is not someone else."
—From the jacket copy for *Getting Even*

■ ■ ■ ■ ■ ■ ■

In the sixties, when he was trying to develop his comedy act, Woody got back at his parents by stitching them into his routines. His mother, he riffed, left a live teddy bear in his crib. When he got older she warned him never to be suspicious of strangers. If anybody with candy beckoned him into a car, he should hop right in. Poking fun at relatives is normal for comedians, but Woody's family evidently offered an exceptionally rich lode of material for put-downs and wisecracks. With age, he mellowed and presented Nettie and Marty almost nostalgically in his coming-of-age movie, *Radio Days*. Even so, his description of their contentious marriage remains basically unchanged.

"His mother," recalled boyhood friend Jack Freed, "had a hot temper and was always taking a whack at him. Whenever he got her goat, she'd start howling and yelling before taking a good swipe at him. If my mother hit me that hard, I'd have run away crying, but he never cried. He had an amazing ability to restrain his emotions. His mother couldn't control herself at all."

In 1986, Nettie was a woman of seventy-eight, a resident of Manhattan's Upper East Side, living rent-free at her son's expense in one of the new apartment high-rises. Woody sat his mother on a chair, facing the camera.

"Did you hit me?" he asked from behind the camera. Making a documentary about her life and the life of Mia Farrow's mother, actress Maureen O'Sullivan, two women who seemed to share nothing in common, seemed like an intriguing idea. "Mia's mother was a movie star all her life and knew nothing else," he explained afterward. "She was Tarzan's mate. She had a Beverly Hills pool and hung around with Bogart and all these people." Maureen was a thoroughbred filly, whereas his own mother was a plow horse, "a typical Jewish-neighborhood cliché in every way," he said.

The tiny, snowy-haired woman was squinting.

"I remember you would hit me every day when I was a child."

Hit him? she asked incredulously. What did that mean? That she whipped him?

"No, but you were always slapping me."

His insistence on dredging up the past made her testy. Of course she smacked him. What did he expect, a saint? He was a stubborn kid, never listening to her when she corrected him, jumping around and pulling off his clothes, making her crazy. But she refused to stand for any monkey business. "You were too active and too much of a child for me," she said. "I wasn't that good to you because I was very strict, which I regret."

Her daughter, on the other hand, had been a cuddly, docile child. "I was much sweeter to Letty than I was to you," she reminded him.

Two Mothers was harder than he anticipated. He never finished it.

CHAPTER TWO

The Purple Rose of Midwood

The year is 1935, the setting a New Jersey factory town on a wintry afternoon. Cecilia, a timid waitress at a diner, is watching the new picture at the Jewel for the fifth time. By this time she is drawn willy-nilly into the lives of the screen people, whose existences are defined by penthouses, black maids, and the inevitable white piano. Over sounds of laughter and clinking glasses, the guests sip dry martinis and hold forth about excursions down the Nile. Wearing a safari suit and pith helmet, Tom Explorer-Adventurer-Archeologist-Poet Baxter has been whisked to Manhattan for a madcap weekend. His jaw is square, his smile creamy. He looks even more of a heartthrob than he did yesterday when Cecilia had seen the movie only four times. Pretty soon she is not even thinking about going home to her husband, an unemployed boozer who slaps her around.

While she is slumped in her seat gazing, rapt, at Tom Baxter, something extraordinary begins to happen. Out of the blue he faces the audience and returns her gaze, looking directly into her face, flicking his eyes back and forth over her Lillian Gish hat and neatly buttoned brown coat. And then he speaks, in the coolest screen voice ever manufactured in Hollywood: "My God," he says, "you must really love this picture." And the next thing Cecilia knows, he is hopping off the screen into the dark of the theater and declaring his love for her. Tom Baxter is everything she has ever wanted in a man: good looks, nice manners, devotion, wealth. Of course he is fictional, Cecilia must admit, "but you can't have everything."

Cecilia is fictional, too, a character in the 1985 movie *The Purple Rose of Cairo*. No role Woody Allen created was more Allan Konigsberg's alter ego, his fictional soul mate, than Cecilia, who, like himself, discovers that the make-believe world of the movies is "a total, total joy."

When he was five, he saw *Snow White and the Seven Dwarfs* and took to cinema like an acolyte to the Mass. Over the next ten years, he watched thousands of pictures. After *Pinocchio* and *Bambi* came the war movies, Phil Silvers

29

and Carmen Miranda in *Four Jills in a Jeep,* then all the Bob Hope–Bing Crosby road pictures the week they were released because Hope was his favorite comedian, and tons of Westerns because his father loved cowboys. He cried over little Roddy McDowall in *The White Cliffs of Dover,* and swashbuckling Tyrone Power in *The Black Swan.* A few years later his filmgoing companion became cousin Rita Wishnick, five years older and also a movie addict, and together they sniffled over *Casablanca.*

Within walking distance of his house were two dozen movie houses. The neighborhood's main theater was the Midwood on Avenue J. His other favorites were the Vogue, the Elm, the Triangle, the Avalon, the Kingsway on Kings Highway, and on Nostrand Avenue, the cavernous Patio, whose lobby fountain was stocked with darting goldfish. At the decayed Kent, a double feature cost eleven cents, if you didn't mind the rats scurrying in the dark and the sound of freight trains passing underneath, and years later he shot interior scenes there for *The Purple Rose of Cairo.* In wintertime, on Saturday mornings at eleven, he would be the first shivering person in line at the Midwood for the double feature beginning at noon. But all summer long, when there was no school, he went to the movies every day. His friends had parents nagging them to go out and play in the sun, but Allan hated the hot weather, and his parents seemed not to care what he did. Under a caramel midafternoon sun, when the silvery trolley tracks along Coney Island Avenue were burning hot, he paid twenty-five cents and disappeared into the air-cooled darkness with his popcorn and a supply of Milk Duds. After seeing the double feature three times, he staggered, as he later recalled, "into the ugly light," creeping woozily home with his shirt sticking to his shoulders, expelled from paradise.

All during the war, the Konigsbergs seemed unable to settle down. From the house at Fourteenth and J, they moved a half-dozen times in the neighborhood, usually sharing an apartment with Nettie's sister Sadie and her husband, Joe. Woody remembered "cousins and uncles running in and out of rooms." At one point, they lived almost a year at the beach, a happy time that he would re-create in *Radio Days,* followed by a brief stopover in suburban Port Chester, New York, twenty-five miles north of the city, that would leave him with a lifelong antipathy toward grass and trees. When the family returned to the old Midwood neighborhood in 1945, the Konigsbergs and Wishnicks took a semiattached frame house on a leafy street near the elevated train track, at 1144 East Fifteenth Street. This is the house where Allan would live from age ten to seventeen, sharing a room with his cousin Rita, while his two-year-old sister, Ellen (nicknamed Letty), slept with their parents, and the third bedroom was occupied by his uncle and aunt. The house still stands, spic-and-span, its front entrance moved to the side of the house and a picture window and porch added—now owned by a young couple with three children.

Allan, ten years old, short and underdeveloped, felt insecure about his looks, and he usually wore a sad-sack expression on his pale face. Although he appeared to be timid, and in fact would make a career of playing a born loser, he was neither bashful nor repressed. Like his mother he was high-strung, moody, and prickly edged; around adults he had a fresh attitude. "One day," recalled Jack Freed, who lived next door, "we were playing in an overgrown lot near the old ice company when we noticed this strange red-headed kid lurking around. Just to be ornery we started throwing stones to chase him away." Soon, however, he and Al began chumming around together, against the wishes of Jack's father, who thought that the new friend was a bad influence. "I don't want you hanging around Allan," he warned. "He's never going to amount to anything." According to Jack's older sister, Doris, "He was a wild kid, somewhat of a hellion. He seemed to be constantly in trouble at school."

In the fall of 1940, Woody entered P.S. 99 (now the Isaac Asimov School), the same four-story, redbrick school that his father attended, but showed no aptitude for learning and figured out how to avoid school by pretending to be sick. Behavior problems coupled with bad grades brought Nettie to school so frequently that his classmates knew her on sight. At home, she rode herd on him, to no avail. "He had intellectual capability but he just wasn't interested," said Jack Freed, who continued to hang around with Al despite his father's warnings. "Even in high school, he did just enough homework to get by."

Because he never developed a passion for books, reading was a chore. The only form of literature that gave him pleasure was comic books, and evidently he became an omnivorous speed reader of the Superman, Batman, and Mickey Mouse series, sometimes covering fifty comics in the course of a day. "But lots of kids were big readers of comics," commented Jack Freed. "And he was growing up in a household where nobody directed him toward reading great books." Despite the comics, he found himself able to write "real prose in school compositions. There was never a week when the composition I wrote was not the one that was read to the class." Not until his teens did he accept the theoretical importance of reading, but it was too late by then—he found it boring. The great books that taught him about life—how to talk, to look, to eat, to make yourself attractive—were the movies.

With an academic career largely spent loafing in class, playing truant, and sneaking off to movies, he wound up basically uneducated. It didn't trouble him, and the mature Woody would be proud of having learned "nothing of value in school, in elementary school, high school, or my year of college." Everything of importance came from movies and comics. "All kinds of values, social behavior. Some from radio programs, too. But nothing of value from school. Once they teach you to read and write, forget it." Years later when he was in his thirties, he confided to an interviewer that "I wake up in the morning and clutch on to my bed and thank God I don't have to go to school." Over the years his recollections of school tended to take on a Solzhenitsyn-like gloss. You could almost imagine he had spent twelve years deep in the Urals, in some forced labor camp, consorting with murderers and thieves, curled up with his comic books.

■ ■ ■ ■ ■ ■ ■

Moving Pictures:
ALLAN FELIX: My parents didn't get divorced . . . although I
    begged them to.
                                        —*Play It Again, Sam,* 1972

■ ■ ■ ■ ■ ■

"They were the oddest couple," as a friend of Woody's described Nettie and Marty Konigsberg. "They had nothing whatsoever to say to each other." In fact, Jack Victor added, "I never heard them exchange a single word." Jack was one of Woody's closest friends; the others were Elliott Mills and Gerald Epstein. Later, a fourth boy, Mickey Rose, a transfer student from Crown Heights, would join the group. Typical of the neighborhood, the boys came from various economic backgrounds. Jack's father was a pants presser. Elliott's father worked in Wall Street brokerage houses as a margin clerk. Jerry's father was an attorney whose clients included Rocky Graziano, and his family lived several blocks farther west in the grander section of Midwood in a thirteen-room house. Mickey's parents were divorced, and his mother had been a Rockette at Radio City Music Hall.

Eccentric as Woody always portrays them, his parents may not have differed greatly from the other lower-middle-class, second-generation children of immigrants, struggling to get by during the Depression. For whatever reason they made an imperfect match, but since divorce was not customary, they soldiered on and made the best of the situation. Looking back, Woody's friends report that Nettie and Marty were "a trip," "hysterical," "a riot," which must be true because Woody himself would convulse his audiences by recounting their marital foibles. Growing up as the couple's son was another matter, not the slightest bit amusing. In later life, he complained about never once being taken to a museum or a Broadway show, never owning a piano. But cultural deprivation was the least part of it. Despite the birth of Woody's baby sister, Letty, in 1943, the marriage continued to deteriorate.

Superficially, things seemed much better: The Depression was over, the wartime economy was booming, two incomes made life relatively comfortable. Unlike the Dickensian childhood of his Woody Allen character, Allan Konigsberg received a generous allowance of seven dollars a week, more pocket money than any of his friends had, and his father was always slipping him an extra dollar or two. Finally Marty had settled down to a steady job at Sammy's Bowery Follies, a Gay Nineties saloon offering vaudeville entertainment, located in Manhattan on the Bowery. Known as the poor man's Stork Club, the nightclub was as popular a tourist mecca as the Statue of Liberty. At Sammy's, the Third Avenue el rumbled overhead as bums and drifters mingled with GIs on leave; the walls were covered with framed photographs of its famous patrons, including Harry S Truman and John F. Kennedy. In fact there were so many political and show business celebrities there that Weegee, the legendary news photographer, made the club one of his regular nightly stops. For close to twenty years, Marty worked there as a bartender, bouncer, or night manager. "When we came home from school," said Jack Freed, "he was just getting up and we would find him in his bathrobe watching Westerns on Channel 11."

"Marty was a small-time hustler," said Elliott Mills. "Whatever you wanted, he got. You wanted a typewriter, he got you a typewriter. Of course it had no serial numbers." Not only did Marty mix in the nightclub scene, but he also reportedly toted a gun—supposedly because he had to ride the subway late at night—and carried a police badge. (Nettie's brother, a jeweler, manufactured them for the NYPD.)

Sammy's formed the backdrop of Woody's adolescence. But oddly, his father working in a famous club surrounded by showgirls and vaudeville acts didn't seem to interest him. As far as Jack Victor knew, "he never stepped foot in Sammy's. He certainly never talked about it." At Woody's bar mitzvah party, however, some of the guests were friends of Marty's from Sammy's, and they were delighted when young Allan smeared on blackface to do an imitation of Larry Parks as Al Jolson in *The Jazz Singer.*

Unlike Woody's mother, his father tended to be easygoing and affectionate. To twit his son he would say, "I wish you were the champ of the world."

"Yeah, why?" Woody said.

"Because then I'd be the next champ," his father bantered.

Whatever his son did was perfectly acceptable. Once, Marty bought Allan a chemistry set, and Allan dyed Nettie's Persian lamb coat bright yellow. Marty could not have been more delighted. Recollecting the incident years later, he said that Allan "was always doing funny things like that." Most of the time, though, Marty impressed his son as a man who was completely immersed in himself. "He's never let a thought enter his head," Woody came to believe. "When he was young he spent every cent he ever made. Never thought about whether he could pay the bills. He was an affectionate guy, but he never cared about anything."

When he described his parents' values as God and carpeting, he was probably not referring to his father, who never paid the slightest attention to either religion or home furnishings. Once during the High Holy Days, instead of a trip to temple, Marty boldly marched over to the local Chinese restaurant. When he returned from Joy Fong's, he took a few bites from the cardboard container of his favorite dish of chow mein and began to complain heartily. It was awful. He felt like taking the disgusting mess back. "I'm going to cut off that Chinaman's goddammed pigtail!" he sputtered.

Although Marty had no use for Jewish dietary rules and consumed whatever took his fancy, Nettie kept kosher and sent her boy to Hebrew school. At home, she kept trying to impress upon him the value of work and success. "Don't waste time!" she yelled again and again, a life lesson that would be ingrained in him. With an abundance of almost manic energy, he threw himself headlong into a variety of pursuits as a youngster, teaching himself magic and practicing card and coin tricks obsessively in front of a mirror for six or seven hours a day. Many years later, Ralph Rosenblum, Woody's first film editor, would marvel at the "Prussian discipline" that enabled him to complete a film one day and then get back in the harness the next to start a new screenplay.

"His mother was extremely naggy," recalled Jack Victor. "Sometimes Woody couldn't take it and would say very cruel things. When she had cataracts and a patch over one eye, he said, 'Shut up, Mom, or I'll blind your other eye.' "

■ ■ ■ ■ ■ ■ ■

Eyewitness:
"He was small, he was funny, he was smart enough but not exceptionally smart, not an A student. He wasn't going to be a great scientist. But he had this powerful need to be recognized."
—ELLIOTT MILLS

■ ■ ■ ■ ■ ■ ■

More than thirty years later, when Woody was asked which fictional character he'd most like to be, he picked Colette's little prepubescent charmer Gigi. He wanted to be in France, "to meander, feather-light, down the boulevards of belle epoque Paris in a little blue sailor dress, my sweet face framed by a flat, disk-shaped hat with two ribbons dangling mischievously past my bangs." He imagined himself awakening in Gigi's little bed with the silk embroidered sheets and eating Gigi's breakfast of soft-boiled eggs with cherries. For dinner there would be a cup of thick chocolate beaten up with an egg yolk. Perhaps toast and a bunch of grapes. Each new day would be a joy. If he couldn't be Gigi, then he wanted to live his life over as a black athlete or a black musician or, better yet, as both, dribbling and shooting for the Knicks and when he got too old for basketball, playing the saxophone or clarinet. Instead, the gangly kid on East Fifteenth Street holed up in a prison of his own making. "I'd eat in the cellar or my bedroom, read my comic books, lock myself in my room and practice the clarinet and my card and coin tricks. It would drive my mother crazy—she'd hear things dropping for hours in the room." Years later, his mother would reassure him he had been a sweet, happy-go-lucky little boy until around the age of five. Then, an amazing thing happened. His personality suddenly changed, and practically overnight, he turned sour and antisocial, she reported. His melancholy made no sense to her. And Woody, having lived under a blanket of sadness for as long as he could remember, could recall no specific incident either. His basic character, he said, has always been "pessimistic, depressed." By his own admission, he regarded all people with suspicion. "I never did believe in any of that business where love is everything."

What he thought about most often, as he approached puberty, was sex, not unusual for a thirteen-year-old boy. Besides sex, he thought about becoming famous, even though nothing in his personality seemed to augur a special destiny. But more frequently he thought about dying, a subject seldom uppermost on the minds of young boys. Without a trigger for his sense of impending doom, he nevertheless had no trouble articulating his apprehension. "I have memories of being very young, probably 6 or 8, and being put to sleep at night." Lying in the dark, thinking "someday I will be dead," he would force himself to imagine the finality of it and suffer hideous depression. In addition to his fear of oblivion, he was also terrified by the dark. Not until much later—his early forties—would he be able to sleep without a night-light, or come home at night without ritually checking every single closet in his apartment to make sure "there wasn't an enemy there out to get me." He unburdened himself years later to Roger Ebert, the film critic, that "not a day goes past when I do not seriously consider the possibility of suicide." At the time of this statement, he was a fifty-one-year-old titan of the movie business, who had been in psychoanalysis for twenty-eight years.

Occasionally he caught a glimpse of what seemed like happiness. On a school trip to Washington, D.C., his class spent the night at a monastery on the outskirts of the city. For Woody, the cloister was an oasis of tranquillity, and later he would recall wistfully how each morning the monks shuttled calmly up and down the paths, how they knelt and prayed. Their serenity was so "seductive" that he almost wished he could become a Catholic.

According to Woody, he felt such an intense sense of failure that "everything dissatisfied me." He must have soft-pedaled his insecurities because around his friends he seemed sure of himself. One of those friends, thirty years hence, walked out after seeing *Manhattan* feeling "very depressed because I never realized how unhappy he was—so much of him was in that movie." To Elliott Mills, "he was full of enthusiasm. He was interested in so many things. And whatever was going on, he had something clever to say." Of course, Mills added, "everybody we knew was funny. His whole family, even his sister, was comical because it was considered a good thing to be funny and come up with a great line. There was a kid in the neighborhood we called Tut. One day some joker phoned the funeral home and reported that Tut was dead. When the mortuary sent a hearse to his home, his mother went hysterical. For years, all somebody had to say was 'Tut is dead,' and we'd pee our pants." Granted, it was not Woody who thought up the Tut caper, but it was the kind of joke the merry pranksters appreciated. In terms of making life funny, Mills said, Woody was "at the further end of the curve."

Making people laugh was nothing special when it was the air you breathed. "It was just something I could always do," Woody explained, "like some kids had an ear for music, I could be funny." Coming so easily, however, it seemed a gift of no particular value. It surely did not confer on him the respect he craved. Indeed, the laughs that he drew from his classmates in school only annoyed his teachers.

The Soviet Union exploded an atomic bomb in 1949. The following year, the war began in Korea and Senator Joseph McCarthy declared war against communists at home. Alger Hiss denied furnishing official documents to the Soviets and was convicted of perjury. Shortly, eight sleepy years of the Eisenhower era would begin. The events and people that formed the paranoia of the fifties seemed to have small impact on the wholesome pace of adolescence in Midwood, home to Wingate Field, Cookies on Avenue J, Capri Pizza with its jukebox in the corner and its single bald waiter. "It was a golden age," reminisced Elliott Mills. "Nobody had a lot of money but everybody had brains and everybody was funny. Our heroes were the Dodgers and jazz musicians. There were no drugs or gender problems. Nobody got laid until they got married. It was an idyllic childhood." With both of Woody's parents working, the gang usually congregated at his house, where they hatched complicated plots to get dates and watched the Konigsberg television set, one of the first on the block. Never again would Woody enjoy such satisfying relationships, a camaraderie based on "exchange of intimate feelings and discussion of what motivated people and how the psyche worked," described Jack Victor. "We dissected everyone we knew."

At fourteen, Woody had begun to develop a passionate interest in Sidney Bechet, the New Orleans clarinetist and soprano saxophonist whose music he had first heard on a crackly Saturday morning radio show. Immediately enraptured, he bought all Bechet's records he could find. "I'd come home from school, and put on those records and just do nothing else for hours but play them and replay them," he said. On Sunday afternoons, he and his friends were in the city at Child's Paramount, listening to the house band led by Conrad Janis and dining royally on full-course dinners of Salisbury steak or veal parmigiana for two dollars. One Sunday, they were thrilled to hear Bechet himself, who was making a rare visit back to the States from France and passed through New York. Introduced by Orson Welles, he played the soprano sax. After the concert, Woody went up to shake hands, one of the most unforgettable moments of his life. Half a century later he would proudly tell people that he had seen "Sidney Bechet live."

He bought a soprano sax and tried to teach himself to play but found the instrument too difficult and switched to clarinet. An aspiring musician, he began lessons at an upstairs studio on Kings Highway, run by a man who wore a patch over one eye, and later he negotiated two-dollar clarinet lessons from one of Fats Waller's sidemen, who agreed to come to his house, an hour-and-a-half trip from the Bronx. Nobody practiced more diligently. For all Woody's effort, he wasn't, as he later ruefully admitted, "born with the real equipment," a fact he refused to face for many years. And when he did, he nonetheless continued the habit of practicing every day, rain or shine, at least a half hour, but more often two hours.

The summer he was seventeen, word got around that a stag film was coming to the Jewel—a Swedish movie that actually showed a woman swimming stark naked. Excited, he made sure to be the first customer in line on opening day, to get a seat with an unobstructed view of the screen. *Summer with Monika* was about a girl (Harriet Andersson) who runs away to spend the summer with her boyfriend and gets pregnant. Woody, rapt and horny, had no idea who directed it, "nor did I care," he wrote later. The power of the movie, its erotic poetry and sadomasochistic undertones, escaped him entirely. The only scene that remained in his memory was the shot of Harriet Andersson disrobing. Following his first exposure to Ingmar Bergman, he was soon captivated by another of his films, *The Naked Night*. This time, as he "sat forward for an hour and a half, my eyes bulging," he did notice the name of the director, then promptly forgot it when he walked out. Finally, several years later, he saw *Wild Strawberries* and developed what he called "a lifelong addiction" to Bergman's films.

During high school, he and his friends were regular visitors to the Jewel, where they saw all the so-called art pictures: Chaplin's *Limelight,* the work of Jacques Tati, Rene Clair, and Jean Renoir. They took an instant liking to Terry-Thomas and Alastair Sim, in fact to all of the British comic actors, and they also loved American classics, too. When *Gone With the Wind* was revived at the Midwood, Woody was eager to see it again because he was in love with Scarlett O'Hara, who "drove me crazy." "Because he was the dominant person in our crowd," Jack Victor remembered, "we all saw it every day that week, twice each day, ten times altogether."

■ ■ ■ ■ ■ ■

Memorabilia:
Roses are red,
Violets are blue,
Alan Ladd is handsome,
So what!
—ALLAN KONIGSBERG, 1949,
written in the autograph book
of a P.S. 99 classmate

■ ■ ■ ■ ■ ■

After graduating from P.S. 99, Woody went to Midwood High School and entered the college-preparatory program. Academically one of the first-rate schools in the city, Midwood was a competitive place full of high-achievers, the postwar optimists and competers, well-off white kids who hadn't the slightest doubt they were the best and the brightest and whose second- and third-generation Jewish parents, having made the world safe for democracy, were pushing them to excel. Students regularly won Westinghouse science scholarships, and it wasn't unusual for 99 percent of the senior class to go to college. Alan Lapidus, one of Woody's schoolmates, said that Midwood "was the kind of school where everybody was involved in something but Allan got involved in nothing. He was a short, funny-looking kid, too scrawny to be athletic, although he definitely tried." As editor of both the school newspaper and the yearbook, Lapidus was a class leader and one of the cool crowd, who also happened to be a close friend of Bryna Goldstein, the object of one of Woody's crushes.

Loathing Midwood even more than P.S. 99, Woody arrived there at the very last minute in the morning and left the minute the bell rang. "He was bright and knew how to talk, but he never did a lick of work," said Gladys Bernstein, a math and science teacher. "He was a slippery rascal who came late to class, carried on, and got a lot of 65s." Throughout his life, he painted the school as a sewer presided over by "emotionally disturbed teachers," for which Midwood faculty would never forgive him. Years later he would dredge up his favorite childhood memory of "getting up in the morning, having my big piece of chocolate cake and milk for breakfast, my parents still asleep, going out, presumably to Midwood High School but *not* going to Midwood High School." Instead, he took the train to Times Square, arriving just in time for the first show at the Paramount Theater, independent behavior that impressed his friends. "He appeared to be confident of himself and his intellectual capability," said Jack Victor. "All of us thought he was destined for great things."

Having missed so many classes, Woody repeatedly required tutoring to pass courses. In his sophomore year, presumably hoping for a way to make him buckle down to his studies, his mother decided to get him a typewriter. Not one of Marty's hot deals without serial numbers, but a brand-new Olympia portable, an expensive German model that sold for forty dollars and looked like a tank. In the store, Woody demanded to know if the machine was worth the price.

"This typewriter will last longer than you will," promised the salesclerk. (Most likely an accurate warranty because he still uses it.)

If Nettie expected the Olympia to improve his grades, she found it didn't make a scrap of difference. If anything, it pushed him further from his studies. But as it turned out, the typewriter changed his life in an odd way that nobody could have predicted. Shortly after acquiring the Olympia, he began tapping out jokes. A distant cousin of his in public relations thought the one-liners were clever and suggested sending them to newspaper columnists, who were always looking for free material to fill space. Before sending out anything, however, Woody decided that he needed a pen name, something that sounded more professional than Allan Konigsberg. "It was an ongoing discussion for months," said Elliott Mills. "We'd be walking along Avenue K to play stickball in the 99 schoolyard, talking about what would sound best. Early on he decided to use his first name as the last name. The problem was the new first name. 'Miles' was a candidate but not a strong one. It dropped out of contention fast when 'Woody' came up."

In the fall of 1952, Allan-Woody began his senior year of high school, with his mind elsewhere as usual. Under his new nom de plume, he began mailing out batches of jokes with a businesslike note: "Enclosed are some gags for your consideration and sent exclusively to you." The first columnist to bite was Nick Kenny at the *New York Daily Mirror*. Woody, utterly thrilled but never satisfied, aspired to better. The hottest Broadway columnist was the *New York Post*'s Earl Wilson, the crew-cut, bow-tied homeboy from Ohio who had made good in the big city with his Earl's Pearls quips, his fictitious showgirl Taffy Tuttle, and his B. W. (Beautiful Wife) Rosemary and son

Slugger. On November 25, 1952, Wilson first published a joke of Woody's about a much-maligned government agency, the Office of Price Stabilization, which was trying to control inflation long after the war's end. The joke ran as follows: "Woody Allen figured out what OPS prices are—Over People's Salaries." As the columnist quipped later, "Knowing a sucker when he saw one, he mailed me one-line jokes with postage due."

There was no indication that Wilson's new jokesmith could be a sixteen-year-old. For one thing, he sounded sexually sophisticated. "It's the fallen women who are usually picked up, says Woody Allen." Mostly the jokes swung back and forth between topical subjects, typically observations about the business of living. Already he was working with an attitude, the same one he shared with family and friends, all of whom tended to see things in a ridiculous light without even trying. Eager to be accommodating, Woody was regularly tailoring bons mots for Wilson's showgirl: "Taffy Tuttle told Woody Allen she heard of a man who was a six-footer and said, 'Gee, it must take him a long time to put his shoes on.' "

He couldn't get over his good luck. There was his new name "in a column that I had read a million times before with news and gossip of people whose lives I couldn't imagine I would ever touch. But there it was." Woody Allen in the same lofty company as Taffy Tuttle. In the insular little world of Midwood High, word of his adventures quickly spread. On February 27, 1953, there was an article about him in the Midwood *Argus* praising the "carrot-topped senior" who has made "quite a name for himself as a gag-writer." Asked for the secret of his success, Woody said, "I just sit down at the typewriter and think funny." By February, he had two dozen clippings. "When Bryna Goldstein first showed me Earl Wilson's column," recalled Alan Lapidus, "and said that Woody Allen was Allan, I was shocked. Nobody had given a second thought to this little schlemiel." Lapidus, who dreamed of being a writer but wound up an architect like his father, would conclude that "Allan was smarter than all of us. We were focused on being wonderful, but the best and the brightest of us never amounted to anything. It was Allan who was looking at the outside world, knew what he wanted, and did it."

Toward the end of his senior year, his uncompensated contributions to Earl Wilson suddenly paid dividends with a part-time job at a Madison Avenue public relations agency representing celebrities such as Arthur Murray, Guy Lombardo, and Sammy Kaye. To attract attention to their clients, David O. Alber Associates planted newspaper items that made them sound witty, as if funny lines automatically popped out of their mouths. In fact, when Woody in his saddle shoes finally met Dave Alber, he already had a reputation. Recalled then publicist Eddie Jaffe, "There were dozens of people submitting gags but Woody was one of the best." Alber offered him twenty-five dollars a week for twenty hours of work, more money than he could earn delivering for Padow's Pharmacy or pinning at the bowling alleys. He was ecstatic. Until he became acquainted with Wilson and Alber, he had never known adult praise, but with his new parent surrogates, "my life began being special." With classes on the early shift, he was dismissed at one. "I would get on the subway," he said, "the train quite crowded, and straphanging, I'd take out a pencil," and by the time he got off he'd have whipped up forty or fifty jokes. It was "no big deal."

When he graduated from Midwood High in 1953, the *Epilog* yearbook carried a blank space alongside his photograph. Of the 720 students in the Class of '53, he was the only one who had not participated in a single extracurricular activity. If there had been a student voted least likely to succeed, he was it.

In September Woody's friends went to college: Jack and Elliott to City College of New York; Jerry to Dickinson; and Woody was accepted at New York University. Determined that her son make something of himself, Nettie planned for him a career in pharmacy, completely disregarding his aversion to school, which he would always think of as "a terrible, terrible nasty experience." She also dismissed the fact that he had acquired a manager, Harvey Meltzer, the older brother of a classmate, with whom he signed a five-year contract that gave Harvey a 25 percent commission. So far no work had materialized, and in any case, Nettie never considered show business a sensible job. But what made her imagine Woody would be happy as a pharmacist is hard to fathom.

As a compromise, he enrolled at New York University as a film major, not because of any desire to make films but because it was an easy course. Hoping to get by with a minimum of effort, he took what the school called a limited program—three courses, including Spanish, English, and Motion Picture Production. However, riding the subway to school was too great a temptation for a consummate truant. As the train approached West Fourth Street in the Village, the stop for N.Y.U., a voice kept telling him, "Don't get off here. Keep going." In Times Square he spent the morning skylarking at the Automat, with coffee and the morning papers, browsing in the Circle Magic Shop, then slipping into the Paramount for an early feature. In the afternoons, he trekked across town to the Alber office, where his salary had been increased to forty dollars. Half the time he never got to class; to make matters worse, he seldom cracked a book. At the end of the first semester, he flunked Spanish and English, and barely passed motion picture production. N.Y.U. dropped him. Taking a defiant stance, he insisted that he "couldn't care less." His mother, he later joked, ran into the bathroom and tried to kill herself with an overdose of mah-jongg tiles. Nettie was not the sort to fall apart. What she actually did was swing into action and push the university to give him a second chance. The administration agreed, on the condition that he enroll in the summer session and bring up his grades. But one of the deans said pityingly that he just didn't seem to be college material and predicted what a grim future would befall him unless he started studying. In his opinion, the dean added, since Woody seemed to be maladjusted, it might be a good idea for him to see a psychiatrist.

Woody strenuously objected to the idea that he might be a misfit. He was already a person of some small importance, he told the dean. He was gainfully employed as a writer for a show business publicist and also sold jokes to the television comedian Herb Shriner. But that news only seemed to confirm the dean's opinion of his instability. Theatrical people are, he is said to have replied, "all strange."

That winter of 1954, to please his mother, he enrolled in a night course in motion picture production at the City College of New York, where he lasted an even shorter time than at N.Y.U. After only a few weeks, "I was given a Section Eight," he laughed, "the only one awarded by a nonmilitary institution." Nettie was understandably upset. Here she had bent over backward to give him a college education, but he threw it all away.

■ ■ ■ ■ ■ ■ ■

Snapshots: *Outside a friend's house with Bryna Goldstein, he poses in a Marlon Brando slouch, with the actor's trademark white T-shirt, jacket, and tight jeans. His hands are stuffed into his pockets, his hair slicked back, his jaw thrust forward in surly rebellion. He is bursting with sultry sexual aggression.*

The pretty, desirable girls at Midwood High want the tall boys, muscular six-footers with chunky chins. Physically, Woody is exactly the kind of conventionally geeky-looking guy who can't get a date for the high school prom. With 120 pounds packed on a skinny 5 foot 6 inch frame, he will soon get even odder-looking when he has to get glasses that fall and selects a pair of big black horn-rims.

■ ■ ■ ■ ■ ■ ■

When he was eighteen, Woody met a neighborhood girl at the East Midwood Jewish Center. Harlene Susan Rosen was small and string-bean slender, with an olive complexion, lovely black eyes, and a cascade of straight dark hair. She had a sweet face, and her only physical defect was a slight ski nose from a less than perfect rhinoplasty. At fifteen, she was attending James Madison High School, where she was an excellent student and also showed some talent for art, piano, and recorder—not surprising, since the Rosens were an artistic household. Woody gravitated toward the Rosens, whom he considered sophisticated, well-off people. Harlene's father played the trumpet, and her mother had once sung with a band. Julius Rosen had become a successful merchant who owned a children's shoe store on Kings Highway, a big corner house at Twenty-third and Avenue R, and a boat. His wife was an attractive, ambitious woman, who, not unnaturally, assumed that her two daughters would marry wealthy men. As for Harlene, she was probably dazzled by the attentions of a worldly older boy, who regaled her with his adventures in the overheated world of show business. Soon they were going steady.

However, in keeping with the fifties disapproval of premarital sex, they remained virgins. Woody's main interest in any female at this time was hormonal. To get what he wanted, he proposed marriage and bought an engagement ring, much to the dismay of both families, especially Judy Rosen, who had no desire to see one of her daughters with a college dropout earning forty dollars ($243 today) a week. Woody was not deceiving himself, either. Earning money for writing jokes was, he said, "like getting paid to play baseball or something," thrilling but also fool's luck. His drawer full of clippings amounted to the ability to hold the coats of David Alber's clients and make them sound funny. He wanted to be somebody, but he feared ending up as a nonentity: "I don't know what—a delivery boy or a messenger," he later said.

That bleak winter of 1955, there was an engagement dinner at the Konigsbergs. Unfazed by the occasion, Nettie began hectoring him about getting over his joke-writing foolishness, returning to college, going into a respectable business. How could he support a wife? Finally, Woody could no longer stand Nettie's needling. He grabbed the engagement ring and ran out of the house.

CHAPTER THREE

Stand-Up

I n the winter of 1956, Woody's life took an unexpected turn when he got a chance to go to Hollywood as a comedy writer on the *Colgate Variety Hour,* NBC's answer to the top-rated *Ed Sullivan Show* on CBS. Living at the Hollywood Hawaiian Motel, on his own for the first time, he felt confident that he had escaped his humdrum life with his family in Brooklyn. Proudly he raved to friends back home about the lush, sun-soaked good life of southern California; he loved the palm trees rising above the swimming pools, and bragged about stepping out at night to dine at world-famous restaurants such as the Brown Derby.

Yet, for all his enthusiasm, he felt intense loneliness and wrote several letters a day to Harlene, a freshman at Brooklyn College. In March, he could stand it no longer and impulsively summoned her to Hollywood to get married—a grand, dramatic gesture "as romantic as a movie script," in the eyes of his friends. Harlene, dewy-eyed, dying to get away from home, needed little persuasion to drop out of school and rush to Los Angeles, the elopement guaranteeing automatic transformation into a married lady of independence. On March 15, a rabbi married them at the Hollywood Hawaiian Motel. He was twenty, she was seventeen.

Hardly had the ink dried on the marriage certificate before Woody regretted his decision. Only days later, he was talking about divorce, sourly referring to his bride as "her," and predicting that the relationship had absolutely no chance of working. If not for the stigma of divorce, and the pain it would cause his parents, he let it be known that he was ready to walk out at once. Sex was important to him, but the reality of marriage must have been unnerving. At twenty, he was as well prepared for the day-to-day intimacy of living with a spouse as the average adolescent boy. As though that weren't bad enough, poor ratings caused the Colgate show to fold a month later, and they were forced to return to New York, homeless and broke but pretending to be happy newlyweds. Not only did the entire Hollywood adventure fizzle out prematurely, not only was their teenage marriage off to a terrible start, but Harlene had to ask her parents for her old room so that they would have a place to stay.

That fall they moved into the city and rented a one-room efficiency in a brownstone at 311 West Seventy-fifth Street, just down the block from Riverside Park. In the days before co-op gentrification, rents on the Upper West Side were dirt cheap. Broad boulevards were flanked on either side with Kafkaesque apartment houses, inhabited largely by refugees still speaking in heavy European accents. Crisscrossing the avenues were narrow streets lined with blighted row houses, now chopped up into makeshift walk-ups. Their building had been originally a one-family house, and the apartment presumably a parlor, or at least half of one, because now from the ceiling an elegant chandelier hung smack up against a wall. The long, narrow room made Woody joke about furnishing the place with hurdles.

Harlene resumed her education at tuition-free Hunter College, and Woody kept busy selling one-liners to radio stars like Peter Lind Hayes. For the time being, they put aside the idea of separation and tried to make a success of married life. Harlene learned how to cook, not always successfully, because Woody complained that everything she made, even coffee, tasted like chicken, and Elliott Mills remembered a dinner of boiled beef hearts and overcooked string beans as the worst meal he had ever eaten. In companionable moments, Harlene and Woody played their recorders together and went to movies.

It took almost three years before they could afford to move. Their new apartment, in a dinky brownstone at 4 East Seventy-eighth Street, was not much of an improvement over their old place, but at least it was on the East Side.

On the subway Woody ran into a kid from the neighborhood with whom he'd gone through P.S. 99 and Midwood High. He was miserable, he confided to Jimmy Moore, and had recently begun seeing a therapist. Moore was surprised. "In those days I'd never known anybody so unhappy that he would go to a psychiatrist. But if you did, you certainly didn't talk about it. I wondered what could be bothering him." Woody didn't really know what was bothering him, except "a continual awareness of seemingly unmotivated depression." He found a clinic with sliding-scale fees, all he could afford at the time, and went four or five times a week at fifteen dollars a session.

In spite of depression, his fortunes began to improve after making the acquaintance of several veteran writers who took a professional interest in him. More than anyone else, his most important mentor was Danny Simon, head writer on the Colgate show, and older brother of future playwright Neil Simon. Even though Woody had become a whiz at turning out jokes for Dave Alber's clients and for Herb Shriner, Danny warned him that writing jokes was not enough. He had to build on the gags to create characters and eventually learn how to write sketches. Later Woody would say that everything he knew about the craft of comedy writing—how to do a straight line, how to cut jokes that don't move the plot, and, most important, how to keep rewriting—he had picked up from Danny Simon.

As Simon's protégé, he began to wriggle his way slowly into big-league television comedy, though, to be sure, as a novice without good credentials or track record. After returning from Hollywood, his first job was *Stanley,* a half-hour sitcom starring Buddy Hackett and Carol Burnett. On his writing staff, the roly-poly Hackett had a stable of aces, including Larry Gelbart, Danny Simon, and Lucille Kallen. Intimidated, Woody sat quietly as a baby bird and spoke in whispers. "He was a very timid kid who didn't say much," remembered Hackett. "He was so damned serious about everything." After *Stanley* bombed, Woody worked on Pat Boone's musical variety program, *Chevy Showroom,* another frustrating experience. Many times, Boone remembers, "we'd be standing in the hallway during a break and Woody in his agitated, insistent way would be proposing some wild, drawn-out idea that we both *knew* was never going to make it. I would dissolve in helpless laughter and slide down the wall until I was sitting on the floor. Yet not one of those sketches was ever used on the show."

Like every comedy writer in the fifties, Woody was dying to work on Sid Caesar's *Your Show of Shows,* but there were never any openings. Finally, in 1958 Caesar used him for two NBC specials, which were both broadcast as "Sid Caesar's Chevy Show." Woody, thrilled, found himself in the company of writers such as Larry Gelbart, again, and Mel Brooks. The writers' room, Gelbart recalled, resembled "a playpen" full of all-white, all-Jewish, primarily male writers, who were trying to please a time bomb of an employer who habitually drank himself sick. Impossible to work for, Caesar once dangled Mel Brooks from the eleventh-floor office window by his ankles. Brooks, himself manic, habitually referred to young Woody as "that rotten little kid." Asked about Woody in 1997, he characterized him as a person who "never communicated anything memorable. I guess he was truly hiding his light under a bushel." Nevertheless, the rotten little kid was beginning to get a reputation, because in 1958 he and Larry Gelbart won a Sylvania award for the year's best television comedy.

In spite of his aversion to the country, he began leaving the city every summer to work at Tamiment, a resort in the Pocono Mountains of Pennsylvania, renowned as a borscht belt farm club for writers. (Herman Wouk memorialized the resort as South Wind in *Marjorie Morningstar.*) For many years, Max Liebman had produced the Saturday night shows at Tamiment Playhouse with the fresh young talents of Danny Kaye, Carol Burnett, Sid Caesar, Jerome Robbins, Mary Rodgers, and Danny and Neil Simon. The productions were said to be the equal of Broadway theater. Helping to write and stage—and sometimes act in—a different show every weekend, Woody found himself toiling around the clock. In his spare hours, he sat on the porch, chewing packs of spearmint gum, practicing his clarinet, and reading. "People joked that the books were marriage manuals," said Mary Rodgers, who, with Marshall Barer, was there at Tamiment working on the music and lyrics for a one-hour version of what eventually became *Once Upon a Mattress*. Woody, at the tender age of twenty-three, "already had a reputation for being a genius," said Rodgers. Actress Jane Connell agreed that he was impressive, "confident of what he had to offer and even though very shy, never kowtowing to anyone."

For Woody, the atmosphere at Tamiment was irresistible, a "George S. Kaufmanesque stage door feeling" that made him feel part of show business. Less enamored of the place was Harlene, called "Mrs. Woody" by the staff, who earned extra money typing scripts and "always had a cold," recalled Mary Rodgers. "Actually, I think it was an allergy to the mountains, or maybe to Woody." Like the other performers, Harlene and Woody lived in a one-room cabin and shared a toilet with the cabin next door, but the lack of privacy didn't seem to bother them. They were "Hansel and Gretel," said Jane Connell, "little kids who seemed more like brother and sister than passionate lovers. Harlene looked a bit like Olive Oyl in the comics." Behind his wife's back, slyly mocking their marriage, Woody told the other players that he knew nothing about sex on their wedding night and talked to a rabbi, who advised him not to worry. "All you do is mount her like a young bull." The story, despite many repetitions, never failed to make people laugh. The sniffling Harlene did not utter a word, "didn't show her feelings," reported producer Moe Hack. "She could take a lot of punishment."

In four years Woody became a successful writer for television's biggest comedy stars. In 1960, he went to work for the *Garry Moore Show* at a weekly salary of $1,700 (the equivalent of $9,300 today). It was quite a lot of money, but, characteristic of his negative attitude, Woody was still miserable. The greater his success, the more impatient and dissatisfied he was. Writing for others, he decided, was "a blind alley," not much different from working in Macy's. Around friends, he made no secret of his boredom in the comedy trenches. He was just writing "to earn a living," hacking around from show to show, always worried that the star would be dropped for poor ratings. In no time, he began treating the Moore show like Midwood High, a place to avoid if at all possible. When he did show up, he arrived late, goofed off, and needled the other writers. His manager, Harvey Meltzer, was a cautious man who warned him to take it easy and develop his talent slowly and systematically, advice that Woody stubbornly refused to follow. When their five-year contract expired in 1958, Woody dumped his manager, to the relief of Meltzer, who later complained that Woody was "making me sick what he was putting me through." On the recommendation of a friend from Tamiment, Woody then hooked up with two agents who did not require him to sign a contract. Unlike Meltzer, Jack Rollins and Charles Joffe took only a flat 15 percent commission.

The other thorn in his side, not as easy to remove as Meltzer, was Harlene. Now twenty-one, adopting a beatnik uniform of black skirts, leotards, pierced ears, and no makeup, she was a junior at Hunter, where she studied philosophy and German. By this time she held show business in low regard. It pained her to see her husband, a man obviously capable of serious work, wasting his talent on the lowest form of writing. Every so often her disdain reached the point where she would entice Woody into high-flown intellectual debates, which only infuriated him. However, it was probably her browbeating that shamed him into filling the gigantic craters in his education. To build his vocabulary, he began keeping lists of new words, and he also followed her courses, either by reading along with her or engaging a tutor from Columbia University to help him delve into the great works of philosophy and literature he had once considered impenetrable. Even so, it must have been grueling for a man whose best reading experiences had been comic books. "There have been very few things I can say in my life that were fun to read," he was to admit. "Even a great book like *Crime and Punishment* was not a joy to read." More enjoyable were magazines such as *The New Yorker,* which published the prose of S. J. Perelman, an "unremittingly hilarious" humorist in his opinion.

There was no question that their marriage was a mistake, but he could not bring himself to break free. Bitterly angry at being trapped in a situation he could not resolve, he took out his frustration by constantly diminishing his wife's talents and achievements, belittling and rebuking in much the same way his mother had treated him. Harlene, depressed, redoubled her efforts to please him.

All day he had been unable to eat, and now it was a little before ten and his heart was pounding. He felt as if he would pass out from stage fright. Waiting backstage at the Blue Angel, one of New York's most sophisticated supper clubs (the cover was $3.50), he listened while Shelley Berman introduced him as a funny young television writer who wanted to try out some of his own material. Neatly dressed in a suit and tie, he trudged out to the microphone and shot a sad-eyed glance at the audience through his thick Harold Lloyd spectacles, looking as startled as a fawn caught in headlights. Customers, drinking Scotch and smoking at the little pink-and-black tables and the banquettes along the quilted walls, stared back and smiled. Standing stiff and frightened under the draped velvet curtains, he began to robotically recite the thirty-minute audition monologue that he had spent months writing and polishing, tightening and rehearsing and timing. Once he got going, he plunged ahead fast and furious, as if he were reciting "The Charge of the

Light Brigade"—monotonous, mechanical, looking neither left nor right, what one of his managers would later describe as the equivalent of "a child doing show-and-tell." After a while, the blasts of laughter were coming less frequently until finally the crowd fell eerily quiet, eyes at half mast. At 10:30, fingers still pecking at his jacket, he walked offstage, feeling completely deflated. On that Sunday evening he learned an important lesson: There was a big difference between being funny and creating a comedy act. Killer material meant nothing without personality.

■ ■ ■ ■ ■ ■ ■

In His Own Words:
"It was unspeakably agonizing. All day long I would shake and tremble, thinking about standing up that night before people and trying to be funny."

—WOODY ALLEN, 1966

■ ■ ■ ■ ■ ■ ■

In 1960 the narrow streets of the West Village, Bleecker, MacDougal, and Sullivan, were a neon blur of clubs and coffeehouses offering all kinds of entertainment to middle-class couples from the outer boroughs and slumming uptown couples. The Cafe Wha, the Bitter End, and the Village Vanguard presented a roster of beatnik poets, amateur folksingers, and aspiring comics, all of them holding on to their day jobs because the clubs paid a going rate of five dollars a set. A few weeks after his catastrophic debut at the Blue Angel, Woody began working two shows a night, six nights a week at the Duplex, a club on Grove Street. It was a tiny walk-up on the second floor, with tables bunched together, a postage-stamp stage, and air sooty with cigarette smoke. Solely responsible for his being there were Rollins and Joffe, who were determined to push him into performing. Entering his life at its lowest point, they recognized that he had the originality but not the skill and immediately adopted the role of surrogate parents, babying him, holding his hand virtually every evening. "We *smelled* that this shy little guy could be a great performer," said Rollins.

Jack Rollins, eleven years Woody's senior, old enough to be a father figure to him, was born Jack Rabinowitz in 1914 and grew up in Brooklyn. A tall, forlorn man with pronounced dark circles under his eyes, he looked like a depressed raccoon who had got hold of a cigar. Early ambitions to become a theatrical producer got sidetracked when he met a folksinging short-order cook and began devoting all his time to developing the career of Harry Belafonte. Charles H. Joffe, twenty-nine, also from Brooklyn, attended Syracuse University and briefly tried to make a living as half of a song-and-comedy act. He then became a junior agent at MCA, one of Hollywood's biggest talent agencies, where he was not particularly successful, either. The two men met when Joffe noticed Rollins trudging along the halls of MCA, hustling his folksinger—no easy task in the days of segregation.

Together Rollins and Joffe made a splendid team: Rollins had the kind of sweet personality that made him a sensitive handler of people's feelings; Joffe was a fast-talking negotiator. Working out of a messy one-room office on West Fifty-seventh Street, a hole in the wall stacked high with old newspapers, they had a tiny stable of clients. Besides Belafonte, they represented two comics just starting out, Elaine May and Mike Nichols, but no writers because they were not lucrative. Before long, they broached the idea to Woody of doing stand-up. Why drop his best lines into someone else's mouth when he could perform the material himself?

Woody thought the suggestion was preposterous. Getting up in front of an audience terrified him. Not only did making a spectacle of himself require a kind of nerve that he definitely didn't possess, but, he pointed out, he was earning good money as a comedy writer. By now he had made his Broadway debut as well, with the contribution of two skits to *From A to Z,* a revue starring Hermione Gingold that had run for twenty-one performances. On the other hand, his whining about his dead-end job, his hellish marriage, anything and everything, intensified. For the next two years, he continued to write for Garry Moore, while Rollins and Joffe continued to hound him.

The advantage of a cut-rate club like the Duplex was that Woody could be really bad but nobody would know. (And he didn't have to pay for the privilege of performing.) There was no salary, cab fares, or wardrobe. There weren't even many customers, eight or ten maybe, most of them juiced and more interested in talking to one another than hearing him. Rollins recalled the audience response as "zero." Woody would remember "a Godforsaken, mostly empty club at 1 A.M. and then nobody would laugh. I wanted to die." Having no idea how to move onstage, he grabbed the microphone and ambled up and down like a caged ferret. No performance was complete unless he tangled the cord around his neck. Sometimes Rollins worried that "he was going to choke himself." Basically, he had the body language of a schoolboy called upon to recite.

Oblivious to hecklers, he would "stoically go through with his lines and do his 25 minutes like they weren't there," remembered Rollins. He passed the time between sets huddled at a table with Jack and Charlie, sighing deeply, endlessly grumbling about having to perform for a bunch of "dogs with high-pitched ears." It was insane. He had a knot in his stomach, he was earning nothing. Look how terribly he was suffering. "Listen, fellahs, do you think I should continue this?"

If it's too difficult, he should quit, Rollins and Joffe told him. After all, it was him on the stage, not them. But Woody ignored them. He enjoyed whining. It was the essential Allan Konigsberg. The next night the "why me?" lamentations would begin all over again. Did they think he should go on? And they would repeat, like good straight men, "Well, we think so if you can bear it."

Frequently Woody's high-school gang came by to offer encouragement and act as laughers. "He got sick and threw up," recalled Elliott Mills. "It wasn't easy. He was never a traditional borscht belt comedian. He couldn't spritz. All he could do was tell stories."

Woody's last show was at 12:30, and an hour later he would be out on Sheridan Square with Charlie Joffe. Uptown there were always places to go, Eddie Condon's on Fifty-fourth Street, the Wilbur De Paris Band on Fifty-second. At 2 A.M. Broadway was jumping. You went to Jack Dempsey's clam bar, or to the Optimo cigar store with its window of phone booths facing the street, or you could sit in Hanson's Drugstore, specializing in Max Factor No. 2 pancake and burgers—full of showgirls from the Latin Quarter. Lindy's and the Stage Deli were clubhouses where comics and their agents and flacks convened for bagels and nervous yocks until all hours of the morning, a scene that Woody would paint so brilliantly twenty years later in *Broadway Danny Rose*. There was no reason to go home.

The city after midnight was not a place you saw comedians' wives, not a place wives wanted to be. Between the *Garry Moore Show* by day and the Duplex at night, Harlene got frozen outside of Woody's life.

Shortly after Woody began performing at the Duplex, an actor friend from Tamiment, Bob Dishy, came to see the show with a date who had been, until recently, a student at Brandeis University. Although Louise Lasser majored in political science, she always won a featured role in student musicals—not surprising because she was also a talented singer with a Judy Garland–type of voice (two years later she would replace Barbra Streisand in the musical *I Can Get It for You Wholesale*). After her junior year at Brandeis, suffering from bouts of depression, she returned home to study acting. Immediately enamored of the petite strawberry blonde with the endearing toothy smile, Woody invited her and Dishy to his apartment. Then, on New Year's Eve, 1960, Louise invited him and Harlene to celebrate the evening at the apartment of her parents, who lived just a few blocks away on Fifth Avenue. At the party, Louise tried to befriend Harlene but sensed her hostility and concluded that she must have "known something." But at that point there was nothing to know, except that Louise had developed a huge crush on Woody.

By the spring of 1961, however, it was a different story. By then they had been seeing each other secretly for months, meeting at the Metropolitan Museum of Art and taking carriage rides through Central Park. The fact that he was married and living with his wife put a damper on the romance. Whenever the twenty-year-old Louise brought up the subject, he offered the standard explanation of husbands in the process of switching women: He and his wife had grown apart. As soon as Harlene graduated from Hunter in June, they planned to separate. Reassured, Louise felt "that was the nice thing about Woody," who could always take control of situations and defuse her anxiety by saying "exactly what was going to happen, the reasoning behind it, and when." Harlene would not actually graduate until June of 1962, finally getting her degree after six years because periodic shortages of money had forced her to drop out for some semesters and work. Woody and Louise continued to tryst in Central Park, but contrary to Louise's suspicions, it is doubtful that Harlene knew of their affair. Even after the separation, when Woody moved his things to a studio apartment a block away at 14 East Seventy-seventh Street that summer, she continued to wonder if they had done the right thing; maybe with more effort it could have worked out.

Not that Woody had any regrets. Continuing his pattern of attraction to women above him, he had moved on. Louise represented everything he associated with the brittle Nick and Nora Charles world of Upper East Side wealth and sophistication. If he could have his way, he would have been her. Born in 1940, the only child of a noted tax expert, S. Jay Lasser, and his wife, Paula, Louise grew up living in a Fifth Avenue building and attending exclusive private schools and progressive summer camps. "Whenever I got off the bus," she joked, "Pete Seeger was standing there with a guitar." But despite her privileged upbringing, Louise had emotional problems that seemed to be inherited from her mentally unstable mother, whose illness resulted in repeated hospitalizations. In 1961 Paula Lasser attempted suicide. Emerging from a five-day coma, she demanded to know who had been responsible for saving her life. Informed that it was Louise, she cried, "I'll never forgive her." Three years later she would try again and succeed.

Louise, "the smartest of all Woody's women," according to a friend of Woody's, was well read, and Woody had to hustle to keep up with her. As he himself was to admit later, "It was only when I started going out with women who were more cultured and made great demands on me that I started to feel I had to keep my end of the conversation up."

■ ■ ■ ■ ■ ■ ■

In His Own Words:
"I never set out to create any image at all."
—WOODY ALLEN, 1964

■ ■ ■ ■ ■ ■ ■

Little by little, the act caught on. By the summer of 1961, Woody moved on to a Village coffeehouse, the Bitter End, where he was paid a pittance, in the high two figures he joked. To the *New York Times Magazine,* he tried to make everything sound easy. "The simple fundamentals of working in clubs can be unequivocally learned in a month," he declared. In fact, transforming himself into a stand-up comic had taken nearly a year. During those months of experimentation, he accomplished the most creative work of his entire life and invented a verbal comic strip known as "Woody Allen." In some respects, his character was the classic Little Man Against the World—the slender sparrow body, the cartoon face, the thinning red hair, the sorrowful eyes behind thick glasses, the nervous mannerisms: dribbling fingers and the shuffling feet, the mumbled wells, uhs, ums, and ahs, in a singsong New York cadence (which he was working hard to lose). But the material was so surrealistic that he managed to reinvent the little schnook genre and make it his own. Anyone who knew him could see that his awkwardly appealing stock character was "an exaggerated version" of Allan Konigsberg, one that blurred the line between autobiography and comedy.

Of course, his urban neurotic did not appear full-blown. In the beginning, all he had was funny material and a woebegone appearance that provoked laughter in itself, but he lacked a theme. His own account of giving birth to his character is not completely trustworthy: "Gradually, the character evolved," he explained at the time. "It didn't evolve deliberately. I just wrote stuff that seemed funny. But the character was assigned to me by the audience. They laughed more at certain things. Naturally I used more of those things." The critics also shared in his creation because, he observed, they "wrote about me as a certain type. So I put more material in the act that would fit that type." In other words, he found his good-boy persona through trial and error.

What he failed to acknowledge, at least not then, was how much his gropings owed to specific individuals, one of them being Bob Hope and his WASP schlemiel character, the vain, cowardly womanizer who ends up the winner. Only seven years old when his mother took him to see *Road to Morocco,* Woody knew every Hope film by heart and automatically copied Hope's smart-alecky attitude and superb timing. To Hope's fast one-liners and ad-libbed asides, Woody layered the nervous, stabbing delivery of Mort Sahl, the comic he idolized above all others. However, as he became slightly more comfortable in front of an audience—goaded no doubt by reviewers who had dubbed him "Son of Sahl"—his own unbuttoned personality began to emerge, and the material became more psychological. (Woody, who couldn't care less about JFK and Nixon, steered clear of Sahl's topical material and instead joked about chasing gorgeous women.) In addition to borrowing from Hope and Sahl, he sprinkled his style with bits and pieces from other humorists—S. J. Perelman, Robert Benchley, Groucho Marx, Charlie Chaplin, Jerry Lewis—until what finally emerged was a plum pudding distinctly recognizable as the Woody Allen style.

The political satire of Sahl and the social satire of a hipster such as Lenny Bruce could be appreciated anywhere, but Woody staked out territory that was local and familiar: His neighborhoods existed inside the city limits of Jewish New York, both the Brooklyn of his youth (he joked of pollution destroying German subs off Coney Island) and the exclusive Upper East Side, where as an adult he was easily mugged in the lobby of his Park Avenue building. But in one way or another, the subject of nearly all his humor would be Allan Konigsberg, his complaining little-boy self, with fanciful semiconfessional bits that evoked his own emotional geography: his mother whom he swore must have breast-fed him through falsies; his parents who rented out his room after he had been kidnapped, his screwball grandfather who sold him a gold watch on his deathbed, his experiences at N.Y.U. where he cheated on a metaphysics exam by peeking into the soul of another student.

In time, the construction of his routines would grow more complex. The fantasy "Down South" tells of his visit to an unnamed southern city. Setting off to a costume party dressed as a ghost, he is offered a lift by a car full of men in white sheets. Soon the Klansmen discover he is worse than bogus, he is a New York Jew. They are not amused, and decide to lynch him on the spot, but Woody manages to calm them with an eloquent discourse on brotherhood. Typically, his routines had conclusions as quietly unexpected as a bang on the head. "Not only did they cut me down and let me go, but that night I sold them two thousand dollars worth of Israel bonds."

In his most memorable monologue, "The Moose," Woody begins by offering the audience a story they won't believe. "I was hunting in upstate New York and I shot a moose." He straps the moose on the fender of his car, but on his way home, driving through the Holland Tunnel, the moose wakes up. What's more, the moose begins signaling for an illegal turn. As the routine unfolds and one line collapses hilariously into the next, Woody tries to get rid of the moose. In desperation, he takes him to a sophisticated East Side costume party where the moose mills sociably with the other guests. Not only does he blend in easily, he wins second prize for his costume, first prize having been awarded to a certain married couple named the Berkowitzes who came dressed in, of all things, moose suits. Woody's moose is understandably irritated and during the ensuing confrontation becomes unruly. The three moose knock one another unconscious. Woody grabs two of the moose, straps them to his fender, and hurtles back up to the woods, where he dumps them. The next morning, waking up in their moose suits, the poor Berkowitzes are shot. We then move to a bastion of the Establishment, the New York Athletic Club, where the Berkowitzes have been stuffed and mounted prominently on a wall. In the end, the joke is on the fraternity of WASPs, whose bylaws exclude Jews from membership.

•••••••

March of Time:
"It must have been 1963 or 1964 when David [Brown] and I first heard him perform at the Blue Angel. He was just starting. I remember being so annoyed because there were some out-of-towners from Wisconsin or the South Bronx talking and talking through the jokes and they wouldn't stop. So I threw buttered rolls at them."

—HELEN GURLEY BROWN

•••••••

By 1962 Woody was establishing a national reputation as the hottest comic in the country. While the earliest notice of him came from influential local papers such as the *New York Times,* which suggested he might be potentially a special comic ("a Chaplin-esque victim with an S. J. Perelman sense of the bizarre and a Mort Sahl delivery"), he kept dogging the big national magazines for coverage. Grateful for any scrap of attention, he greeted each article in *Time, Newsweek,* and *The Saturday Evening Post* with joy and turned into a relentless writer of thank-you notes. To Rogers E. M. Whitaker, the railroading buff who covered the club scene for *The New Yorker,* he wrote that his favorable reviews were "by far my most satisfying achievement" in his nightclub career. A local newspaper reporter received a mannerly, typed bread-and-butter note: While he was usually disappointed by the way his interviews read, he found her piece both enjoyable and helpful. To almost everybody he extended a standard invitation to meet him for a drink.

An old hand at press agentry and hype, he easily borrowed the tactics of David Alber to promote his own career and diligently embarked on what would become a lifetime of self-marketing, manipulating the media to his own advantage. His coquettish handling of the press—coyly standing in the paparazzi line of fire, pleading for attention while feigning reluctance—would become known as Woody Allen Disease. As a newcomer, however, the shrewdest weapon in his arsenal of stratagems would be down-home modesty. He said solemnly to the *New York Times Magazine* that his reactions to everyday situations "seem normal to me, but completely hilarious to everyone else, and most of the time I can't figure out why."

*　　　　*　　　　*

Not long after Harlene flew to Chihuahua for a Mexican divorce in November of 1962, he mentioned her onstage for the first time. He and his wife, he confided, couldn't decide whether to vacation in Bermuda or file for divorce; they settled on divorce because a holiday lasts two weeks, but a divorce is forever. Sure enough, the line got a laugh.

As part of the separation agreement, he promised to pay a lump sum of $1,750, followed by an extremely modest $75 a week in alimony for the rest of her life, or until she remarried. Should he be continuously employed with a running contract, the sum would be increased to $125. "Leaving when she did, just as he was about to make it, she got a bad deal out of the whole thing," said a friend. "The settlement was peanuts." After the divorce, all contact between them ceased and so when his alimony payments became erratic, Harlene apparently couldn't bring herself to complain.

Judging by some of Woody's statements to the media over the years, Harlene's behavior during their six years together could not have been more exemplary: She was a studious young woman who ground away at her studies and got straight A's at Hunter, when she was not playing the piano or painting. The starter marriage had been "really a great experience," but their interests grew "diverse" until they finally went their friendly ways. That was not exactly the truth because, according to Louise Lasser, never did Woody have a kind word to say about his former wife in private. And in public, even though he and Harlene were no longer married, she continued to play a major role in his life. Unable to resist the urge to punish her, he slyly began adding Harlene one-liners to his act on a regular basis, until at times these mischievous bad-boy zingers threatened to become the centerpiece. Lobbing verbal grenades, he regularly referred to her as Quasimodo, the hunchback of Notre Dame. At various times, he described her as a "weird woman" who had half a dozen sex-change operations "but couldn't find anything she liked." Marrying her was a stupid mistake because when he first introduced her to his parents, "they approved but the dog died"; the first time she cooked him a dinner he almost choked to death on a bone in her chocolate pudding; on her birthday he gave her an electric chair that he passed off as a hair dryer; the American Museum of Natural History used one of her shoes to reconstruct a dinosaur; she was so bumble-brained that after burning herself on a hot stove, "it took her two minutes to think of the word ouch." The nastiest joke, however, imagined her being raped: "My first wife lives on the Upper West Side and I read in the paper the other day that she was violated on her way home—knowing my first wife, it was not a moving violation."

These sorts of jokes follow in the tradition of Milton Berle, or Henny Youngman with his "Take my wife, please!" or any of the older borscht belt comics who regularly insulted Jewish women, usually their wives or mothers-in-law. Woody, too, was unkind to his mother, but there was no one he treated so scornfully as the spurned Harlene. So unmistakable was his hostility that sensitive patrons could not help noticing. At the Blue Angel one night, a heckler yelled, "Who keeps you warm at night!" But that was rare. Usually his Harlene jokes guaranteed huge laughs. Even his friends who had always been enormously fond of her found themselves laughing uproariously, then feeling guilty. The trouble was, admitted Jack Victor, "the jokes were funny."

Upon leaving Harlene, Woody continued to live in the same neighborhood with Louise. After the studio on Seventy-seventh Street, they took a bigger apartment on East Eightieth Street before renting at 784 Park Avenue, an expensive doorman apartment building at the corner of East Seventy-fourth. The fancy address pleased him, but the apartment itself turned out to be dingy because it faced a brick wall. Living with Louise had its ups and downs, too. For all her fairy-tale façade—her beauty, talent, intelligence, and wealth— she was emotionally frail, an insecure young woman who knew of no other way to relate to a man except in a child-father relationship. Her mother's illness meant she had been brought up mostly by her father, a controlling man who indulged and pampered her. Woody, too, began to treat her as a kittenish little girl in need of supervision. Her low sense of self-regard seemed excessive. When he was working at the Bitter End and they were still living in the studio, she insisted on taking a waitress job at the club to be near him. The sight of her hustling around with coffee while he was doing his act was terribly distracting, he protested. But she enjoyed waiting tables, she replied. He suggested, "Why don't you be my maid instead?" and offered her fifty dollars a week to clean the apartment.

As it happened, he could have paid Louise a lot more than fifty dollars. With the days of the little oddball places behind him, Rollins and Joffe were booking him into the best clubs in the country: the Blue Angel and the Americana Hotel's Royal Box in New York, Caesars Palace in Las Vegas, Mr. Kelly's in Chicago, the Crescendo in Los Angeles. He was pulling in $4,000 to $5,000 a week, which translates into $21,000 to $26,000 today. But through the winter of 1963 and the spring of 1964, it was television that triggered his breakthrough into significant wealth and fame. As a guest on the late-night shows hosted by Johnny Carson and Steve Allen, he quickly established himself as the most talked-about comic of the season, famous for droll one-liners and scintillating off-the-cuff repartee. Ironically, Woody had a low opinion of TV, which he dismissed as "junk." It made no difference, because its viewers could not get enough of him. Once he was able to attract the attention of the entire country, exposure that only television can afford, his career blasted off like a rocket shimmying toward the Milky Way.

CHAPTER FOUR

What's New, Pussycat?

On a steamy afternoon just before the Fourth of July weekend in 1964, Woody arrived at Washington National Airport. In the men's room he changed from jeans and sneakers into a rented tuxedo and proceeded to the White House, where he was invited to attend a state dinner in honor of the president of Costa Rica.

Woody detested parties, which were always full of people he had never met before, indeed, never particularly wanted to meet. For him, he liked to say, telling jokes for a living was the perfect job because it meant he didn't have to be around people. "I go up on stage, I do my act, they laugh, I go home." Of course, an invitation to the White House was altogether different. For a working-class boy brought up on Fifteenth and K in Midwood, two generations removed from Leon Cherry's luncheonette on East Eighteenth Street, it was an enormously surreal moment, proof that he had made it. Shaking hands with President Lyndon Johnson at the reception, he strolled around and chatted with some of the eminent guests, among them Reverend Billy Graham, Jimmy Durante, and Richard Rodgers. Awestruck, Woody later said that the magnificence of the eighteenth-century mansion and the dignity of the military band almost made him feel as if were stepping into a scene from *Gone With the Wind.*

But midway through the evening, the bubble showed signs of bursting. Suddenly his tux began to itch, and his shoes, also rented, were rubbing blisters on both feet. To make matters worse, there was little to eat on his dinner plate but a filet mignon the size of a half dollar. Before he could make his escape, the band was playing a fox-trot, and Lady Bird Johnson insisted on sweeping him around the dance floor. Mrs. Johnson examined his Raggedy Andy hairstyle. When she inquired jokingly if he might be wearing a wig, he found himself so flustered that he could think of no sufficiently comical comeback. At midnight, he rushed back to the airport and fished his jeans out of the locker, scolding himself for having behaved like "a wallflower." As it turned out, his performance anxiety was completely unjustified because six months later he would be invited to entertain at LBJ's inauguration.

The next week after his dinner at the White House, his career got another boost. Earlier NBC had asked him to substitute for a vacationing Johnny Carson as guest host of *The Tonight Show.* All that week he was scrambling to put together material. Before each day's taping, the couch in his office would be blanketed with manila file folders bulging with scraps of paper, jokes scribbled on dog-eared yellow sheets, on cocktail napkins and matchbook covers. Pawing through the odds and ends, he claimed that he hadn't the faintest idea what he was going to say. He was guaranteed to mess up. Moaning about his plight to a *Newsday* reporter, he said: "What the hell am I doing here anyway?" (Making $2,400 for only five nights' work was the correct answer.) For all his endless offstage self-flagellation, he was never at a loss for words on camera with guests such as comedian Godfrey Cambridge. One evening he invited Louise to appear on the show, without of course informing *The Tonight Show* audience that she was his live-in girlfriend. By week's end, he had approving television critics joking that Johnny Carson had better get back to New York fast.

Woody's secret contempt for television did not prevent him from accepting every booking that came his way: *Candid Camera, What's My Line,* even a folk music series called *Hootenanny,* he did them all. Most embarrassing was *Coliseum,* in which he exposed himself in bathing trunks to introduce a magic act called Mr. Electric, "what my wife called me the morning after our honeymoon night," he quipped.

If *Coliseum* fell at one end of the spectrum, *The Ed Sullivan Show* on Sunday night was at the other. Once you had been on *Ed Sullivan,* the whole country knew who you were the next morning. Although Woody would be booked many times, his first appearance in 1962 was very nearly his last. At the run-through, he decided to keep his performance fresh for the show and chose to do "Private Life," one of his most popular routines, which included a bit about his wife's cousin who had taken out "orgasmic" insurance. ("If her husband fails to satisfy her sexually, Mutual of Omaha has to pay her every month.") Sullivan, unaware that Woody was making a substitution and why, watched with mounting agitation. If there was one thing Sullivan hated, after commies, homosexuals, and women wearing trousers, it was smut. No sooner had Woody finished than Sullivan began screaming at him. He was a dirty pervert. How dare he pull that filth! But he wouldn't get away with it because he was off the show. "Attitudes like yours are why kids are burning their draft cards," he shouted. Finally, turning to the rehearsal audience, Sullivan begged their pardon.

Woody was amazed. His impulse, he later confided to Dick Cavett, was to "respond nastily." Instead of shouting back, he "apologized like a shrinking violet. I charmed the pants off him." After that Sullivan was "wonderful" to him and invited him back many times, but Woody would never forget how he had been "humiliated."

Not so long ago, he was taking any gig offered to him. Now, at twenty-eight, he was a headliner who continually worked the club circuit. A vagabond life on the road, however, meant late nights and empty hotel rooms. In spite of his fear of flying, he went out "for six, seven months at a time without a night off," he said. "I mean seven nights a week. I would go from the Blue Angel to the Hungry i to the Crystal Palace." The worst part was doing two or three sets a night, being absurdly exhausted "and then you have to do it again at two in the morning." As he wrote Groucho Marx, his television appearances coupled with the need to change his act for every nightclub reappearance took a lot out of him. Still, he knew he shouldn't complain because it was better than bagging groceries. At the A&P, of course, you didn't often get Scotched-up wiseguys. After being heckled one night at the Hungry i, Woody turned his back on the audience and did the rest of his act facing upstage. The audience, feeling shortchanged, stomped out. Afterward, the club manager called him into his office. "Don't do that again," he warned. "I had to give thirty refunds."

Yet, there were also bright spots. One evening in Chicago, he and Jack Rollins got to talking with a young couple at a coffee shop across the street from Mr. Kelly's. Rollins mentioned that he had to leave town and worried that Woody might get lonely. Soon Woody was seeing the couple almost every night. John Doumanian, thirty-three, was a big teddy bear of an Armenian, good-humored and jolly. He worked for Capitol Records, and his pretty wife, Jean, was a buyer for a small women's boutique. Jean Karabas was born in 1937 and grew up in Chicago, where her parents, Greek immigrants, operated a restaurant. With long jet-black hair and pale skin, a very thin figure and elegant wardrobe, every stitch of it black, she had the anorexic look of an *Addams Family* character. One of her detractors likened her to "a Greek widow, who dresses dark and eats black strap molasses," an allusion to her preference for organic food. Woody enjoyed their company, especially the twenty-seven-year-old Jean, who, he thought, had a surprisingly great sense of style and sophistication for a midwesterner. It was tough to make her laugh though. Instead she would say, "That is *soo* funny."

As it turned out, Woody and Jean were similar. Both had grown up in traditional households, both burned hot with ambition, both had made mistakes and married young. They had the same tightly wound personalities, precise and meticulous, and tended to have difficulty relating to people. There was "a wonderful side to her," said Laurie Zaks, a television producer who worked for Jean in the seventies. "She was great to her family and friends. But there was also her angry side. I sensed that she'd been through tough times along the way. There was a lot of old anger she had never dealt with."

A few years after their meeting, Woody remained on friendly terms with the Doumanians when they moved to New York and got a divorce. For Jean, he arranged a job booking celebrities for Dick Cavett's popular television talk show. Over the years John Doumanian would appear as an actor in several of Woody's pictures. It was Jean, however, who would become Woody's most trusted confidant, a sounding board for just about every step he took in life thereafter, from how to dress to how to conduct his love life. "She's pretty, she's intelligent, she's loyal; she's everything you could want," Woody would rave about her. "She's a dream friend." And when they were together, she took charge. "To know Woody, just look at his friends," said writer Peter Tauber. "Jean is emblematic of his very controlled, very orderly side. You can see that he doesn't have room in his life for crazy people."

As the repository of his confidences and kvetches, Jean saw or spoke to him daily, always seeming to be taking his emotional temperature. Late at night Louise would wake up and hear him talking on the phone. Some people assumed there had once been a romance—or that Jean had wanted to marry him—but this was apparently not the case. The relationship, which has turned out to be the longest of his life, remains platonic, and they continue to meet for dinner several times a week. In middle age, he still depends on her as his "closest friend in the world." For him, she is "the person you want to be with when you're waiting for the results of your biopsy." If Woody has a soul mate, it's been Jean, the only woman he has been able to respect as an equal. "He's very lucky to have her," remarked one of her friends, Stephen Silverman, an editor at *People* magazine. "She's been a real crutch."

■ ■ ■ ■ ■ ■ ■

Stand-Up:

AUDIENCE QUESTION: Would you accept the vice-presidential nomination?

WOODY: I'm apolitical. I have no political convictions whatsoever. I'm a registered pervert.

—"Question and Answer Session," Monologue

■ ■ ■ ■ ■ ■ ■

Comedy albums were taking a sizable slice of the entertainment market in the sixties. People spent money to stay home and listen to Jonathan Winters, Nichols and May, and Lenny Bruce on their living-room hi-fis. In March 1964, Woody recorded his first album live at Mr. Kelly's. *Woody Allen*, released by Colpix Records, contained thirty-seven minutes of original material; altogether, eleven routines that included "Private Life," "N.Y.U.," "My Marriage," "My Grandfather," and "Brooklyn." Although the album was nominated for a Grammy, sales did not satisfy Woody, who complained incessantly. How come his career was going great, he grumbled to his publicist Richard O'Brien, but no one bought his album? That didn't stop him from recording two more.

Slowly but surely, his earnings continued to mount, to $250,000 a year ($1.3 million today) by the time he turned thirty. Woody attributed his success to "just the throw of the dice." Much of that luck had to do with appearing at precisely the right moment, when the postwar baby boomers, now come of age, were seeking new values and unlikely heroes in unusual places. A decade of so much self-consciousness that it was packaged as a sign of the zodiac, the age of Aquarius was a time in which his comic sensibility proved irresistible. To those who characterized the idealistic sixties, Woody represented a new breed of man, the quintessential misfit, the heroic frog who had turned into a prince. Clearly he was a man ever-faithful to his principles, who relied on his own moral compass, however out of whack it might be. People said they wanted to be like him. Metaphorically, wrote the critic Diane Jacobs, the Woody persona held up a mirror to his times by embodying "the struggles of late-twentieth-century urban man."

All the same, his grip on the consciousness of the sixties is ironic because in many respects his values clashed with the wildly anti-Establishment, psychedelic, miniskirted, love-in and freak-out temperament of the decade. Woody, anti-anti-Establishment, had virtually no interest in the social and political upheavals of the time: segregation in the South, equality of the sexes, the Vietnam War, the student protest movement, the Cold War, or the space race. His political position was to have none. Everyone assumed that as a New York Jew, he must be a meat-and-potatoes liberal Democrat, and that is how he tended to see himself. More accurately, he was a political naïf who had lived through the McCarthy years without knowing exactly who McCarthy was. The day John F. Kennedy was assassinated, Woody was in Los Angeles playing the Crescendo, and he spent that evening with Mort Sahl and Dick Cavett—all of them wisecracking that nobody was going to show up but then nobody had showed up before the assassination either. After agreeing to take part in an actors' antiwar demonstration in 1969, he failed to put in an appearance. During the 1972 presidential campaign, he was invited to perform at a George McGovern fund-raiser but declined because he'd rather "do something beyond humor" like ringing doorbells or handing out leaflets. He did neither. "I'm not really a political person," he told the sixties activist Jerry Rubin, and went on to describe himself as more interested in "the real issues—

philosophical issues of life and death," big questions that he would continue to pose time and again as part of his act. (He had no answers.)

Equally heretical in his personal tastes and habits, he was never a citizen of the permissive Woodstock Nation. He was against doing drugs, and only smoked pot once or twice, which is not surprising because he needed to be in control at all times. Once a smoker of cigarettes and thin cigars, he now smoked nothing. He drank no hard liquor, and wine only sparingly. As for music, he was passionate in his dislike of Elvis, Dylan, and the Beatles. "I hate rock," he once declared.

In the heyday of sex, drugs, and rock and roll, of the three his only interest was sex.

■ ■ ■ ■ ■ ■

Tales of New York Life:
EARL WILSON: Do you know all about sex?
WOODY: I know enough to get through the evening.
—Interview, 1972

■ ■ ■ ■ ■ ■

On a wintry night in 1964, at the Blue Angel, the actor Warren Beatty was sitting at one of the ringside tables with a debonair middle-aged man in a conservative dark suit and tie. Practically everything Woody said made Beatty howl with laughter. Afterward, he turned to his companion to say he really ought to hire Woody. He was positively brilliant. The man in the dark suit, however, had hardly been laughing at all. He was thinking.

Charles K. Feldman was born for the Hollywood high life. At the age of sixty, he was a connoisseur of the best real estate in Hollywood and on the French Riviera, the most beautiful women, the finest wines, the most lavish hotels and casinos. For all these exotic trappings, he was a consummate businessman. Orphaned in childhood and raised by a wealthy New York couple, he graduated from the University of Michigan, then law school at the University of Southern California, and set up a Hollywood law practice. In 1932, aged only twenty-eight, he became president of Famous Artists, a huge talent agency whose clients over the years had included superstars such as Marlene Dietrich, Greta Garbo, and John Wayne. In the forties, he turned producer with partner Howard Hawks, and eventually became known for high-quality pictures—for example, Billy Wilder's *The Seven Year Itch,* a tremendous commercial success starring Marilyn Monroe.

That winter in New York, he was seeking a writer for a picture he wanted to make with Beatty, a former client and close friend, who was almost a surrogate son to him. After his debut in *Splendor in the Grass,* the twenty-seven-year-old Beatty had suddenly become a star big enough to turn down seventy-five scripts a year. As a result of his virile good looks, he also had the women running after him. Answering his phone, he had a breezy stock greeting for his female callers: "What's new, pussycat?" It was, Feldman decided, the perfect title. Feldman decided to make a movie about a natural Don Juan, like the satyrish Warren, who wanted every woman he spotted, and Beatty had agreed to star, but the project had hit a road bump. Optioning a creaky Don Juan comedy, *Lot's Wife* by Czech writer Ladislaus Bus-Fekete, Feldman turned over the property to Billy Wilder's frequent collaborator, the top screenwriter I. A. L. Diamond, to turn into a modern farce but Diamond's script proved to be a disappointment.

Several days after Feldman saw Woody perform at the Blue Angel, he delegated the photographer Sam Shaw to make inquiries. The picture of nonchalance, Shaw strolled into Charlie Joffe's office dressed in sneakers and grungy pants. How much, he asked, did Joffe want for his boy Allen to write a film script? Joffe, unimpressed, barely giving Shaw the time of day, answered $35,000. Shaw nodded approvingly (Feldman had authorized $60,000) and said Feldman would be in touch.

In the end, after much haggling, Joffe was able to increase the sum by throwing in Woody's services as an actor, hardly a deal sweetener because Woody, who had never sold a screenplay, had never acted, either. Meanwhile, an astonished Woody regarded Feldman's offer as nothing less than an unexpected godsend. As his long-suffering friends and managers could attest, he was continually grumbling about how much he hated being a stand-up, bleating that he'd never had any talent for public performance in the first place, that performing comedy was just as indescribably horrible as writing it. Bemoaning his fate, Woody always had a litany of complaints about fame not being everything it is cracked up to be. Unfortunately, success as a stand-up had turned out to be, as he put it, "a ride I couldn't get off." So this emissary from Hollywood's magic kingdom with his Warren Beatty screenplay was nothing short of the answer to his prayers.

In July of 1964, that same summer he dined at the White House, he left for London in a particularly good mood and checked into the Dorchester Hotel. Finishing a screenplay, it turned out, had been unbelievably easy and now he looked forward to the satisfaction of watching his creative efforts translated to the screen. He quickly discovered, however, that the life of a screenwriter is not all blue skies and sunshine, because Feldman asked for rewrite after rewrite. With each draft, Woody revealed his pique by making his own role fatter and funnier and Beatty's tinier, until the actor backed out in disgust. Feldman promptly stuck Peter O'Toole in the part. As the plot goes, the editor of a Parisian fashion magazine (O'Toole) consults a psychiatrist about curing his addiction. With "pussycats" falling all over him, he has more sex than he can handle. Before long, it is the shrink, Dr. Fritz Fassbender (Peter Sellers), who, dying of horniness, is going berserk trying to figure out the secrets of his compulsive patient's success. Woody turns up as O'Toole's buddy Victor Shakapopolis, who dresses and undresses strippers at the Crazy Horse saloon for twenty francs a week.

"Not very much," consoles O'Toole.

"It's all I can afford," replies Woody.

Through the summer of 1964 and into the new year, as production got under way in Paris, the realities of moviemaking came as a painful shock to Woody. Misunderstanding the nature of the picture business, he had fancied that his story would reach the screen intact. He no more expected Feldman to change his script than he expected the mogul to have rewritten his club act. In fact, the plain truth was that nobody paid a bit of attention to what he thought about the movie. During the months of production, making no attempt to adapt to his loss of control over the situation, he lived in raw misery. In his hotel room at the Hotel George V, he practiced his clarinet, and every night he patronized the same bistro where he supped on soup and fillet of sole. In Woody's estimation, the script now belonged to Feldman, who had weakened and butchered his work as he turned it into commercial dreck, the idea of movies as a business being a concept Woody would never really comprehend. "They just killed it completely. I fought with everybody all the time." In a fury during rushes one night, he shouted "fuck off" at Feldman, who ignored him. Later, however, he asked Charlie Joffe to make Woody stop cursing. It hurt his feelings.

Humiliated, Woody returned to New York in January 1965 and announced that the picture was so awful he had no intention of seeing it. "It would only bother me," he told the *New York Morning Telegraph*. Privately, he promised himself that he would never do another film "unless I had complete control over it."

What's New, Pussycat? opened in June to frightful reviews. A disgusted Judith Crist of the *New York Herald Tribune* dismissed the picture as smut, "a shrieking, reeking conglomeration of dirty jokes." Stung by her scornful comments, Woody sent her the original script, then invited Crist and her husband to his home for a dinner that concluded with six desserts. "It was a delightful evening," recalled Crist, who, completely charmed, would remain devoted to Woody from that day forward. In *The New Republic*, Stanley Kauffmann described Woody as an amateur who had no idea how to write for the screen. His material "probably reads hilariously but does not play successfully," an astute observation because this would remain one of Woody's major problems for the next ten years. Almost alone among the critics was Andrew Sarris, the influential *Village Voice* columnist who had introduced American audiences to the French "auteur theory" (the director is the real "author" of a film). Sarris could not remember seeing "a more tasteful sex comedy." Familiar with Woody from clubs, he considered him "a terrific stand-up comic, very charismatic, fast on his feet when it came to improvisation. And with his great ear he knew how to deflate pomposity." Sarris admitted seeing *Pussycat* four times.

Probably it was to be expected that *What's New, Pussycat?* failed to impress Woody's mother. Attending a screening with Mickey Rose and some of her son's other friends, Nettie saw nothing to make her laugh and afterward dismissed the picture as moronic.

In spite of bad reviews, there was no denying Feldman's business acumen. *Pussycat* turned out to be a solid success, grossing $17.2 million, the fifth biggest moneymaker of the year, and its title song, written by Burt Bacharach and sung by Tom Jones, was also a popular hit.

On the strength of *Pussycat,* Woody received $75,000 to develop *Kagi No Kagi,* a Japanese James Bond–genre spy picture that, unsuccessfully dubbed into an English version, had proved an incredible mess. He wrote loony new dialogue, completely contrary to the action, which he put in the mouths of the Japanese actors. (Heroic spy Phil Moskowitz searches for the world's best egg-salad recipe.) Afterward, Woody disliked the film so much that he sued to prevent its release but changed his mind when *What's Up, Tiger Lily?* received decent notices. Andrew Sarris thought it was "one of the funniest movies of the year and the most creative job of dubbing dialogue" he had ever heard.

Thanks to Charles Feldman, Woody now had two screen credits and a budding career as an actor, a line of work for which he had no particular native talent. Still, two years later he appeared in his second Feldman film, *Casino Royale,* a spoof of the James Bond films, with Peter Sellers and David Niven. Woody is 007's nephew, Little Jimmy Bond, who is eventually unmasked as the evil head of the crime organization SMERSH. (The sex-obsessed Dr. Noah is planning to release a bacillus germ that will make all women beautiful and destroy all men over four feet six.) An outstanding supporting cast (Orson Welles, John Huston, and William Holden) could not save *Casino Royale* from turning into "an unredeemingly moronic enterprise," Woody said. Watching the dailies during shooting provided him with a valuable Baedeker, "a handbook of how not to make a film."

■ ■ ■ ■ ■ ■ ■

Rashomon:
"He was very loyal. If you were his friend and if he said he had a commitment to you then you were his friend 24 hours a day. It was a lifetime commitment. He would write you every day or call

you every day, and I believe that is why he has such a good reputation with the people he knows."

—Bryna Goldstein Eill

"WOODY ALLEN at various places and times unknown to me
in shows, broadcasts, in conversation and otherwise, did deface
and ridicule me, his former wife."

—Harlene Allen

"If I were to close my eyes and imagine Woody, something I
would keep with me is just the image of him watching *Cries and
Whispers*. . . . Him being swept away. I've seen it on his face. I've
seen it. It's moved me. It makes me love him."

—Diane Keaton

"Many things about him were hidden from me and I was always
frightened of him and I didn't fully understand him. I thought he
was shy, but there are sociopathic tendencies. . . . I had a limited
grasp of what he was."

—Mia Farrow

"Every day I raced home from school hoping to find one of the
brown envelopes in our mail box. When there wasn't one, I was
despondent, and when there was, I felt a thrill I have not since
experienced—except perhaps when getting an unexpected check.
Either way, I would spend the afternoons composing and polish-
ing another letter to my mentor."

—Nancy Jo Sales

"He's dependable, helpful, he works hard, he's ethical, he saves
string."

—Marshall Brickman

"Life is difficult for Woody. He's one of the unfortunate tormented people. His mind is working all the time. So is a sweet
side and a silly side and a sexual side. One night I couldn't sleep,
and I thought, 'I'm lying next to one of America's foremost
humorists.' "

—Louise Lasser

■ ■ ■ ■ ■ ■ ■

It was a gray Wednesday in February 1966, with two to four inches of snow being predicted. Around eight that evening, Woody arrived at the Americana Hotel on Seventh Avenue and Fifty-second Street to do two shows (for $6,000 a week). Regardless of the weather, the Royal Box was almost sold out—among the intrepid patrons, Jack Victor and his fiancée, whom Woody had invited for dinner. After the first show, a waiter came over bearing an invitation to go upstairs to Woody's suite. There, they were surprised to find a makeshift wedding reception in progress because Woody and Louise had been married that afternoon.

Several weeks earlier, they took blood tests without telling anyone. Both of them had misgivings. The decision to go through with the marriage was made at the last minute, so spur-of-the-moment that Woody had to run out and buy a $1.98 wedding band at a Times Square novelty shop. It is hard to tell which of them was more reluctant. After living together for five years, it was probably Louise.

"We both decided to do it," she explained later, "because the relationship wasn't moving forward and we thought that maybe marriage would make things different." The ceremony took place in the living room of her father and new stepmother's apartment at 155 East Fiftieth Street. Nettie and Marty Konigsberg were not invited. The only witnesses were Mickey and Judy Rose, and Woody's new best friend, Jean Doumanian. Supreme Court Justice George Postel, a personal friend of the Lassers, had never seen Woody's act, indeed had never heard of Woody Allen. During the ceremony, Postel turned to Louise and intoned, "Do you take Woody Herman to be your husband?"

"No!" she exclaimed.

Afterward, Postel assured them that no couple married by him had ever divorced, words that Louise never forgot because minutes after the ceremony she could not help asking herself, "Should I stay married?"

On the surface, they seemed extremely happy together. In the months following the wedding, they moved into a $900-a-month, six-room apartment on the top two floors of a townhouse at 100 East Seventy-ninth Street. Their new home, decorated by a fashionable interior designer, Olga San Giuliano, had Aubusson rugs, designer window treatments, and silk-covered walls hung with three Gloria Vanderbilt oils and drawings by Matisse and Kokoschka. There was a formal dining room furnished with French antiques, a billiard room, and upstairs, for their bedroom, they had picked out a four-poster canopy bed. But for all the fine furniture and the art, the duplex remained mostly unfurnished. A wood-paneled room, with a magnificent Aubusson on the floor, was sort of a storeroom containing nothing but a ragtag collection of useless presents they had given to each other (a jukebox and a Hammond organ), and in the corner a movie projector and screen were untidily stacked next to an air conditioner in a wicker clothes hamper and a couple of unopened cartons.

Overseeing the household was a staff of two, a cook and a Filipino valet who turned out to be a drinker and had to be dismissed. Attempting to be social, Woody and Louise dutifully entertained journalists and critics with dinners of scrod, peas, salad, and several choices of dessert. On New Year's Eve, 1966, they planned a disco party. Special invitations designed by Louise went out to 150 of their friends. The day of the party, however, a mention in Earl Wilson's *Post* column resulted in more than five hundred gate-crashers. When Louise saw all the people she began to cry, and Woody took her outside. In despair, they sat down on the curb and then, he recalled, "we went down to the corner and had a sandwich at the drugstore. We had to get out of there." When they got back to the house, people were still pushing their way inside. "Whose party is this?" Louise overheard someone asking. The next day, a neighbor returned one of their Matisse drawings he had found on the stairs.

On their first wedding anniversary, Louise thoughtfully presented Woody with a traditional paper anniversary gift of an autographed letter from Sir Arthur Conan Doyle that mentioned Harry Houdini, which Woody framed. (It still hangs on his wall.) But after a year, the relationship was already unraveling. Like Houdini, Woody became an escape artist by disappearing behind a wall of hobbies. Increasingly silent and reclusive, he installed an old billiard table that he bought from McGirr's pool hall and had taken to playing by himself. During this time, Louise would describe Woody's response to her attempts at starting a conversation: "He keeps shooting billiards. It's sort of hard to talk to him that way."

In the fall of 1967, she played a leading role in a Broadway musical, *Henry, Sweet Henry,* opposite Don Ameche. On opening night, Woody sent her a sweet telegram: "I'm bringing 500 mice to your opening. Please be grand." Louise, greatly talented, was also greatly troubled, and Woody had his work cut out for him. Extremely depressed, subject to disturbing mood and weight swings, she kept herself afloat with a variety of pills and daily sessions with her analyst, who warned that marriage to Woody was killing her artistic fulfillment. Actually the burden of sustaining the marriage fell on Woody, who would worry when she slept all day and wind up calling her analyst to check on her medication. Louise's condition, depicted in the Dorrie character (Charlotte Rampling) in *Stardust Memories,* would seriously affect their marriage. In those years, he told Eric Lax, Louise was extraordinary but "crazy as a loon." At first, it was worth it because he could be sure of her having two good weeks a month. Eventually, however, she was having two good *days* a month. When he saw *After the Fall,* Arthur Miller's 1964 drama inspired by his marriage to a near-psychotic Marilyn Monroe, he immediately saw the similarities between the two women.

Of course, Woody, admittedly "finicky and touchy," was a difficult husband. Aside from his crabby moods, he demonstrated a junkielike addiction to work that alarmed Louise. In the morning while she was still asleep, he woke up early and began writing. All day long he was sealed off in his workroom. If she knocked, he usually called out, "Hiya, Louise, come on in," in the tone of a cranky father to his little girl. And barely three months after the wedding, he bolted off to London with Charlie Joffe for the filming of *Casino Royale*. To pass the time, he shopped for jazz records, played poker, and, lounging on his hotel bed with a pad and pencil, began writing a play about a family from Newark, unsophisticated folks like the Konigsbergs, who are accused of spying while vacationing behind the Iron Curtain. *Yankee Come Home* is full of oddball characters and comic touches that make it seem like a dramatic version of his nightclub act, with one laugh on top of the next.

Renamed *Don't Drink the Water,* the play opened on Broadway in the fall of 1966, with Lou Jacobi and Kay Medford as the American couple and Tony Roberts as the ambassador's son who falls in love with their daughter. As the opening had approached, Woody was filled with dread. Displeased with some of the actors, he had premonitions of disaster, which were confirmed in Philadelphia during the pre-Broadway tryout when his efforts were critically mauled. There were plenty of laughs, reported *Variety,* but "the story and staging format suggest pre–World War II farce." Woody would never take rejection well. Hoping the comedy would work in New York but fearful of the critics, he conveniently disappeared on opening night and wound up playing billiards at McGirr's pool hall on Eighth Avenue. In what would become a lifelong pattern, he fled from the painful prospect of seeing his work judged while insisting that he cared nothing for the world's opinion.

There was no doubt it was "a terrible play," he said later, "just a group of a million gags all strung together." New York newspaper critics tended to agree. But audiences seemed to enjoy it, and the show had a respectable run of eighteen months. Joseph Levine purchased film rights but rejected Woody's request to direct and instead hired Howard Morris, a television comic from *Your Show of Shows.* Released in 1969 with Jackie Gleason, it proved to be a dud at the box office, maybe because it looked like just another episode of *The Honeymooners.* After selling the film rights, Woody took no further interest and refused to see it.

Some people anesthetized with booze; Woody wrote. For years he had been jotting down ideas on slips of paper and tossing them into a drawer. Unlike most writers, he never saw a blank sheet of paper that intimidated him, never suffered a moment of artistic paralysis. In 1965 he hired a private secretary, a woman from Joplin, Missouri, by the name of Norma Lee Clark, and the first thing he did was empty his makeshift archive and deliver a valise stuffed with paper. Typed, the material came to nearly two hundred pages.

Aside from typing, Norma Lee's duties were to screen his calls, sort mail, and arrange appointments. She worked out of the Rollins and Joffe office on West Fifty-seventh Street and communicated with her employer by intercom several times a day, "every 20 minutes if he's in a nervous state," she reported. Their relationship remained strictly impersonal. Not only did he see Norma Lee infrequently, he seemed to be totally uninterested in her as a person. Asked about Woody in 1980, after fifteen years in his employ, she said that he was a "very easy and undemanding" boss who didn't encourage intimacy. "I don't think Woody has ever asked me a personal question."

Outside of her regular job, Woody's secretary was an aspiring writer of Regency Romance novels. Clients visiting the Rollins and Joffe office remember her poring over stacks of Harlequin paperbacks as she taught herself the novelistic formula. Over the next twenty years, working in the shadow of a prolific celebrity, perhaps inspired by the productivity of her employer, Norma Lee would publish sixteen titles, including *The Impulsive Miss Pymbroke, The Daring Duchess,* and her most popular, *Lady Jane* ("She was once a nobody. Now she was a woman with a past. . . .").

In the fall of 1965, *Playboy* asked Woody to submit a story. He did an essay on chess, about a pair of refined but dotty gentlemen by the names of Allen and Mittleman playing an increasingly nasty game by mail. When Louise read their exchange of letters, she thought the story was much too literary for what was essentially a girlie magazine.

"This is a good piece of writing," she said. "It's the kind of thing *The New Yorker* might be interested in."

He doubted it. To him, *The New Yorker* was "hallowed ground." Giving in to Louise's urging, however, he turned the story over to Norma Lee Clark for typing and mailed it out "just as a lark."

Woody's chess piece landed on the desk of the fiction editor who knew Woody only as a funny stand-up comic. Reading the piece, Roger Angell thought it was "obvious he could write a sentence." But several things bothered him, primarily that "his writing was *exactly* like S. J. Perelman's." Returning the manuscript, he notified the author that he could resubmit the piece if he made some changes in the second half. "The insults and exaggeration after page 6 [sound] forced and reminiscent of Perelman," he explained.

Never had Woody dreamed of being published in *The New Yorker.* Awestruck, he set out to the *New Yorker* office to meet the editor, a man some fifteen years his senior. A child of *The New Yorker,* Roger Angell was the son of legendary fiction editor Katharine Sergeant Angell White and the stepson of the author of *Charlotte's Web,* humorist E. B. White. After an interoffice affair, his mother had divorced his father, New York attorney Ernest Angell, and married White, seven years her junior. A member of an old Boston family, august in manner, Katharine White could be so formidable that Roger Angell, in the office, referred to his mother as "Mrs. White."

Angell wasted no time setting Woody straight. "This is very funny but we already have one of these. We have the original." This brought no argument from Woody, who, having deliberately copied Perelman's style, had apparently succeeded only too well. But Angell's next objection floored him.

"The piece is too funny," Angell said. There was a laugh in practically every line.

"Fewer laughs?"

"Yes, I'm afraid so." The piece read as if it were a stand-up routine, Angell explained, and written humor didn't work that way.

"The Gossage-Vardebedian Papers" was published on January 20, 1966, followed shortly by two more Perelmanesque essays: "A Little Louder, Please" (a cultured intellectual admits he hates pantomime), then "Yes, but Can the Steam Engine Do This?" (a history of the invention of the sandwich). It was not until the following year that Angell reported to a friend that Woody had almost entirely overcome his compulsion to write like Perelman. (Some critics felt he switched to copying the deceased Robert Benchley.)

Woody's extraordinary discipline amazed Angell. Not only did he accept corrections without argument, but he completed them with lightning speed, often returning the piece promptly the next morning. "In many ways, he was the ideal contributor because he was so quick to respond to suggestions." Sometimes Angell's acceptance letters included crumbs of praise: "Mr. Shawn is delighted." William Shawn, the revered editor-in-chief who had been chosen to succeed the magazine's founder, Harold Ross, genuinely admired Woody's writing. From its inception the magazine had always been short on humorists, and by this time Perelman was practically the only great one left. Mr. Shawn, said Angell, "regarded Woody as a gift from God. He loved his work." Shawn recognized Woody's comic literary gift, but it was Angell who had forced him to be specific and precise—and therefore as funny as he could possibly be.

Publication in *The New Yorker* not only lifted Woody's confidence tremendously, but it also eventually would cement his reputation as a master literary humorist. Ever after, many would regard him as a legitimate successor to giants such as S. J. Perelman and Robert Benchley. In the period between 1965 and 1980, he turned out twenty-eight stories in which he roved wildly, taking aim at a variety of targets (the Dead Sea Scrolls, insurance salesmen, UFOs, God, and the Holocaust), and sprinkling his prose with a variety of brand names: Hannah Arendt, Proust, Flaubert, Bellow, O. J. Simpson, and Elaine's restaurant. Perhaps the single most clever piece is "The Whore of Mensa," which recounts the efforts of a private investigator, Kaiser Lupowitz, to break an intellectual call-girl ring, specializing in hookers for the mind instead of the body, whose clientele is made up of johns with a taste for brainy women, preferably with master's degrees in comparative lit. Into Kaiser's office walks a nubile redhead named Sherry, whose hindquarters remind him of two scoops of vanilla ice cream.

"Shall we begin?" he asks, leading her to the couch.

Dragging on her cigarette, Sherry gets right down to business. "I think we could start by approaching *Billy Budd* as Melville's justification of the ways of God to man, *n'est-ce pas?*"

Not all of Woody's submissions were accepted. "When he turned somber, it was disappointing," said Angell. "It really wasn't stuff we wanted to run."

Once, during a conversation, Angell got a disturbing glimpse into Woody's thinking. Angell said to him, "I certainly hope you're not one of those writers who think humor isn't important enough for a man to be remembered for."

"I am."

"Writing humor is a serious business," Angell argued. "Do you mean it's not serious enough for you?"

"I do mean that," Woody insisted.

In 1980 Woody stopped writing for the magazine because, he informed Angell, the demands of filmmaking simply left him no time. It was only half true. Writing "little souffles" had begun to bore him. He noticed that "guys like S. J. Perelman and Robert Benchley, guys who I idolize, ended up with endless volumes of 'casuals' and it was a dead end." As always, dead ends depressed him. Just as he had lost interest in being a stand-up comedian, he also became dissatisfied with writing for *The New Yorker*, although, Angell recalled, "there was no falling out or cooling off. We would have been distressed if he had continued to write for anyone else." In the fifteen intervening years their correspondence catches the tone of a literary partnership that seldom—maybe never—rose above the impersonal. Woody's letters always began "Dear Roger" and always ended "Woody Allen," as if he were writing to his accountant. The gentlemanly Angell, as much a mentor to him as Rollins and Joffe, treated him with unfailing cheer and diplomacy. As the years passed, he displayed increasing affection. Woody, on the other hand, remained completely businesslike, always keeping a distance. Outside of the magazine, the two men observed the usual author-editor amenities: Woody asked Angell and his wife Carol to movie screenings and New Year's Eve parties; the editor invited his author to Christmas parties and stopped by Michael's Pub to hear him play Dixieland jazz.

By the late seventies, the magazine was regularly rejecting about half of his submissions. In cover letters, Woody would urge Angell to discard unsatisfactory pieces. Some stories, such as "My Speech to the Graduates," read as if written by a nightclub comic, Angell noted, and continued apologetically, "Sorry to let you down." Some stories ("The Condemned" and "Confessions of a Burglar") were rescued by heavy editing; others, such as "The Lunatic's Tale," in which a man switches the brains of his scholarly wife and sexy mistress, were returned because "almost every sentence seemed to need some kind of revision." Among the pieces subsequently sold to other publications such as *The New Republic* and *The Kenyon Review* were "Remembering Needleman," "Nefarious Times We Live In," and "Retribution." Departure from *The New Yorker* marked the end of his prose-writing career.

■■■■■■■

Stand-Up:
"I kid my ex-wife all the time but she was animal. She was not technically animal officially. Officially she was reptile."
—"What's New, Pussycat?" Monologue

■■■■■■■

Though a divorcée at twenty-three, Harlene did not sit around pining. Hoping to lead the bohemian life, she settled down in Italy, where she studied art in Florence and reportedly enjoyed several exciting romances. Returning to the United States, she moved into a modest apartment in the West Village, dressed like a hippie, and hung around with people who practiced meditation and yoga. Despite a first-rate education, she seemed unable to find a position commensurate with her abilities and eventually supported herself by secretarial jobs, one of these in the psychology department at Yeshiva University.

It seems unlikely that Harlene was unaware of Woody's jokes about her. Nevertheless, she chose to ignore the situation until 1964, when he displayed photographs of her and her sister on a national television show "while holding me up to ridicule," as she put it. Making sport of her in inconspicuous nightclubs was annoying; demeaning her on prime-time television made her mad, so much so that her attorney formally protested. Woody promised to stop.

Three years later, Harriet Van Horne, television critic for the *New York World Journal Tribune,* devoted an entire column, "Woody Sways on His Pedestal," to his mean-spirited treatment of his ex-wife. "So you thought women were the vindictive sex?" Van Horne wrote. "Well, you haven't heard Woody Allen discussing his last duchess." The previous night she had watched him on two shows—*Perry Como* and *The Tonight Show*—"licking his wounded pride with the tongue of an adder." If his ex-wife had to endure his antics in silence, Van Horne hoped it was sweetened by "a splendid settlement and throngs of dashing beaux." Because unless she bought an hour of prime television time, what recourse did Harlene have?

Harlene lost no time rushing to court with a $1 million lawsuit charging Woody, the National Broadcasting Company, and its affiliates with defamation of character, citing repeated acts of libel described as "statements attributing to me lack of chastity and morality." She meticulously compiled examples of the "wicked and malicious" material, including the crack about rape and the moving violation. (And by the way, he owed her nearly $8,000 in back alimony.)

Woody, dumbfounded, refused to admit any wrongdoing. He had meant no disrespect. The only purpose of his "good-natured fun" and "harmless jokes" was to make people laugh, he argued in his reply to the complaint. Nobody takes comics seriously. Suggesting that some conniving attorney had put her up to it, just to squeeze money out of him, he wondered why Harlene waited so long to object.

Privately, he thought she was being too sensitive, and decided there was nothing to worry about. In any case, his attention was drawn to more important problems, such as his current wife: Their relationship had become so rocky that most of their time together was spent quarreling. It seemed that divorce would be unavoidable. Then that summer, in Central Park, he was playing a charity softball game on a team with George Plimpton and Tom Wolfe, when he was hit in the right hand and had to be admitted to the emergency room. The following week he opened at Caesars Palace with his hand in a cast. The accident upset him far more than Harlene's suit, which he continued to ignore.

Woody's mother felt sure that he would lose. Her advice was to "settle for half," $500,000 seeming like a bargain, everything considered. But Woody, feeling fireproof, brushed off her advice, and as a result, Harlene increased the amount to $2 million. Six years later, the matter was settled out of court, when he made a financial settlement and vowed to drop the jokes if she agreed not to discuss their marriage or the terms of the settlement. For three decades, Harlene has kept her word. How much she collected is unknown, but it has been sufficient for her to live comfortably ever since.*

---

*Whatever the precise nature of the scars, this much seems clear: Woody would never forget or forgive Harlene. She seems to be the model for the archetypical castrator throughout his films: Allan Felix's ex-wife, Nancy, in *Play It Again, Sam*; Alvy Singer's ex-wives, Alison Portchnick, the political activist, and Robin, the literary-intellectual social climber, in *Annie Hall*; Isaac Davis's ex-wife, Jill, the lesbian memoirist in *Manhattan*; and Harry Block's ex-wife, who resembles the Nazi German heavyweight champion, Max Schmeling, in *Deconstructing Harry.*

■ ■ ■ ■ ■ ■

Caught on Tape:

WILLIAM F. BUCKLEY, JR. (reading a question): Mr. Allen, do you think the Israelis should give back the land they won from the Arabs?

WOODY: No, they should sell it back.

Asked to host a *Kraft Music Hall* special, "Woody Allen Looks at 1967," he invited as his guests Liza Minnelli, Aretha Franklin, and Buckley, the well-known conservative editor of *National Review.*

"But I'm not a comedian," Buckley said.

"Oh," said Woody, "don't worry about that."

Fortunately, Buckley has a good sense of humor.

■ ■ ■ ■ ■ ■

At thirty-two, Woody stood at a crossroad. Afflicted with boundless energy, he had bounced from television writer and nightclub comic to movie actor, screenwriter, essayist, Broadway playwright, even fashion model because he posed for a series of magazine ads for Smirnoff vodka and Foster Grant sunglasses. That year his various projects earned a half-million dollars—but was he becoming too successful for his own good? The superman output staggered his friend Groucho Marx. "For God's sake," Marx wrote the flashy overachiever in the spring of 1967, "don't have any more success—it's driving me crazy."

CHAPTER FIVE

The "Coatcheck Girl"

It was 5 A.M. and chilly on a June morning in San Francisco, and in his excitement Woody cut his nose while shaving. Within the hour, he was heading toward San Quentin, the city's famous maximum-security prison, where he was scheduled to shoot in the laundry and dining hall, with the cooperation, he hoped, of a hundred inmates. If he could not help feeling trepidation about the convicts, who, he reminded himself, "hadn't seen a woman in years, much less a fair-skinned Jew," the fact remained that he had every reason in the world to feel lucky. After frustrating months of haggling, in which Jack Rollins and Charlie Joffe had failed to convince United Artists that their client needed absolute artistic control, they finally cobbled together a deal with Palomar Pictures. The newly formed subsidiary of the American Broadcasting Company put up roughly $1.5 million for the novice film-maker to write, direct, and act, notwithstanding the fact that he had no directing experience, no discernible acting talent, and only a single real screenwriting credit. The day before beginning principal photography, Woody seemed relaxed about his first picture. "The way I look at it," he told the unit publicist, "the less I know, the better. Directing and acting will be no harder than just acting." Since he wrote the script, he knew exactly what he wanted. "So," he continued, "I don't anticipate problems."

Actually, he was flying by the seat of his pants. Not only did he require the help of Mickey Rose, his high-school friend from Midwood, to complete a shooting script, but he also felt shaky about most aspects of film production—rudimentary decisions like where to put the camera and how many takes. Insecure, but brimming with chutzpah, he wired Carlo Di Palma, the Italian director of photography for Michaelangelo Antonioni, and one of the most well-known cinematographers in the world at that time. "Can you come and shoot my first movie?" he inquired. (He had to settle for a television photographer whose biggest credit was *Bonanza*.) As for directing a movie, he was better equipped to direct traffic. In fact, he dreaded the thought of daily contact with a bunch of people he barely knew. "That's the worst problem of movie directing for me," he said, "the fact that I loathe group activity," which by its very nature was the heart and soul of film production. To avoid directing, he first asked a British director, Val Guest, whom he knew from *Casino Royale*, then approached an American icon, Jerry Lewis.

Lewis was diplomatic. It was "a great honor" and he was "thrilled to be asked." Unfortunately, he had "other commitments."

But it wouldn't take much time at all, Woody wheedled. Only eight weeks.

Lewis just laughed. "Woody, I spend twenty-eight weeks in prep. Shooting in eight weeks? We're talking thirty-six weeks." Do it yourself, he suggested.

Take the Money and Run is a pseudodocumentary that traces the career of a neurotic petty criminal, Virgil Starkwell, and his ambition to make the FBI's Ten Most Wanted list, an unlikely fantasy because Virgil is hopelessly incompetent when it comes to planning and executing crimes. In one memorable scene, he waits in line to rob a bank and finally hands the teller a note: "Please put $50,000 into this bag and act natural." But the teller can't read his handwriting.

Virgil courteously proceeds to read the holdup note to him. "Because," he continues, "I am pointing a gun at you."

Meanwhile, the teller is continuing to examine the note. "That looks like 'gub,' " he replies. "That doesn't look like 'gun.' " What happens next is that Virgil is sent to the bank manager's office because none of the tellers can dispense $50,000 without proper authorization.

By means of interviews with his friends and family, the picture describes Virgil's early childhood, his failed music career, and his relationship with a pretty girl (Janet Margolin) he meets on a park bench. After fifteen minutes he wants to marry her; after thirty minutes he has forgotten about stealing her purse. Despite his marriage, the bumbling Virgil eventually ends up in prison again, this time serving an eight-hundred-year sentence.

The idea for the stickup scene might have originated in 1965 during an interview with *The Realist*. Editor Paul Krassner mentioned having seen a recent news item about a botched robbery in Painesville, Ohio. The teller, smiling politely at the gunman, announced, "I'm sorry but my window is now closed. You'll have to take this to another teller." According to the interview, Woody replied, "I can empathize with the robber."

■ ■ ■ ■ ■ ■ ■

Moving Pictures:
Virgil Starkwell: In prison the psychiatrist asked me if I had a
    girl and did I think sex was dirty. I said, "It is if you do it right."
                                        —*Take the Money and Run*, 1969

■ ■ ■ ■ ■ ■ ■

The main lesson Woody learned from Charles Feldman, who died in 1968, was that functioning inside the Hollywood system was impossible for him. In his heart he knew that the whole "body rhythm of the place," the time-wasting lunches with ten different writers, the mandatory negotiations with actors who weren't available for six months, would surely drive him crazy. "I don't like the way studios make films," he said in 1998. Instead, he wanted nothing less than total independence.

He was not the only one. By 1968 a clutch of rebellious young filmmakers was becoming known to the public—Dennis Hopper, Robert Altman, Francis Ford Coppola, Martin Scorsese, Peter Bogdanovich, Steven Spielberg, Warren Beatty, George Lucas—all of them talented newcomers who identified with Woody's mistrust of the studios and his determination to control his work. Recognizing that the studio system was collapsing, the new generation of directors resembled fuzzy chicks just poked from their shells, scurrying around to figure out how to play the power game, how to push aside the old boys' club and become Warners and Zanucks themselves. Several months earlier, Arthur Penn and Warren Beatty had released *Bonnie and Clyde*; now Dennis Hopper and Peter Fonda made *Easy Rider,* and soon there would be a drove of extraordinary films to herald Hollywood's new golden age: *Five Easy Pieces, The Last Picture Show, McCabe and Mrs. Miller, The Godfather, Mean Streets, Taxi Driver, American Graffiti,* and still later, *Chinatown, Star Wars,* and *Raging Bull.* With a kind of religious fervor, directors like Dennis Hopper proclaimed themselves spiritual innovators, revolutionaries who had overthrown the oppressor and intended to use the Hollywood system to make "little, personal, honest films," a sentiment endorsed by George Lucas with the Marxist cry of "the power is with the people now. The workers have the means of production!" Suddenly nothing seemed impossible for this latest bunch of young movie junkies with their gargantuan ambitions.

Meanwhile, Woody was hoping to carve out a niche for himself, no easy task because of several noticeable handicaps. In spite of intuitive comic talent, he had trouble with the basic techniques of screenwriting. At this time, he remained ignorant of timing and motion, how the great film comedians—Chaplin, Keaton, the Marx brothers—used a plot as a base upon which to build their jokes and keep the comic energy flowing. One analyst of his early work belittled him as "the master of coitus interruptus of cinematic humor," which was harsh but not inaccurate. In *Take the Money and Run,* for example, Woody had no idea how to end the bank-robbing scene; and the prison-breakout sequence in which Virgil is chased by guards also goes nowhere because Woody couldn't figure out the visual comic opportunities (think about Buster Keaton in *Cops* and how he expanded and milked a similar situation for fifteen minutes). At a loss for an ending, Woody shows Virgil being led back to his cell. Challenged to master the craft, Woody lazily fell back on filming his nightclub routines. In *Take the Money and Run,* in fact in every film until *Annie Hall,* his characters tend to be stick figures, the stories verbal cartoons. In time he would improve as a screenwriter—and be nominated for an Academy Award thirteen times (a record) in the category of best original screenplay—but all too often, his early scripts were clumsy.

Another of his weaknesses was his acting. In *What's New, Pussycat?* he squeaked through by presenting himself as a stand-up comic doubling as an actor. But in *Take the Money and Run,* in the leading role, it was hard to overlook his twitchy mannerisms, especially the frenzied gestures that suggested "a bad case of St. Vitus dance" to Stanley Kauffmann, who thirty years later still saw Woody as "a frantic amateur."

Returning from San Francisco in August 1968, after bringing in his first film on schedule and under budget, Woody appeared to be a man without a care in the world. Through the fall of 1968 and early winter of 1969, he worked with an editor to whittle *Take the Money and Run* into a sensible story. By this time, he had a finished print, complete with titles, music, and sound effects, but something had gone terribly wrong, and so he was almost tempted to give up. At no screening did an audience laugh, not even the servicemen they enticed from the USO in Times Square, guys with presumably nothing better to do. Not until Palomar Pictures threatened to shelve the picture did Woody acknowledge the serious trouble he was in.

Ralph Rosenblum was ten years older than Woody, a bearded, burly six-footer with a leonine head. Born in the Bensonhurst section of Brooklyn, the film editor had a reputation for being difficult and opinionated, a combative man whose temper had been known to erupt explosively in the cutting room. In January 1969, at a dilapidated screening room on West Forty-third Street, Rosenblum got his first look at *Take the Money and Run.* It was, he thought, primitively shot and yet "very unusual," because it rocketed from the high brilliance of the Marx Brothers all the way down to "a slapped-together home movie." However choppy and uneven, it was nevertheless "packed with funny material," clearly the work of a "very fresh mind." So the situation was not hopeless. As the lights went on, a jittery Jack Rollins and Charlie Joffe hurried over to get his reaction. Could he fix it? Joffe asked. Rosenblum made a point of stalling. "He asked to see the script," recalled his widow Davida Rosenblum. "Before deciding, he wanted to know what had been discarded."

At a restaurant on Madison Avenue, Woody and the editor met for the first time. When Rosenblum arrived, Woody was alone at a corner table eating his dinner. While Rosenblum was not exactly anticipating a head-on conflict, he had edited two dozen features and known plenty of first-time prima donna directors ashamed to show their ignorance but relieved to dump their messes on his doorstep. Woody, however, hiding his mouth behind his napkin as he chewed, did not seem to be a bit arrogant and proceeded to spill out his troubles in the most self-effacing way. Rosenblum could not help being taken with the modest young director. *Take the Money and Run,* Woody said sadly, had turned out to be a "negative experience," and now he was "stuck with a bad picture" just when he was scheduled to go on the road with a play. Several days later, a truck delivered two hundred boxes of film to Rosenblum's office and the next two weeks, a period he would remember as "one of the most pleasurable in all my years of editing," were occupied screening the outtakes. While Woody was away, Rosenblum performed deep surgery in the editing room. He carefully moved scenes around, restored others that had been cut, extended still others, and replaced music. Given Woody's haphazard plotting, it "didn't matter too much where one scene or another ended up." Only the closing shot, a grotesque *Bonnie and Clyde* scene showing Virgil Starkwell's bullet-torn body, offended him, and he suggested shooting a new ending. When Rosenblum finished, Woody had more than a movie. He had a hit.

In his debut as a filmmaker, Woody established a signature cinematic style—a style seemingly inspired by such humorists as Robert Benchley and S. J. Perelman—whose most distinctive features were equal amounts of absurd parodies and anarchistic gags, delivered by means of the kind of wild, comic pacing usually associated with Looney Tunes animation. The *Newsweek* reviewer called the movie "a silly symphony that can put the zing back into life." While visually inventive (Virgil plays cello in a marching band) and chock-full of ingenious verbal gags, the shortcomings of *Take the Money and Run* were obvious as well. The picture was choppy, repetitious, and unpolished. What's more, it often came across as a stand-up routine, a problem immediately pointed out by the *New York Times* critic Vincent Canby when he labeled the film "the cinematic equivalent to one of Allen's best night-club monologues." Yet these flaws counted for little in the end. What made the movie special was precisely its rough amateurism, combined with Woody's awkward performance replete with stuttering ums and ahs. Hopefuls longing to make a movie of their own—and there were many—came away inspired. Those content to watch films had the refreshing impression that the filmmaker, a real person for a change, was actually having fun, and it was true. As Woody later told critic Diane Jacobs, he got "more of a personal kick out of just being funny" in movies such as *Take the Money and Run* than he ever would later on.

That summer of 1969, when *Take the Money and Run* opened, Woody had reason to feel encouraged. Of course, reviews were mixed but few critics seemed immune to the freshness of a thrilling new talent. Embracing him as their new darling, some major magazines were left hungering for more and predicting, as did *Newsweek,* that "the results ought to be brilliant."

In the history of film, *Take the Money and Run* had a special significance: Woody's first feature marked the introduction of a much loved stock character of the movies, the nebbishy neurotic who would take his place alongside Chaplin's Little Tramp and Keaton's Great Stoneface.

More than fifty actresses came to read for the part. Among the finalists was a pretty twenty-two-year-old girl with long brown hair, blue eyes, and high, round cheekbones. Obviously high-strung, she was a bundle of physical tics: She fiddled with her hair, rubbed her nose, fluttered large hands that seemed barely under control. Inside her cheek bulged a wad of gum, which she kept chawing on like a baseball player with a tobacco habit. At the Broadhurst Theater, Woody climbed up onstage to read with her. The girl was good, he decided, but too tall. To measure her, he stood her up against him, back to back. "It was like being in third grade," he remembered. "But we were just about the same height." Not quite. In her stocking feet she was five feet seven. He was five feet six in shoes. No matter: He was very taken with the big girl.

Not long after returning from San Francisco, he had begun production for his second stage play. *Play It Again, Sam* is a romantic comedy about a daydreaming film reviewer who gets a girl by taking advice from the ghost of Humphrey Bogart. Allan Felix is a twerpy intellectual living in Greenwich Village, a graduate of Midwood High, who writes criticism for *Film Quarterly.* He has just been abandoned by his sexy young wife who finally got fed up with his movie fantasies. Shattered, he begs his best friend, Dick, and his wife, Linda, to fix him up with women but manages to bollix up his dates. Before long, he finds himself attracted to Linda, a woman who is just as neurotic and insecure as he is (her neglectful husband is obsessed by his business deals). When Dick is out of town on business, Allan and Linda sleep together, but the next morning, both of them have second thoughts. Allan feels guilty cuckolding his best friend and—in a parody of the closing scene in *Casablanca*—decides to do the right thing. He gives up Linda for the higher moral value of friendship. As the credits roll, Allan walks into the fog to the strains of "As Time Goes By."

Since the Allan Felix character was obviously a fictionalized version of himself, Woody decided to play the part in spite of his lack of training as a theatrical actor. The role of Allan's friend was given to Tony Roberts, and that left only the part of the wife to be cast. The role went to the big gawky girl with the gum. Later Woody claimed that Diane Keaton had made him feel insecure. "She was a Broadway star and who was I? A cabaret comedian who had never been on stage before." Keaton was hardly a Broadway star. In fact, she had done little of note. Her stage experience was limited to the rock musical *Hair*, in which she was a member of the chorus and understudied the lead. Only a few weeks before auditioning for Woody did she get to take over the role. In *Hair*, she was known less for her talent than for being the only cast member who refused to go nude during the finale.

Diane Keaton's childhood was conventional southern California. Born Diane Hall in 1946, she grew up in Santa Ana, a city south of Los Angeles, where her father was a civil engineer and owner of a consulting firm. In the Hall household—there were two younger sisters and a brother—the star was Dorothy Hall, a great beauty who had been Mrs. Los Angeles in the Mrs. America contest. From her early years, Diane would remember sitting in the audience and watching her mother in the spotlight. "Oh God, it was so amazing," she thought. "I want to be on that stage, too." After a year at Santa Ana College, still aching to have her name in lights, she headed for New York to study at the Neighborhood Playhouse, which led to a job in summer stock. Joining Actor's Equity, she learned the union already had a Diane Hall and changed her name to Dorrie Keaton, her sister's name and her mother's maiden name. Not long afterward she changed it a second time, to Diane Keaton. When she met Woody, she was living alone on the Upper West Side in a shabby one-room, roach-infested apartment with the tub in the kitchen.

During rehearsals, Woody and Diane clicked immediately. It was obvious that she had a crush on him. "I'd seen him on television before and I thought he was real cute," she later recalled. Woody thought she was "very charming to be around and of course you always get the impulse with Diane to protect her." He was still married, but after Christmas, when the company moved to Washington, D.C., for the pre-Broadway tryout, he and Diane became lovers.

On stage and off, Keaton was a mix of eccentricities. Her acting leaned heavily on a collection of dithering and blithering mannerisms that would so annoy one critic that he awarded her, a decade hence, "the Sandy Dennis Prize for Instant Deliquesence." In personal conversation, jittery and inarticulate, she tended to flutter through a rich repertoire of stutters and stammers and giggles—"God!'s" and "Well, uhs"; "gees" and "sures." Unconventional in appearance, she dressed herself in clothing purchased in thrift shops. "She was the type," Woody recalled, "that would come in with, you know, a football jersey and a skirt . . . and combat boots and, you know, over mittens." Few woman would have felt truly comfortable in some of her outlandish getups—including a tiny minidress with brilliant green tights, and orange clogs with three-inch soles—but Diane had the flair to pull them off. Woody was openly smitten.

"When I first met her," he said later, "her mind was completely blank." Far from being a drawback, this was precisely the sort of unequal relationship he preferred. There is no doubt that his newly beloved, eleven years younger, was unformed and guileless, lacking in formal education. But underneath she was not "a coatcheck girl," as he seemed to think, nor was she "a complete idiot." As a self-appointed mentor, he suggested books to improve her mind and psychotherapy for her immaturity, even offering to pay for her sessions. She seized the opportunity.

Woody's throat hurt. In his dressing room, on the makeup table, alongside paperbacks of *Selections from Kierkegaard* and *Basic Teachings of the Great Philosophers,* he kept a blender, a can of chocolate syrup, and a jar of honey. The highbrow books were for show. The other paraphernalia had a serious purpose; he was whipping up malteds to gain weight and the honey was medicinal because his throat was usually raw from the strain of trying to project his untrained voice across the footlights.

Aside from preoccupations with his voice, life as a stage actor turned out to be surprisingly pleasurable for Woody. He had his days free to write or relax. In the evenings, he and Diane would walk together to the theater district, strolling down Broadway to Forty-fourth Street. Shortly after eight o'clock, the curtain went up, and he spent the next ninety minutes onstage in the company of people he liked. Now that the play was doing nicely at the box office, he had stopped biting his nails and felt completely comfortable about the text. Afterward, cast members went out for a late supper before heading home. "It was the easiest job in the world!" he said years later.

Broadway critics tended to be lukewarm. Some dismissed Woody's play as little more than a diverting evening at the theater. Clive Barnes of the *New York Times* wished he had treated the subject more seriously, while Walter Kerr thought he had copied George Axelrod's seven-year-itch fantasy of a lonely man, sexually obsessed and dreaming about babes. However, none of the nitpicking criticisms mattered to theatergoers, who found the work funny and entertaining. As a result, *Play It Again, Sam* settled in for 453 performances on Broadway, and a London production starring Dudley Moore had an equally successful run.

Playing opposite Diane, Woody came across as an immensely attractive performer. Even though he continued to portray the nebbish, and would do so until he made *Annie Hall* in 1977, audiences glimpsed a more earthy side of him with Diane, who obviously liked him. It was easy to see why: He was smart, confident, and absolutely sexually appealing, despite his glasses and funny clumps of red hair. And it was not hard to imagine him in bed with a woman, in contrast to the typical comic, whose character was usually about as erotic as Mr. Magoo.

The special chemistry between Woody and Diane worked beautifully for both of them but would have an even greater impact on Keaton's career. In the long run, her association with Woody would mean more important film roles and eventually an Oscar for *Annie Hall*. On the other hand, it would take years to erase her public image as Woody's girl.

Four years later, *Play It Again, Sam* would be released as a film starring Woody and Diane. The rights were sold to Paramount Pictures, which initially intended to cast it with stars, but a number of actors turned down the roles. By the time the project finally got rolling in the fall of 1971, Woody was sufficiently famous from *Take the Money and Run* and *Bananas* to be perfectly eligible. Although he agreed to write the screen adaptation, he had no interest in directing the finished script. Because he had put *Sam* behind him and moved on to new projects, Paramount hired the experienced Herbert Ross, who made a few notable changes, chiefly shifting the locale from New York to San Francisco. Lavishly praised as a funny, smoothly made situation comedy, *Play It Again, Sam* would become Woody's biggest box-office success so far and make him a mass-audience star. The picture has become a classic.

Throughout the run of the stage play, obsessively in love with Diane, he was intent on disentangling himself from his marriage. Even though he and Louise had amicably agreed to separate, they continued to live together. When she finally moved out in June of 1969, he could not bear to inform his parents of the breakup. At the very moment when the movers were loading up the van, hoisting some of Louise's bookcases out of a window onto Seventy-ninth Street, Marty Konigsberg arrived at the door.

"What's happening?" he asked.

Not a thing, Woody told his father.

While calling the separation a trial, neither one of them expected to get back together, and Louise would eventually take a twentieth-floor co-op on East Seventy-first Street. After almost ten years together, three of them as Woody's wife, she counted on retaining his allegiance. For a time, this turned out to be the case because he felt protective. After giving her a cameo in *Take the Money and Run,* he took pains to cast her in three additional films. What's more, they were still sleeping together. For all their problems living under one roof, there had never been any trouble with their sex life. Together they traveled to Mexico for the divorce in the spring of 1970 and spent the night in the same hotel room. Next morning, they appeared in court nervously holding hands. Louise would recall the trip as a larky "good time"; whereas Woody said, deadpan, that the divorce was a "protest against the Viet Nam War."

Nevertheless, he continually fueled Louise's jealousy of Diane Keaton. About a month after the divorce, the summer Woody was in Puerto Rico filming *Bananas* and living at the San Juan Sheraton with Diane, Louise came to visit. In his hotel room, he pointed to a bureau. "That's Diane's drawer," he said, then began to extol her virtues. Diane was, he insisted, the greatest actress in America and responsible for the best relationship he'd ever had. Louise took the lavish praise for Diane personally and interpreted it to mean that she lacked talent. His flaunting of Keaton that day in San Juan would continue to rankle Louise twenty years later.

Her confidence buckling, she fell into a slump. That Woody was romantically attracted to Diane could not be disputed, but she refused to acknowledge that he loved Diane, or felt any physical passion for her, beliefs that Woody seemed to have encouraged. Once, when Diane returned to California for a month to visit her parents, he invited Louise to stay with him.

In 1970 Woody's income topped $1 million ($4.2 million today). Now that he had a checking account that seemed about as large as the federal budget, he stopped carrying cash and relied on friends for pocket change, nor did he cash checks or visit banks. All such mundane transactions were left to his accountant. Looking for ways to spend his money, he splurged on a Picasso lithograph and German Expressionist paintings, Jacobean furniture, leather-bound volumes of Franz Kafka's work, and a Rolls-Royce complete with driver. An ardent New York Knicks fan, he asked sportscaster Howard Cosell to help him get season tickets at Madison Square Garden (then located at Forty-ninth Street). Even though the seats were "way up in the balcony," he felt lucky to get them and over the years moved down to courtside.

With money rolling in, he was able to afford the penthouse of his dreams. Even before Louise moved out, he decided to buy a co-op in the neighborhood, something not more than "ten blocks from the mainstream." Among the glamorous properties that Realtors showed him were a pair of adjoining penthouses on Fifth Avenue, located about a block north of the building where Louise's parents once lived, whose doorman examined his scruffy clothes and made him wait for Louise in the lobby.

The building at 930 Fifth Avenue turned out to be exceptionally conservative. Its co-op board, fearing that the presence of a person such as himself—that is, a person in show business—would inject a sleazy element into the building and upset other tenants, had "grave reservations" about accepting Woody, recalled one of the shareholders. In an interview with the board, Woody argued that he was not the usual show-business person at all; in fact, he was basically asocial, either writing all day or rising early each morning to go out and make movies. He insisted that he had "practically no friends" and would cause no trouble. After numerous reassurances, he was accepted, at which point he turned around and made a request of the board: that he would never be approached in the lobby for an autograph. (This pact was immediately broken when an elderly dowager, living in the building for many years but unaware of the no-autographs agreement, trotted up to him and exclaimed, "Are you Woody Allen?" "No," he said, and turned away.)

Renovations to convert Penthouses A and C into a suitable duplex—a project running into tens of thousands of dollars—meant gutting the property. On the lower floor, a warren of small rooms surrounded by narrow terraces, walls were razed to create spacious living and dining rooms, a library, and a private elevator foyer. External walls were also knocked down and small windows replaced with giant floor-to-ceiling solar glass to provide sweeping views of the park and skyline. There was only one bedroom, which along with its adjoining dressing room took up the entire top floor (no doubt signifying this was the home of a confirmed bachelor). The upper terrace wrapping around the airy master bedroom was turned into a small garden park of lush plants and trees with a pond. (Years later, complaining of bugs, he hardly ever ventured outside.) When *Architectural Digest* ran a photo spread, Woody's interior designer Olga San Giuliano explained how she worked with the "fantasies and inner life" of her client, so that the penthouse might reflect "who he is privately."

During these years, the relationship with his parents remained as ambivalent as ever. Seldom did he show up at family gatherings, and when he did, it was for only a few minutes. After saying hello, he usually disappeared into the bedroom to watch television before beating a hasty departure. For the most part, however, he was a dutiful son and brother who made sure none of the Konigsbergs had to do without. Proudly, he moved Nettie and Marty into the city and bought them a co-op on the Upper East Side as well as a vacation home in Hallandale, north of Miami Beach. His mother, after more than thirty years, retired from her bookkeeping job at the florist shop. His father, still spry at seventy, kept busy with a variety of odd jobs; he sometimes did engraving for a jewelry shop on the Lower East Side or else he breezed around the city delivering packages for the Rollins and Joffe office, where people affectionately called him "Mr. K."

Living comfortably now, neither of the Konigsbergs was in any position to object when their son kidded them in public. They were proud of him, they would insist. Whether Nettie actually saw all of Woody's films is doubtful. But evidently Marty did, going to the box office and paying for a ticket like anyone else. He was not always thrilled, and once remarked to a relative, "I don't understand that crap he's writing."

Another recipient of Woody's generosity was his sister, Letty, a petite redhead with a perky sense of humor and yappy mannerisms reminiscent of her mother. Eight years apart in age, Letty and Woody, as children, seemed to be neither rivals nor equals. Their relationship was affectionate; she worshiped her brother, who in turn felt protective of her. As a grown-up, Letty was always included in the select group invited to see rough cuts of Woody's pictures. In times of crisis, she was one of his most passionate defenders.

After graduation from Brooklyn College, Letty became a teacher. When her first marriage to a neighborhood boy ended in divorce, she married the principal of her school, Sidney Aronson, and had a son, Chris. By the seventies, Letty and Sidney were living comfortably in Manhattan, on Park Avenue, only a few blocks from Woody. Having grown disenchanted with teaching, Letty decided that she wanted a career in television. She managed to find minor positions on Robert Klein's television comedy series and later on *Saturday Night Live*. Throughout the 1980s, she was employed by the Museum of Television & Radio, where her duties included publicity and exhibitions.

When it came to financial support, Woody would be as generous to Letty as he was to his parents. On the other hand, according to Mia Farrow's recollections, he was privately disparaging and avoided her company. Is it coincidence that in every film in which the Woody Allen character has a sister—films such as *Stardust Memories* and *Deconstructing Harry*—the sister character is written to be a perfect horror? It may be that this was the only way Woody could express his resentment of the adorable baby sister doted on by his mother.

■ ■ ■ ■ ■ ■

The March of Time:
"The inequality of my relationship is a wonderful thing. The fact that I'm with a much younger woman, and much less accomplished woman, works very well. By luck, it's a very happy situation."

—WOODY ALLEN, on his relationship
with Soon-Yi Previn, 1997

■ ■ ■ ■ ■ ■

For all their affection for each other, Woody and Diane Keaton were incompatible. As time went on, the relationship grew progressively difficult, in part because he was reluctant to face the truth: She was not the "coatcheck" girl he first perceived. Once young and naive, without "a trace of intellectualism when I first met her," he recalled, she turned into an enthusiastic pupil who worked hard at self-improvement. She read, took classes, and studied photography. Five times a week she visited her therapist. Woody, however, stuck in the role of mentor, still needed her to be subservient. By the time the stage run of *Play It Again, Sam* ended in March 1970, their affair was over. A brief period of living together ended with Diane renting a place of her own. She began to see other men—including Warren Beatty and Al Pacino in the seventies. In some respects she remained, as Woody once depicted her, "a real hayseed, the kind who would chew eight sticks of gum at a time." She still loved to chew gum. Otherwise, she was her own person.

CHAPTER SIX

The Medici

Arthur Krim was a solidly built man, five foot ten, with glasses and dark hair streaked gray. Avuncular in manner, he was an intellectual who could have easily been mistaken for a college professor or a doctor. Born in Manhattan in 1910, he graduated from Columbia Law School, then joined a prestigious New York law firm where he rose rapidly to partner. After serving in the army during World War II, he became president of Eagle Lion Films, his first motion picture experience. In 1951 he and his friend Robert Benjamin took over the venerable United Artists, a one-of-a-kind studio that dated back to 1919, when it was founded by four silent-era superstars—Charles Chaplin, D. W. Griffith, Mary Pickford, and Douglas Fairbanks—for the express purpose of retaining control over their enormous earnings. By the late forties, however, the company was losing $100,000 a week and the two surviving owners, Chaplin and Pickford, were only too relieved to sell. Among the classics released by a revitalized UA were *The African Queen, High Noon, Marty,* and *Some Like It Hot.* In the 1960s, which brought across-the-board declines in the industry and all-time-low box offices, UA nonetheless continued to prosper with the James Bond, Pink Panther, and Beatles movies.

United Artists was a New York–based motion picture company that seemed made to order for someone like Woody. An oddity in the Hollywood system, a film studio without a physical studio, it had no lot, no wardrobe or property departments, no contract players or star salaries. Its corporate headquarters was located at 729 Seventh Avenue in midtown Manhattan, 3,000 miles from the movie industry's nerve center. There was a pronounced feeling of family among chairman Krim and his top executives, Bob Benjamin, Eric Pleskow, William Bernstein, and Mike Medavoy. With minimal overhead, they functioned essentially as a financing and distribution company that leased its features from producers for a period of seven years.

In 1966 Woody tried to interest United Artists in financing his first picture, but the studio was unwilling to put up more than $750,000. On the strength of *Take the Money and Run,* Rollins and Joffe were able to hammer out a three-picture contract that would give their client modest two-million-dollar budgets and fees of $350,000 for writing, directing, and acting. David Picker, head of production, told Woody to go ahead and write whatever he liked. Taking Picker at his word, he submitted *The Jazz Baby*, a period drama set in New Orleans. The bewildered UA brass went into shock, and Eric Pleskow, for one, would blank out the script so effectively that he lacks all recollection. Woody, untroubled, promptly came back with another screenplay titled *El Weirdo* (again coauthored with Mickey Rose), which read like a fast-paced cartoon.

Possibly the first draft for *El Weirdo* was "Viva Vargas! Excerpts from the Diary of a Revolutionary," a story Woody had submitted to *The New Yorker* the previous year. William Shawn rejected the piece because he felt it ridiculed Ernesto "Che" Guevara, the charismatic guerrilla leader who had been killed in Bolivia two years earlier, but the story was finally published by *Evergreen Review*. Whichever in fact came first, the story or the script, the idea was appealing enough that Woody determined to tell it in one form or the other.

In *El Weirdo*, eventually titled *Bananas*, a sex-starved tester of useless products (for instance, coffins with stereo systems) falls hopelessly in love with a plump blond political activist named Nancy (Louise Lasser), only to be rejected by her because he lacks leadership qualities. "Who's she looking for, Hitler?" Fielding Mellish wonders. But Fielding, having survived constant near-electrocution by his electric blanket during a childhood of habitual bedwetting, is tougher than he appears. Desperate to win Nancy's love, he travels to San Marco, a banana republic whose president has just been assassinated in a revolutionary uprising. Joining a band of rebels, he becomes president and returns to the United States in a red-bearded, Castro-type of disguise to promote foreign trade for his country (locusts at popular prices), and gets himself arrested and pardoned. *Bananas* ends with Fielding's wedding night, covered on television with sports commentator Howard Cosell supplying a live play-by-play.

"Arthur was very much concerned about the irreverence vis-à-vis certain religions," recalled Eric Pleskow. (Certain scenes made fun of the United Jewish Appeal.) "Apart from being in the movie business, he had other dimensions, his activity in Democratic politics, and so he was always concerned with image. In the end, however, *Bananas* was well received and did us no harm."

Once again, the critics took special notice of Woody. In the *New York Times,* Vincent Canby gave early evidence of loving anything Woody did because "when he is good, he is inspired. When he is bad, he's not rotten, he's just not so hot." Others, however, pointed to his still-crude filmmaking and took a dim view of his determination to be an auteur. By confusing the ability to write comedy with the ability to perform it, he ensured that *Bananas* would be dashed to bits on "the rocks of his acting and direction," wrote Stanley Kauffmann in *The New Republic*. Kauffmann acknowledged in 1998 that he viewed *Bananas* as "on-the-job training. Woody was learning how to direct by making pictures. There wasn't a film student in the country who couldn't have better directed *Bananas*. He was a gifted writer whose acting was crude. His idea of acting was to wave his hands. Serious drama meant waving his hands more quickly." As for love scenes, Kauffmann could not appreciate Woody playing a lover. "Watching him kiss a girl—any girl—made me want to look the other way."

Bananas was not a huge moneymaker but it would establish a blueprint for Woody's relationship with UA, who did not expect his films to earn much. In fact, as the years passed and film costs increased (and Woody spent more), his pictures would become even less profitable. "That wasn't the point," a former UA executive said impatiently. "He was our prestige item."

■ ■ ■ ■ ■ ■ ■

Hollywood Vignettes:
"Arthur was not a self-made man. He was a born prince."
— JUDY FEIFFER, former Orion executive

■ ■ ■ ■ ■ ■ ■

A special relationship soon developed between Woody and Arthur Krim. A bachelor most of his life, Krim finally married in his fifties. His wife, Mathilde, a physician who was one day to cofound the American Foundation for AIDS Research (AmFAR), had a daughter from a previous marriage. But Krim would never have children of his own. That fact, some people said, was the reason he showered Woody with what amounted to an adult version of a deluxe train set plus any other toy his heart desired. This plot, a scenario that L. B. Mayer would have approved, was pure Hollywood: Celebrated older man mentors brilliant younger man; ambitious protégé repays his powerful benefactor with loyalty and prestige. According to the UA mythology, a "mystical glue" bound the two men together. It was very simple, said one executive: "Woody was the emotional son Arthur never had."

In Woody's eyes, the cultured and magnetic Krim was a heroic personality. Unusual among entertainment moguls, he lived an entirely separate existence as a political activist. He had been a close personal friend and adviser of John F. Kennedy's. It was at Krim's town house on East Sixty-ninth Street that President Kennedy, in 1962, celebrated after his forty-fifth birthday party in Madison Square Garden, when Marilyn Monroe crooned a sultry "Happy Birthday, Mr. President." Later the Democratic fund-raiser, who reportedly turned down cabinet posts and ambassadorships, would become an adviser to Presidents Johnson and Carter in the fields of civil rights, arms control, and Middle Eastern relations.

This unusual man, and his UA colleagues, bestowed on Woody an extraordinary production deal with patronage that was unprecedented for a commercial artist. Basically, he could make any film he liked on any subject he liked. Woody, however, viewed the blank-check arrangement with restraint and vaguely presented it as "a nice, simple gentlemen's agreement." Once he tried to explain it to an editor at *Cinema.* There was no interference from his financial backers, he said. "I have absolute control. They don't have approval of the script. They don't have casting approval, they have absolutely nothing." Once in a great while "they"—Krim, or possibly Bob Benjamin or Eric Pleskow—would have something to say. "I always try and give them the courtesy of listening and talking with them. It never comes to anything. They always ask for permission just to come to the set." If he displayed condescension, it was not out of ignorance. He understood full well that the nice gentlemen's agreement, the money with no strings, was an amazing idea for Hollywood. "Had there been no Arthur Krim and UA, Woody's structure could not have evolved any other place in the world," believes Steven Bach, who was to join the studio in 1978 as senior vice president and head of worldwide production. Stanley Kauffmann calls his deal "sui generis, an independent filmmaker who never had to scrounge for money from a father-in-law, whose taproots are in the big money streams of Hollywood. There's been no one else in that position."

The people at UA were well aware of their largess. "Sometimes I felt like the Medici," mused Pleskow, alluding to the princely Florentine family who patronized art and literature during the Renaissance. Granted, films such as *Bananas* and *Sleeper* did not really qualify as high culture, but this was Hollywood, and the idea of commissioning an independent filmmaker to develop whatever he fancied was exhilarating. By giving him his head, UA was likely to get a few duds along with very good pictures. Who could imagine what new ideas might flower? And, as Pleskow said with a smile, "we didn't poison anyone."

"He knew how to handle us," explained Steven Bach. "He would ask for things, like the latest equipment in a private screening room, things that seemed a little outrageous. But we felt he deserved them. At the worst, you would take a tax deduction. At best, you would keep him happy." Of course Krim and Benjamin gave him "carte blanche," said another person. "He was their family."

At the outset, the gentlemen's agreement did not seem at all extraordinary. He impressed the Medici, Pleskow recalled, "as an intelligent young man. No one could foresee that he'd do a film every year." But UA underestimated Woody.

With two pictures under his belt, he was raring to do more. His second film for UA was loosely adapted from *Everything You Always Wanted to Know About Sex* (*But Were Afraid to Ask),* a best-selling manual by sexologist Dr. David Reuben that supposedly answered patients' dumb questions. Acquiring the option from Paramount (who intended the vehicle for Elliot Gould), Woody never bothered to read the book. Glancing at Reuben's chapter headings, he structured an episodic script using seven questions ("What's a sex pervert?" "Do aphrodisiacs work?"). Then he proceeded to concoct the answers in a series of lunatic sketches that spoofed all sex manuals, Dr. Reuben's in particular. In one sequence, "What is Sodomy?," an uptight doctor (Gene Wilder) enters into an obsessive affair with a sheep named Daisy, a devotee of frilly lingerie, and winds up in the gutter drinking Woolite. The final sketch, "What Happens During Ejaculation?," a clever parody of *Fantastic Voyage,* shows what happens in the male body during an orgasm. Woody, complete with horn-rimmed glasses, plays a neurotic sperm who worries about what will become of him. What if this turns out to be ordinary masturbation? What if he winds up on the ceiling?

With the release of two hit films back to back, Woody was having a very good year. In May of 1972, the screen adaptation of *Play It Again, Sam* followed *What's Up, Doc?* into Radio City Music Hall. Critics split into two camps: the negative, who had been expecting another Marx brothers cartoon like *Bananas,* and the positive, who thought Woody's decision to broaden his appeal with a personal romantic comedy had paid off. Only four months later, *Everything You Always Wanted to Know About Sex* opened to stinging notices and packed theaters. Soaring on word of mouth, it would become one of the top ten moneymakers of the year, despite the fact that notices universally panned it for tasteless material and too few laughs. At a Chicago screening, embarrassed critics even walked out, one of whom loudly sputtered "Yuck!" Woody's champion at the *New York Times,* Vincent Canby, deemed it clever but not particularly funny, and Dr. David Reuben was offended. (Eventually he endorsed its "humor, charm, and good taste, the best movie Woody Allen ever made.") None of this counted at the box office, however, where audiences found Woody's sex manual utterly irresistible.

■■■■■■■

Moving Pictures:
LUNA: It's hard to believe you haven't had sex for two hundred years.
MILES: Two hundred and four if you count my marriage.
—*Sleeper,* 1973

■■■■■■■

In 1973 Miles Monroe, a former clarinet player with the Ragtime Rascals, is part-owner of the Happy Carrot Health Food Store on Bleecker Street in Greenwich Village. One morning, he goes into St. Vincent's Hospital for what is supposed to be routine surgery on a peptic ulcer, but complications develop and he fails to regain consciousness. The doctors wrap him in aluminum foil and freeze him. Two hundred years later, society has retooled and the United States is a totalitarian state run by an albino fascist dictator. Rebel scientists trying to overthrow the government decide to revive Miles, the only person alive without an identification number. The bespectacled Miles, resembling a giant baked potato wrapped in tin foil, comes to in the year 2173. Expecting to wake up at St. Vincent's, he is naturally confused, more worried about his rent, now 2,400 months overdue, than about being a revolutionary hero. To avoid being captured by the thought police and reprogrammed, he disguises himself as a robot and winds up working for a socialite poet named Luna (Diane Keaton), whose work has been influenced by Rod McKuen. They join the underground movement and kidnap the Leader's nose (all that is left after an assassination attempt) before he can be reconstructed by cloning.

Again Woody used a collaborator, this time a thirty-one-year-old television producer named Marshall Brickman. Born in Rio de Janeiro, the son of a Polish Jew who came to the United States by way of Brazil, Brickman grew up in the Flatbush section of Brooklyn and graduated from the University of Wisconsin with a degree in music. In 1963 he met Woody at the Bitter End in Greenwich Village, where Brickman was a banjo player with the Tarriers, folksingers managed by Rollins and Joffe, and Woody was performing stand-up. Brickman, who also played guitar and bass, later toured with John and Michelle Phillips before they joined the Mamas and the Papas, and finally switched to television comedy writing for *Candid Camera* and *The Tonight Show,* before producing *The Dick Cavett Show.* Although Brickman and Woody seemed to be opposite in temperament, with Brickman generally sociable and cheerful, they shared a similar comic sensibility. When someone once asked him to compare himself to Woody, he answered, "I'm taller."

Unlike Woody's collaboration with Mickey Rose, in which they worked on a script together, Woody and Brickman worked out the plot to *Sleeper* during long walks, often through Central Park. Then Woody went home and wrote the draft, which Brickman would later read and comment upon. A talented craftsman, Brickman's strength was in understanding how to structure a story, an area in which Woody did less well.

Sleeper was not their first attempt at collaboration. Several years earlier, there had been another script, but it failed to find a producer. This time there was no problem getting UA's approval and a budget of $2 million. With seven weeks allotted for filming, shooting began in Denver in the spring of 1973, and by summer had moved to Hollywood, to the old David O. Selznick lot in Culver City, where *Gone With the Wind* was filmed. Nestled amid the gigantic concrete buildings, Woody noticed a three-room cottage surrounded by a garden of daisies and a picket fence. Told that it had once been Clark Gable's dressing room bungalow, he promptly commandeered it for his office.

Sleeper, a complicated picture requiring intricate sets and special effects, fell behind schedule, and additional photography soon depleted Woody's $350,000 fee. Under pressure to meet a Christmas release date, he frantically shot and edited simultaneously. Ralph Rosenblum, urgently summoned to Culver City in August, discovered that "tension pervaded every aspect" of the production. Nevertheless, *Sleeper* managed to open as scheduled on December 18 at Radio City Music Hall and received sensational reviews. It was Woody's first big critical and commercial success, one of the biggest moneymakers of the year. A delighted United Artists signed him to a new five-picture contract that extended his original deal to seven years.

Not until *Sleeper* did Woody begin to attract generally respectful attention from large-circulation newspapers and magazines, some of whose critics now began to view him as the best comic director and actor in the country. Foremost among his admirers was Vincent Canby, the *New York Times* critic whom Woody would credit as one of the significant figures in his career. A reporter for *Variety*, Canby arrived at the *Times* in 1965 to cover show business and succeeded Renata Adler as film critic four years later. In the meantime, he had seen Woody perform stand-up at the Americana Hotel, where he made a point of talking to him "informally between shows one night. I had known little about him and I was knocked out." *Take the Money and Run* impressed him positively as "a night club routine but still a very good movie, and remains one of my favorites. Certainly I had a suspicion that he was up to something unusual." With *Sleeper*, Woody finally crossed over from stand-up to the screen.

At *The New Yorker*, another important review medium, the film department had been shared since 1967 by Pauline Kael and Penelope Gilliatt, whose styles could not have been more dissimilar. As the most influential critic of the seventies, Kael redefined film criticism, and critics who followed her thinking would be dubbed "Paulettes." More often than not, her brass-knuckle reviews sounded angry, as if she felt personally offended by a film that did not meet her standards. She wrote as if she were being chased by a posse, which may have been what prompted Warren Beatty to nickname her Ma Barker, after the bank-robbing public enemy. Born in Petaluma, California, she was a tiny, argumentative woman, nondescript in appearance, three times married, who once had been fired by *McCall's* for knifing *The Sound of Music*. When she arrived at *The New Yorker*, she was almost fifty.

Over the years, Kael would be tight with a number of directors who asked her opinion on scripts, invited her to their sets, and arranged special screenings. If electrified by a picture, she became its personal advocate and went on television to drum up enthusiasm. Crossing the line between criticism and film production, she resigned from *The New Yorker* in 1978 and took a Hollywood job developing film projects for Warren Beatty. (She soon returned to *The New Yorker,* however.)

Among the new-wave directors, Kael's darlings were Arthur Penn, whose *Bonnie and Clyde* she single-handedly rescued from a premature demise, and Robert Altman, whose *Nashville* she had championed as virtually a perfect film. While Woody was not one of her pets, she did appreciate his work, to a point, because she thought his movies made people feel less insecure about their imperfections. In her eyes, *Take the Money and Run* had been nice but nothing special, "a limply good-natured little nothing of a comedy, soft as sneakers." For several years they maintained cordial relations, sometimes appearing together to collegially trade repartee on TV talk shows, but friendship counted for nothing to Kael at her typewriter. After giving *Sleeper* a couple of preliminary swings—"a beautiful little piece of work," "a small classic"—she administered an unexpected jab: If *Sleeper* was the best slapstick comedy of the year, it was only because "there hasn't been any other." Then she moved in for the knockout. Woody's films lacked an antic quality, in fact his humor reminded her of "strip-mining" because he scratched the surface without ever getting close to the mother lode. Psychologizing, she mocked him as hopelessly anal and reserved special scorn for his choice of the clarinet, "an instrument that appeals to controlled, precise people."

The intensity of Kael's attack embarrassed Roger Angell, who urged Woody to ignore her and reminded him of a forthcoming profile by Penelope Gilliatt. By contrast, Gilliatt's film critiques tended to be literary, kindhearted, sometimes loopy. She admired Woody, recalled her close friend Andrew Sarris, "beyond belief." A vivacious, red-haired British writer who had once been married to the playwright John Osborne, she had visited Woody the previous summer in Culver City. A boozy dinner at Trader Vic's resulted in whispered confidences over rum punches (virgin punches for himself) and Chinese spareribs. Even then, at the age of forty-two, Gilliatt was known to have a weakness for alcohol, which would eventually contribute to her undoing. Sipping rum punches, she rapidly formed an extravagant opinion of her subject. In New York that fall, Woody invited her to his apartment for more cozy talks. Plying her with chocolate pudding, he confided choice secret tidbits about his first marriage, his analyst, his pigeon problem, the maid he was planning to fire, and his lifelong addiction to Hershey bars.

In writing her *New Yorker* profile, Gilliatt got so carried away by Woody's puppyish vulnerability that she apparently began to think of him as a pet dog, a cuddly pooch with long red hair hanging around his neck "like a setter's ears." He had "no idea of how nice he looks," she added. *The New Yorker* published the rum-punch piece with a straight face, though some of the writers there found it as nutty as a cuckoo clock. Ved Mehta would later describe this incident as one of those occasions when Gilliatt's work exhibited "a touch of the surreal." Afterward, Gilliatt invited Woody to her daughter Nolan's birthday party, and he deigned to accept. Another guest, Vincent Canby, recalled that "two dreadful little boys rushed over and one of them asked him to autograph a dollar bill. Woody obliged, and the other kid chimed in, 'Now it's worth two dollars!' and ran off. It was embarrassing but Woody was most gallant about it."

As Woody once admitted in a letter to Roger Angell, Gilliatt's reviews never made much sense to him. In fact, if someone set out to deliberately satirize film criticism, her writing would be the easiest place to begin. On the other hand, he much preferred her to Kael, who despite her brilliance allowed personal problems to color her judgments. But the critic whom he had never liked, he went on, was Stanley Kauffmann, with his schoolmarmish harping on his amateur acting and directing. Kauffmann's deadserious advice on how Woody could make funnier comedies made him laugh. If Kauffmann ever made a comedy he'd be eager to see it, he chortled. In any case, he needn't worry about Kauffmann's reviews because, he said, few people read *The New Republic* anymore.

■ ■ ■ ■ ■ ■ ■

On the Couch:
"He's made his lunacy work for him. It takes a special kind of genius to successfully use your insanity."

—Walter Bernstein

■ ■ ■ ■ ■ ■ ■

Spending the better part of the year away from New York meant missing his daily psychotherapy sessions. Undeterred, he would locate a pay phone and talk to his doctor for forty-five minutes while timing himself on his watch. In Freudian analysis for fifteen years, he was now on his third psychiatrist, not counting the clinic he used when he was broke in 1958. (No longer did he actually go to therapy; it came to him, in the evenings or at any hour he preferred.) And yet, those thousands of hours on the couch had not resulted in "one emotionally charged moment," he confessed to the writer Francine Du Plessix Gray in 1974. He never cried, not once. His tearless sessions were blithely dismissed as "in, whine for fifty minutes, out again." The previous year he had switched to a woman, Dr. Kathryn Prescott. "I had these fantasies of what would happen if I was locked in a room with a beautiful, fascinating woman." Nothing happened. He cut back from five to three times a week. Still nothing. Therapy was hideously "dull, dull, dull."

Even though he complained incessantly about analysis, just as he raged and whined about practically everything else in his life, treatment was a definite lifestyle for him. Growing celebrity was accompanied by an even greater need for a shrink, somebody to whom he could unload his grievances each and every day. On top of his childhood phobias (death, darkness, kidnapping, boats, airplanes, most elevators) were now layered a host of fresh fears, typically a cleanliness phobia that prevented his taking baths because immersion in dirty water disgusted him, and eating habits so rigid that at times he could get down nothing but fish. Dining in pizzerias, when his friends ordered pies loaded with sausage and mushrooms, he always stuck to plain cheese.

All of his denials to the contrary, treatment was one of the keys to his professional success. "Underneath," remarked one of his actors, "he has the little twerp syndrome. But look how well he has used it!" Deliberately milking his analysis until being a professional neurotic became part of his persona was as much a schtick as Jack Benny's stinginess. Acting the part came easily. And pretending treatment was a waste of time allowed him to keep the shades drawn on bigger problems. Although he claimed to be depressed, it never interfered with his work. "I'm disciplined," he admitted. "I can go into a room every morning and churn it out." He might be crazy but he wasn't dysfunctional.

■ ■ ■ ■ ■ ■ ■

Commentary:
"If he took three or four years to make a film, it would be a mess. Not at all funny. His mind works fast. The pace of his life matches the pace of his films."

—VINCENT CANBY

■ ■ ■ ■ ■ ■ ■

After completing *Sleeper*, Woody sent Eric Pleskow a note saying he was almost finished with his next script, a contemporary murder mystery about a New York couple who stumble across a crime. Two weeks later, Pleskow was surprised to receive the first draft of a screenplay about the Napoleonic wars, set in Czarist Russia.

"What happened?" he asked.

"I tore it up," said Woody. At a meeting in the UA offices, he explained to the top executives that he wanted to make an early-nineteenth-century picture about the meaninglessness of existence, and he planned to shoot it in Russia. "Krim was one of the most intelligent men ever to head a movie company," said Steven Bach. "He may have been listening with a straight face but I suspect he was thinking, 'Sure disaster. How could this picture possibly attract teenagers in Omaha?' But this was his son and if that's what he wanted to do, that's what he wanted to do." Contrary to what the title suggests, *Love and Death* was neither serious nor depressing. Boris Dmitrivich Grushenko is a schnook of a pacifist (and a militant coward), who from the moment he enlists in the Czar's army seems headed for trouble. Embroiled in a plot to assassinate Napoleon, he is executed. According to Pleskow, UA regarded Woody as "an exceptional animal in our business, comparable only perhaps to a man like Chaplin. He was never excessive in his demands for himself. That's why we were his people and he was our man."

Their man spent seven months on location in France and Hungary. Though he went over budget by $1 million, the result was his most polished film yet, with none of the home-movie jerkiness of *Bananas* or *Sleeper*. Notices were, for the most part, enthusiastic. Judith Crist in *New York* magazine noted approvingly that he was "going for the character rather than the cartoon" (and she also applauded his acting as "perfection"), while Penelope Gilliatt viewed *Love and Death* as his "most shapely" film. Vincent Canby raved about "Woody's War and Peace," as personal a film as "any American star-writer-director has made since the days of Keaton, Chaplin, and Jerry Lewis." Even Stanley Kauffmann gave him credit for putting the camera "in the right place most of the time."

■ ■ ■ ■ ■ ■ ■

The Box Office:

Year		*U.S./Canadian rentals in millions
1969	*Take the Money and Run*	2.6
1971	*Bananas*	3.5
1972	*Play It Again, Sam*	5.8
1972	*Everything You Always Wanted to Know About Sex (But Were Afraid to Ask)*	8.8
1973	*Sleeper*	8.3
1975	*Love and Death*	7.4

*Not adjusted for inflation.

Note: As Woody became popular overseas, foreign earnings climbed steadily during this period.

■ ■ ■ ■ ■ ■ ■

"What about the kid?" said Martin Ritt.

"What kid?"

"You know, the funny kid." Ritt finally remembered the name. "Woody Allen."

For a number of years, Martin Ritt, the director, and Walter Bernstein, the screenwriter, had been trying—without success—to make a picture about screenwriters suspected of being communists or Red sympathizers during the House Un-American Activities Committee investigation into the entertainment industry. During the McCarthy era, a few of these writers, in order to earn a living, hired fronts, nonpolitical people who handed in scripts and passed themselves off as the authors, in return for a percentage of the fee. Both Ritt and Bernstein had been among the blacklisted, which meant this semiautobiographical project was in the nature of a personal crusade for them. Originally a serious drama about a man who was blacklisted, the script was made more salable as a blackish comedy featuring the "front" as the protagonist. Then the project languished for several years because "Columbia wanted a star," said Bernstein, "somebody like Dustin Hoffman or Robert Redford, nobody we wanted." It was obvious to Ritt that Woody's range as an actor was severely limited, yet he was clearly right for the part of Howard Prince, a street-smart coffee-shop cashier and part-time bookie who prospers by fronting for a blacklisted TV writer.

In the fifties, when he seldom read newspapers except for the sports section, Woody knew vaguely of Senator McCarthy as a man with a five o'clock shadow. It was not until 1963 that he became aware of the ugly climate of that period. Appearing at the Hungry i in San Francisco, he got friendly with the stage manager, who was none other than Alvah Bessie, one of the Hollywood Ten "unfriendly" witnesses. In 1950 Bessie was cited for contempt of Congress and sent to prison after declining to say whether he was or ever had been a member of the Communist Party. Although Bessie was thirty years older than Woody, he treated him as a peer. After returning to New York, an appreciative Woody wrote to thank him for his kindness. During the filming of *Love and Death,* Woody read Bernstein's script and immediately expressed interest, not only because it was "one of the best pieces of material offered to me," but also because he felt drawn to a subject that "expresses me politically." Without his participation, making *The Front* would have been difficult, even though Bernstein said they would surely have tried to satisfy Columbia with Hoffman or George Segal.

In one scene, Woody asked Bernstein to remove a Jewish mother character, but otherwise he made no attempt to impose his ideas on the script. With direction it was a different story, however. Handing over control of the picture to Ritt made him unhappy. On the set, he was "never disrespectful," said

Andrea Marcovicci, who played Woody's idealistic girlfriend, "but I sensed it was hard for him to table his thoughts." According to Walter Bernstein, "Woody is never deliberately cruel but there's a certain lack of tact, to say the least. He's one of the most insensitive sensitive people I know." At the rushes, Bernstein recalled, "he drove Marty crazy by criticizing things in front of everyone, and Marty finally had to ask him to stay away because he was hurting people's feelings." Woody expressed amazement. "It's the problems that we should be talking about," he told Bernstein. "We don't need to mention the good stuff." It never occurred to him that people needed recognition for a job well done. One problem never mentioned was Woody's costar, the famously irrepressible Zero Mostel, an actor of Falstaffian proportions. Actors passing by his dressing room would hear him bellow, "Shut up out there, I'm farting!" His antics made Woody cringe, recalled Bernstein. "Woody shrinks when anybody touches him. He was always polite to Zero, but it was clear he didn't want to be around him. In the film, you can read it in his body language."

Critics attacked *The Front* for trivializing and romanticizing the blacklist. Other reviewers felt that the credibility of the project was destroyed by casting Woody in a straight role. He dragged down the rest of the cast, Stanley Kauffmann thought, "because they are trying to act and he is doing his night club stuff."

On Monday nights, the tables at Michael's Pub were jammed together so tightly that waiters could barely squeeze through the sea of green-and-white-checked tablecloths. Out in the tiny bar, a hundred jostling fans were penned behind a velvet rope, spilling their $3.20 drinks on one another, just to hear Woody and his clarinet. In the late sixties, he had begun playing New Orleans jazz with a half-dozen musicians, most of them nonprofessionals, including a stockbroker, two teachers, and the owner of a burglar-alarm business. At first they got together in their apartments "for fun," he recalled, but in 1970 made their public debut at Barney Google's, a beer garden on East Eighty-sixth Street. On the strength of Woody's fame as a comedian, the New Orleans Funeral and Ragtime Orchestra moved on to other clubs but no place kept them very long until they met Gil Wiest, the owner of Michael's Pub on East Fifty-fifth Street. Wiest shrewdly recognized the drawing power of a clarinet-playing celebrity and wondered if presenting the group on a regular basis might attract business, even if the music was strictly amateur. That guess proved correct, with name recognition making up for lack of musical expertise, and now every Monday the restaurant was packed. Whenever a number ended, the crowd applauded wildly, and the bar drinkers tapped their feet, but Woody looked tight-lipped and grim. "Come on, Woody," a woman yelled. "Smile." Seldom did he acknowledge their presence, let alone mingle or smile at them. In fact, one of Wiest's jobs was to make sure nobody got close enough to touch him. It was only Groucho Marx, making a surprise visit one night, who took it upon himself to reach up for Woody's hand and tinkle a tip of a few pennies into his palm.

Throughout his thirties, Woody's career flourished, but his personal life was stalled. There was no emotional center. After breaking up with Diane, he dated constantly, very often actresses, because they were usually the women he met in the normal course of his work. In show-business circles, he had a reputation for being something of a stud. "Put it this way," said Tony Roberts. "Harpo Marx probably chased the most girls, I chase the second most, and Woody is a close third." Girl chasing seemed to go hand in hand with casual sex. In 1980 he was to admit that for nine years there had not been a single romantic relationship lasting longer than two months.

Though he knew hundreds of people, he had few *friends,* as most people interpret that word. There were several cronies who joined him for various activities—Tony Roberts for tennis, Marshall Brickman for writing—but he was not really on intimate terms with these men. Closest to him of all remained Jean Doumanian, who had been his best friend for almost a decade. With Woody's support and connections, and her own talent, she gradually moved up in television from Dick Cavett's talk show to Howard Cosell's variety show on ABC, for which she booked celebrities. In 1976, once again with Woody's help, she rose to a similar position as talent coordinator for *Saturday Night Live,* performing her job with consummate efficiency and style. At *SNL,* a casual place where clean jeans and T-shirts were considered formal wear, Jean wore designer suits and came across as "a very stylish person with a moneyed style that seemed rather French," recalled Karen Roston, the show's costumer. Despite the couturier outfits, Jean was not popular. According to one colleague, she suffered from certain grating mannerisms "as if she had just read Michael Korda's book *Power!* She turned off a lot of people." Another co-worker called her "the kind of person who makes you crazy. I used to tell myself, 'The day will come when I'll be able to get back at her.' "

Highly dependent, Woody was in the habit of telephoning Jean at work several times a day. In the evenings they met for dinner, very often at an Italian restaurant in an unfashionable neighborhood of brick tenements on Second Avenue near Eighty-eighth Street. So seldom did Woody spend an evening at home that Elaine's served as a comfortable and convenient kitchen away from home. The owner, Elaine Kaufman, was a strapping woman with thick eyeglasses. The daughter of Russian-Jewish immigrants, who grew up in Queens, she had a knack for self-promotion and preparation of unexceptional meals. In 1963 she opened her Yorkville tavern that soon became a cherished sanctuary for a number of writers, among them Tom Wolfe, William Styron, Gay Talese, and Norman Mailer. Never could the proprietress, a high-school graduate whose first job was clerking in Woolworth's, be considered an intellectual, but she read omnivorously and adored gifted young male writers, whom she called her "boys." (She was "Big Mama.") Against all odds, Big Mama's Algonquin Round Table began to flourish.

Of all her literary pets, Woody was her favorite. She doted on him, flattered him, and finally bestowed on him a table of his own—Number 8—in the front, which was reserved every night until ten. In return, he publicized the restaurant by his continual presence and later by shooting scenes for several movies there. By the late seventies, Elaine's had become a renowned restaurant that defined itself as being the popular place to see and be seen, if you had any status at all. Patronized by a mixture of prominent writers and movie stars, politicians and ballplayers, the place filled up night after night with celebrities and the rubberneckers who paid to gawk at them while tucking away giant veal chops, one of the house specialties. (Woody, a picky eater, always ordered fish or pasta.) Hard-pressed to explain why he spent so much time at the city's most obvious celebrity outpost, a kind of Eiffel Tower of mediocre fare, he claimed that he enjoyed the food. What Woody enjoyed was being the center of attention so long as he didn't have to interact with other people, and Elaine Kaufman kept people from bothering him while he ate.

CHAPTER SEVEN

"A Picture About Me"

His birthday was still several days away, but the *New York Times* noticed Woody would be celebrating forty on December 1. Or, as the paper would indelicately word it, entering middle age. Taking a break from filming *The Front,* Woody seemed to be in a truly bubbly mood as he chatted with reporter Mel Gussow during a commemorative interview. Costumed for the role of Howard Prince, in a 1950s business suit, with his tousled hair neatly cropped, Woody looked like a boyish twenty-five. But forty, he insisted, was a marvelous age. Professionally, he took pride in the fact that he had five films under his belt. Physically, he was in pretty good shape, too. "I'm becoming more attractive with age," he said, because he looked less like "a punk." At this rate, he would probably be gorgeous by fifty.

Would he ever consider a face-lift? "I don't even have my teeth filled," he laughed.

When the conversation turned to his next picture, he disclosed that it would be shot in New York. Otherwise, he couldn't talk about it. "I'm afraid my enemies will come out with the same film," he smiled.

Judging by the *Times* interview, which could not have been more relentlessly upbeat, there was no question that Woody Allen felt pretty good about himself. In fact, despite his success, he did not feel good at all. Reaching forty simply intensified his lifelong terror of death. Getting older, he believed, was "the worst thing that could happen to anyone," rather like "drawing the ace of spades." Other than his demise, he was acutely aware of being short and skinny, and now he was also losing his hair. Moreover, although he would never admit it publicly, he still felt like a failure. His accomplishments as a filmmaker were unsatisfactory, he decided, and his work sophomoric. His personal relationships were especially poor. After two troubled marriages and more women than he could count, he had actually grown weary of the chase. He found himself mourning his affair with Diane Keaton, and looking back, decided that she had been the love of his life after all.

Looking ahead, he felt a sense of foreboding. Surely he should be contented because he had everything a man could want. Yet, there was not a single thing that seemed to give his days any fizz. All was flat. As he had discovered, there was a psychoanalytic term for the I'm-Not-Having-Any-Fun syndrome: *anhedonia,* the inability to experience pleasure.

In the months prior to his birthday, he began working on a screenplay that attempted to penetrate the air of unrelieved gloom hanging over him. Unlike his previous stories—about bumbling bank robbers and health-store proprietors with ulcers—this was like nothing he had ever attempted before. "It was a picture about me," he said later. "My life, my thoughts, my ideas, my background." As much as he disliked the idea of using autobiographical material, he felt the need to take risks and try something different. What he envisioned was a film that would make people take him seriously.

Once again, he collaborated with Marshall Brickman. "The first draft," remembered Brickman, "was the story of a guy who lived in New York and was forty years old and was examining his life." The guy is Alvy Singer, a comic by trade, a whiner by nature, who can always find something to fuss about. To keep up his morale, he reminds himself that being unhappy isn't so terrible because life is a mixture of troubles too horrible for words (blindness, terminal illness) and garden-variety misery (everything else), and so all of us should feel lucky to be merely miserable. Woody and his collaborator worked together almost effortlessly. Their routine was to trudge down Lexington Avenue, discussing ideas, sometimes crossing over to Madison, sometimes stopping for Häagen-Dazs, Woody writing down dialogue, then more brainstorming. Among the various strands in Alvy's life were a love relationship gone wrong, the meaninglessness of life, and "an obsession with proving himself and testing himself to find out what kind of character he had," recalled Brickman. What resulted finally was a long opening soliloquy that repeatedly cut away to a series of more or less disconnected events that explicated his discontent and self-loathing, and also showed him trolling for women.

With an initial operating budget of $3 million (rising to $4 million), Woody's "picture about me" went into production in the spring of 1976. After five pictures, filmed in California, Colorado, Puerto Rico, Paris, and Budapest, he finally got to live at home and shoot his first movie in New York City—become, in fact, a completely New York–based filmmaker. Drawing from the pool of local production people, he gathered a select circle of crew members who would stay on as regulars for the next twenty years. Working with a creative casting director, Juliet Taylor, he was able to make good use of New York's stage actors, people such as Colleen Dewhurst, Christopher Walken, Sigourney Weaver, and Danny Aiello. His new cinematographer was the New York–born Gordon Willis, a brilliant forty-seven-year-old who filmed, among others, *The Godfather* and was known in the business as "The Prince of Darkness" for his underlit films.

To play Alvy Singer's two ex-wives, Woody cast Janet Margolin (who actually resembled Harlene) and Carol Kane. For Alvy's current girlfriend, Annie, Woody gave the part to Diane Keaton, on whom, of course, the character happened to be based. This girlfriend, referred to in Alvy's opening monologue, did not actually appear on-screen for fifteen minutes. No matter. Annie Hall was not the main character.

Diane Keaton was living in a stark white apartment, in an Art Deco building on East Sixty-eighth Street. It boasted a white-on-white living room, which contained a white-on-white painting. The kitchen was also white: not only its walls and floors and Braun and Osterizer appliances, its crisp white telephone and white watering can, but even the Keri lotion was in a white container perched on a white shelf. "White is very cleansing for me," she explained. Except for her two cats, Buster and Whitey, she lived alone.

Keaton, now thirty, could look back on a film career that had run hot and cold. Her drab role as Kay Corleone, the downtrodden wife in *The Godfather* and *The Godfather, Part II,* did not suggest any great acting range. "She was abysmal in the *Godfather* films," Stanley Kauffmann said. "Obviously Woody was crazy about her. Sometimes that can be detrimental. When a director is infatuated with his leading actress, he can go mad in licking her with the camera. But Woody managed to transform his feelings into good evocative use of her talent." Still, in *Play It Again, Sam; Sleeper;* and *Love and Death,* Woody was the star who got all the good lines, and she remained in his shadow, at times little more than ornamental window dressing. During long periods of unemployment, she kept busy taking classes—singing, acting, dancing—and working out at the gym every other day. She supported herself by doing the "Hour after Hour" underarm deodorant commercial on television and acting in TV series such as *Mannix* and *The FBI,* and she also made two films that were less than stellar.

In the first cut of Woody's new movie, Alvy Singer meets Annie Hall after a doubles match at a tennis club. Dressed in street clothes, they stand around talking. Annie is wearing men's clothing: a white men's shirt tucked into baggy tan trousers, a black vest, and a long polka-dot tie (all of which came out of Diane's own closet). On her head is a floppy black hat. Within thirty seconds of her appearance, she laughs, shakes her head, throws up her hands, looks bewildered, giggles, reproaches herself, then calms down. "Oh, well, la-de-dah," she trills. "La-de-dah." Like Alvy, who *lerves* her, *lo-oves* her, *luffs* her, who has to invent words because *love* is too weak to express his feelings, the audience likewise *lerves* her immediately.

The end of Woody's real affair with Keaton was protracted and painful. If he resented her therapist and teachers, she disliked his condescension, pecadilloes, and zombie moods. Repeatedly separating and reuniting, they finally went their own ways and settled into a companionable friendship, catching foreign movies and Knicks games together. Once they were at his apartment after a game, and she was hungry, even though she had just dined on steak and potatoes and marble cheesecake at Frankie and Johnnie's. She went to the freezer and took out frozen waffles and heated up three or four. Then, no sooner did she finish the waffles than she was back in the kitchen, fixing tacos. Woody decided that she had "the largest appetite of anyone I've ever known."

Woody continued to look back nostalgically on their romance, even though he treated her in a manner expressly designed to sabotage the relationship. Still, there were times when he missed her terribly. Nobody had really taken her place.

That September, Ralph Rosenblum found himself running smack into the same sort of problems that had confronted him on Woody's first picture. When he started sifting through the 100,000 feet of footage, he smelled big trouble. In his opinion, it was "an untitled and chaotic collection of bits and pieces that seemed to defy continuity," and he held little hope for popular success. The film opens in Woody's old Brooklyn neighborhood and shows his mother's consternation when a black family moves in. Among other scenes there is a guided tour through the nine layers of Hell with the Devil (Level Five: organized crime, fascist dictators, and people who disapprove of oral sex), an idea that would resurface twenty years later in *Deconstructing Harry* when Billy Crystal gives Harry the very same tour. An admittedly disheartened Marshall Brickman could see that the film was "running off in nine different directions" and the first twenty-five minutes didn't work at all.

By the end of October, however, Rosenblum had a bloated first cut, which ran about two hours and twenty minutes. Yet, in spite of dozens of brilliant skits and laughs galore, there was no plot. In a stream-of-consciousness monologue, reminiscent of *Take the Money and Run,* Woody skidded from one vignette to another—from the absence of God to fear of the void to his fascination with nymphets to his fear of impotence. "The thing was supposedly to take place in my mind." Like a dying man watching a mosaic of his life float by, he tried to cover every base.

To find a story that worked, Rosenblum began trimming Alvy's relationships with his first two wives, and as he did so, Diane Keaton began to dominate the footage, so he "kept cutting in the direction of that relationship." Before long, the whole concept of the picture began to change, moving steadily from a story of Alvy complaining about his difficulty with relationships in general to his love affair with Annie in particular. What remained was a tidy love story about a neurotic New York comedian and his equally neurotic girlfriend, and how they met and fell in love, and how, eventually, they drift apart. Relationships, like life, Alvy muses afterward, are full of loneliness and misery but unfortunately "it's all over much too quickly." Because Alvy knows that his craving for love will assure another relationship, and another, he tells the old joke about the man who goes to a shrink because his crazy brother thinks he's a chicken.

Turn him in, advises the doctor.

"I would, but I need the eggs."

Annie, after living in Los Angeles for a while, returns to New York. Alvy and his date bump into her and her date outside the Thalia theater, which is showing *The Sorrow and the Pity.* They get together for a nostalgic lunch at a restaurant opposite Lincoln Center, and afterward Alvy watches Annie cutting across the trafffic on Columbus Avenue. She was "a terrific person," he thinks to himself. It's never clear how Annie, at the end, feels about Alvy. Diane Keaton would later observe that Annie, possibly the best women's role Woody ever wrote, is "basically stupid," in her estimation. Perhaps, but Annie is too smart, too ambitious, to waste her life with Alvy.

All that remained to do, finally, was choosing a title. Woody favored calling the picture *Anhedonia,* while Marshall Brickman countered with equally silly titles *(It Had to Be Jew, Me and My Goy).* Woody, however, could not have been more serious about *Anhedonia.* Brickman recalled that when Arthur Krim first heard the title, he "walked over to the window and threatened to jump." Eric Pleskow remembered getting a phone call from Gabe Sumner, vice president in charge of advertising and promotion at UA.

"Listen, I have Woody here," Sumner said. "Did you hear the title of the movie? *Anhedonia.*"

"You can't be serious," replied Pleskow. He hung up the phone, looked up the word in the dictionary, then sped down to Sumner's office on the floor below, where the discussion became more heated. Woody refused to budge. Finally, Pleskow politely put his foot down. "For you and me, it will be *Anhedonia,* but for the rest of the people we need to find a title." He wasn't joking.

During a series of test audience screenings, Woody diligently tried out a different name each night. *Anhedonia* got blank stares; *Anxiety* produced a few chuckles. Finally it was a toss-up between *Annie and Alvy* and *Annie Hall* (which Eric Pleskow never considered "a catchy title" either). Even so, *Annie Hall* is not really about Annie, but about Alvy and his inability to relate to her or any other woman. The title could just as easily have been *Alvy Singer,* or *Allan Konigsberg.*

Despite editing problems, the movie had already begun generating heat, and word of mouth said the picture was simply marvelous. In their enthusiasm for what they figured would be a box-office breadwinner, the studio wasted no time making plans. But Woody began to give them a hard time. In the UA offices on Seventh Avenue, there was plenty of griping over his inflexibility. Some people grumbled that advertising a Woody Allen picture was like committing suicide with a smile on your face. Contractually, Woody did not have advertising approval, only the right of consultation, but "he actually did have approval because he took it," observed a UA executive. Woody had no use for the Hollywood system of marketing films, including common strategies such as promotional tours. (When he met with the Toronto press, asked if he enjoyed the filming, he answered, "No, it was a boring movie to make.") According to another UA veteran, "He figured people would decide on the basis of reviews. I don't think he cared if his pictures made money or not. Sometimes I thought he would have preferred to publicize his pictures by installing billboards in front of theaters." He remembered hearing Woody once say, "Either people will come or they won't."

They did.

Out of Woody's inner despair, kept carefully masked from public view by quick-witted banter, emerged a motion picture that would bring cheer to millions of moviegoers. *Annie Hall* gave people permission to feel good about themselves, even when they were feeling like failures. In the "picture about me," Woody appeared in every scene, almost every frame, parading his insecurities, phobias, and deep self-deprecation. Then, unexpectedly, he came even closer by directly addressing the audience, mulling over the troubles besetting his relationships, the ordinary hang-ups that all of them could identify with. By sharing his most intimate experiences in this way, he endeared himself to audiences of the seventies. Stanley Kauffmann, remembering *Annie Hall* twenty years later, said, "There was accuracy and flavor, along with a sense of rightness and fulfillment. It was as if he had sunk a taproot into an era and its people."

When Penelope Gilliatt saw *Annie Hall,* she bestowed her highest compliment and compared Woody with the genius of Buster Keaton (her all-time cinema hero) and *Annie Hall* with *The Navigator;* Woody "technically pushes far ahead of anything he has done in the cinema before, playing with ideas in film which he has been experimenting with in prose." This time the enthusiastic Gilliatt was joined by the great majority of critics busily dragging out their superlatives. One of the few exceptions was John Simon, the crusty *National Review* critic, who refused to consider the movie as a fable for his times. Instead, he wrote, *Annie Hall* told him "everything we never wanted to know about Woody's sex life and were afraid he'd tell us anyway." Later, he admitted his difficulties watching any film in which Woody played a romantic role. "I'm obsessed with looks. Some people like to eat and I happen to like good-looking people, female or male. Even children. Even dogs. Woody has a good face for a comedian but not for a romantic film. Looking at his face depresses me."

Annie Hall would become a classic that measured against the best films in history, ranking Number 31 on the American Film Institute's 1998 list of the best one hundred movies ever made. It established Woody's reputation as an important artist, catapulting him into the pantheon of great film comedians, where Chaplin, Keaton, Fields, and the Marx brothers dwelled virtually alone. In that spring of 1977, he went from a cerebral neurotic appreciated primarily by sophisticated urban audiences to a new star embraced by the middle class throughout the country. Women in particular seemed to be crazy about the film, and for the first time Woody began to attract a devoted female audience. Even before the movie was released, women's service magazines began hopping on the bandwagon, unaware of his contempt for their typical readers, who "just junk their lives being a housewife raising kids," he thought. *Redbook* arranged for one of its editors to share a tête-à-tête dinner at his penthouse. After martinis, mixed by Woody himself, they adjourned to the dining room, where his housekeeper served a delicious meal, which the editor would describe as "a subtle first course with an egg on top; lovely encircled-with-vegetables fish; hot apple souffle." But in spite of the candles and the classical music, she departed four and a half hours later without asking many questions at all. Apparently reluctant to disturb his Zen-like reverie, she seemed to know little more than when she arrived; indeed, Woody said so little worth quoting that *Redbook* found it necessary to dig up a few humorous quotes from his *New Yorker* pieces. There was "an almost moatlike space" around him, the magazine lamely observed.

Probably no celebrity of the seventies was more socially autistic than Woody. But the media presented him as a lovable eccentric, giving no hint of his disturbing side. As a result, he developed a pristine image in the popular imagination. The feminists were the only group he was unable to charm. Sensing his hostility toward women, both as a filmmaker and a man, they were beginning to view him as something more than a charming oddball. Shortly after his fortieth birthday, in preparation for an article in the *Village Voice*, Vivian Gornick paid a visit to Woody's penthouse. The writer, who is exactly the same age as Woody, came from the same background. The child of working-class Jews, she grew up in the Bronx. Gornick supposed the offscreen and on-screen Woody would be the same man. "I expected to find him living in one room and eating tuna fish out of a can," she said. "I was shocked when I saw how he was living." They sat in his Fifth Avenue lair and sipped chilled white wine and argued about women and men. A long time ago, one night in 1964, she and her friends had seen him perform at the Bitter End. He was, she felt back then, nothing less than "us." His humor, his anguish over growing up smart and anxious were "great stuff. He's a fantastic mimic and he did our lives to a T. It was wild." But over the years his perfect pitch made her laugh less and less. "I began to see the arrested quality of his movies. The shocking thing was that he was forty and still chasing girls, still a schlep who was obviously stuck in his adolescent pursuit of sex."

"Tell me," she said over the wine. "You create out of a woman a foil who ultimately is the object of ridicule. Don't you see that?"

He did not.

"Don't you get enough flack from enough women so that you can see that?"

"Listen," he said, "when you're a comic, you're always offending someone. Jews are offended by my rabbi jokes." And besides, he was no chauvinist. He loved women. He couldn't understand why she found his pictures sexist.

She had been watching him trying to get laid for fifteen years, as she struggled to explain, and didn't want to see it portrayed on film one more time. When she viewed *Annie Hall* a few months later, she thought to herself that "Alvy is not much brighter than Annie but he comes out on top. In Jewish comedy, the wild street comics like Berle and King and Brooks would make fun of Jewish women—their wives and their mother-in-laws; Woody Allen made a fool of the shiksa."

After publication of the *Voice* article ("You're Not a Schlep Anymore"), Gornick felt guilty about giving him such a hard time. He could not have been more hospitable, "sweet-tempered, utterly forthcoming." Sometime later, when he called to ask her for a date, she refused to go out with him because "it was one-up-manship. I was sure he wanted to bring me down."

∎ ∎ ∎ ∎ ∎ ∎ ∎

On the Couch:
"When you do comedy, you're not sitting at the grownups' table, you're sitting at the children's table."

—WOODY ALLEN, 1978

∎ ∎ ∎ ∎ ∎ ∎ ∎

Annie Hall was in postproduction when Woody was ready to move on to the next project. In early 1977 Eric Pleskow received a call from Sam Cohn, Woody's agent at International Creative Management (and an addition to Woody's personal managers, Rollins and Joffe). A crusty, middle-aged, chain-smoking man fond of dressing in sweaters and loafers, Cohn was one of the most powerful talent agents in the business. Operating almost independently as an agency within an agency, he handled actors as well as directors, producers, and writers. Speaking to Pleskow, Cohn cautiously explained that Woody had some material that was not a typical Woody Allen script. Reading the atypical script, Pleskow and Arthur Krim understood immediately what he meant. Several days later, the UA officers met with Cohn, Charles Joffe, and Jack Rollins. According to Pleskow, "I'm sure they were all set for a knock-down, drag-out fight. But we simply said 'Cool,' or the 1977 equivalent of 'Cool.' We felt that all the great work done by Woody entitled him to do *Interiors*. We cherished the association." So Woody's new project received the green light.

What Arthur Krim and his associates honestly thought of the script for *Interiors* is unclear. But around 729 Seventh Avenue, office clowns began to call Woody "Ingmar Allen." From the viewpoint of Steven Bach, shortly to inherit Krim's yes-or-no script approval, it was not a thrilling script but he agreed with the studio's decision. "Woody needed to get it out of his system. I felt, in the long run, something good would come of it." In the business, people expressed themselves bluntly. "The *Interiors* script was really a piece of shit," said an executive, "but everybody said it was wonderful. Woody was their darling, and so he could do anything."

Among those who felt it was a mistake was Woody's editor. One Friday, a copy of the script arrived by messenger as Ralph Rosenblum was preparing to leave for the country. Over the weekend he settled down to read it but, after a few pages, turned to his wife and said, puzzled, "I think they sent me the wrong script."

Skimming the manuscript, Davida Rosenblum had a similar reaction. She remembered saying to her husband, "Oh, my God, how could this happen?"

A few days later, still upset, Rosenblum met Woody for lunch to discuss the new picture, which he thought was "indescribably dreadful." As usual, he was blunt-spoken. "Don't make it."

"Well, I want to," said Woody.

For Woody, the amassing of wealth meant nothing compared to his real ambition, which was to be taken seriously. Making a movie for grown-up people was the kind of work that he considered "the real meat and potatoes." His ambition, he told Gene Siskel in 1981, was to make "a series of great films. I would like to try and overreach myself and challenge the great filmmakers. In the next 10 or 15 years of my life, I'd like to make some really wonderful films. Not just commercially successful, but films that I could look at with, say, the films of Akira Kurosawa and Jean Renoir, and say 'Well, my films are perfectly acceptable in that class of filmmaker.'" The success of *Annie Hall* presented him with the opportunity to change his image.

■ ■ ■ ■ ■ ■ ■

Moving Pictures:
OG: You want to do mankind a service? Tell funnier jokes.
—*Stardust Memories,* 1980

■ ■ ■ ■ ■ ■ ■

"That's my mother," Louise cried. "And that's my father."

But plenty of people told him that *Interiors* was the story of their family, he replied.

"Oh yeah? They must have all been relatives of mine!" Louise, who had just returned from seeing Woody's new film, was shocked at the exploitation of her own family tragedies, including her mother's suicide. In any case, she continued, "I don't think you got my mother right."

Eve is a tormented woman in her early sixties who has poisoned the lives of her children and turned into an impossible burden for her husband. An interior designer by profession, she is, in Woody's words, "a New York woman with incredible good taste, style, breeding." Having cracked up more than once, she is also a graduate of several sanatoriums and a few bouts of electric shock treatment. A compulsive perfectionist, who worries about placing the right vase on the right table, she has created a kind of temperature-controlled biosphere where everything—and everybody—must be perfect. When her ex-husband falls in love with another woman, she loses her fragile grip on sanity and walks into the ocean. Her three daughters—played by Diane Keaton, Mary Beth Hurt, and Kristin Griffith—are left to react to their mother's suicide while figuring out how to pick up the pieces of their own wrecked lives.

Principal photography commenced on October 24, 1977. For the first time, Woody remained behind the camera. There was no role for him in this picture, he said (actually he had fragmented himself into all three sisters, plus the icy, judgmental mother). And besides, his presence in a serious drama might invite undesired laughter and dilute the tragic meaning of the story. In the past he always tried to cast friends, people with whom he felt comfortable, but this time he daringly hired two of the theater's most brilliant actresses, Geraldine Page and Maureen Stapleton, to play the mother and the second wife. "I was very intimidated by the cast," he said. Certainly there was nothing comfortable about directing Page and Stapleton, who made him feel as if he had been thrown into "a snake pit." In contrast to Page, the great grande dame of the theater and the ultimate professional, Stapleton was informal and unpretentious, in some ways even more frightening to Woody, who never encouraged intimacy on the set and never socialized with his actors off the set. People seldom stepped over the line.

On location in Southampton, Long Island, Stapleton spotted the unapproachable Woody in the hotel lobby one evening. Warned of his peculiarities, she was not the type to let that stand in her way. "I just grabbed his arm and dragged him into the bar. We sat down and had a few beers and we talked. Later some of the guys were stunned because nobody did that. I said, 'What's the big deal?'"

The headline in *Variety* read HIGH NOON AT UA.

In late January 1978, around the time that *Interiors* wrapped, Arthur Krim stunned Hollywood by abruptly storming out of United Artists and taking with him his top-tier management. Krim in 1967 had sold UA to Transamerica Corporation, a San Francisco–based multibillion-dollar conglomerate whose income derived from operations such as insurance, rental cars, and turbine engines. Disgruntled over Transamerica's management practices and its economy measures, most of all its attempt to run UA like a budget rental-car company, Krim tried without success to buy the company back. By the end of 1977, the situation had apparently become intolerable. Three weeks later, the Medici formed a new company, Orion Pictures, named after the great hunter constellation.

Krim and his associates were instantly hailed as the white knights of the industry, but this shake-up in the executive suite created a dilemma for Woody, who had three pictures remaining on his contract. He decided to stay but nobody in the industry, or at UA, believed that he would hang around once his contract ended. The exception was Andy Albeck, the new chief executive, who was determined to keep him. "Albeck," reported Steven Bach in his memoir, *Final Cut,* "had seen *Interiors* and privately assumed it would be a failure. That wasn't the point." Interestingly, Woody agreed with Albeck. "It's not going to make a dime," he predicted. "I've seen the picture. And I know."

■ ■ ■ ■ ■ ■ ■

Commentary:
"What man in his forties but Woody Allen could pass off a predilection for teen-agers as a quest for true values?"
—PAULINE KAEL, 1980

■ ■ ■ ■ ■ ■ ■

In *Annie Hall* there is a brief scene, cut during editing, in which Alvy Singer fantasizes about a certain high-school student to whom he was sexually attracted. Playing the role of the student was a pretty, dark-haired, seventeen-year-old from Stuyvesant High School, Class of '77, whom Woody met for the first time on the set. Their romance, unknown to the public, was common knowledge to patrons of Elaine's and readers of New York gossip columns. The *New York Post* reported that "Woody Allen's beautiful new and very young girlfriend is proving quite a distraction for the little genius. They were in Elaine's the other evening—someone said Woody was carrying her books—and only had eyes for each other."

Stacey Nelkin considered herself an "extremely sophisticated" girl who had "never dated boys my own age." Born in New York, raised partly in Europe, she was a bright child who was selected for Stuyvesant, one of Manhattan's so-called elite public high schools, by a grueling competitive examination. Ambitious to be an actress, she auditioned for Woody's new movie while still a junior and soon became involved with him off the set. She admitted to being "crazy about him." Friends of Woody's would characterize the besotted young girl as kind of a sex toy for him, expendable at any time. But she believed it was "a real relationship and a mature one that was perfectly normal." Indignant, she reported that "I wasn't underage when I dated Woody. I was 17 and he was 41 but the age difference didn't come up. It was a non-issue." The two-year affair was, she added, "a very moral relationship," not "just about the bedroom."

However, it seems to have been a one-sided involvement. If Stacey was in love with Woody and fantasized marriage, he made it clear that he was a committed bachelor. Because he never wished to acknowledge her publicly, she had to practically sneak into his apartment building and was never permitted to spend the night. He insisted she get dressed and go home. Once the sexual attraction died away, he broke off the relationship. In her place, he began to see Jean vanden Heuvel, a forty-four-year-old divorcée and mother of two, whose roots in the film business went deep since her father, Jules Stein, headed MCA, the entertainment conglomerate that owned Universal Studios. Crushed, the cast-off Stacey fled to the West Coast to forget, and even though Woody sent her plane fare to come back and visit, nothing came of the reunion. By that time, he was working on a new script about a middle-aged man dating a seventeen-year-old Dalton student, and there was another young girl in his life, one who was even younger than Stacey.

Somebody left a white bunny with the doorman. Worshiping fans liked to drop off unsolicited gifts, homemade layer cakes and knitted sweaters, never anything of value, but this was the first time a living creature had been plopped on his doorstep. He hated animals. The elevator operator conveying the news found him to be in high dudgeon. Surely the building didn't imagine he would bring the animal up to his apartment? And what did he know about taking care of a rabbit? In the end, his secretary, Norma Lee Clark, had to call the ASPCA. It was also Clark's job to screen Woody's mail, which had grown to mammoth proportions. Seldom did fans receive a reply. Usually Woody never saw the mail.

Months after *Annie Hall,* an enterprising thirteen-year-old from Coral Gables, Florida, who had a crush on Woody, somehow managed to obtain his home address and send him a fan letter. Amazingly, he responded; a few days later, she received a plain brown envelope without a return address. Dear Nancy Jo, the letter read,

> Hard to believe you're 13! When I was 13 I couldn't dress myself, and here you write about one of life's deepest philosophical problems, i.e., existential boredom.

He wanted to know all about her life. What kind of a city was Coral Gables? What did her parents do for a living? What time did she get up in the morning? Did she get depressed? If she decided to reply, he'd like to know what books she had read and the music she liked (not pop, he hoped). As for himself, he was reshooting scenes from his next movie *(Interiors),* "which have not come out so good."

Nancy Jo Sales was a precocious redhead, tall for her age, the child of divorced parents, who had something more in common with Woody than the color of their hair. For a thirteen-year-old, she was remarkably discontent. Apparently a misfit at school, she read nineteenth-century novels and watched Barbara Stanwyck movies. (In her high-school yearbook, she would be inelegantly labeled a "Geek/Freak.") At home, when her mother needed help in the kitchen, she disappeared. Obsessed with Woody, she wrote him several times a day while hiding behind the stacks in her school library. After school she would race home to get mentoring letters that contained reading lists (Proust and Kierkegaard) and instructions on shopping (Mahler's Fourth Symphony, the Bernstein recording, of course). The student-teacher exchange of letters was passed off to Nancy's mother as correspondence with a girl she met at camp.

In New York, on a shopping trip with her stepmother and one of her stepmother's friends, Nancy Jo decided to send a note to Woody, who immediately telephoned the hotel and invited them to visit. When they arrived at his door, he seemed unsure which one of the three women was Nancy Jo (the stepmother and her friend were barely thirty). In the living room, the older women dominated the conversation with talk of real estate deals and celebrity-watching at Elaine's. As she listened in mortification, Nancy Jo fixed her eyes upon the tray of individually wrapped candies on the coffee table.

The New York visit marked the end of Nancy Jo's secret life with a movie star. The letters from Woody abruptly ceased. She was never sure why, or what she had done wrong. "It took me a long time, in my teenage way, to get over him," she wrote in 1993. When Woody, the following year, described his nymphet pen pal to an interviewer from the *New York Times Magazine,* he called her "a nice, intelligent girl" whose letters were precocious in the extreme. He distinctly remembered telling her that "if you're really the age you say you are, it's phenomenal. If you're not, don't write to me again and waste my time. Finally I met her whole family." She was eleven, he thought, no more than a child.

In January 1978, the prestigious New York Film Critics voted the best picture and screenplay awards to *Annie Hall.* At the awards dinner, the presenter of the writing honor was to be the famous humorist S. J. Perelman, one of Woody's longtime idols. Having seen the picture three times, Perelman composed some tart remarks chosen especially for Woody's ears. He was not exactly happy, therefore, to arrive at Sardi's and learn that Woody had decided not to accept his award in person. Unlike the Oscars, indisputably a televised circus, the New York critics ceremony was a high-class, low-key private dinner. Perelman couldn't imagine why anyone would boycott it.

The previous year, Walter Bernstein had hosted a dinner party so that Woody could meet Perelman, who happened to be a friend of Bernstein's. Of course, Perelman was well aware that Woody's *New Yorker* pieces mimicked his own literary style. Known to be crabby about imitators, the older writer ignored Woody's prose and chose to regard him as a splendid filmmaker. The party turned out to be a disappointment, however, "not completely a disaster," Bernstein recollected, but Woody was withdrawn "and the two men didn't connect in some essential way." At dinner, Bernstein began carving a roast that was resting on a silver platter when the knife began scraping against the bottom of the dish. At the sound, Woody "went berserk, as if hearing nails scratching on a blackboard I guess, and he leaned over and grabbed my arm to make me stop."

The Sunday after the New York Film Critics awards, Woody and Perelman bumped into each other at Elaine's. Perelman, who had just turned seventy-four, was being treated to a birthday dinner by a friend, Delta Willis. "It was the first time that Mr. Perelman had ever been to this so-called literary establishment," Willis recalled. "When we came in, Elaine Kaufman didn't recognize him and so we were seated around the corner in what is known there as Siberia." A short while later, spotting Woody eating with Marshall Brickman, she encouraged Perelman to send over his calling card. "My dear Mr. Allen," he scrawled. "Won't you please join us for a Dr. Brown's Cel-Ray Tonic?" When a waiter delivered the unsigned card, Woody crumpled it up.

Forty-five minutes later, he rushed back to their table. By then, Perelman and Willis had finished dinner and were drinking espresso. "I thought it was a joke," Woody said sheepishly. Realizing that his absence at the critics dinner might have offended Perelman, he attempted an apology. "There were too many critics there," he deadpanned. Perelman was not amused.

Accolades and awards for *Annie Hall* kept coming: the New York and Los Angeles critics, the National Society of Film Critics, the Directors Guild of America, the British Academy, and the Golden Globes. It also received five Oscar nominations—including best picture, actress, actor, director, and writing. The likelihood of *Annie Hall* winning best picture was considered remote because the competition was exceptionally strong: *The Turning Point, Star Wars, Julia,* and *The Goodbye Girl.* Not only had no comedy won best picture since 1960 *(The Apartment),* but United Artists had won two years running for *One Flew Over the Cuckoo's Nest* in 1975 and *Rocky* in 1976, and never before had a studio taken top honors three years in a row. Nevertheless, United Artists re-released *Annie Hall* on four hundred screens and began putting together a campaign to publicize the picture's Oscar nominations, the standard ballyhoo in the film industry.

Resisting vigorously, Woody opposed any mention of the nominations in ads, particularly in New York. As the tug-of-war continued, he reluctantly agreed that UA might mention Oscar outside New York. Red-faced UA publicists, arms twisted out of their sockets, attempted to explain this bizarre procedure as a deliberate creative decision, a refreshing change from the traditional trumped-up Oscar nominations. But Woody had his own way of making his point. Should any local theater take it upon itself to mention the Oscars in its *Annie Hall* ads, he warned, he would do his best to have the picture yanked from its screen.

The fiftieth annual Academy Awards were scheduled for Monday, April 4. The previous week, Woody announced he would not be attending the ceremony. "The whole concept of the awards is silly," he told the *Los Angeles Herald-Examiner.* Holding up to ridicule Hollywood's biggest night as "a popularity contest," he inveighed against the Academy for being a crass trade association and the Oscars as ego candy "bought and negotiated for." Should he win one of their stupid awards, he didn't want it. That night he planned to be in New York playing jazz because he couldn't let his band down. In an interview with NBC film critic Gene Shalit, he merrily offended the 3,375 members of the Motion Picture Academy of Arts and Sciences, along with everyone else in the movie-factory town. "If it were a special occasion or something, I might do it," he said. "But I'm not interested in an inanimate statuette of a little bald man. I like something with long, blond curls." While the Oscars may be a popularity contest, that had nothing to do with his true reasons for not attending the Academy Awards presentation. Perhaps fearing rejection, he could not bring himself to be present when the fate of his picture was announced to his peers in the industry, as well as millions of television viewers worldwide.

On Monday evening, in Los Angeles, Diane Keaton arrived at the Dorothy Chandler Pavilion at 6:30, rigged out in what *Annie Hall* might have worn to the Oscars, a Victorian gown, a long skirt with layered tunic, a high-necked blouse with a rose pinned to the bodice, and boots. Accompanied by her sister, she flapped along the red carpet and made her way to her seat. In New York, meanwhile, Woody pulled up to Michael's Pub wearing his standard winter uniform, a Ralph Lauren plaid shirt with rolled-up sleeves, rumpled corduroy slacks, and sneakers, with his scraggly red hair falling in clumps over his ears. Immediately he began to fume because the place was overflowing with photographers and reporters. Throughout the evening, he refused to speak with anyone. At 12:15, he packed his clarinet, grabbed his combat jacket, and ran out a side door to his waiting Rolls-Royce. Usually when he got home on Mondays, he liked to unwind by watching television. That night he did not turn on the set because the Oscars were still being broadcast. Instead he climbed into bed. "I turned my phone off and went to sleep."

CHAPTER EIGHT

Vanity Fair

The next morning Woody went down to the kitchen, where he poured orange juice and heated up a croissant. Once the coffee was brewing, he opened the front door to take in the *New York Times*. As he glanced at the front page, he noticed a small news item in the lower right-hand corner (4 AWARDS TO ALLEN FILM) and started to laugh. "You've got to be kidding," he thought. Hastily opening the paper, the first thing he saw was Diane's photograph, and he couldn't help thinking it was "all very funny." In a major upset, *Annie Hall* had done the inconceivable and walked off with Oscars for best picture, actress, director, and original screenplay. Only in the acting category was he beaten, by Richard Dreyfuss for *The Goodbye Girl*.

Checking his answering service, he found "a million messages from people who'd been calling all night," especially from the media, who hounded him for reaction statements. To admit that he was happy went against his nature, and so he said that he felt pleased "for Diane and for everyone involved," but the Oscars meant nothing to him personally.

Woody's reaction puzzled even those who knew him intimately.

"No joy?" asked Charles Joffe, incredulous.

"I don't have time for that," Woody muttered. It was sad, thought Joffe, who, at the Oscars ceremony, scampered up to the podium with a proud Jack Rollins to accept the best picture award from Jack Nicholson. Joffe, bouncing up and down in excitement, delivered a speech perfectly suited to the occasion. "United Artists had said to Woody, 'Woody, do your thing.' They have allowed Woody to mature into a fine filmmaker." Considering how much Woody owed Arthur Krim and the Medici, it was a fitting tribute but one that many people in the film industry felt he should have made himself.

He did not bother to pick up his Oscar statuettes. Several months later, he confessed to having "no idea" of their whereabouts. Finally the Academy shipped the awards to the Rollins and Joffe office. Norma Lee Clark called her employer.

"What do you want to do with them?"

"Well," he said sarcastically, "I'm certainly not going to put Oscars in my house!" His parents, nevertheless, made room in their china cabinet.

In its first year of release, *Annie Hall* grossed $25 million (domestic), a figure that climbed to an estimated $100 million (worldwide) over the next decade. As Woody is fond of pointing out, however, the picture earned less than any other Academy Award–winning best picture.

■ ■ ■ ■ ■ ■ ■

Eyewitness:
"He hit his high point with *Annie Hall*. That scene in the LA parking lot is truly funny. And also the picture [*Everything You Always Wanted to Know About Sex (But Were Afraid to Ask)*] where the psychiatrist's in bed with a sheep, and not just any sheep but a sheep who's wearing a garter belt! But the serious films don't work because Woody doesn't know a lot about interpersonal relationships and so he doesn't have a lot to say—he's not philosophically profound."

—ELLIOTT MILLS

■ ■ ■ ■ ■ ■ ■

For years Woody had been currying favor with the major film critics—people such as Penelope Gilliatt, Judith Crist, even the acerbic Pauline Kael—women whom he saw socially for lunch and dinner, and for whom he arranged special previews of his pictures and handwrote funny little complimentary notes on yellow-lined legal paper. But it was Vincent Canby, the powerful *Times* critic, whose good opinion he most craved and who championed him over the years with the same kind of rah-rah cheerleading Pauline Kael had given to Warren Beatty and Robert Altman. Canby's notices were to mystify a younger generation of film critics. "Everybody is entitled to their opinion but Canby was a fanatic about Woody," said Neil Rosen, a New York television movie critic. "New Yorkers would line up around the block solely based on his accolades. Sometimes it was warranted because the guy is a comedic genius but not in every movie. Woody Allen could make a movie called *The Barking Dog* and Vincent Canby would compliment him on the brilliance of the barking. He could film a piece of human excrement and Canby would write about the brilliance of it all and people would pay money to watch it."

A few days after seeing *Annie Hall*, Canby wrote a column in which he called Woody "America's Ingmar Bergman," a notion that generated instant sneers and jeers but would be forgotten by neither reviewers nor filmgoers. In the estimation of the pugnacious John Simon, Canby's remark "helped ruin Allen" because he took it as gospel. "John has no sense of humor whatsoever," said Canby, who, waving a dismissive hand, stands by his words. "Once you write words like 'comic genius' or 'American Bergman,' you immediately think oh my god, what have I done. But what I meant was that his place in American cinema is like Bergman's in Sweden. As a personal filmmaker he towers over everybody else. Nobody has ever come close to him."*

When *Interiors* was released in the summer of 1978, after a year of advance hype, Canby devoted four columns in the daily and Sunday *Times* to a discussion of the film. Two decades later, he admits that "I didn't like the picture at the time. It was not his natural form. However, I warmed to it later because making *Interiors* took great courage."

No other critic gave Woody credit for courage, or for anything else for that matter. It was almost universally panned. Even though Penelope Gilliatt called the film "a giant step forward" in American cinema, her predictable enthusiasm was drowned out by dissident colleagues merrily dismantling Woody's efforts. *Interiors* reminded Pauline Kael of "a handbook of art-film mannerisms," so chilling that it might have been directed by the suicidal Eve herself "from the grave." Similar Grand Guignol images were conjured up by Stanley Kauffmann, who called it a "tour of the Ingmar Bergman Room at Madame Tussaud's" wax museum. It took John Simon two columns to adequately document the magnitude of the "disaster" perpetrated on a gullible public by a man with "a Bergman complex." The "hackneyed" dialogue, the "derivative" camera work, and the sorry acting of Diane Keaton ("a vacuum cleaner in heat") made him "roll over with helpless laughter." Such snotty cracks would eventually make Simon persona non grata at Woody Allen screenings. Looking back, Simon said recently that he was "tough on everyone, but I like to think I'm fair. I was no harder on Woody Allen than I was on others. He was desperate to have it both ways, the little Jewish schmuck, who was the epitome of a loser and yet comes out on top. That was too much

---

* In 1978, Woody had an opportunity to meet Ingmar Bergman when the Swede, together with his wife and longtime companion, Liv Ullman, was visiting New York. Ullman's suggestion that they meet for dinner reportedly made Woody anxious. Aside from his limited social accomplishments, he disliked one-on-one meetings with celebrities because it always turned out to be, he said, a meaningless exchange of compliments. When he hesitated, Ullman assured him that Bergman appreciated his work and had requested the meeting.

To Woody, Bergman was the greatest filmmaker who ever lived. Still, for all his eminence, the sixty-year-old director's career seemed to be in decline. In 1976, he had angrily left Sweden for several years after being charged with income tax fraud, charges that were eventually dropped.

The evening turned out to be perfectly pleasant. At Bergman's hotel room, dinner was ordered from room service, and the two men spent the entire time talking shop, mostly commiserating about the frustrations they faced as personal filmmakers whose pictures never managed to generate big lines at the box office.

cake." The blisteringly negative press for *Interiors* put Woody in a bad mood. The critics, he grumped, were not "charitable."

If reviewers were mean to him, so were moviegoing audiences, because the picture that cost United Artists $10 million would earn back only $4.6 million in rentals. What's more, some of Woody's personal friends and biggest admirers could only shake their heads. To Roger Angell, *Interiors* was "that sad, miserable movie, the Jewish idea of how Protestants view death."

The question is, What happened? *Interiors,* a study in muted beige and earth tones, its silent tableaux photographed by Gordon Willis against blank walls or the rolling ocean, could not have looked more stylishly handsome. It was finely performed for the most part, too, winning Maureen Stapleton an Oscar nomination. Nevertheless, it was stupefyingly dull, "a bore," said UA's Steven Bach. "I just hated it." A possible explanation may be that, unlike *Annie Hall,* where the writing came out of Woody's own life and the people he knew, his *Interiors* characters appeared to be strangers to him. Except for Stapleton's character, they were people that other writers—Ingmar Bergman or Eugene O'Neill—knew best. Detouring in from distant works of art, confused and lost, they seem to be searching for their authors.

During the cutting of *Interiors,* Woody and Ralph Rosenblum ate lunch at a Hunan restaurant on Broadway, not far from Rosenblum's brownstone on Eighty-fourth Street. As they approached the restaurant one day, a teenage girl spotted Woody from across the street and dashed gleefully toward them. Charging through the plate-glass doors, she arrived breathless at the table to ask for an autograph just as they were sitting down. Woody, studying the menu, didn't look up.

No, he murmured.

Crushed, she slunk out.

"Why don't you give her the autograph?" asked Rosenblum, sympathetic.

Woody's anxiety about the new film exhibited itself in an unusually high level of tension between them. "By the time we finished *Interiors,*" Rosenblum wrote, "we both sensed that our decade-long collaboration was nearing an end." Not only did he have little enthusiasm for the film, but after *Annie Hall,* there seems to have been a falling out. Some in the business held Woody responsible for the fact that Rosenblum was passed over for an Oscar nomination, and perhaps Rosenblum himself believed this to be true. In any case, around this time he began to write a book (with Robert Karen) about film editing, *When the Shooting Stops . . . the Cutting Begins,* including much of his personal history, and asked Woody to write the preface. But when Woody saw the galleys, he angrily reneged. Not only did Rosenblum take a great deal of credit for much of Woody's best work but he also described outtakes from *Annie Hall* in such detail that Woody felt they would be unusable in another film. And besides, he always assumed that relations between a director and editor would be confidential, and here was Rosenblum broadcasting his personal affairs, making critical remarks about his foibles. In ten years, Rosenblum wrote damningly, "we've never shared a heartfelt concern, an uninhibited laugh, an open display of despair or anger."

After Rosenblum's departure, Woody set up his own editing room in a suite of offices in the Beekman Hotel on Park Avenue. A knowledgeable editor himself by this time, he knew what he wanted, which was to be the boss. He hired Susan Morse, one of Rosenblum's assistants, who was in her mid-twenties. Unlike Rosenblum, Sandy Morse was a comfortable person, easy to get along with.

∎∎∎∎∎∎

Moving Pictures:
MARY: What do you do, Tracy?
TRACY: I go to high school.
　　　　　　　—*Manhattan*, 1979

∎∎∎∎∎∎

In Woody's next film, *Manhattan,* the hero is a forty-two-year-old television comedy writer working on his first novel (by dictating his prose into a tape recorder) and a divorced daddy sowing his postmarital wild oats with a new girlfriend. Tracy, seventeen and a student at an East Side private school, sexually liberated, is deeply infatuated with her middle-aged lover. Isaac Davis's best friends are a happily married couple: Yale, a college professor, and his wife, Emily, who don't find anything peculiar about Isaac's affair with a teenager who still does homework. Isaac, however, is shocked to learn that Yale is having an affair with Mary Wilke, a member of the local intelligentsia who is reviewing Tolstoy's letters for a literary magazine and tossing off a novelization. Then things happen: Yale breaks off with Mary for the sake of his marriage; Isaac discards Tracy to take up with the snobbish Mary; then the partners change again when Yale leaves Emily for Mary. Alone again, Isaac mourns his lost chance and tries to win Tracy back, in vain.

The starting point for this unconventional fable of a May-December romance, another collaboration with Marshall Brickman, is clearly Woody's affair with Stacey Nelkin. But plenty of pageantry got added along the way: Gershwin's "Rhapsody in Blue," bursts of fireworks flaring over the towers of Manhattan, the notion that Woody regretted the loss of his nymphet. As Stacey herself would remark, "the thing that always seemed strange to me is that Mariel Hemingway played it much younger. She acted in such an innocent and naive way. That just wasn't me." Evidently Nelkin did not know about the existence of Nancy Jo Sales. Woody seems to have seamlessly woven together the two young women to create the character of Tracy, who has had affairs with three boys before meeting Isaac.

By casting the gloriously six-feet-tall, sixteen-year-old granddaughter of Ernest Hemingway as the mistress, Woody made viewers forget that Isaac was barely on the right side of statutory rape. Of course, Mariel, in real life much more than a coltish child, had made her film debut at fourteen, and by this time she and her older sister, Margaux, a successful model who lived life in the fast lane, happened to be the toasts of swinging New York. After principal photography and retakes were completed, Mariel invited Woody to come out west and visit her family in Ketchum, Idaho. As luck would have it, the next day it snowed and Mariel's father proposed they take Woody for a hike to show him the natural beauty of the land.

"So I'm off like a goat to the top of the mountain," Mariel Hemingway recalled, "and this poor little man is schlepping through the snow. It's not like he was out of shape, but this was high altitude." Every so often, she yelled back, "Are you OK?"

All Woody could answer was, "Ayyyy." First thing next morning, he telephoned for a private jet to rescue him.

Back home in the safe countryside north of Bloomingdale's, he and Sandy Morse were finishing up the editing of "Woody Allen No. 3," and then catastrophe struck again, when he woke one morning stricken with complete loss of hearing in one ear. Having just spent several days on the sound track, he could not help remembering that George Gershwin's dizziness and headaches had led to an expected—and rapid—death due to a suspected brain tumor at the age of thirty-eight. (Gershwin, like Woody, was a notorious hypochondriac.) Within hours, Woody was scheduling tests and preparing for the worst. That weekend, lying motionless in his bed, asking himself "if this is it," he wondered if the thing had spread to his spine and should he attempt to sleep with every woman he knew. The prospect of his life going down the tubes was "terrifying to me, absolutely terrifying."

Although the tests found no sign of illness, he would never forget the worst experience of his life, which he converted into comedy in *Hannah and Her Sisters* ("I'm dying! I'm dying! I know it!"). Soon his attention turned to matters even more strenuously scary: the screening of twenty-one Bob Hope films from start to finish. That spring, the Film Society of Lincoln Center was planning to honor Hope's achievements, and because Woody repeatedly claimed that Hope had been his major influence, the Society asked him to compile and narrate a sixty-minute film tribute to the comedian, an anthology that he titled "My Favorite Comedian." Avery Fisher Hall on the night of the black-tie gala was sold out, the 2,700 ticket holders including a swarm of celebrities—people such as Diane Keaton, Kurt Vonnegut, and Andy Warhol, everybody but Woody himself, who was conveniently in Paris. Dick Cavett, conarrator of the film and emcee of the gala, explained that the thought of appearing at this sort of gathering made Woody "break out in a rash." One of the attendees, Andrew Sarris, recalled that "lots of people who bought tickets were under the misapprehension Woody would appear." Having spent $250 for a seat, some were annoyed but none more than the guest of honor.

The previous day, at the Waldorf Towers, journalist Stephen Silverman had asked Bob Hope what he thought about Woody watching his old pictures.

"Hey," Hope drawled with a curl of the lip, "how 'bout that guy?" and squinted, as though hard of hearing, when asked for his opinion of Woody's films. Finally, he said, "I saw that"—he fumbled for the title—"*Annie Hall.*" Then he lost interest and quickly changed the subject to the Johnny Carson roast he was emceeing that evening. Twenty years later, Hope sounded more charitable about Woody's pilfering of his comedy style. "Hey, it's an honor to be copied," the ninety-three-year-old comedian said. His favorite Woody Allen picture was, he said, *Take the Money and Run.* "The idea of a cello player with a high school marching band is comic genius. Woody is more than a 'comic.' He's a comedy guru." If Woody offered him a substantial role (but not a cameo), "I would probably say yes. Good sex-symbol roles are hard to come by."

At the Lincoln Center tribute, however, strolling on stage to deliver a twenty-minute monologue, Hope stung like a hornet. Woody Allen, he said contemptuously, was a wonderful kid who wrote, acted, and directed, which would make him "a *near* genius. Not a whole genius but a near genius." Woody's best friend, Jean Doumanian, sitting in the audience, took umbrage at that remark. As the crowd filed out afterward for a cheese-and-dessert reception, she turned indignantly to Stephen Silverman. "Have you ever heard anything so insulting in your life?" she sniffed.

On Saturday evening, April 14, 1979, United Artists was screening the new picture, now titled *Manhattan,* for Woody's friends in the tiny blue screening room on the lobby floor of the MGM Building, on Sixth Avenue. Steven Bach, one of the few people to have seen the script, had flown in from the West Coast, on his way to London. The spring day was mild, and the sky over midtown that afternoon a perfect blue. Quietly Bach slid into his seat. He later said that if there had been two hours in his three years at United Artists that remain in his memory as "pure, unambiguous pleasure, they are those two." After the lights came up, he nodded wordlessly to Jack Rollins and Charlie Joffe, then strolled down the nearly deserted avenue, humming Gershwin and grinning. In a rush, "all the reasons I had always wanted to live in New York" came back, "all the reasons I had wanted to be in the movie business."

Like Bach, audiences everywhere were bewitched because possibly no other film has conjured up more perfectly the essence of the big city. Even the critics, most of them at least, found the picture irresistible. Andrew Sarris in the *Village Voice* raved that *Manhattan* was "the only truly great American movie of the 1970s." Asked recently if he still ranked it as the outstanding film of the seventies, Sarris thought it was "not the only one. There are others I like from that period. But my test of a movie is whether or not I can look at it again and again. Can you stand to see *The Bridge on the River Kwai* another ten times? Or *Lawrence of Arabia*?" But perhaps the ultimate compliment was offered by Maureen Stapleton, who thought *Manhattan* was so beautiful, so romantic that "it almost makes you forget all the dog poop on the streets." It would be his biggest commercial success, earning a healthy $45.7 million ($137 million in today's dollars).

Manhattan, Woody's third script with Marshall Brickman, would turn out to be their last collaboration for more than a dozen years. Like Ralph Rosenblum, Brickman had made key contributions to Woody's success as a filmmaker. Just as Rosenblum tightened rambling footage and turned potential flops into hits, it was Brickman who helped Woody find strong structures to support his inspired stories. In terms of craftsmanship, Woody's most outstanding scripts would be *Sleeper, Annie Hall,* and *Manhattan,* the films he wrote with Brickman. While Woody never had a shortage of creative ideas, he was apt to go off the track whenever he had to construct a story by himself.

Always self-effacing, Brickman never made a peep about his second-class status in the collaboration. Rosenblum, however, was not the sort to take a backseat and took credit for having more or less single-handedly saved *Annie Hall* and *Take the Money and Run,* which was probably one reason for Woody's annoyance over Rosenblum's book. The truth, of course, is that nothing Rosenblum did in the editing room mattered had not Woody shot brilliant material in the first place. Similarly, Brickman's talent for organization was irrelevant without Woody's original creativity.

∎∎∎∎∎∎∎

Tales of New York Life:
EARL WILSON: What kind of girls do you like?
WOODY: Uh . . . yeah . . . well . . . practically all kinds.
WILSON: Any kind, just so they're breathing?
WOODY: No, it isn't even necessary in my case. I've had some that
   didn't breathe and it didn't bother me.
                                    —WOODY ALLEN interview, 1972

∎∎∎∎∎∎∎

The tall, moony girl with the tattersall vest and the long braid down the middle of her back looked like an *Annie Hall* paper doll. Once he had scrawled his signature, she bent over him and planted a tender kiss on his cheek, then handed him a white rose. The place was full of fabulous young creatures lined up quietly near the bandstand, bobbing up and down to "Shine On, Harvest Moon," waiting with their paper and pens. They stood primly, like young ladies in a debutante receiving line. The next one, overcome by his presence, left her ballpoint behind. Down the line he could see a pre-Raphaelite beauty in a gauzy white-lace dress sprigged with violets, but reaching him she turned out to be a chatterbox.

The man who once had trouble getting a date never had to go home alone. If he wanted sex, there was Michael's Pub, his personal Deer Park, a hunting preserve teeming with women. Since there was no dressing room, he sat at a ringside table between shows, accessible to predatory groupies. (Woody never denied the propositions but claimed he didn't respond.) If picking up women failed to satisfy him, neither did his brief relationships with women such as Teri Shields, a tall, blond, heavy-drinking divorcée, who had made a profession out of managing the modeling career of her nubile eleven-year-old daughter, Brooke, who had posed nude for *Playboy* before Woody cast her as an extra in *Annie Hall.* He was also involved with Jessica Harper, the actress who appeared in *Love and Death.*

These should have been the best years of his life. Instead, he felt that his entire existence had been warped by success. He never got used to the gawkers, freaks, and mutants who looked as if they had escaped from a Diane Arbus photograph, ghouls who ran up to him, shouted his name from buses, collared him in restaurants, stalked him home, even touched him, which made him recoil. Sometimes he felt like "a prisoner in my own home, when I feel like, oh, I don't want to go down and get the papers because some people will say hello to me. So I stay in." When he did go out, especially if it meant walking alone, he felt exposed. Never mind that he had hungered to see his name in lights. Now there was "no place to hide."

Fame, once his motive for living, then "an inconvenience, a pain in the ass," had now turned into a raging beast. Ultimately, he developed the knack of subtracting himself from the picture. At Michael's Pub he zoned out and fiddled with his mouthpiece, never making eye contact with the audience. Tucking his chin into his armpit, he gazed down or up or to one side, looking less like a jazz musician than a schoolkid hoping not to be called on. To disguise himself on the street, he began wearing a tan fishing hat, which he kept scrunched over his ears like a Saxon helmet, as if dressed for battle. With his face obscured he felt less vulnerable. In time, however, the hat became a trademark around town, and then he hid inside a hooded parka. "He was full of contradictions," said Eric Pleskow. "He didn't want to be recognized but he had a white Rolls. I could never figure it out."

Most of his fans were harmless, but some of them truly scared him. One night, he was chatting with Vivian Gornick at Michael's Pub, when a man planted himself next to their table. "Love you," he told Woody, who didn't even look up.

"No, I mean it," the man said. "I just love you. You're my favorite, you're the greatest." He didn't budge.

"I appreciate it," Woody said at last, "but you can see we want to talk."

In the blink of an eye, for no reason, the scene shifted and turned ugly. "I don't give a fuck what you want," the man said. As Gornick recalled, "it happened in a second and it was terrifying." She saw a piece of the picture; Woody saw it whole. Since the mid-1960s, when he first tasted fame, he always had "a fear of being shot by a girl or a psychotic fan who imagines some connection between us." Ten years later, after his face appeared on the covers of *Time* and *Newsweek,* the likelihood of a bullet in his head seemed more real than ever. It was little wonder he developed stomach problems.

The cross was gone. It was a Christian seaside resort, and one Friday afternoon in early November 1979, disgruntled townspeople were looking up at the Ocean Grove Great Auditorium, where yesterday a crucifix had dangled. In its place, a sign blinked HOTEL STARDUST. Ocean Grove is a tiny community of gingerbread houses next door to Asbury Park, New Jersey, where just about everybody is a practicing Methodist, a town so religious that it's illegal on Sundays to drive a car, ride a bicycle, or fly a kite. The sight of Woody's production crew and a platoon of security guards crawling all over their house of worship elicited angry grumbling. It was terrible how the campmeeting association had sold out to Woody Allen just to get $25,000 and a new cross.

Throughout the seventies, Woody socialized regularly with Judith Crist, attending her postholiday "Survival Party" every January, entertaining Crist and her family at his apartment or at Sardi's. In addition to reviewing for *TV Guide* and the *Saturday Review,* the fifty-seven-year-old critic hosted monthly film weekends at the Tarrytown Conference Center thirty-five miles north of the city. At an orgy of food and film in a rustic setting, some two hundred movie buffs would gather Friday evening in time for cocktails and dinner, then spend the next two days watching movies (many of them as yet unreleased), conducting postmortems, and rubbing elbows with creative artists invited to analyze their work. In its eighth season, by now practically an institution, the Judith Crist Film Weekends drew the same kind of knowledgeable people, Crist explained, "who went to art houses on a Saturday night." Woody had appeared several times as the honored guest and made sure to give Crist advance copies of his films to screen for her confreres.

In early 1979, he telephoned Crist at her country home in Woodstock. He was thinking about setting his new picture against the background of a "film weekend" and hoped she would have no objection. Crist was thrilled. Naturally, he went on, the story itself would be purely fictional; in fact, he was planning to change the sex of the host. Crist immediately objected. And when she insisted her part be played by a woman, Woody, shrewdly, suggested she herself undertake the role. Crist promised to think about it. As he might have predicted, she declined because she was not an actress and "couldn't spend six months in New Jersey." (In the end, she agreed to do a cameo for $250.)

Sandy Bates, like his creator, is a former stand-up comic turned superstar comedy film auteur, who now wants to concentrate on serious drama. "It's about malaise," Woody explained. The story takes place in the mind of a spiritually bankrupted individual poised "on the verge of a nervous breakdown." A first cousin of Alvy Singer's, "he's accomplished these things yet they still don't mean anything to him." To make sure he was not mistaken for Sandy, Woody took special precautions to minimize comparisons. In case anyone imagined he might actually be Sandy Bates, he argued loudly that everything in the picture was invented: He never had a girlfriend who had been institutionalized, never dated a French woman with children, fought with studio executives, or employed a chauffeur arrested for mail fraud. Maybe not. But believing that Woody was not Sandy was a lot to ask of audiences who were not, after all, idiots. They took the picture at face value as the most openly autobiographical movie he had ever done.

There was nothing particularly startling about the exterior parallels between Sandy's career and Woody's. What was shockingly revelatory, however, were the interiors. Sandy, a suppurating pustule of hatred, despises himself and his success and eviscerates just about everybody he knows, not only his women and the condescending Hollywood moguls, but even his sister's pitiful fat friend who has been raped. At the Stardust Hotel for a weekend retrospective of his work, he is besieged by freaks: the pretentious film critic and her tiresome students, a camp follower who bribes her way into his bed after her husband has driven her from Bridgeport, the man who lurches up to tell him "I'm your biggest fan," before shooting him dead (or so Sandy hallucinates). At the end, Sandy is alive and whining, still a gloriously rich crybaby.

■ ■ ■ ■ ■ ■ ■

Hollywood Vignettes:
"Directors can get just about any girl they set their sights on. And if they don't have time to look for themselves, they have pimps

scouting for them. The presence of pimps in a social setting can be very unpleasant."

—Pauline Kael, 1998

∎∎∎∎∎∎∎

One Wednesday night in November of 1979, Woody was at Elaine's, hunkered down at his table along the wall. As the hour neared midnight, the noise was bouncing off the ceiling, and a fetid cloud of smoky air was hanging over the nobodies stacked up three-deep at the bar. Just as Michael's Pub served Woody in more than one capacity, Elaine's likewise was both restaurant and playground, an uptown annex of the Deer Park. The place was always loaded with attractive women, and Elaine Kaufman would introduce Woody to anyone he fancied. So would Robert Zarem, a regular at Elaine's and a well-known publicity agent for show-business celebrities whom *Newsweek* christened "Superflack." When Jean Doumanian first arrived in New York from Chicago, she worked for Bobby Zarem. The volatile pitchman, now middle-aged and rolypoly, fueled by an inexhaustible tank of hot air, had become an important cog in New York's publicity machine by his talent for feeding material to gossip columnists. The son of a Savannah shoe distributor, he suffered panic attacks and emotional outbursts, and visited his therapist on Tuesday and Thursday afternoons. Like Kaufman, Zarem easily fell into the role of serving Woody.

This particular night, the publicist made a point of bringing over a blond actress, Mia Farrow, who had just walked in with Michael Caine and his wife, Shakira. The Caines had come from the Barrymore Theatre, where they had seen Mia and Anthony Perkins in a new play, Bernard Slade's *Romantic Comedy,* and were about to join Mick Jagger for dinner. Mia, having done matinee and evening performances, said she was exhausted and should have gone straight home to bed because she knew it would take forever to get served. She did not appear tired. Pale blue veins showed through skin so milkily translucent that it made her look like an anorexic Botticelli. She had a whispery baby-doll voice, the same silken little-girl manner of Jackie Kennedy. When she was twenty-two, she had been on the cover of *Life,* which depicted her as "a small forsaken animal that snuggles its way into your lap," the kind of creature that men wanted to cuddle "not in an embrace, but fatherlike, because she seems so hopelessly fragile." In truth, Mia was not the sort to snuggle, nor was she "hopelessly fragile," being more accurately a Lolita of vaulting ambition, who pulled off the considerable coup of marrying Frank Sinatra. Yet, at thirty-four, she still retained some of her superficial childlike qualities.

Woody knew Mia's sister Tisa, a minor actress whom he had cast in *Manhattan* as Polly, the girl who had the wrong kind of orgasm. (To whom Isaac replied that even his worst orgasms were smack on the money.) Suddenly remembering that after *Manhattan* Mia had written him a fan letter, he told her how the compliments had made his day.

Afterward, whenever Woody or Mia talked about how they met, they invariably mentioned Michael Caine. Never was there a reference to Bobby Zarem, who in the world of the mega-famous was a kind of shoeshine boy, providing an essential but anonymous service. In fact, nothing could have been more perfect than a superflack playing Cupid to a superstar director and the godchild of the poisonous Louella Parsons.

Several months earlier, a photograph of Woody had appeared on the cover of the *New York Times Magazine* one Sunday morning. Posing on his roof deck, he was clutching a large black umbrella and gazing into the middle distance with the lugubrious expression of a funeral home director. The flattering article, "The Maturing of Woody Allen," predicted that Woody would become "one of America's major serious film makers." Better yet, it offered him a perfect platform to separate himself from his West Coast contemporaries, the Coppolas and Scorseses with their sex-drugs-and-violence pictures, and to position himself as the American Ingmar Bergman for the eighties. Throughout the interview, in his airy living room filled with plants, against a backdrop of movie-star opulence, Woody sat, barely moving on the edge of his favorite chair. The only time he stood up was to change a Mozart recording to a Beethoven. Of particular interest to him now, he insisted, were feelings, not laughs. In *Manhattan,* for example, he cut a number of funny scenes because they were "superfluous. They stopped the flow. And sometimes they were too funny." It was an audacious idea, a comedian tossing out material because it was too funny.

A half mile away, in her apartment on the other side of the park, Mia Farrow tore out the article and slipped it into her dictionary. It was not that she sought out powerful men, but they were the only people who thrilled her.

■ ■ ■ ■ ■ ■ ■

Memorabilia:
Woody Allen
requests the pleasure of your company
for New Year's Eve
on December 31st, at ten o'clock
4 East 75th Street
New York
R.S.V.P.

■ ■ ■ ■ ■ ■ ■

Helen Gurley and David Brown, after a preparty dinner at Elaine's, whisked over to the Harkness mansion, home of the Harkness Ballet Foundation, where Woody was hosting a party to ring out the seventies and welcome the eighties. The event was, Helen Gurley Brown said, "a hard ticket. If you were invited you went." Among those who were invited and went were Gloria Vanderbilt and her two boys, and Robert De Niro, looking shockingly fat for a new boxing movie. And Mick Jagger, George Plimpton, Lauren Bacall, and Lillian Hellman. And Norman Mailer, Vincent Canby, Pauline Kael, Kurt Vonnegut, and Bette Midler. And Stephen Sondheim, Arthur Miller, Arthur Schlesinger Jr., and Robin Williams, plus hundreds more. Afterward, people talked about it as the last great party of the seventies, perhaps one of the great parties of several decades, as thrilling as Truman Capote's legendary black-and-white ball back in 1966. The evening was masterminded by Jean Doumanian, who had drawn up the guest list—the pop stars of politics, music, literature, fashion, and Hollywood—with the same assiduous attention she applied to booking guests for *Saturday Night Live*. Woody, dressed in tux and tennis shoes, assumed his post at the foot of the grand staircase, looking like a wobbly Ashley Wilkes on the day of the barbecue at Twelve Oaks. While many of the party guests he barely knew, or had never met, probably never wished to meet, there were a few whose presence genuinely thrilled him. "Earl 'The Pearl' will be here any minute," he whispered in Roger Angell's ear. Besides Earl Monroe, he also invited another of his favorite Knicks stars, Walt Frazier.

Harkness House was filled with hyacinths, "everywhere in beautiful jars," remembered Andrea Marcovicci, "tons and tons of hyacinths in the middle of winter on every floor. For the cool and hip, there were discos on two of the upper floors. There were buffet tables with filet mignon and shrimp and lobster. At four o'clock in the morning, a breakfast of eggs and bacon was served. I've never seen a party handled more beautifully." In his diary, Andy Warhol admitted that he was impressed. Woody's party was "the best." It was "wall-to-wall famous people," and he added, "we should have gone earlier."

· · · · · · ·

The March of Time:
"Mia gets what she wants."
—Maureen O'Sullivan
(Mia's mother), 1967

· · · · · · ·

Following the introduction at Elaine's, Woody added Mia Farrow's name to the guest list for his New Year's party. She showed up with her sister Stephanie Farrow and Tony Perkins and his wife, Berry Berenson, but dashed out scarcely a half hour later, before ringing in the new year. Woody, wrapped up in his guests, barely said hello.

A few days after the party, she sent him a bread-and-butter present, *The Medusa and the Snail: More Notes of a Biology Watcher* by Dr. Lewis Thomas, who had previously written the best-selling *The Lives of a Cell.* No intellectual herself, Mia was nonetheless skilled at selecting a gift for one, and the Thomas work, a collection of science essays, had been chosen with particular care. Aside from its serious subject, the book itself was a message: She was available. Woody, however, failed to pick up on it. *The Medusa and the Snail,* along with the bouquets and bottles of champagne sent by other guests, was politely acknowledged by Norma Lee Clark, who phoned to say that Mr. Allen sent a thank you and hoped they could have lunch one day.

Another bleak New York winter went by. The unhappiness in Woody's personal life, still a shambles, spilled over into his Fall Project, the most risky picture he had attempted because it portrayed his fans as freaks, a sideshow carnival of distorted faces resembling Weegee grotesques. Any person who truly admired him, he seemed to be saying, was a moron. Principal photography began on September 11, but by December, Woody had slipped five weeks behind in the twenty-two-week shooting schedule. The buzz around New York suggested the picture was in trouble. A *Village Voice* columnist tried pumping Charlotte Rampling, one of the leads, who refused to divulge anything because, she told Arthur Bell, Woody "would kill me if he thought I was talking to you." Seeking out less cautious sources (an extra who played a Martian in a UFO sequence), the *Voice* cobbled together a report of the filmmaker holding up a mirror to his dark side, in a parody of Fellini's *8½* that could easily turn out to be a masterpiece or a disaster. Of one thing the paper was certain—it sounded "depressing." Nervous about public reaction, Woody was determined to keep the plot secret.

In the spring, eager for relaxation, he decided to sandwich in a few days in Paris with Jean Doumanian and her new boyfriend, Jaqui Safra. At *Saturday Night Live,* Jean's diligence paid off when the show's creator and executive producer Lorne Michaels resigned and NBC named Jean as his replacement. To assure a brilliant debut for his friend when the new season began in November, Woody was full of ideas on how Jean could reinvent television's foremost comedy show.

In the meantime, there was no further contact with Mia Farrow, whose large family must have sounded like some kind of weird baby factory. Usually he shied away from mothers because he and they had nothing in common. He had as much interest in family life as any sixteen-year-old, which is why he once blurted out that "it's no accomplishment to have or raise kids. Any fool can do it." Most of the time, with a straight face, he claimed that the only reason he had no children was because "I've never had a marriage that has worked." But that was precisely his problem—maintaining a relationship was impossible. Navigating the decade of the seventies, a golden age of one-night stands, he symbolized the single, kiddie-phobic, narcissistic male, over forty but still pulling girls' pigtails, the connoisseur of casual sex, not yet ready for commitment. The last thing this type of bachelor wanted was the aggravation of squalling kids. On-screen, he didn't know how to behave around children. In *Manhattan,* the scenes between Alvy and his son were clumsy, and in *Stardust Memories,* the Sandy Bates character, quintessentially self-involved, loves a French woman but is painfully ill at ease with her two small children. Offscreen, Woody did not particularly enjoy spending time with youngsters, either, not even his sister's two children, Chris and Erika.

Nevertheless, a few days before leaving for France, he impulsively decided to get in touch with Mia. Rather than calling himself, he asked Norma Lee Clark to set up a 1 P.M. lunch at Lutèce on East Fiftieth Street. He arrived early and ordered a bottle of 1949 Château Mouton-Rothschild. In a tweed jacket and tasteful tie, he had dressed appropriately for a first date with a Hollywood princess, at one of the city's great restaurants. Mia blew in, breathless and disheveled, sporting an outfit entirely suitable to a day on the moors: Irish sweater, skirt, sensible walking shoes with leggings and socks, because she had just tramped down from the Upper West Side. Her hair, washed but not set, looked as though it had been styled by a lawn mower. Later, trying to recall the lunch, she could not remember the food, only the conversation about W. B. Yeats (Woody's favorite poet), Plato and Christianity, James Agee, and classical music—Mahler's slow movements and the Heifetz recording of the Korngold Symphony. After a decade with Andre Previn, a prominent musician and a first-rate jazz pianist, it was a subject she knew something about. Although the *New York Times* profile of Woody that she had tucked into her dictionary included an eyewitness account of him at Michael's Pub, Mia pretended to know nothing of his clarinet-playing, but he was happy to tell her about Sidney Bechet and Jelly Roll Morton. When they left the restaurant, it was already getting dark. Woody gave her a lift in his Rolls and promised to call when he returned from Paris.

Afterward, he could never recall the date of that first lunch, except that it was a few days after the death of Jean-Paul Sartre. Mia, however, remembered exactly. She commemorated the occasion by embroidering April 17, 1980, on a needlepoint sampler.

CHAPTER NINE

Beware of Young Girls

Maria de Lourdes Villiers Farrow seemed to be a character out of the pages of *Photoplay*. She was born in Beverly Hills on February 9, 1945, the third of seven children belonging to a glamorous couple: John Farrow, a director at Paramount, and Maureen O'Sullivan, an Irish starlet under contract to MGM. Mia's godparents were Hollywood royalty: George Cukor, the so-called woman's director, and the feared and famed Hearst gossip queen Louella Parsons. Mia's dog Billy was the grandson of Lassie. On exclusive Beverly Drive, on the half-acre grounds of the Farrow home, the seven beautiful children lived in a separate wing of the house, where they were bathed, dressed, and pampered by a staff of nannies and governesses. Meals were prepared in their own kitchen. Weekends were spent at the beach house in Malibu. While the Farrows took pains to create for their children the idyllic type of childhood that existed only in the cinema, there was a certain emptiness at the heart of all this grandeur. The children lived apart because John Farrow could not tolerate noisy kids underfoot. He was a strict disciplinarian with "an almighty temper," recalled Mia, who as a toddler could not pronounce Maria and would be known by her childhood nickname. Her father believed in corporal punishment and thought nothing of whacking her across the room or beating her with his walking stick. "I didn't know my parents very well," she admitted.

John Villiers Farrow was an interesting minor director of forty-two pictures, notably the 1943 war film *Wake Island*, and a thriller, *The Big Clock*, starring Ray Milland. Skilled at getting good performances, he was also widely disliked for his tyrannical treatment of actors.

An Australian by birth, whose mother died in childbirth and whose father seems to have abandoned him, he was raised by relatives and ran away, first chance he got, to join the merchant marines. In his early twenties, Farrow impregnated a seventeen-year-old San Francisco girl, Felice Lewin, but was brought to heel by her father, a mining tycoon who insisted that he marry Felice before she gave birth to a daughter. Undoing this union in order to marry Maureen O'Sullivan in 1936 required a special dispensation from the Vatican.

During her career in Hollywood, Mia's mother made seventy pictures, including *The Barretts of Wimpole Street* and *David Copperfield,* even a Marx Brothers film, *A Day at the Races.* But she is remembered best for her association with Edgar Rice Burroughs's apeman in six Tarzan movies, playing opposite Johnny Weissmuller as Tarzan's scantily clad mate, Jane, in the jungle series. In the 1940s, semiretired, she was almost constantly pregnant, and gave birth to three sons and four daughters within the space of a dozen years. Although Maureen Farrow liked the idea of having babies, she had absolutely no idea what to do with them afterward. A next-door neighbor, Maria Roach, daughter of comedy producer Hal Roach and Mia's best friend, remembered Mrs. Farrow as a distant exotic figure who was not involved in her children's daily lives and spent most of her time out of sight, like the Wizard of Oz, in her bedroom, which was painted dark green and resembled a religious shrine.

With the arrival of one baby after another, a marriage that was never Ozzie and Harriet in the first place grew progressively unhappier. In Hollywood, where sex was a matter of supply and demand, there was nothing but supply for studio executives and directors, especially men as good-looking as the tall, blond Farrow, a legendary fornicator. A snake tattooed on the upper inside of his left thigh appeared to be emerging from his genitals. Exercising droit du seigneur, with a sense of entitlement about sex from the actresses he directed, Johnny Farrow and his snake would prove memorable for some of Hollywood's biggest stars. By the early fifties, Mia's mother and father were sleeping in separate bedrooms. So that her rest would not be disturbed when her husband came home in the middle of the night after tomcatting around Beverly Hills, Maureen insisted on a separate entrance to his room.

At the age of nine, Mia contracted a mild case of infantile paralysis, a mysterious ailment that, before the Salk vaccine, was crippling and killing thousands of children. After six days in the polio ward at Los Angeles General Hospital, surrounded by children unable to breathe without a respirator and confined in iron lungs, she returned home to find everything changed, in order to safeguard the other children. "The dog had been given away," she recalled. "Our swimming pool had been drained. The lawn had been reseeded. The whole house had been repainted, the couch reupholstered, the carpets cleaned." She was terrified about contaminating her brothers and sisters. The following year there was another crisis when Mia's oldest brother, fifteen-year-old Michael, was hit by a car, and four years later he would die in a plane collision while, unbeknownst to his parents, he was taking flying lessons.

Throughout her life, Mia would be possessed by an overriding need for her father's approval. His reputation as an adulterer masked a serious, scholarly man, a fervent Roman Catholic who wrote a massive popular history of the papacy and a biography of Sir Thomas More. For his services to the Church, the Vatican awarded him a Knighthood of the Grand Cross of the Order of the Holy Sepulchre. More significant, however, was his obsession with Father Damien, a Belgian priest who founded a leper colony in Hawaii, where he eventually contracted the disease and died in 1889 at the age of forty-nine. Culminating years of research, Farrow published a biography, *Damien the Leper*, an inspirational work that would go through thirty-three printings. His preoccupation with the leper saint's selfless work among the Hawaiians would have a pronounced impact on Mia, who, in her adult life, would endeavor to re-create Father Damien's colony in her own home, by adopting nonwhite children who were blind, crippled, or otherwise medically disabled.

In the fall of 1962, beyond humiliation, tired of the papal knight's indefatigable philandering and heavy drinking, the long-suffering Maureen O'Sullivan turned her back on the wreckage. In New York, she acted in a Broadway comedy, *Never Too Late*, and had a romance with its seventy-five-year-old director, George Abbott. With the family fragmented, Mia joined her mother at Christmas. One night when Maureen was spending the evening with Abbott, her husband telephoned, and Mia made excuses. Throughout the night, Farrow called repeatedly, but Mia let the phone ring. Eventually, the calls stopped because John Farrow, clutching the receiver, had died of a heart attack.

No event shaped her future more than the death of her father, who had expressed withering disdain for actresses, whom he treated like pieces of meat, and opposed Mia's acting ambitions on the grounds that it would certainly make her miserable. Almost immediately after his death, she joined the cast of *Peyton Place*, the first daytime soap opera to be aired in the evening. The TV version of Grace Metalious's novel, about a small New England town and its citizens, would become one of 1964's biggest hits and make Mia, as its brooding heroine, Allison MacKenzie, famous overnight. What she lacked in acting ability—sometimes requiring ten takes to film a single line—she made up for in other respects. With her father's looks, she was a beauty whose best feature would be her extraordinary skin, as diaphanous as if her flesh were a package done up in Saranwrap.

■ ■ ■ ■ ■ ■ ■

March of Time:
"There were four sisters and three brothers and we all used to fight to kill. I'm serious. I have scars all over my body. We used knives, bottles."

—Tisa Farrow, 1970

■ ■ ■ ■ ■ ■ ■

The year after her father died, Mia met Frank Sinatra on the 20th Century-Fox lot while filming *Peyton Place*. During lunch breaks, she had taken to planting herself on the doorstep of the soundstage where he was filming a train scene for *Von Ryan's Express*. With her fair hair styled in waist-length braids, attired in a long white nightgown, she quickly captured Sinatra's notice. He dispatched one of his underlings to find out how old she was.

"Nineteen," she said. Sinatra was fifty.

Minutes later, while being introduced to the singer, she spilled the contents of her straw bag, including her retainer and a box of tampons, on the floor in front of his chair. Sinatra, charmed, saw an adorable little girl who needed to be cared for, like an exotic plant in danger of wilting, the helpless image she would convey to practically every man she ever met. Walking her to the stage door, he asked for a date.

In a darkened screening room, they held hands and as she said later, she began to love him the moment she first smelled him. He was wearing the same brand of aftershave lotion as her father had used. The next day, Sinatra sent his Learjet to bring Mia and her deaf cat, Malcolm, to his compound in Rancho Mirage, California, where he induced her to part with her virginity a few hours after the aircraft touched down at Palm Springs Airport. A pretty redhead wept by the pool. She had been expecting to share Sinatra's bed but had been passed along to Yul Brynner at the last minute. Sinatra, like Mia, was addicted to high drama.

Hollywood was as picaresque as a feudal barony where a lord could share a woman sexually with a rival, then turn around and vengefully deflower the enemy's daughter after his death. Years earlier, Sinatra first entered Mia's life one evening when she was eleven and having dinner with her father at Romanoff's. Walking by their table, Sinatra glanced at Mia and remarked to her father "pretty girl," whereupon Farrow looked at him as if he were a worm. "You stay away from her," he warned. There was more to this exchange than its face value. After the breakup of Sinatra's tempestuous marriage to Ava Gardner, John Farrow directed her in *Ride, Vaquero!*, a Western filmed in southern Utah. At first, the sex goddess disliked Farrow. On the weekends, carousing with hookers imported from Los Angeles, he would spend all day Sunday in bed and then report to the set on Monday mornings with a hangover. However much she was put off by his whoring, as well as his sadistic treatment of horses in the film, she subsequently changed her mind, and it was this relationship that prompted Maureen O'Sullivan to install the separate entrance on Beverly Drive. Although the Farrow children had no full knowledge of their father's indiscretions, Mia happened to know about Gardner because one day she accidentally caught them together in his office.

Mia's upbringing had imprinted a layer of rich fantasy over the pathology of a damaged family playing out various themes of religion, infidelity, alcoholism, and physical and emotional abuse. Giving up her virginity to the ex-husband of her father's mistress was simply the sort of extravagant theatricality that had become second nature.

One of Mia's friends, Liza Minnelli, was shocked to hear about her unlikely new boyfriend. "You're not dating Uncle Frank!" she exclaimed. But Mia's mother considered Uncle Frank "a nice man" likely to take good care of her daughter, a clue to the extent of her maternal guidance. Self-absorbed, unable to assume responsibility for her children's upbringing, Maureen allowed all of them to do more or less as they pleased, frequently with disastrous results. As a widow, her own desperate quest for affection led her to contemplate marriage to a twenty-three-year-old French rabbinical student. The boy's horrified parents, faced with a Mrs. Robinson situation, hastily put an end to the relationship.

In the summer of 1966, Mia married Sinatra in Las Vegas. No family members or friends attended. Their wedding photograph was described in detail by the *New York Post*: "The groom, his retreating hairline camouflaged by one of his sixty toupees, his face tanned almost to the bronze of Max Factor's theatrical makeup Number 11-N but a trifle jowly, his chin just visible in duplicate, was beaming." For better or for worse, Mia had re-created her parents' marriage. This became obvious a few months later, during an opening at the Sands Hotel, when Frank asked her to stand and take a bow and informed the audience that he had married again. "Well, you see I had to," he said. "I finally found a broad I can cheat on," which caused gasps even from the blasé Las Vegas crowd. Mia, head lowered, smiled. She would soon retreat into needlepointing and marijuana. In her fifties, still full of unresolved feelings about Sinatra, she remembered loving him "with all the powers of my infantile, hungry, myopic self," and at Sinatra's funeral she sat sobbing next to his first wife, Nancy.

While her husband's voice—his timing, phrasing, and matchless interpretation of a song—had made him a colossus among popular entertainers, he was also a flawed human being whose nastier side was suggested by his friendships with hoodlums, his treatment of women, whom he referred to as cuff links or broads, the ring-a-ding misogyny of his partying Rat Pack sidekicks, his high-priced hookers and gutter brawling. Angry, restless, he always had a chip on his shoulder, never bigger than when comedian Jackie Mason repeatedly made jokes about him and Mia ("Frank soaks his dentures and Mia brushes her braces"). Ignoring a number of warnings, Mason found three bullets fired into his hotel room, followed several months later by an unknown assailant breaking his nose and crushing his cheekbones. Sinatra's temper reminded Maria Roach of John Farrow, who "could be so charming and wonderful, and turn around and be somebody else," the Jekyll and Hyde syndrome typical of the alcoholic personality.

What Sinatra wanted most was a dependent wife, whose only interest would be satisfying his every desire. According to comedian Tom Dreesen, a close friend of Sinatra's, his stooges and yes-men flattered him as if he were the Sun King. "You have to understand that when you are with Frank Sinatra, it's his world and you are living in it. If you can revolve around his energy, you benefit." But Mia, who expected to be dominated by men, nevertheless showed surprisingly little aptitude for being a yes-woman. To spite him for excluding her from his fiftieth birthday party, given by his ex-wife Nancy and their children, she pitched a tantrum and chopped off her hair to the length of a boy's. In 1967 she was offered her first starring role in *Rosemary's Baby,* a horror film directed by Roman Polanski, based on Ira Levin's widely popular novel about an innocent young housewife who lives in a spooky New York apartment and gives birth to the son of Satan. When shooting was delayed, and Sinatra ordered her to walk off the set, she refused, no doubt counting on a short-lived conflict. Instead, he instructed his lawyer to draw up divorce papers. On the Paramount lot, Mickey Rudin appeared with a brown envelope, and took Mia into her trailer, leaving a few minutes later without a word. "Sending Rudin was just like firing a servant," thought Roman Polanski. If Mia's marriage to Sinatra ended badly, it also lasted sixteen months, which was about a year longer than some people expected.

■ ■ ■ ■ ■ ■ ■

Eyewitness:
"When you look at her, you are convinced that she has only just stepped out of a convent, all scrubbed and holy and chaste. It is sometimes a shock to remember who she really is, and what."
—PETER YATES, 1970

■ ■ ■ ■ ■ ■ ■

After her divorce from Sinatra, Mia made numerous sexual conquests. Wild living and immaturity combined with a slew of men, lots of sex, and a miscarriage brought loneliness. "She was a real sad little girl," recalled an actress friend, "the walking wounded." Mia would describe her malady as "a touch of Zelda Fitzgerald in me."

In Palm Springs, she visited John and Michelle Phillips of the Mamas and Papas, who had just become parents of a baby girl, Chynna. Suffering from exhaustion and postpartum depression, Michelle was having a hard time. Leaving her to fend for herself, Mia and John slipped away to Joshua Tree and checked into a hotel. John Phillips, completely infatuated, saw Mia as "gentle and flighty," a "real Flower Child." Decked out in beads, granny glasses, and funky muumuus, as if dressed for a masquerade ball, she liked to go around barefoot and sit on the floor. According to his memoirs, their relationship seemed to be fueled by taking mescaline together and engaging in boisterous pillow fights. One day as they were tripping, Peter Sellers pulled up to Phillips's house and found them stoned. Sellers, another man who had fallen hard for Mia, after breaking up with his wife, Britt Ekland, was gripped by such a raging obsession that Roman Polanski, who introduced them, figured they must be soul mates. Finding his soul mate whacked-out with John Phillips, Sellers let out a maniacal squeal, "I'll get you down from that drug if I have to pull you down by the pubic hairs." Barely two years later, Mia married again.

Andre Previn was born in 1929 and accepted into Berlin's most prestigious conservatory after showing signs of genius as a piano prodigy at age six. His father, an attorney, was not unduly disturbed when Hitler came into power because, even though he was Jewish, he thought of himself first of all as a German. One evening in 1938, however, on his way home from work, he noticed a sign: NO DOGS OR JEWS PERMITTED IN THIS PARK. Arriving home, he told his wife to pack for a weekend trip to Paris. They never returned. Andre Previn remembered that "we took one bag and left everything behind." From Paris, the Previns emigrated to Los Angeles, where they had a cousin who was a musical director at Universal Studios. While still a student at Beverly Hills High School, Andre began working for MGM and graduated to contract composer, arranger, and orchestrator of film musicals during the studio's golden age. In his sixteen years in Hollywood, a period he would call his "Esther Williams days," he scored a total of sixty films, won four Academy Awards for Best Music Score (*Gigi, Porgy and Bess, Irma La Douce,* and *My Fair Lady),* and bought "a pretty house." Despite his hugely successful career as a film composer, he refused, he said, "to spend the rest of my life manufacturing music that would be played while Debbie Reynolds spoke," and lived for the day when he could become a symphonic conductor. Within a few short years, he was principal conductor of the London Symphony Orchestra, the first American to lead a major British orchestra. The English press dubbed him "the British Leonard Bernstein."

Previn's looks were unconventional. He was short, with thinning black hair, a prominent nose, heavy circles under his eyes that made him look owlish, and he walked with a stoop that gave him an old-man quality. "There was nothing appealing about him at first," said an acquaintance from his Hollywood days. "But the minute he opened his mouth he had women eating out of his hand." After a first marriage to jazz singer Betty Bennett, and two daughters, he then married Dory Langdon, a talented lyricist four years his senior whom he met at MGM. An abusive family history resulted in a troubled adulthood for Dory: affairs with married men, two abortions, an annulled marriage, and a mental collapse that landed her in an institution, where she apparently was diagnosed as schizophrenic. Her marriage to Andre would be clouded by crippling breakdowns that necessitated hospitalization, interspersed with periods in which she functioned normally.

They first encountered Mia at the home of their next-door neighbor, the director Alan Pakula, when she bounced over to them and exclaimed sweetly that everyone she loved also loved them, and so she just had to say hello. She was holding in her hands a square of tapestry on which she was needlepointing a rose pattern. Dory, sizing up the twenty-four-year-old actress, studied the texture of her skin, as translucent as if "she were still wrapped in the gauze of her placenta." Listening to the whispery voice that had been "gently buffed" by good schools and money, Dory, at forty-three, felt quite over the hill. "No pig in the parlor, she," Dory wrote in an autobiography. "This was lace-curtain Hollywood." Mia persisted in trying to befriend the Previns, and once when Andre was away with the Houston Symphony, she invited Dory to her home in Bel Air. Confidences were exchanged. Why didn't she accompany Andre on tour? Mia wondered. Dory said that she rarely ventured out of Los Angeles because flying terrified her, a problem because Andre got lonely on the road and she feared he might fall under the spell of some sex kitten. Taking a youthful approach to Dory's dilemma, Mia advised worrying less about death by air crash and living her life more fully.

In months to come, Andre kept his distance from Mia. Sixteen years her senior, he seemed to be irritated by her flower-child flakiness. One evening, he and Dory were driving to a restaurant with Mia and Mike Nichols, when Mia suddenly declared she'd be perfect to play Peter Pan because she'd visited never-never land many times. That annoyed Andre, who told her that "if you ever say anything so stupid again, I'll personally throw you out of the car." Another night Mia and Liza Minnelli paid a call on the Previns, and Andre accompanied Liza on the piano, while Mia sat quietly in a corner listening. As the evening progressed, Dory began to seethe at the way Liza kept touching her husband and vowed that she would never be invited back. It never occurred to her to worry about Mia, because she always drove Andre nuts.

Not long afterward, in London, Andre and Mia accidentally ran into each other at a party. Andre, feeling claustrophobic, came out to the sidewalk for a breath of air and spotted Mia leaving. She couldn't stand it any longer, she said.

"Well, that's interesting because I can't stand it either," he replied. "How about going out to dinner?" According to Mia, Previn was unattached that evening. According to Dory Previn, he was still attached to her. And so when Mia became pregnant in May of 1969, Andre had difficulty informing his wife, who learned about it when a gossip columnist telephoned to ask for her reaction. Despite her fear of the air, in an attempt to join her husband and save her ten-year marriage, she hastily booked a flight to London. As the plane was sitting on the runway at Los Angeles International Airport, she tore off some of her clothes and ran bare-chested up and down the aisle. Screaming threats at other passengers, including a priest, she was removed from the aircraft and hospitalized.

Andre hesitated to press for a divorce until Dory came to her senses. But, said a friend from that time, "Dory was not OK before she found out. She would never be OK." Meanwhile, Dory, now released from the sanatorium, continued to hope that Andre would eventually come back to her, but after Mia delivered nonidentical twins, Matthew and Sascha in February 1970, she had no choice but to agree to a divorce. However, her hatred for the third Mrs. Previn was unabated. Convinced that Mia set out to marry her husband by deliberately becoming pregnant, she wrote and recorded an album of personal songs, including the pointed "Beware of Young Girls," which told of a wife's bitterness when a career homewrecker burrows into her marriage and steals her husband. (Mia thought the song was tasteless.) Two years later, Dory and Mia accidentally passed each other in the ladies' room at the Hillcrest Country Club in Los Angeles. They did not acknowledge each other. "I started to say something and got choked on my own words," Mia recalled. "Maybe it was better not to."

In the seventies, the Previns lived on a twenty-acre country estate in Surrey. Surrounded by woods and streams at "The Haven," their family kept growing. During a concert tour in South Korea in 1970, Andre accompanied another musician to an orphanage for Vietnam war victims. The sight of hundreds of babies lying in cardboard boxes, covered with newspapers, upset him so greatly that he wanted to scoop up "as many as I could carry out." He and Mia adopted two-month-old Kym Lark in 1973, another Vietnamese baby, Summer, the following year, and a Korean orphan, Soon-Yi, in 1977. A third biological son, Fletcher, was born to them in 1974.

In the beginning, the marriage was sometimes happy, sometimes not. Married not yet two years, Mia was complaining to *Photoplay* about trying to work out "a lot of problems," adding that "maybe being every man's third wife is a jinx." Previn, a man of immense charm and charisma on the podium, radiated sweetness and witty humor but in private could be frosty, guarded, and withholding. Mia also discovered that Andre, though not traditionally handsome, was attractive to women. As time went on, there was increasing gossip about him and other women, including the music critic of the *Financial Times* of London. But in the end it was not his black moods or his alleged dalliances that broke up their marriage but the fact that he was hardly ever home. As one of the most prominent musicians in Britain, he was either on the road or performing on television. During the second year of their marriage, Mia was shocked to realize that he had spent only a total of fifteen days with her. Andre despised Hollywood and didn't want his wife to work there, and besides, her children needed her at home. But with a husband who was always absent, life could become humdrum, and so she acted in several British films that contributed nothing to her reputation.

Among the Previns' close friends was an English couple, Heather and Michael Jayston, and their three children. Michael, an actor who played Czar Nicholas in *Nicholas and Alexandra,* had appeared with Mia in Carol Reed's *The Public Eye* (1972). His wife, a tall woman with high cheekbones and shoulder-length auburn hair, was a glass-and-jewelry etcher. She was a good friend of Mia's, whose example resulted in the Jaystons' adoption of a Vietnamese war orphan as well. By the time that the Jaystons divorced in 1977, Andre had developed more than friendly feelings for the thirty-year-old Mrs. Jayston, who would become his fourth wife in 1982. Mia, too, began having relationships, with Roman Polanski and then Sven Nykvist, Ingmar Bergman's director of photography.

An enterprising teenager who grew up too fast, Mia once revealed her aspirations to gossip columnist Hedda Hopper. Being anonymous, she confided, "just 'one of the Farrows,' third from the top and fifth from the bottom," couldn't possibly satisfy her. Instead, she planned to think big, because that was how she could achieve her heart's desire—"a big career, a big man, and a big life." Mia may have been immature and greedy, but she was also a show-business brat, tremendously savvy in the ways of Hollywood. That men would be her entrée to the big life was obvious—it was the expected role of women, even in the swinging sixties—but Mia also grasped a crucial fact: What counted was connecting with rich, handsome older men. Already prospecting for a suitable candidate, casting flirtatious glances toward Yul Brynner and Kirk Douglas, she sensed that nice girls finish last.

By her mid-thirties, Mia had been married to and divorced from two big men. Like any woman who presents herself as a fragile gamine in need of care—another traditional female role—Mia tried to avoid competition with men, indeed was careful not to suggest she could ever be an equal. Personally, her assets were meager. She learned to act at the Liz Taylor Academy of Dramatic Arts, although she steadily improved with age and eventually developed into a capable comedienne. Average intelligence and a sketchy finishing-school education, but few skills of concentration, made unlikely any fulfillment of her childhood fantasy of becoming a pediatrician. Primarily, she was a pretty woman with a breathtaking complexion.

While Mia had no problem winning the affection of prominent men, keeping them proved more difficult. Big men plus big money plus big egos equaled big trouble. Without fail, they fell victim to forces beyond their control, usually the allure of other women, and meandered away. "I believed in my husbands/partners," Mia said. "I trusted them absolutely, automatically, and I failed to see the full picture."

CHAPTER TEN

Woody in Love

During Saturday matinees, Woody liked to slip into the Barrymore Theatre, where *Romantic Comedy* was now in its eighth month. Once the curtain fell, he would make a beeline for the stage door and whisk Mia away for a quick bite before the evening show. By now the whole company knew she had a mad crush on him and he was crazy about her.

Even a blind person, he thought, could appreciate Mia's beauty, but that was only part of the reason he found her thrilling. Her exotic pedigree, sublimely trailing the mythology of Hollywood's gilded era, conjured up for him the ecstasy of Midwood's old movie palaces and long dark afternoons with giant boxes of Milk Duds. She seemed a fantasy in the flesh, whose connections to the glamour personalities pasted on Cousin Rita's wall of pinups overwhelmed him. It was hard to believe that her mother was the same sexy starlet from the Tarzan movies. For that matter, the last person he ever expected to love was the ex-wife of Frank Sinatra, who had been a god to his cousin.

In the months after their lunch at Lutèce, on Sundays when there was no performance of *Romantic Comedy,* they explored the city's offbeat neighborhoods on foot, holding hands and carrying a bottle of Château Margaux and two wineglasses in a brown paper bag. And when they got tired, the Rolls materialized à la *Breakfast at Tiffany's* and took them home. In cozy East Side art houses playing Bergman and Goddard films, they hugged and kissed. Apart, Woody yearned for Mia and dispatched his chauffeur to Central Park West with lover's gifts to be dropped off with her doorman, his favorite recordings and romantic e. e. cummings poetry, and once an antique postcard showing a man in a bowler hat with five children that had been inscribed by some unknown lover, "Your future husband—Your future children."

The one thing he could not manage to do, however, was pick up the phone and call her. From May to August, Norma Lee Clark continued to schedule their meetings by dialing Mia with dates and times when her employer would be available. As they were lovers by then, this arrangement seemed ridiculous, but Mia made no objection. His reluctance to phone her ended when she checked into New York Hospital for emergency abdominal surgery resulting from complications following peritonitis, and from there convalesced in Martha's Vineyard. While she was away, he began calling two or three times a day.

Aside from his telephone phobia, Woody's biggest problem was her children. In this matter, they totally ignored each other's messages. Woody, at the beginning of their relationship, warned that he'd never dated a mother (apparently forgetting Teri Shields) and had "zero interest" in kids, giving her to understand she must not expect anything of him. And Mia, only a few weeks after they began dating, while sitting in a theater watching a new Australian film, *My Brilliant Career,* suddenly turned to him and whispered, "I would like to have a child with you." Woody, taking the remark as a joke, looked at her and laughed. After all, she had seven children. What he failed to understand was that, above all else, Mia adored babies. "She never met a baby she didn't like," said an intimate.

Not only had Woody not yet met her children, he expressed no interest in meeting them. Since the divorce, Mia had been living at the Langham on Central Park West, in a spacious eight-room apartment that combined her mother's six-room apartment with the unit next door. Woody had never been there. Whenever he picked her up, he waited downstairs in the Rolls. It was not until late September that the first encounter took place, accidentally, when he arrived to pick up Mia just as she was entering the building with her family, like a mother duck trailed by ducklings: the ten-year-old twins, Matthew and Sascha; seven-year-old Lark; and Soon-Yi, who was also around seven or eight; and the two six-year-olds, Daisy and Fletcher. To these half dozen was recently added a seventh, Misha, who suffered from cerebral palsy on his right side and had to wear a leg brace. Abandoned in a phone booth in Seoul, South Korea, Misha was two when Mia took him in earlier that year, after specially requesting a handicapped child. The children were returning from the playground, all of them holding dripping ice-cream cones. They were shy. Woody fidgeted. Later, ill at ease, he told Mia they were cute.

In September, shortly after Mia's return to the city, Woody prepared for the release of *Stardust Memories.* Unlike previous years when he alleviated his anxiety over the openings of *Interiors* and *Manhattan* by fleeing to Paris, this year Jean Doumanian was not available, and so he invited Mia to accompany him. Paris happened to be the one European city she couldn't stand. What's more, being separated from her children always upset her, and she had barely recovered from surgery. Nevertheless, she could not bring herself to refuse the pleasures of a romantic week with her new lover.

*   *   *

The previous summer, Joan Didion noticed that a number of her friends were busy seeking a recipe for "the perfect vegetable terrine," a normal seasonal activity. But others were waiting in long, hot lines to see *Manhattan,* which left her incredulous. In the pages of the *New York Review of Books* soon afterward, Didion disemboweled the picture, and, by extension, the narcissism of its creator. Like a little boy who has never been unfairly scolded, Woody didn't quite believe anyone could pan *Manhattan,* by this time a huge commercial success.

A native Californian who in her youth had romanticized New York as extravagantly as Woody, the forty-four-year-old Didion had constructed an impressive career as novelist, journalist, screenwriter, and essayist. Training her critical eye on *Manhattan,* she immediately began finding fault. Woody's characters impressed her as whiny elitists constantly moaning about their lives over expensive meals at Elaine's, perpetual adolescents whose concerns "are those of clever children, 'class brains,' acting out a yearbook fantasy of adult life." Their bad manners were appalling, likewise their eternal dissatisfaction over relationships and their tiresome habits of name-dropping. As for their obsession with externals, Didion especially loathed the scene that everyone seemed to adore, the famous monologue (purloined from Bob Hope's theme song "Thanks for the Memory") in which Isaac lists his reasons to go on living—Groucho Marx, Frank Sinatra, Cezanne's apples, Swedish films, Louis Armstrong's "Potato Head Blues." (Most middle-aged adults would have included their children.) Woody's trivial pleasures, all of them passive, Didion concluded, amounted to nothing more than "the ultimate consumer report." There was nothing in *Manhattan*—or for that matter in *Annie Hall* or *Interiors*—for reasonable people to admire.

Didion's pitiless essay, immediately famous among the *Review's* highbrow readership, naturally got under Woody's skin. Didion quickly forgot both the movie and her article because having once written about a film, with a few exceptions, "it leaves my mind altogether." Her sniping didn't leave Woody's mind. As a loyal subscriber of the *New York Review of Books,* he usually read the paper on the day of arrival, "or else it piles up, and becomes a matter of guilt." Didion's review was sufficiently enraging that two years later, still smarting, he fussed to Gene Siskel that Didion "accused me of things that clearly are not fair. And I felt that just wasn't right." Never would he understand that fairness per se was not the critic's mission, just as never would he devise a surefire way to manipulate them, although in *Stardust Memories* he got some measure of revenge by depicting them as braying jackasses.

The disdain of Joan Didion, sweetheart of the New York literati, proved to be merely a warm-up for the hurricane of denunciation that was to follow. Vincent Canby championed *Stardust Memories* as "marvelous" and "breathtaking," but his reaction was atypical. Pauline Kael, who did a drive-by shooting of *Annie Hall* ("the neurotic's version of *Abie's Irish Rose*"), thought *Stardust Memories* was an ugly work that degraded the people who liked Woody's pictures, then turned around and presented its creator as their victim. She decided he must be "crazy." The hostility of a stand-up comic toward his audience was remotely understandable, but the contempt of a filmmaker for fans who revered him, whom he bloodied as big-nosed, fat-lipped grotesques, was simply incomprehensible. "The Jewish self-hatred that spills out in this movie could be a great subject, but all it does is spill out," she wrote. If Woody found success so painful, *Stardust Memories* "should help him stop worrying" because he had just pulled the plug on himself.

Years later, Kael told friends that her pummeling of *Stardust Memories* ended her friendship with Woody Allen. "What a shame that he took it so personally," someone commiserated.

"Oh no," Kael replied. "It was vicious."

Emerging from the press screening, Andrew Sarris thought that "the way in which he put down both his own family and also people who were swarming over him was very knowingly nasty." His review blasted *Stardust Memories* for being "the most mean-spirited and misanthropic film I have seen in years and years from anyone" and recommended Woody's latest only to "people who would consider it a privilege to pay $5 to watch Woody gargle in the men's room at Elaine's." In *National Review*, John Simon branded Woody an "existential sniveler" whose "small, Jewish, and ugly" hero, Sandy, like Woody himself, "has an insatiable yen for big beautiful shiksas, to be conquered as plentifully and publicly as possible." Undoubtedly, Simon's comments about Woody's sex life were injudicious. Likewise, equating Michael's Pub with the Hotel Stardust, Woody's real-life and fictional hunting grounds, was not really fair, either. But when Simon went on to mention personal details—such as Woody's affair with Jessica Harper—that didn't belong in a film review, he went too far. As for Judith Crist, the Tarrytown movie queen memorialized in the film, she first saw it at a critics' screening, where she came down with a sudden case of myopia. "I didn't see myself," she remembered. "Then I paid admission at the Little Carnegie. The second time I also missed myself. I am devout about Woody's talent but I can't remember a single line of the movie. I hate to say it but it is my least favorite Woody film." In the *Saturday Review*, referring caustically to blatant similarities to Federico Fellini's *8½*, Crist called the picture Woody's *9½*, and concluded that "what we have here falls into the category of kvetch."

Generating similar degrees of hostility in customers as well, *Stardust Memories* did disappointing business. Outside of New York, it opened and closed in three or four weeks. Woody regarded the controversial picture "the best I ever did," and certainly it was his most honest in trying to convey a truth about fame, but nobody wanted to hear it. He expected to catch "a lot of flack." All the same, he was surprised about the extent of the animosity. "So many people were outraged that I dared to suggest an ambivalent love/hate relationship between an audience and a celebrity. This is what happens with celebrities. One day people love you, the next day they want to kill you." Woody had it right. Ten weeks after the opening of *Stardust Memories,* about a half mile from Woody's house, John Lennon was shot and killed by a fan who had asked for his autograph earlier in the day.

■ ■ ■ ■ ■ ■ ■

Caught on Tape:
"I'm a spartan. I have no bad habits whatsoever."
—WOODY ALLEN interview, 1977

■ ■ ■ ■ ■ ■ ■

As a result of *Stardust Memories,* the press began gunning for him. In a scathing cover story assigned to one of their crackerjack metropolitan reporters, the *New York Times Magazine* ripped Woody's Boy Scout image to tatters. Before coming to the *Times,* Tony Schwartz had been a political columnist at the leftist magazine *New Times.* Now he specialized in celebrity profiles that exposed clay feet. In Woody's case this meant shining a light into the dark corners of his life, illuminating the spartan Jewish boy next door from Brooklyn, who wore famously rumpled clothes and put art ahead of commerce. Predictably, Schwartz's investigation hit pay dirt. "What Mr. Allen says is often at variance with the way he really lives," he wrote in "The Conflicting Life and Art of Woody Allen."

According to Schwartz, the spartan lived the extravagant life of a movie star. He had a luxurious penthouse duplex on Fifth Avenue with floor-to-ceiling windows overlooking Central Park, and it was stuffed with Persian rugs and French provincial tables. He had a trained Cordon Bleu cook doubling as a full-time housekeeper, and a secretary screening his calls. He had a chauffeur driving a new Rolls, cream-colored, about a block long, with smoked windows so that nobody could see him. He had Ralph Lauren make his jackets, Cartier engrave his party invitations. Schwartz uncovered much else, including the personal publicist on retainer solely for the purpose of turning down interviews supposedly because Woody hated discussing his private life. He had the best table at Elaine's. And he had his personal sex buffet full of "young, unattached women, who stood back by the bar" at Michael's Pub, smoking and drinking white wine. About the only possessions Schwartz managed to overlook were Woody's four VIP courtside season tickets at the Garden, behind the scorer's table, choice seats that set him back more than most people earned in a year (the seats in section 16, row B, cost $232,000 in 1999).

· · · · · · ·

· · · · · · ·

"Studio 8H," answered the production assistant.

"Hi. This is Mo Golden calling. Is Jean there?"

The PA put the call on hold. "Jean!" he screamed. "Woody's on the phone!"

Everyone at *Saturday Night Live* knew the identity of the mysterious Mo Golden. When Jean was talent coordinator, Woody made regular, frequent calls to her private number. After she became producer in the summer of 1980, he was a huge unseen presence hovering over the seventeenth floor. Because earlier he had helped her get the booking job, there was speculation that he was in some way involved in her promotion to producer. That her qualifications were shaky seemed to be reinforced by the incessant phone calls, a virtual Woody hot line, the impression that she could do nothing without consulting him. Aside from the "Mo Golden" calls, she accepted his suggestions about hiring writers and gave his sister a job as researcher.

From the start, Doumanian alienated her staff. It was not the redecoration of her office (everybody did that), or the robed swami who came up to deliver herbs. It was not even her mispronunciation of words such as *Oedipus* (she pronounced it "Ode-i-pus"), although this generated plenty of unkind titters. Rather, it was her abrasive management style. People at *SNL* did not cut other people dead in the hall.

One day, making conversation, a newly hired writer inquired, "Where are you from?"

"Why is that important to you?" Jean said suspiciously.

"Just a friendly question," replied Peter Tauber, who concluded that talking to Jean "was like talking to the great Inca sun god. Jean's office was like a throne room. During writers' meetings, she made us sit on the floor while she sat behind a black onyx desk. Sometimes she would rotate her chair and take a telephone call for a half hour. She'd go out to dinner and leave us waiting. Like we were inferior beings." The friendly Tauber would find himself fired before the new season got under way.

"She pissed off a lot of people," said Laurie Zaks, who was Jean's secretary before Jean rose to power. "She didn't treat people well. For obvious reasons, it was the wrong job for a person who is not really creative. She was just not equipped to be producer of *Saturday Night Live.*"

In revenge, the staff adopted Tauber's name for her, the "Ayatollah Doumanian," and leaked nasty stories to the media. As a result, Marvin Kitman of *Newsday* would respond by nicknaming her "Jean Dobermanpinscher." "Anyone who replaced Lorne Michaels would have been in the hot seat," pointed out costumer Karen Roston. Sure enough, the press gleefully mashed Doumanian when the season began in November, wisecracking that the show's trademark opening ("Live from New York, it's Saturday Night") ought to be changed to "Dead from New York, it's Saturday night!"

In spite of her connections to Woody (and her discovery of Eddie Murphy), Jean Doumanian failed to survive the season. In March 1981, she was replaced by a man. Recalled Karen Roston, "One day I went in and she was not there." According to staff gossip, Jean received a million-dollar settlement.

■ ■ ■ ■ ■ ■ ■

Moving Pictures:
VOICE-OVER: "The first time I ever saw Radio City Music Hall . . . it was like entering heaven."
—*Radio Days,* 1987

■ ■ ■ ■ ■ ■ ■

Crowning them "The Couple of the Year," the *New York Daily News* chronicled Woody and Mia's shopping and dining habits as they cruised around Manhattan. Among Mia's romantic purchases was $260 worth of old movies at Video Shack (including Fritz Lang's *Metropolis* and *M*). At Christmas, she was seen in Bloomingdale's, buying a Woody doll. A connoisseur of fine wines, he began running up hefty bills at the D. Sokolin vintners on Madison Avenue. To avoid prying eyes in restaurants, they hid behind menus. No matter, because the press managed to obtain details of their breakfast orders at the Carnegie Delicatessen—where Woody would order Rice Krispies and soft-boiled eggs; Mia, sturgeon on rye bread—and spied on them at Pearl's, his favorite Chinese restaurant, to report them holding hands, crossing their arms over the table. By the end of 1980, the *News* had Woody proposing.

When the proposal came it was not of marriage. For Woody, commitment took the form of creating a movie role for Mia, transforming her into his leading lady just as he had with Louise Lasser and Diane Keaton. After *Rose-*

mary's Baby, Mia had struggled to become an accomplished actress. All told, she had acted in seventeen motion pictures, performed Chekhov and Gorky with the Royal Shakespeare Company, and played Peter Pan, opposite Danny Kaye as Captain Hook, on a *Hallmark Hall of Fame* television musical in 1976. (Julie Andrews's singing was dubbed in to replace hers.) Her most memorable role was in a big-budget Hollywood production of *The Great Gatsby,* in which she played F. Scott Fitzgerald's ethereal heroine Daisy Buchanan, opposite Robert Redford as Jay Gatsby. "Every major actress wanted the part," recalled Robert Evans, then head of production at Paramount. "Like Scarlett O'Hara, no matter how big the star, they all had to lower themselves to be tested. Not one actress refused. One morning I opened a letter and a pressed daisy fell out; the note read, 'May I be your Daisy? Love, Mia.' " Mia stole the highly coveted role away from Ali McGraw, Faye Dunaway, Candice Bergen, and Katharine Ross because the producers decided only she had the right vulnerability, that hint of "spoiled arrogance," Evans recalled. Several weeks into production, however, the executives at Paramount were outraged to learn that Mia was pregnant. Rather than replace her, which would have cost a fortune, the studio was forced to shoot her scenes before her condition showed. In *The Great Gatsby,* Mia looked so radiant that Time, Inc., chose her as the cover girl for the first issue of its new weekly magazine *People.* The movie, unfortunately, turned out to be a box-office flop, and Mia's acting proved little more than adequate, causing her dream of superstardom to recede like the green light on Daisy Buchanan's dock.

"It was an impossible situation," recalled Steven Bach, who was head of worldwide production for United Artists at the time. "I knew it and he knew it but neither one of us could say so."

One afternoon in the fall of 1980, Woody met with Bach at the Russian Tea Room on West Fifty-seventh Street, next door to the Rollins and Joffe office. He was polite but poker-faced. Finally his contract with UA was coming to an end. In 1978, when Krim and the Medici formed Orion Pictures, Woody clung to an old-fashioned sense of honor about professional commitments and stayed on to make *Interiors, Manhattan,* and *Stardust Memories.* All this time, Jack Rollins and Charles Joffe played dumb and kept telling UA they knew nothing of Woody's plans and had no influence over his decision. However, they kept repeating like a mantra, "Arthur is like a *father* to Woody."

"It was perfectly clear to me that we were not going to get to keep him," Bach said. "But *trying* to keep him was my most important single function in three years, more important than *Heaven's Gate* [the notorious thirty-six million dollar debacle that helped sink the studio and became a generic term for calamity]. If *Heaven's Gate* had opened as disastrously as it did on one day, and Woody had agreed to stay at UA the next day, United Artists would still be in business as of old. It was that important."

In spite of an extremely generous counteroffer, Steven Bach and UA failed, and in December 1980, Woody decamped to Orion. The new deal paid him 15 percent of a picture's gross receipts, which he would divvy up with Rollins and Joffe and Robert Greenhut, his producer since *Annie Hall.* Soon after, he began developing his first film project with the twin themes of conformity and celebrity, a subject he had explored in *Stardust Memories* but that continued to preoccupy him. Despite the drubbing he took for that picture, he was not finished with the issue of unhappiness born of success and fame and refused to drop material that the public cared nothing about. In his first offering for Orion, smarting from accusations that he relied too heavily on Bergman and Fellini, he came up with a concept that was original from start to finish. And for good measure, he quietly remade *Stardust Memories.*

Set during the late '20s and early '30s, the story purports to be a real documentary about Leonard Zelig, a man who wants so badly to be liked that he tries to fit in everywhere. Insecure and anxious, he can't help assuming the personality, even the appearance, of people he meets. For example, contact with a black musician makes him change into a black musician; conversation with a psychiatrist transforms him into a learned doctor, and so forth. As a consequence of this miraculous talent, Zelig the Human Chameleon quickly becomes an international celebrity feted with ticker-tape parades and merchandised with board games and dolls, songs and dance crazes. At the same time, fame takes its toll and "the price he paid was being an unhappy, empty human being," Woody explained. In the end, Leonard walks off into the sunset after falling in love with his psychiatrist (played by Mia). Cured, he loses his neuroses and becomes an ordinary man.

Technically, the film was brilliant. To integrate a modern-day character into historical footage, Woody, his cinematographer Gordon Willis, and editor Sandy Morse used more than thirty hours of stock footage from old newsreels, photographs, and radio broadcasts, as well as seventy-five hours of newly shot black-and-white footage that simulated historical scenes. To capture the sounds of the past, they recorded them using microphones made in 1928, when sound technology was in its infancy. By use of mattes (optical devices), new material could be superimposed on old footage, resulting in a startling scene showing Leonard at an actual rally for Hitler. In order to embed Woody's image into a thirties newsreel, new footage had to be painstakingly aged to match the graininess of the old. The result was a seamless match that demonstrated Woody's consummate skill as a technician.

*   *   *

In the spring of 1981, before principal photography was scheduled to begin on his human chameleon picture, Woody grew panicky. He was pathologically fearful of free time and here he was, becalmed, with nothing to do. To sustain himself, he decided to toss off "a bon-bon, a little dessert," basically a home movie to show off the delicate beauty of his photogenic new girlfriend. It would be a homespun, summertime idyll with people chasing butterflies and playing badminton and show the country "the way I want it to be, with golden vistas, and flowers, animals, moon, stars, all in 1906," he told Roger Ebert. In six days he completed the script for *Summer Nights,* a romantic comedy set at the turn of the century that brings together three couples for a weekend. Woody plays Andrew, a stockbroker who dabbles as an inventor (his latest: a flying bicycle), and Mary Steenburgen is his sexually inhibited wife. They are joined by Andrew's best friend, Maxwell, a lecherous doctor accompanied by an oversexed nurse (Tony Roberts and Julie Hagerty), and a pompous elderly philosopher and his sexy young fiancée (Jose Ferrer and Mia). No sooner have these free-thinking couples assembled than they begin regrouping in a game of sexual musical chairs. By mid-June Woody was preparing to shoot in pastoral Pocantico Hills, New York, on the grounds of the Rockefeller estate in Tarrytown.

Working for Woody showed Mia an entirely different side of her lover, who could be severe and sarcastic with his actors. In a scene that required Jose Ferrer to say, "These are not my teeth," Woody was unhappy with his reading of the line and put Ferrer through the ringer by shooting it over and over. Tension began to build. The seventy-two-year-old Ferrer, a widely respected actor and director of stage and screen, grew increasingly upset. After take number thirty, he finally refused to do the scene one more time and yelled angrily that Woody had melted him into a mass of fears. Woody, observed Andrew Sarris, "is almost a ventriloquist and all his actors are marionettes. It's his nature. He has to be on top."

If Woody could intimidate Jose Ferrer so easily, he had no trouble making Mia feel like "a rank amateur," she would write. Worried about her acting, she began frantically fishing for reassurance, but no comfort was forthcoming. As a world-class whiner himself, he lacked patience with women who complained. Suffering second thoughts about her Woody film debut, she told him that on future pictures she did not want to act but would like to be his assistant, to which he retorted, "It's hard work." Understandably, this blistering rebuke magnified her jitters. Before long, Mia found plenty of other reasons to worry. The weather was miserably hot and humid, and she had to be encased in a sweaty iron corset for the frilly period costumes; her hair was set in torturous curlers to produce Mary Pickford ringlets. She developed fierce headaches, and by the middle of shooting, she also had an ulcer and dosed herself every four hours on Tagamet. To make matters worse, there were unexpected problems with her sister Stephanie, who had been hired as her stand-in. Mia was close to Steffi, who was divorced and lived with her son only a few blocks away, but Mia soon regretted her presence on the film because she straggled around after Woody in a flirtatious way. During breaks the two of them would go off together, laughing and relaxing under a tree, while Mia, confined to her camper with corset and curls, boiled with jealousy. Their flirtatious camaraderie made her so suspicious that she wondered if they were sleeping together.

Woody retitled his erotic comedy *A Midsummer Night's Sex Comedy*. In fact, it owes more to Bergman's *Smiles of a Summer Night* than to Shakespeare, although Woody scoffed at the notion that he had deconstructed the Swede's turn-of-the-century boudoir farce with its sexual chases and carnal round dances. Photographed so beautifully by Gordon Willis that it seems to be a painting in motion, an animated Renoir's *Luncheon after the Boating Party, Sex Comedy* is the most visually gorgeous of all Woody's films. Stanley Kauffmann thought the picture was "easily his best-directed film, much better than his last, *Stardust Memories*, which finished last in the Fellini Sweepstakes"—but still found Woody to be an inept writer. Unlike his previous films, Kauffmann was later to say, which had been "cobbled together," *A Midsummer Night's Sex Comedy* had "a sense of control and fluency. He now knew how to use a camera gracefully and was becoming a very good director." Nearly everyone else found fault. "Watching Woody in the woods wasn't much fun," grumbled Gene Siskel in the *Chicago Tribune*. "Little sex and less comedy," John Simon huffed in *National Review*. Pauline Kael took Woody to task for presenting "tableaux that suggest the Nelson Rockefeller collection of imitation works of art." At the box office, the bon-bon proved an expensive financial disaster, and Mia's performance resulted in a Razzie Award as Worst Actress of 1982.

For the first time in his show-business career, Woody received back-to-back pans. He badly needed a hit.

To give authenticity to his pseudodocumentary about the chameleon man, Woody wanted to use guest-star interviews with real people, interspersed with archival newsreel footage and antique photos. It was intended to be a takeoff of *Reds*, a picture that costarred Warren Beatty and Diane Keaton (his current girlfriend) as American journalist John Reed and his lover, Louise Bryant. Embellishing Beatty's film were interviews with Rebecca West and other witnesses to the history of the Bolshevik revolution. Unlike Beatty's real-life witnesses, Woody's intellectuals were asked to utter serious opinions on a fictional figure from the twenties, a man supposed to be more famous than Charles Lindbergh. Trolling for celebrities, Woody wrote to Greta Garbo and asked if she would like to be in one of his movies. She did not reply, nor did a letter to Jack Dempsey produce results because the Manassas Mauler, now in his late eighties, was suffering from poor health. Woody was more successful with Lillian Gish, whose career had spanned the entire century. The First Lady of the Silent Screen, now an energetic eighty-five and still working, was happy to comply. The interview was disappointing, however, and he decided not to use it in the film.

Finally he persuaded Saul Bellow, Susan Sontag, Irving Howe, and Dr. Bruno Bettelheim to discuss Leonard Zelig's place in history. Bellow, for instance, was given lines like: "Therefore his sickness was also at the root of his salvation. It was his very disorder that made a hero of him." As usual, Woody failed to reveal what the film was about, and by the time Bellow found out it was too late. Had he known, he would have backed out of it because the picture made him look "foolish," he thought. The $5,000 payment did not compensate for being taken advantage of. If the Nobel prize winner couldn't figure out what Woody was up to, neither could Susan Sontag. Years later, she was appearing at an Oregon arts program when a member of the audience asked about the *Zelig* cameo. Sontag got snippy. "Next question," she said impatiently.

A moderate commercial hit, *Zelig* turned out to be a critical winner; its sophisticated special effects received glowing reviews, the best since *Manhattan,* and some writers compared it to *Citizen Kane.* Looking back, Andrew Sarris thought that critics probably oversold the picture to their readers. To begin with, he said, "we New York critics tend to identify with Woody. We have roughly the same kind of politics and we laugh at the same things. He has us in his pocket." In 1983 Woody singled out several critics, Sarris among them, and arranged private screenings for them, a shrewd move that paid off nicely. Afterward, Sarris felt he "had been had by Woody" and should have been more cautious in his estimation of *Zelig.* In any case, its sophisticated special effects succeeded in dazzling viewers. *Newsweek*'s Jack Kroll spoke for the majority when he called *Zelig* "a brilliant cinematic collage that is pure magic," and to Vincent Canby, it was nothing less than the perfection of ideas Woody had been systematically exploring in every film since *Take the Money and Run.* Few critics or viewers realized how intensely personal the picture was for Woody, nor did they associate its themes with *Stardust Memories.* Like Leonard Zelig, Woody was a famous figure who, forced to battle the beast of celebrity, continued to feel like a poor lost sheep once known as Allan Konigsberg. Only Pauline Kael was impolite enough to bring this up, writing that despite Woody's claims to the contrary, his films could not be more autobiographical; he is constantly showing audiences how bad he feels about himself. All the adulation in the world could not keep Woody—and Charlie Chaplin—from feeling "utterly alone and lost, like wormy nothings," she concluded in her best Ma Barker style.

The most peculiar admirer of *Zelig* was Oona O'Neill Chaplin, the widow of Charlie Chaplin, now an elderly, bedridden alcoholic living in Switzerland. One evening, in a boozy stupor, she excitedly watched a *Zelig* videotape four times, under the illusion that each viewing was the first. Delighted with footage that showed her husband clowning with Marion Davies on a tennis court at William Randolph Hearst's San Simeon, she instructed her daughter to send Woody a telegram. "Say he's incredible," she said.

CHAPTER ELEVEN

Pushing the Baby Cart

In the gloom of the Russian Tea Room on a bright July afternoon in 1982, Woody was sitting in his usual booth up front by the bar with Roger Ebert, expounding on the perfect love affair. "You've got to realize," he said in a serious tone, "that a relationship is always better if you don't actually have to live with the other person."

The *Chicago Sun-Times* critic was listening politely. "Really?" he said, as if studying the mating rituals of a Yanomami Indian.

"Oh, of course," asserted Woody, wise in the exotic ways of seventies dating, as practiced on the Upper East Side. "This means you can be in a constant courtship." During the day Mia had her kids to look after, "but in the evenings we'll meet and it's like a date." Then, after sex, she went back to her place. "It's ever so much easier to get along with somebody if you aren't always having to go to bed with them, when you're tuckered out, and get up with them, when you're still sleepy." As he unburdened intimate details to a virtual stranger, he could not help revealing the deep-seated fears of a man with two failed marriages, who was wary of intimacy with a woman—any woman—lest he fail once again. After two years, he still had a problem sleeping the entire night with Mia. Permitting her to simply leave a robe in his bathroom represented a major breakthrough, as was allowing her hairbrush and shampoo to sit in the cabinet alongside toiletries belonging to Diane Keaton, preserved there like so many fossilized relics in King Tut's tomb for more than a decade.

But even as Woody was speaking to Ebert, his life was changing dramatically. Settling into a relationship with Mia made him feel loved and aroused special feelings of belonging that he had never before experienced. As he would write about the Mia character in *Hannah and Her Sisters*, she made him feel connected to the human race. Making efforts to please her, efforts that already involved major practical concessions, he began to move forward and leave his adolescence behind.

Still, patterns of a lifetime were hard to break. In the habit of sleeping in his own bed, he refused to spend the night at Mia's apartment because the place made him uncomfortable. In contrast to the opulence of his co-op, her sprawling rental at the Langham was well-worn, homey, the kind most New York families with children could only dream of. Overlooking Central Park were three sunny front rooms decorated with woven baskets and needlepoint pillows, floors carpeted with Oriental rugs, and walls lined with books and photographs of the children and Walt Disney characters. In the sitting room stood an old spinet piano heaped with sheet music, because five of her children took lessons. A playroom was filled with a rocking horse, toys, and arts-and-crafts materials. The family ate in the kitchen at a Parson's table, and the housekeeper, Mavis Smith, always left a special baked treat (peanut-butter brownies were a favorite) before going home. "I expected to walk into a noisy, cluttered place," recalled Lorrie Pierce, the children's piano teacher for many years. "But Mia ran an exceptionally organized, orderly household. The apartment was so quiet you could hear a pin drop."

Maybe so, but it could not have compared to the monastic silence of Woody's empty penthouse. Conditions at Mia's, where the bedrooms were stuffed from floor to ceiling with bunk beds, may have brought back unpleasant childhood memories of overcrowded houses and rooms shared with relatives. Equally distasteful were the animals that roamed Mia's apartment as if they owned it. Along with the dog, Mary, and several cats, there were three chinchillas, two hamsters, six mice, four frogs and a turtle, a tank of tropical fish, and several birds—a canary, a parakeet that warbled, and the parrot, Edna. The place always smelled a little stinky to him. "The pets, the cat and the dog, would jump on the kitchen table and eat off the plates," he remembered. Disgusted, he refused to use any utensil in Mia's kitchen and made her keep a supply of paper plates and cardboard cups especially for him.

Disliking her house, he instead invited her for sleepover visits at 930 Fifth Avenue. With all seven children (and sometimes their friends), she would arrive on Friday nights toting sleeping bags, toothbrushes, and toys. The next morning, she dismantled the bivouac and hustled them home for breakfast because Woody needed to write or see his analyst. However, during basketball season, they often met again in the afternoon at the Garden. Woody's explanation of the game was frequently interrupted because he and Mia wound up kissing, "cooing, cuddling, and hugging" at a Philadelphia 76ers game, according to the *New York Daily News*. For the sake of her sons, Mia endured the Knicks but never appreciated sports and quickly tired of pretending she did.

Of all Mia's brood, Woody got along best with the two youngest boys, eight-year-old Fletcher, who begged for play dates with him, and the four-year-old Korean boy who wore big glasses just like Woody. The boy's adoptive name was Misha Amadeus Farrow (Misha was Russian for Michael, Mia's dead brother, and Amadeus because he was born on Mozart's birthday), but Woody found it effeminate and suggested a more manly name, in honor of the Philadelphia 76ers star Moses Malone. The only one of Mia's children who was not the child of Andre Previn, little Moses was always begging hugs and kisses from Woody, whom he worshiped as a father from the first. Whenever he accompanied his mother to work, he wanted Woody to play games and draw pictures, and as he grew older, Woody taught him chess.

Like it or not, Mia's children became part of Woody's existence. His efforts to make friends with them were not easy because he was no more comfortable around children than around adults. But his weekend parenting, such as it was, liberated him from routines that had grown rigid, and this made him feel pleased. He was always telling people about how well he got along with the Previn children. From Mia's point of view, however, he had little regard for her family. Whatever he did—trading his Rolls for a capacious stretch limousine to transport the kids—was never enough. What bothered her most were the distinctions he made between her biological offspring and her adopted Asian youngsters, who, to him, didn't seem like real brothers and sisters to Mia's own kids, no matter what they called one another. It was hard for him to imagine them as one family. To his way of thinking, according to Mia, she seemed to be baby-sitting for UNICEF, without getting paid for it.

In the summer of 1981, shortly before the filming of *A Midsummer Night's Sex Comedy,* Mia fell in love with a sixty-acre farm, Frog Hollow, on the outskirts of Bridgewater, Connecticut, a slumbery country town of 1,600, boasting a post office, a general store, and a gas station, as well as a bank and library. "But if you blink while driving through the town center you would miss the whole thing," said a resident. A rural community with working farms, Bridgewater was situated in wealthy Litchfield County, where celebrities such as Ivan Lendl owned homes. Nearby lived close friends of Mia's, Casey and John Pascal and Bill and Rose Styron. Frog Hollow's two-story, white-frame Colonial house faced a lake that had a small beach, a rocky island in the middle, and two log cabins on the far shore. Hemmed by acres of rolling fields and deep woodlands, it was set back from the main road, but just in case, Mia nailed a white sign to a tree: CAREFUL—CHILDREN PLAYING. That the house was slightly creaky made no difference. Everything about the place enchanted her.

Woody came up to tour the new house. After tramping all over, he found fault with the bathroom, which contained a big antique tub but no shower. Mia installed a new bath and shower just for him.

On his next visit, carrying a white rubber mat, he entered the bathroom only to burst out seconds later.

"The drain is in the middle," he said, taking her to task. Germs would not wash down efficiently without a side drain. Since he was unable to shower, he said, he would be forced to leave first thing in the morning.

Mia sought to please. A new bathroom was built with a shower whose drain was placed in the corner. The children called it "Woody's bathroom" because they were not permitted to use it. But even special plumbing never made him feel at home in Mia's country house. During the day, to protect himself from insects, he would wander around wearing a beekeeper's hat and netting. At night, wishing he had "a gun under the bed," he was too terrified to get a good night's sleep.

At the time Mia was settling down in Bridgewater, Woody suddenly decided that he, too, needed a little hideaway of his own, about an hour from Manhattan, just to get out of the city and perhaps use for location filming as well. With Jean Doumanian as his guide, he paid $3.5 million for a six-bedroom oceanfront estate in Southampton called the Ark, complete with sauna, Jacuzzi, and Nautilus weight room. Throughout the winter of 1982, landscapers carted away a Victorian greenhouse and cut down the beach grass. The manse was renovated, painted, and furnished in pine antiques and Laura Ashley prints to Jean's impeccable standards. But the paint had scarcely dried on the place when Woody changed his mind. "I hated it," he said later. After spending one night at the Ark, he decided to sell, although it took several years to find a buyer for his seaside white elephant.

It was Sunday, the Fourth of July, and Woody sat alone in the air-conditioned darkness of the 86 Street East, watching Steven Spielberg's new thriller *Poltergeist*. After the movie, "I walked around the empty streets," he said. The city was the way he liked it, hushed and practically deserted. All traces of summer heat and humidity suddenly cleared away and the cool, cleansing air hit him in the face. For a change, there were no curious New Yorkers staring at him; nobody stopped him for an autograph. That weekend, Mia and the children were at Frog Hollow, and despite her efforts to make her house comfortable for him, he remained pathological about the place. Sitting hours in traffic just to arrive at a glorified summer camp full of bugs and screeching kids was not his idea of relaxation. He was just as happy spending the holiday in his solitary bedroom with the air conditioner on full blast and the curtains drawn.

For Mia, the dark side of Woody could be frightening. One day while they were strolling down East Seventy-third Street, he pointed out the residence of William Buckley, a maisonette in a Park Avenue building. People like Bill and Pat Buckley represented to him the essence of the 10021 ZIP-code elite. Stopping in front of the Buckley home, he proceeded to give Mia an impromptu tutorial on the local blue bloods.

Several months later, on another walk through the same neighborhood, Mia looked at a building and foggily tried to remember if it was Buckley's address. It wasn't. But what seemed like a perfectly innocuous question—or maybe it was something else entirely—made Woody furious. He lashed out at her for acting stupid, until she broke down in tears on the sidewalk. After that Jekyll and Hyde outburst, she would always be wary of him. Woody understood how much he owed Mia. But however rewarding the relationship, it was accompanied by bonds that chafed, sometimes unbearably. Then, out of the blue would swim blackest rage. In these moments, to get his own way, he thought nothing of throwing tantrums, or more often, withdrawing into his chronic anhedonia, which made normal existence impossible. Because of all this, Mia discovered, his world was more circumscribed than anyone imagined.

Together they might have been the reigning couple of the city's show-business social circuit. On a first-name basis with the cream of New York artists, they were invited everywhere and could have entertained on a grand scale had they wished. As a couple, however, they had a limited circle of joint friends. In a dozen years, about the only couple with whom they ever managed to establish a friendship was the pianist Vladimir Horowitz and his wife, Wanda Toscanini Horowitz, but even that relationship was impersonal and unequal. Woody enjoyed Vladimir's eccentricities and Wanda's offbeat sense of humor. (In 1988 he gave her a small speaking part in *Crimes and Misdemeanors*.) During a typical evening together, they picked up the elderly couple at their brownstone on East Ninety-fourth Street and took them to dinner at Le Bernardin, a midtown seafood restaurant. Since Vladimir ate nothing but fillet of sole and asparagus, Woody's assistant always phoned ahead to make certain that sole was on the menu. After dinner, Horowitz insisted on picking up a copy of the next day's *New York Times* before Woody's chauffeur could drive them uptown. Although Mia always misspelled the eighty-two-year-old pianist's first name, she bore sole responsibility for maintaining the friendship with birthday greetings, bread-and-butter notes, and words of condolence to Wanda when Horowitz died in 1989.

For female companionship, Mia had a coterie of girlfriends dating back to her childhood, but Woody's boyhood gang from Midwood had long since ceased to occupy any place in his life. He had lost contact with Elliott Mills, a research scientist at Duke University Medical School, who lived in North Carolina. However, Jack Victor, a research psychologist, and Jerry Epstein, a psychiatrist, were living in New York. When one Monday Jack showed up at Michael's Pub with his teenage son, Woody handed him his private phone number, but Jack hesitated to use it. Over the years, Jack and Jerry occasionally saw Woody from afar at Madison Square Garden but never approached him.

*   *   *

One of Woody's regular dining spots was Rao's, a tiny Italian restaurant at 114th Street in East Harlem with home-style food and only eight tables (and no credit cards accepted), which was always filled weeks in advance by celebrity customers. Both he and Mia enjoyed the owner's daughter-in-law, Anna Rao, a woman with a towering bouffant hairstyle, stiletto heels, dark glasses, a cigarette hanging out of her mouth, and a wry sense of humor. When one evening Mia remarked that she had always wanted to play that type of woman, Woody was happily amazed. Never would he have imagined such unusual casting. Soon, however, he was busy working on a screenplay with an Anna Rao–type character for Mia.

In his third picture for Orion, he returned to the years before he had made it, when as a struggling comedy writer in the fifties, he hung around joints such as Lindy's and observed the usual cast of characters: the small-time agents, the third-rate singers, the women who looked just like Anna Rao. Danny Rose, an unsuccessful theatrical manager, is known for making virtually any sacrifice to nurture his acts. Trying to make a comeback is Danny's biggest client, Lou Canova, an overweight, over-the-hill Italian pop singer with a big ego and a drinking problem, who, though married, is having an affair with the widow of a mafioso. Danny Rose is grooming Lou for the big-time, but Lou can't perform unless his mistress, Tina Vitale, is present. Against his better judgment, Danny agrees to play his decoy.

To portray the floozy girlfriend, hard as nails and straight out of *Guys and Dolls,* Mia got busy transforming herself into an Italian-American with teased blond hair, dark glasses, and a nasal Brooklyn accent. She was no problem. The problem was casting the singer. To get a cross between a third-rate Vic Damone and a Buddy Hackett, Woody saw scores of candidates, even considered well-known ethnic actors such as Robert De Niro and Danny Aiello. Nobody seemed right. In desperation, his casting director cruised Colony Records on Broadway, scooping up all the schmaltzy albums she could find. One of them, *Can I Depend on You?,* containing original compositions, including "Agit'a," a novelty song about indigestion, was by an Italian-American singer by the name of Nick Apollo Forte. "So we started tracking him down and found him singing in Waterbury," Juliet Taylor recalled. "It's as though he had been waiting for this big break."

Taylor's discovery in person was a beefy, dimpled crooner of forty-five, precisely right for the part of Lou Canova. According to Forte, "they just went bananas over me." As Jack Rollins remarked to him, "It was a great day when you met Woody but it was a better day when he met you." Forte felt reborn.

Nick Apollo Forte had never acted before. A nightclub singer, cocktail pianist, songwriter, and part-time tuna fisherman, he lived in Waterbury, Connecticut, with his wife and seven children. Forte was frustrated. His club act and ethnic and country albums enabled him to educate his kids and put in an octagonal, in-ground swimming pool in his backyard, but he was tired of working Holiday Inns for $100 a night. His dream was to play Las Vegas and Atlantic City, with luck, maybe even the Grand Ole Opry. According to Forte, he had never seen a Woody Allen picture.

Principal photography on *Broadway Danny Rose* began in the fall of 1982. Typically, Woody did few takes, on average four, but he preferred two. Most actors caught on immediately but if not, Woody corrected them or rewrote the lines. Or fired them. In the case of Nick Forte, not easily replaceable, he found himself giving acting lessons. Forte, who considered himself "easy to work with," didn't hold this against Woody, who he concluded must be "a perfectionist." In one scene, Danny Rose and Lou Canova are supposed to cross the street, but Forte, as Woody recalled it, "just couldn't get it." After plodding through the scene fifty times, the greatest number of takes Allen had done before (or since), the singer finally got it right, by which time Woody was ready to dial his therapist.

No matter, because Forte, quite rightly, received raves from the critics, who felt he stole the movie with a standout supporting performance that should earn an Oscar nomination. His telephone would not stop ringing. He was signed by International Creative Management, one of the biggest talent agencies in the business. Johnny Carson invited him to appear on *The Tonight Show,* and Gene Siskel wrote him up for the *Chicago Tribune.* Fielding job offers, he got four nights at the Sands Hotel in Atlantic City, and, from NBC, a forty-thousand-dollar contract for a sitcom pilot. Just to be on the safe side, however, he sunk his movie earnings into a commercial fishing boat for giant tuna.

Six months later, the brilliant career was over. The phone never rang. NBC replaced him with James Coco, and Johnny Carson forgot him. His agent was fired for mismanagement. Even the giant tunas let him down.

Favorable reviews did not translate into a healthy box office for *Broadway Danny Rose,* which grossed a measly $10.6 million. The picture received two Oscar nominations for Woody's direction and screenwriting, but the Academy ignored Nick Apollo Forte. Mia, for once not playing herself, gave one of the best performances of her career and received a Golden Globe nomination from the Hollywood Foreign Press Association.

In the middle of shooting *Broadway Danny Rose,* Woody hired a personal assistant. Jane Read Martin, a graduate of Denison University, began her career at NBC on *Saturday Night Live* as a girl Friday to one of the regular players, Jane Curtin, before becoming Jean Doumanian's secretary. Martin was a tall, smiling blonde of twenty-four, flexible and conveniently single, but her main qualification for the job seemed to be unquestioning adulation. She was a fanatical admirer of Woody Allen.

Jane's father, Henry, was a *New Yorker* cartoonist, and her older sister, Ann, would shortly became a best-selling author of a paperback series of children's books about baby-sitting (The Baby-Sitters Club). By the mid-nineties, Ann M. Martin would sell 130 million copies, making her the Jackie Collins of preteen-girl readers and a millionaire presiding over a booming mini-industry, with licensing agreements for dolls, board games, and a TV series. Jane, meanwhile, was struggling to make a career in television production.

Martin's duties were extensive. Since her boss disliked talking to people, she became his alter ego, anticipating his needs, fielding requests for his time and attention, straightening up messes. She knew how to get things done. In his personal affairs, she acted as Woody's Swiss guard and shielded him from aggravation, providing a kind of buffer between him and the outside world. She attended to the menial jobs that celebrities need not do for themselves, the thank yous, gifts, flowers, and returned phone calls. When Woody had to travel, it was Jane who planned the itineraries and handled reservations. For good measure, to ensure things went smoothly, she accompanied Woody and Mia on their trips to Europe. As time passed, Jane wielded more and more power.

The competent personal assistant completed the trilogy of Woody's female support system: Mia, his mate at home, Jean Doumanian to provide faithful sororal support, and Jane Martin as his adoring office wife, who fussed over him from morning until night, developing inevitably a powerful rivalry with his home wife. Unlike Norma Lee Clark, the prissy secretary to whom Woody never uttered a personal word in ten years, Martin saw herself as Woody's friend. Holed up downtown at the Rollins and Joffe office, Clark continued to screen calls, sort mail, and write romances. But Martin's ten- to twelve-hour days left no time for anything but Woody. To the joking suggestion that she would be the perfect person to write a book about him, she laughed and said she couldn't because "she would be sued. She knows too much."

■ ■ ■ ■ ■ ■

The Box Office:

Year		*Domestic grosses in millions
1977	*Annie Hall*	39.2
1979	*Manhattan*	45.7
1983	*Zelig*	11.8
1984	*Broadway Danny Rose*	10.6
1985	*The Purple Rose of Cairo*	10.6

*Not adjusted for inflation.

■ ■ ■ ■ ■ ■

Woody had always preferred dreams to real life. By the time he was ten, he discovered his two ideal refuges from reality: the gloomy Konigsberg cellar, where he could thumb through his comic books in peace, and dark movie houses, where he doted on romantic comedies about people whose lives were lived in penthouses and nightclubs. In November of 1983, he began shooting a film in which he used some of this autobiographical material.

The Purple Rose of Cairo is about a waitress living in a small town during the Depression. She is an ardent movie fan who has managed to break through the wall between flesh and fantasy. Cecilia peels a fictional character off the screen and pulls him into the nonfictional audience at the Jewel theater. Of course, film buffs could not help recognizing the plot's similiarity to a previous movie. In 1924 Buster Keaton filmed *Sherlock, Jr.,* about a movie projectionist who, after dozing off, climbs through the screen and is drawn into the celluloid action of the picture. The very mention of Keaton's silent comedy made Woody huffy. *Sherlock, Jr.* was "in no remote way an inspiration," he said a bit testily, and besides, Keaton had never been a favorite of his. Favorite or not, he might well have been copying Keaton's classic, just as he borrowed from Ingmar Bergman and George S. Kaufman, among others. On the other hand, he may have simply been massaging Woody Allen. In his 1977 *New Yorker* story, "The Kugelmass Episode," a college professor achieves a similar type of fantasy when he enters a magician's literary cabinet and finds himself a character in *Madame Bovary.*

Although the movie-fan story seemed to be truly about himself as a kid, Woody decided not to play the starry Cecilia. Emphatically distancing himself—"there was just no part for me," he insisted—he gave the role to Mia.

Principal photography began in Piermont, New York, a small town on the Hudson River that had the correct gritty look of a thirties factory area. (Some interiors were filmed in Midwood, at the Kent theater, where Woody went as a boy.) Shooting got off to a bad start. For his hero, Tom Baxter, Woody hired Michael Keaton at $250,000, a quarter of his normal fee. But after ten days he had second thoughts and abruptly replaced him, which involved scrapping the footage and buying him out. (Woody said Keaton didn't look like a 1935 person after all, but word leaked out from the location that Woody was not pleased with his scenes.) After approaching Kevin Kline, he hastily signed Jeff Daniels, who had been acclaimed for his performance in *Terms of Endearment.*

Never completely satisfied with any of his films, Woody would nevertheless rank *The Purple Rose of Cairo* as his best picture, at least the one that came closest to his original concept. Later on, he also admitted that Cecilia, of all his created characters, was the one with whom he most closely identified. *Purple Rose* received some of the best reviews of his career. In the opinion of

Time's Richard Schickel, it was nothing less than "one of the best movies about movies ever made." For a change, even the hard-nosed Pauline Kael seemed impressed by the writing and characterizations: "This is the first Woody Allen movie in which a whole batch of actors really interact and spark each other." Among the minority was Woody's passionate detractor John Simon, who compared the picture to an unpopular vegetable: "I say a purple rose is a purple rose, whether as film or as film-within-film, and either way, it's spinach and to hell with it." At the box office, however, audiences too must have smelled spinach because they stayed away. Despite superb reviews, the picture lost money.

For Woody personally, *The Purple Rose of Cairo* would be memorable. One day he was auditioning women to play prostitutes in the brothel scene. As he sat in his office and the door opened and closed, bunches of actresses routinely came and went. In one of the groups, however, he was captivated by a particular woman in her mid-thirties, not really young, not traditionally pretty, either. What's more, she seemed to be handicapped by a peculiar squint, a quavery, Minnie Mouse speaking voice, and a dismaying number of nervous mannerisms. Still, she was the one who "lit up the room," and he immediately decided to use her. After displaying Dianne Wiest in a spectacular cameo, he subsequently elevated her to stardom and she repaid him with interest—three Oscars for *Hannah and Her Sisters, Radio Days,* and *Bullets Over Broadway.* He was to describe her, as he once said reverently of Diane Keaton, as "one of the greatest actresses in America," and his flirtatious manner around her would eventually cause Mia to become suspicious about the nature of their off-camera relationship.

At the time, however, it was Mia who occupied the central position in his life and work. *The Purple Rose of Cairo,* her fourth picture with him, firmly established her in the public imagination as Woody's muse. Hereafter, whenever he released a new film, everyone knew the leading character was fashioned for her special capability. Woody never talked of love; he talked of loyalty, dependability, and obedience. Mia would show up on the set and do whatever he asked. "If you ask her to play nasty, she does it," he said. "If you want her to play something sexy, she does it." In Andrew Sarris's view, Mia had been "more interesting in other things" and Woody, by imposing line readings, only "diminished her." But these early Mia-Woody films struck Vincent Canby as "love letters. He obviously admired her tremendously. She'd always been an accomplished actress—though never a comedienne—and he got performances from her that no other director ever could have gotten."

Soon after meeting Woody, Mia more or less stopped looking for work. Her pay was not extravagant by any means—$150,000 a picture with gradual increases to $375,000—but it was sufficient to live on. Twice she ventured off on her own (a voice-over for an animated film, *The Last Unicorn,* in 1982, followed by a cameo in *Supergirl,* a disastrous British offshoot of *Superman*) but he discouraged her from working elsewhere. In practical terms, his shooting schedule made other films difficult. Year in, year out, he would start shooting in September or October and continue right through Christmas, sometimes into February. Then, after a few weeks' layoff, he would begin reshoots, sometimes extensive reshoots, more than half of the picture, as one phase of production seemed to segue into the next. In June, when he began preproduction for his next project, she and the children moved to Frog Hollow for the summer. "And that was my life," she said. In time, she convinced herself that working for another director would have damaged their personal relationship.

For all her experience as an actress, she lacked the single essential ingredient for becoming a big star: ambition. Children were her main priority. Collaboration with Woody meant job security and convenience. Unlike most film actors, who must leave home for extended periods in order to work, she could remain in New York in what amounted to regular nine-to-five employment. Her children, along with their baby-sitters, accompanied her to work, thus turning every set into a nursery and day care center.

■ ■ ■ ■ ■ ■ ■

March of Time:
PLAYBOY: Would you like to have children?
ALLEN: Eight or twelve little blonde girls. I love blonde girls.
—Interview, 1967

In His Own Words:
"Mia has a talent for mothering the way some people have a green thumb for gardening, or an ear for music, or a talent for medicine. It's no chore for her."
—WOODY ALLEN, 1989

■ ■ ■ ■ ■ ■

Along with Donald and Ivana Trump and Lonnie and Burt Reynolds, Woody Allen and Mia Farrow became one of the most famous couples of the eighties, to all appearances the picture of compatibility, a pair so much in love they could spend twenty-four hours a day together as partners on screen and off. But behind the glamorous public image raged a silent struggle dating back to their first months of courtship five years earlier. Mia wanted to marry. Woody resisted. Almost fifty now, he was not receptive to an arrangement that, he told her, boiled down to nothing but an irrelevant piece of paper. Theirs was a more honest form of matrimony, a relationship based entirely on love and trust. Besides, he insisted, didn't he behave as a husband? Angry, but poor at confrontation, Mia pretended to acquiesce. In reality, she possessed iron determination and to get what she wanted, a friend said, she "simply used passive-aggressive tactics." If she could not become Mrs. Woody Allen, she wanted to have a child, even one out of wedlock. Woody's response was guarded. She would have to assume complete responsibility, meaning the child would live with her and require none of his involvement. With that understanding, Mia tried for months to conceive. Finally, worried because she was almost forty, she suggested adoption. Once again, he agreed, although not enthusiastically. Whenever she talked about the adoption, which was constantly, he impatiently changed the subject. He cared nothing about babies, he said, only his work. Undaunted, she forewent her usual international adoption and instead applied for a blond, blue-eyed American female infant, exactly the kind of child, she admitted later, who might be most likely to appeal to him.

In July 1985, Mia and her twelve-year old, Soon-Yi, flew to Texas to fetch the newborn. Mia named her Dylan O'Sullivan Farrow, after Dylan Thomas, and asked her friend Casey Pascal to be godmother. At first Woody ignored the baby, whom Mia carried in a sling over her chest. "I had no pronounced feeling one way or the other," he was to recall. In just a few weeks, however, the bald, apple-cheeked infant was working her way into his heart. "Gosh," he thought, "she's pretty cute."

After years in which he seldom spent any time in Mia's home, he was there every day. He even asked for a key. One evening on his way to Mia's, he found himself stuck in a cab in traffic. Like a man possessed, he jumped out and ran several blocks to get there before Dylan's bedtime. The change in his behavior was extraordinary. "I got a great thrill out of pushing the baby cart and taking walks with her," he said. "I'd set the alarm for 5 in the morning, and get out of bed and be at Mia's house by 6:15. I wanted Dylan to feel that her father was there, even though Mia and I didn't live together." A short time later, he decided that he wanted to coadopt her. But there was a problem: New York State did not allow unmarried couples to adopt children. Woody had one of his attorneys begin working to find a loophole in the adoption law. He also proposed adopting seven-year-old Moses, who felt deprived because his older brothers and sisters had Andre, but he had no father. Knowing that he would be included in the adoption of Dylan meant a great deal to him, and the idea understandably delighted Mia.

Until then, Woody had been adamant about a separate residence. Overnight, he began talking about the possibility of living together as a family. There is reason to doubt that he wanted to cohabit with Mia's entire brood—and the dog, cat, parrot, hamsters, canary, and tropical fish—but in order to be with Dylan, he had to accept the rest of them. He and Mia began looking at houses and duplex penthouse apartments, places that could accommodate eight children and two adults, but still large enough to give Woody private space. One of the properties under consideration was Harkness House, the luxurious four-story mansion around the corner on East Seventy-fifth Street, the setting of his famous New Year's Eve party. The 1886 town house, lavishly renovated in the sixties by the late philanthropist Rebekah Harkness for her ballet school, was for sale. The asking price, $9.75 million, was a record for residential real estate in the city (the market price of Woody's penthouse, for example, was now about $7 million). After three inspections, Woody did not buy Harkness House, nor did he take the mansion on Beekman Place or the five-million-dollar twin town houses in the West Village.

Finally, they saw the house of their dreams on East Seventy-third Street, a property even more splendid than the Harkness mansion. Built on two lots, the house boasted sunny rooms and a small garden, where Mia pictured herself puttering about and planting strawberries and jasmine. She immediately invoked the MGM movie *Meet Me in St. Louis* and a picture of cozy serenity just like that of the turn-of-the-century Smith family. In the garden, Dylan would have her own sandbox and swings, while Woody would happily play Ping-Pong and Mia would lie reading in the hammock, her mother, Maureen, picking out old favorites on the grand piano. There would be no more trips to the park, because the children would be able to run outside whenever they felt like it, and Mia would never have to worry about their safety. It would be living in New York but not living in New York. In their big house on the Upper East Side, surrounded by high walls and apple trees, they would surely be as happy as the Smith clan, laughing and crying in their Victorian house, in their Technicolor MGM musical, directed by Vincente Minnelli. It was a fairy tale. But Mia believed in fairy tales.

By the time Woody bid on the *Meet Me in St. Louis* house, the owner had changed his mind about selling. Several months passed. Woody still loved "pushing the baby cart," but there was less talking of living together and the celluloid fantasy was quietly shelved. Given their incompatibility, he decided, their relationship as it now stood was "a workable compromise for both of us." In any case, there were other considerations. "I like to sleep with the air-conditioning on, while she doesn't like air-conditioning."

■ ■ ■ ■ ■ ■

Moving Pictures:
ELLIOTT (after sleeping with his wife's sister): She's a wonderful woman and I've betrayed her. She came into my empty life and

changed it and I repaid her by banging her sister in a hotel room. God, how despicable. . . .

—Hannah and Her Sisters, 1987

■ ■ ■ ■ ■ ■ ■

In the mid-eighties, Woody wrote two inviting stories about family life: *Hannah and Her Sisters,* a return to the *Interiors* theme of sisters in conflict, and *Radio Days,* in which he re-created the topsy-turvy domestic chaos of his own family during World War II. Making these pair of back-to-back films at this particular juncture in his life reflected his intense exploration into the idea of parenthood during the period when Mia was trying to get pregnant. They also suited the tenor of the decade that saw Ronald Reagan in the middle of his second term and a country that had turned sharply conservative.

According to Woody, he took his inspiration for *Hannah and Her Sisters,* a title he conceived before writing the script, from Leo Tolstoy's 1870s novel *Anna Karenina,* which begins with the familiar observation that all happy families are alike, but each unhappy family is unhappy in its own way. But as Mia knew, *Hannah* was basically a home movie of her Farrow family. The script contained the kind of inside knowledge a wife tells her husband in confidence: the rivalries and petty complaints; infidelities and quarrels; the substance abuse; all the unforgotten traumas that her family pretended did not happen. Reading the sisters script, she felt betrayed. What's more, it rearoused her old suspicions of Woody and her sister Steffi. It was no secret that Woody found sisters fascinating, even sexually arousing; he had often spoken of Janet Margolin and her two sisters, and Diane Keaton and her sisters, Dorrie and Robin. Mia told herself that she was being too sensitive— Woody was an artist and artists always transformed this kind of personal material. However, the thinly veiled portrait of the Farrows embarrassed and outraged others in the family, particularly her mother, whom the script described as "a boozy old flirt with a filthy mouth." In the end, everyone told one another it was only a movie, and pretended to be flattered. The seventy-five-year-old Maureen accepted the part of Mia's mother, her first featured role in twenty years.

Covering two years in the life of an artistic New York clan, the story unfolds around Hannah, one of three sisters, a successful actress who is the bulwark as well as primary enabler of her dysfunctional WASP family. Like Mia, the dependable Hannah has a brood of children, including twin sons and several adopted children. Hannah's younger sister, Lee (Barbara Hershey), is a recovering alcoholic trapped in an abusive affair with a surly SoHo painter (Max von Sydow); another sister is the scatterbrained Holly (Dianne Wiest), a neurotic cocaine addict who skitters from catering to acting to writ-

178

ing. Hannah's quarrelsome parents are played by Lloyd Nolan and Maureen O'Sullivan. For this picture, Woody split himself into two characters: Hannah's former husband, Mickey Sachs (Woody), a hypochondriacal television producer, who represents Woody's good-boy side; and her current spouse, Elliott (Michael Caine), Woody's bad-boy side, who has an affair with his wife's sister Lee.

In the fall of 1984, principal photography began inside Mia's own apartment at the Langham. For several months the production completely disrupted the lives of Mia's children, who found themselves living on a movie set. All of them agreed to appear in the film, but only Fletcher, Daisy, and Moses had lines. Since the Screen Actors Guild required tutoring on the set for principals, On Location Education provided a licensed teacher for the three younger children. The classroom was the girls' bedroom, the only room in the apartment not ripped apart. Tutor Jean Reynolds recalled that "the apartment was chaotic because of the technical people with their equipment and lights, but the classroom was off-limits to them. With all this going on in the house, it was incredible to see how Mia always had time for the children. Woody also stopped by to play with Moses—it was obvious they had a very nice relationship."

More than 80 percent of the film was rewritten and reshot. The original version ended pessimistically with Elliott still in love with Lee but staying married to Hannah. In the revised script, although Hannah and Elliott's marriage is still a farce, the final scene focuses on Mickey and Holly as she sweetly tells her husband she is pregnant—a kind of miracle baby because Mickey believed himself to be infertile. Years later, Woody regretted tacking on the pregnancy, saying he had tied up the threads too neatly.

Hannah and Her Sisters shows a Woody liberated from many of his problems as a writer and director. The main subject remains himself, but he has dispensed with the existential hand-wringing, the ambitious homages to Bergman and Fellini. Instead, the beautifully crafted screenplay shows a heartfelt celebration of family life on the Upper West Side, as close to Norman Rockwell as Woody would ever get. A whirlwind tour of the city's architectural wonders—the Beaux-Arts façade of the Ansonia, the splendor of the Chrysler Building, charming town houses tucked away on Pomander Walk—were photographed by Woody's new cinematographer, Carlo Di Palma, who was known for his work on Antonioni films. (After eight pictures, Gordon Willis left to work for other directors.) *Hannah* shows another side of Woody, not the hard-edged, repressed neurotic but a mature man in love with his partner and taking pleasure in the idea of parenthood. Because the film opens and closes with homey Thanksgiving dinners, it would become an immensely popular television movie during the holidays.

His biggest hit since *Annie Hall* and the one film most in tune with the values of mainstream America, *Hannah* would be nominated for seven Academy Awards, including Best Picture (it lost to Oliver Stone's *Platoon*). It won Oscars for Woody (Best Original Screenplay) and for Michael Caine and Dianne Wiest (Best Supporting Actor and Actress). Although her performance as a sloppy drunk received no awards, Maureen O'Sullivan received the best notices of her entire career. In the *New York Times,* Vincent Canby wrote that she "never had five minutes on the screen to equal her work here." Ecstatic, Maureen praised Woody as "a very wonderful person—kind, good, and straight," and equated him with George Cukor, who was famous for his skill in directing women. Her career suddenly rejuvenated, she was offered a role in Francis Coppola's *Peggy Sue Got Married.*

Hannah and Her Sisters opened to rave reviews. Leading the critics singing Woody's praises were Andrew Sarris, who, after singling out *Manhattan* as the best film of the seventies, now called *Hannah* "the great American film of the '80s," and Woody's friend Vincent Canby, who labeled him the country's "only authentic auteur" and "the urban poet of our anxious age."

For his next picture, Woody paid a nostalgic visit to his old Brooklyn neighborhood during World War II. Narrated by Woody, who does not appear in the movie, *Radio Days* is more an oral history of a family than a real story. With more than two hundred characters and a dozen separate vignettes, it has several plots loosely strung together into a collage: Woody's alter ego, Little Joe (Seth Green), whose favorite show is the *Masked Avenger,* is the son of "two people who could find an argument in any subject"; Joe's spinster aunt, Bea (Dianne Wiest), only wants to get married; and Sally White (Mia) is an ambitious nightclub cigarette girl who becomes a radio star. Using dozens of locations throughout the city, Woody cut back and forth between the glamorous big city, where the radio shows originate, and the everyday lives of listeners, leagues away in the outer boroughs. At its most effective, *Radio Days* is a happy, likable film that perfectly evokes the textures of those years when every living room had a majestic floor model or a tabletop mahogany box, and people sat glued to their radios, listening to *The Major Bowes Amateur Hour,* the adventure tales of *The Lone Ranger,* and contestants trying to guess song titles on *Name That Tune.* But without a story or strong central characters, it tends to be thin and aimless.

Some critics saw *Radio Days* as a retread of Neil Simon's play *Brighton Beach Memoirs* or Federico Fellini's 1974 anecdotal memoir of growing up, *Amarcord.* The nostalgia did not appeal to Pauline Kael, who cruelly anatomized Woody as an old-timey movie pasha from the lump-in-the-throat school of moviemaking. "Woody Allen has found in himself the heartfelt coyness of Louis B. Mayer—without the redeeming vulgar joyfulness." But *Radio Days* had passionate admirers, among them Vincent Canby, who was reminded of Proust, and Richard Schickel, of Chekhov. These grandiose literary allusions on the part of his reviewing colleagues made John Simon roll his eyes in wonderment. "What's left for Woody to look forward to?" he mused. "Shakespeare, I guess."

"I think this may be my last New Year's Eve," Woody said. "I think I've outgrown it."

He was sitting with Gene Siskel, in the Fortune Gardens Chinese restaurant on Third Avenue, at 2 P.M. on December 31, 1985. Foregoing his usual deli tuna sandwich, he was having a sit-down luncheon interview with the personable *Chicago Tribune* critic. Privately, Woody enjoyed poking fun at both Siskel and Roger Ebert, wickedly dubbing them "the Chicago morons," a perverse salute to their enormous influence as leading newspaper critics as well as national tastemakers on their popular "thumbs up–thumbs down" television show *Sneak Previews*. Thrown over a nearby chair lay Woody's green army jacket. In his everyday uniform of faded gray slacks and a lumpy pullover sweater, and a day-old beard, he had an air of stylish scruffiness. When the waiter appeared, he asked for a double order of shrimp dumplings, wonton soup, spring rolls, and a bottle of Heineken beer.

That evening Woody planned to toast the new year with Mia, and Diane Keaton, visiting from the Coast. After dinner they were going to a party. "If I had my way we wouldn't go out," he said. Parties still terrified him, as did elevators. (Sometimes he walked up twenty flights of stairs.) Fortunately the elevator would be no problem that night because the party was at a town house.

Tucking in his shrimp dumplings with a pair of chopsticks, he embarked on a paean to adoptions. "It's a wonderful, wonderful thing," he told Siskel. For the first time he could "see the joy of it" himself because he was "in on it from the very beginning. I was there when she got off the plane from Texas with the baby." Most days Mia brought six-month-old Dylan to the set, usually accompanied by a pretty baby-sitter, Rebecca Miller (daughter of playwright Arthur Miller). No sooner did Woody glimpse Dylan than he dropped everything and ran over to take her in his arms, then continued to direct while holding her. Whenever another person wanted to take her, he became noticeably jealous. To capture her attention again, he would make faces, put his cap on her head, and kiss her belly, until she screamed with laughter.

After lunch, Woody remained in a good mood. With Gene Siskel in tow, he headed back to Julia Richman High School on East Sixty-seventh Street, where he was shooting classroom scenes on the top floor with a group of children. As baby Dylan was not there, Woody read the *New York Times* entertainment section between takes. At 4:30 everyone but Woody gathered for cake and champagne. Already he was on his way to Central Park West. That December afternoon, Gene Siskel felt certain that he was witnessing a turning point in Woody's career. Despite his neuroses, he was "a happy man," and his new picture was "the life-affirming work" of a director at the height of his game.

Nineteen eighty-five, the year Woody turned fifty, was a vintage year. In a few weeks his fourteenth film was scheduled to "open wide" on four hundred screens. Well ahead of time, the media was calling *Hannah and Her Sisters* his best film ever, another breakthrough. Once again he would ascend to the top of the hill, to bask in the glory of a big film and a domestic box-office gross of $40.1 million, his first commercial hit in five years. But for Woody, the year about to close had brought him an experience far richer than mere commercial triumph. Into his life had unexpectedly entered fantastic happiness, someone upon whom he could shower all the love he had to give. If she happened to be a baby, what was wrong with that?

CHAPTER TWELVE

Dead Sharks

Woody told his mother that Mia was pregnant.

"By you?" she said.

"I guess so," he replied.

Nettie was not the only one to react with hostility. Letty, too, was horrified to learn that her fifty-one-year-old brother had fathered a child with "a second-rate actress, a bad mother, a completely dishonest person." There was bad blood between Mia and the suspicious Letty, who always believed, she said later, that Mia had "a grand plan to meet Woody, have a relationship with him, be in his films, and eventually have his child." The person least pleased by the news, however, seemed to be Woody himself, which seems odd given the fervor with which he embraced parenthood with Dylan, who was not quite two years old. Presumably, more children simply did not interest him very much at that point, and he made no effort to hide his annoyance. Just about the only one celebrating the unexpected pregnancy was Mia, who had given up trying to conceive after the adoption of Dylan. Dispirited over Woody's indifference, which she knew was not her imagination, she withdrew emotionally and even considered breaking off with him.

In her own family, the news that she was pregnant with Woody's child shocked the children, particularly Soon-Yi, who "just hated him," recalled her sister Lark. She burst into angry tears and cried that Woody was ugly and awful-tempered, and the baby would be just like him. In the outside world, the news was greeted with skepticism. On *The Tonight Show,* Garry Shandling jokingly predicted that the baby would be born on a Monday night "so of course Woody won't be there to accept it. He'll be playing his clarinet at Michael's Pub."

A few years earlier the pregnancy might have inspired Woody to marry. If he needed no piece of paper to prove his commitment, a child might one day view it differently. But their relationship had grown complicated, and apparently not even Mia felt that the birth of a baby was sufficient reason for marriage. She charged into Woody's dressing room at the Kaufman-Astoria Studios and warned him not to become emotionally attached to the child because, she said, "I don't think this relationship is going to go anyplace," a threat that left him shaking. As he knew full well, he had no parental rights over Dylan. In his bones he must have sensed that should he and Mia split up, she would never let him see Dylan again.

That summer he took the family to Europe, where they toured Paris, Stockholm, Venice, and Luxembourg by van and limo, with the capable Jane Martin smoothing the way. During the days the family went sight-seeing while Woody holed up in the separate room that Jane always booked so that he might have a private bath and privacy for writing. In London, in the middle of an interview with the BBC, he was asked how he felt about becoming a father at his age. He replied, "I hope it's a she. That would be very important for me." Back in New York, those hopes were dashed when amniocentesis showed that the child would be a boy. After hearing the results of the test, he became disinterested in the new baby. Unlike most expectant fathers, he never wanted to touch Mia's stomach or feel the fetus kick. A few weeks before her due date, he told Roger Ebert that "I love Dylan so much that I would be pleasantly surprised if I love the baby we are having as much as the one we adopted." Although he liked to refer to himself as Dylan's adoptive father, he was not her legal parent, nor did the attorneys he had consulted offer hope of that ever happening.

On a Saturday morning, December 19, 1987, a nine-pound four-ounce son was delivered by cesarean section at New York University Medical Center. Because Woody felt reluctant about participating, Casey Pascal acted as Mia's Lamaze coach during labor. At the last minute, however, he overcame his squeamishness and decided to be present in the delivery room, but told Mia that he would leave if he felt queasy. In the end, he remained for the entire procedure, even though, he said later, it was "not my idea of a fun Saturday morning."

In the hospital, he and Mia began fighting over the name for their child. She refused to name the boy Ingmar, and she was not crazy about his second choice, either—Satchel, after Leroy "Satchel" Paige, a black baseball player who was the most famous pitcher in the Negro Leagues in the forties. Woody was adamant, and in the end she went along. But she gave Satchel her own family surnames—O'Sullivan Farrow. Filling out the birth certificate form, she omitted Woody's name altogether, an oversight on the part of the hospital, she told him when he objected. Besides, she was unsure if he wanted his name on the certificate of an illegitimate child. When she came home from the hospital, he tried to be helpful and picked up the tab for a private nurse, but they remained at odds. Mia's recovery from the cesarean was slow. As for Satchel, he was a colicky infant who seemed to scream night and day. During the first week, she used a supplemental nutrition system, thin tubes taped to each breast to carry formula from a plastic bottle to the nursing baby. Ignoring the practical point of the tubes—to assist newborns with sucking problems—Woody regarded the device as unnecessary. The idea of breast-feeding made him uneasy.

Every morning he dropped by Mia's apartment to have breakfast with Dylan. Sometimes he would find her crying outside Mia's closed bedroom door. Usually Dylan glued herself to Mia whenever she was feeding Satchel, which Woody could not help noticing, and he also understood—up to a point—that sibling rivalry with a newborn was normal. Nevertheless, he decided that Dylan was being neglected and that it was his duty to make up for her mother's lack of attention. His efforts to spend even more time with his little daughter was upsetting to Mia. He was monopolizing Dylan, she complained, while at the same time he never touched or held his son. In these conflicts, one thing led to another, and soon, she was accusing him of finding her unattractive, which infuriated Woody. Possibly her complaints cut too close to the bone. Turned off by the process of pregnancy, birth, and lactation, he may not have found her enticing. She also looked matronly, not her usual slender, ethereal self. Eventually the birth of Satchel would expose all the painful fault lines in their relationship.

■ ■ ■ ■ ■ ■ ■

In His Own Words:
"It's a healthy thing to fail a couple of times, because then you know you're on the right track."
—WOODY ALLEN, 1983

Eyewitness:
"He's a magpie who picks up ideas from here and there, and makes something of them."
—WALTER BERNSTEIN

■ ■ ■ ■ ■ ■ ■

"I was numb," recalled Eric Pleskow, one of the Orion officers. Just after New Year 1987, he learned that Woody wanted to scrap his new release, *September*, and start again from scratch because he was unhappy with several of the performances. The news sent shock waves through the studio's executive suites. Discarding a picture that had completed principal photography was unusual, if not unheard of. It had never happened in Pleskow's experience. On the other hand, when had Woody liked any of his pictures? At one point, intensely displeased with *Manhattan*, he offered Orion another film for free if they would agree to junk it. This time, however, he would not be talked out of his decision to shoot the picture twice. "Look at the body of work,"

Pleskow said defensively years later. "We weren't going to destroy a relationship over that one thing."

Instead of taking the matter out of Woody's hands, once again the Orion chieftains based business decisions on personal feeling. "We never rejected anything he brought us," Pleskow said emphatically. "Not once. Not at UA, not at Orion. In any case, his scripts are road maps and they are always unique, *September* included." He added, "This is where the Medici princes come in. There is no other Woody Allen. If you want to be associated with a man like that, you can't apply the ordinary standards and rules of business."

The story idea for *September* came, indirectly, from Mia. Strolling around Frog Hollow with Woody one day, she made an offhand remark that Chekhov had set his plays in a country house like hers. "This would make a great setting for a little Russian play or something," she said. "It would be fun to shoot up here. The kids would love it."

Inspired, Woody wrote a chamber piece with a small cast and a single set, in this case six people in an isolated Vermont summer house who, like the people in *Interiors,* talk endlessly and accomplish nothing. (Woody does not appear on-screen.) He deliberately gave the film a senseless title "that doesn't suggest anything to anybody until the movie is over," and to most viewers not even then. When shooting at Frog Hollow became out of the question because it was wintertime, Santo Loquasto re-created the house on a soundstage at Kaufman-Astoria, where shooting began in the fall of 1986.

September is about a suicidal woman, Lane, who at the age of fourteen accepted the blame for shooting her actress mother's brutish gangster lover (a roman à clef about the Lana Turner–Johnny Stompanato–Cheryl Crane scandal). Twenty-five years later, Lane is recovering from a nervous breakdown, but her boozy movie-star mother is still going strong. Another plot wrinkle involves Lane's unhappiness after she has fallen in love with Peter, an unpublished novelist who lives nearby. In the mother-daughter roles Woody once again cast Mia and Maureen O'Sullivan, and for the writer he chose one of his favorite actors, Christopher Walken (Annie's nutty brother in *Annie Hall*). Although Woody was eager to use Walken again, disagreements arose. "We couldn't get copacetic," he explained afterward. Walken's replacement was the star playwright–actor Sam Shepard, the Pulitzer prize–winning author of numerous serious works as well as a heartthrob actor in popular films such as *The Right Stuff* (he played the astronaut Chuck Yeager). Woody couldn't get copacetic with Shepard, either. Once he gave Shepard permission to improvise a speech, and the actor brazenly launched into a monologue about Montana. Woody almost blew a fuse. In private, he huffed to Dianne Wiest, who was playing Lane's best friend, "Montana? Montana?" No such word was going to appear in his picture.

Once shooting got under way, Woody realized Maureen O'Sullivan was miscast. Spoiled and selfish in real life, she bore similarities to the character but failed to project those unpleasant qualities in her performance. It was an awkward situation, but reshooting meant he could oust Maureen. He first approached Gena Rowlands before turning to Elaine Stritch, who had no idea this was the second version. "We were well into it before I found out," she said. "But what did I care." Reshooting allowed the removal of Shepard as well. For the role of the weakling writer, he substituted Sam Waterston, a less-glamorous actor who had played one of the men in *Interiors*. When the picture wrapped in the spring of 1987, Woody seemed in no hurry to finish it. His only regret, he announced, was not filming a third version to further develop some of the characters, which made John Simon wail in his review, "What is this: the perfectionism of banality?" The final cost of the project was $10 million, 20 percent over budget.

When *September* opened in the fall of 1988, Stanley Kauffmann wrote sadly that the film was a drastic mistake, not worth making even once, not worth seeing, not worth reviewing. He felt sorry for Woody, who wanted so badly to abandon comedy. One of the very few reviewers to appreciate *September* was Roger Ebert, who thought Woody "as acute an author of serious dialogue as anyone now making movies." In his opinion, there weren't "that many people in America smart enough to appreciate a Woody Allen film." But Woody laid his head on the block, and he got it chopped off, even by admirers such as Richard Schickel. From the beginning of his career, Woody had soaked up ideas from his favorite movies, not only those made by masters such as Fellini and Bergman, but also the films in which Bob Hope had starred. *September,* so obviously "Uncle Vanya–Lite," provoked critics into pointing out his fondness for aping his favorite directors. Pauline Kael called the picture "profoundly derivative and second-rate." What a tragic waste of a career, she lamented; by placing a low value on his talent, by trying to imitate Chekhov, he had turned into "a pseud."

Nobody came to see *September,* which closed in short order and left Woody feeling unusually battered. Reviews barely mentioned Mia's name, or brutally criticized her performance for being, as one reviewer wrote, "Allen's little Max von Sydow in bloomers." After seeing the second version, an unmitigated mess, some people were convinced that the first version must have been even worse. Nobody would know because Woody destroyed the footage.

Undeterred, the following year he appeared to be reprising Ingmar Bergman's 1957 masterpiece, *Wild Strawberries,* which would lead some reviewers to christen his seventeenth movie *Wild Raspberries*. The Bergman classic is about a seventy-eight-year-old professor of medicine who travels to a distant university for an honorary degree, meets people from his past along the way, and is plunged back into his childhood. Dr. Izak Borg appears in *Another Woman* in the form of a fifty-year-old professor of German philosophy (Gena Rowlands), who is likewise haunted by memories of her barren past. She has managed her career admirably, but in her private life she is emotionally barricaded from her own feelings. (Woody would describe this chilly character, along with Eve in *Interiors* and Cecilia in *The Purple Rose of Cairo*, as being close to his own emotional makeup.) Through flashbacks and dream sequences, the professor is forced to confront her true self and understand how her coldness and indifference have hurt people.

Mia, seven months' pregnant when shooting began in October 1987, had only a small part as a mealy-mouthed pregnant woman, whose sessions with her psychiatrist drift through the air vent into Marion's office next door. Mia worked up until a week before Satchel's birth, then returned a month later for reshoots, using a pillow to swell her belly. She had so little interest in the film that she never bothered to see it.

For *Another Woman*, Woody achieved a longtime ambition when he was able to work with Ingmar Bergman's former cinematographer, Sven Nykvist. Woody's coup failed to impress Stanley Kauffmann, who thought that engaging Nykvist was "a pathetic, desperately imitative move." Using the work of innovative artists such as Bergman as stepping-stones to one's own experiences was fine, but it was quite another thing to become an expatriate from the real world. Woody "has stopped looking at his world," wrote Kauffmann, and instead looks mostly at Bergman films. (Woody, in fact, lived an insulated existence. In twenty-five years, he had not driven a car, nor had he ever visited a shopping mall or a multiplex movie theater.) The similarities to Bergman evoked widespread derision. David Ansen in *Newsweek* dubbed *Another Woman* "Wild Matzos." Pauline Kael admitted not having liked *Wild Strawberries* the first time. "An homage," she sniffed, "is a plagiarism that your lawyer tells you is not actionable."

■ ■ ■ ■ ■ ■ ■

On the Couch:
"Each person has his own obsessions."
—WOODY ALLEN, 1985

■ ■ ■ ■ ■ ■ ■

Every day around five o'clock, Woody arrived at Mia's house to take Dylan for a walk. "It was like a father coming home from work," recalled Lorrie Pierce, who was at Mia's place to give piano lessons. "Dylan adored him, and very often had made a drawing for him. Together they were extremely intense. When everyone was singing carols on Christmas, he was cuddling Dylan in his lap, kissing her feet and hands. I thought, 'How sweet.' "

At the age of three, Dylan was an adorable plump little girl with pouty lips and a head of golden, Shirley Temple ringlets. "She was cute as a button," recalled a parent whose child went to the same nursery school. By now she was the focus of Woody's life. At all times, he carried around a pacifier in his pocket. If there was a morsel of food too cumbersome for her little mouth, he chewed it first. In the morning he would creep up to her bed and wait for her to wake. At bedtimes, he was there to spin fairy tales about his own childhood, which he called "Little Woody" stories. Dylan made her film debut at the age of six months as the baby sister in *Radio Days* and subsequently would appear in *Crimes and Misdemeanors* and *Alice*. Whatever the picture, she had the run of the set, like a fantasy playground. George Schindler, a professional magician who played Shandu in "Oedipus Wrecks," remembered how she "played on the camera while they were setting up." Somehow the sight of her made Woody seem like an ordinary baby-talking father.

It was no surprise that Dylan became spoiled. Woody hired professional shoppers to purchase toys and games. The sight of the nursery, which began to look like a branch of F.A.O. Schwarz, eventually upset Moses, it seemed so excessive. "Look at that," he would shake his head. "Kids don't have all that." The big loser in all this was ten-year-old Moses, who had depended on Woody for affection and now got to spend only a few minutes with him whenever Woody visited the apartment or Frog Hollow.

If Moses was unhappy, so was his mother, who was observing Woody's behavior with apprehension. Jealous when Dylan paid attention to anyone else, he treated her like a girlfriend. As tensions rose further, Mia complained that he had stopped giving her presents and gave them to the baby.

"She's a child," he fired back. "Of course I get her presents." Did she expect him to come home with a chocolate egg for her? After that heated discussion, he told himself that Mia was obviously regarding her own daughter as a rival.

The way he related physically to the baby struck Mia as unhealthy. Watching television, he would wrap himself around her and ignore everyone else, Mia said. When she was naked, he could not take his eyes off her. Even more upsetting, dressed only in his undershorts, he would nestle in bed while reading to her, and encourage her to suck his thumb. During their trip to Paris when Dylan was two, Mia recalled that she confronted him one night at the Ritz Hotel and accused him of lusting after her child. "You look at her in a sexual way," she said. "You fondle her. It's not natural. You're all over her." Woody thought she was crazy. Dylan was "the single most important thing in my life" and he had been "a wonderful, wonderful father."

Woody's need to be always in physical contact with Dylan made others uncomfortable, too. At Frog Hollow one summer afternoon, Tisa Farrow and her mother noticed the peculiar way in which Woody was applying sun lotion to Dylan. He was rubbing his finger in the crack of the child's buttocks. Maureen O'Sullivan reprimanded him, and Mia hastily grabbed the bottle away. Dylan's godmother, Casey Pascal, said that she could not remember having ever seen a man so infatuated with a child. "If there was a roomful of children, he would focus only on Dylan."

Meanwhile, there was Satchel. Not only did Woody fail to bond with him but he seemed to have no real interest in his son, whom he jokingly called "a little bastard," Mia would recall. Certainly there was no physical resemblance between father and son, who had white-blond, almost silvery hair and blue eyes and was said to look like Mia's dead brother, Michael. From birth, Satchel was a difficult child, colicky and attached to his mother. At three, he remained hyperactive, "wired," said a source close to the family. He was also exceptionally intelligent—talking at the age of seven months—but that seemed to make no difference to his father. At that time, Satch was not yet weaned and Mia rigged up a harness so that he might continue to nurse. The device was nothing that would have bothered the La Leche League but it evidently appalled Woody.

The summer of 1988, Woody again traveled to Europe with Mia and the family. Accompanied by the troubleshooting Jane Martin, they set out on a whirlwind vacation that whisked them to five countries, including the Soviet Union, which they visited for only one day after Woody became upset with the primitive local customs. First-class tickets on the Concorde and accommodations at deluxe hotels made it an expensive holiday that cost approximately $425,000. (The following year he chartered a private jet.) Writing on hotel stationery in cities such as Helsinki and Salzburg, he completed an unusual screenplay that encompassed the stories of two lives. A highly regarded ophthalmologist (Martin Landau) is having an affair with a neurotic flight attendant (Anjelica Huston), who is threatening to destroy his career and marriage unless he marries her. Even though Judah Rosenthal is haunted by a childhood memory of his father warning him that God sees everything we do, he arranges to have his bothersome mistress murdered—with neither detection nor punishment. Tormented at first by guilt, the eye doctor is eventually able to live with his cold-blooded deed. The crime of the doctor who gets away with murder is paralleled by the misdemeanors of an idealistic maker of high-minded documentary films that nobody wants to see. The nebbishy Cliff Stern (Woody) is regarded as a fool by his castrating wife (Joanna Gleason) and rich brother-in-law, Lester (Alan Alda), who constantly put him down. Cliff's infatuation with a kindly television producer (Mia) seems to offer an escape from his sexless marriage, but she decides to marry Lester instead. What Judah and Cliff—and Woody, too—share in common is their ability to justify their actions.

In *Crimes and Misdemeanors,* a brilliant balance between comedy and drama, Woody turned out a successful film that was serious, witty, and bore no resemblance to Bergman movies. Among the ethical questions that his contemporary New York characters ponder are: Is evil punished? Are good deeds rewarded? Despite its focus on moral issues, this complex comedy would be his biggest commercial hit since *Hannah and Her Sisters.* Taking in $18 million at the box office, it struck a chord with both critics and audiences. Although critics debated the meaning of the film, the idea was perfectly clear to John Simon, who hailed Woody's courage for tackling the subject and his "guts" to come up with an honest answer: "There is no justice, no rhyme or reason in the universe, no God." The film was, in Simon's opinion, "Allen's first successful blending of drama and comedy, plot and subplot."

Crimes and Misdemeanors was one of two films Woody released in 1988, quite an accomplishment for even the most industrious auteur. "Oedipus Wrecks" went into production seven months before *Crimes.* Under the umbrella title *New York Stories,* Woody and his producer, Robert Greenhut, decided to make a short-story film, three shorts by different filmmakers, a genre that had fallen into disfavor after the forties. But Greenhut believed they could pull together a project exploring various aspects of New York life. Martin Scorsese agreed to contribute a vignette about a Jackson Pollack–type painter ("Life Lessons"), and Francis Ford Coppola cowrote with his seventeen-year-old daughter, Sofia, an updated version of the Eloise story, about a twelve-year-old living at the Sherry Netherland hotel ("Life Without Zoe").

Woody's forty-one minute contribution, "Oedipus Wrecks," was a return to his earlier films and the kind of pure comedy that his fans had been waiting for since *Broadway Danny Rose.* At the age of fifty-two, he managed to squeeze a few laughs out of his relationship with his mother. Sheldon Mills is a befuddled lawyer whose engagement to a divorced, gentile woman with three children (Mia) horrifies his mother. As Sheldon tells his psychiatrist, he may be middle-aged but his mother still makes him feel like he is in diapers, which is why he wishes she would disappear. Small wonder because Mrs. Millstein (Mae Questel) orders her son around as if she were a prison matron. Sheldon's wish is granted when a magician accidentally dematerializes the matriarch during the course of a magic trick and can't figure out how to bring her back. Sheldon's joy is short-lived, however, because the emasculating Mrs. Millstein reappears as a giant apparition floating in the sky, publicly humiliating him before the entire city. While there was nothing funny

about Mrs. Millstein's prototype, the portrait of Nettie Konigsberg, on celluloid, was full of comic invention that showed what Woody could accomplish
when he looked at his own life instead of Bergman's films.

New York Stories, financed and released by Touchstone Pictures, a subsidiary of Disney, did poorly at the box office. Despite the reputations of the
three superstar filmmakers, it grossed a disappointing $10.8 million against
an estimated negative cost of $19 million.

Over the years, Woody wrote a variety of memorable roles for Mia, but at the
same time that he showcased her talent, he also subtly undermined her self-
confidence. Discouraged from working elsewhere, she came to believe that no
other director would want to use her. Eventually the extensive roster of
Woody's actors who were nominated or had received an Oscar would include
Woody himself, Diane Keaton, Dianne Wiest, Michael Caine, Judy Davis,
Geraldine Page, Maureen Stapleton, Mariel Hemingway, Martin Landau,
Jennifer Tilly, Chazz Palminteri, and Mira Sorvino. But the Academy snubbed
Mia in her ten custom-designed roles. In the late 1980s, as the rift between
them widened, Woody seemed to lose interest in writing meaty roles for Mia.
(Audiences were also sick of seeing her year after year.) He stuck her in nondescript supporting roles: a pregnant patient *(Another Woman)*; a discarded
fiancée ("Oedipus Wrecks"); a bland television producer *(Crimes and Misdemeanors)*. With cheekbones that never seemed to age, her face was still beautiful but she was overweight. In all three of those films, she had to be costumed
in baggy sweaters and raincoats, or photographed from the waist up.

Then, at the end of 1989, Mia suddenly slimmed down to look like her old
self, for a picture that Woody titled *The Magical Herbs of Doctor Yang.* Pampered women such as Alice Tait are common sights in Woody's neighborhood. While their husbands slave away in Wall Street, they keep busy with
shopping, massages, and lunches. Sometimes, in their floor-length mink
coats, they even pick up their children from expensive nursery schools (such
as the ones Satch and Dylan attended). Their luxurious interior-designed
apartments are staffed by cooks, nannies, and personal fitness trainers. Alice,
unhappily married to a cold, selfish stockbroker (William Hurt), suffers from
a bad back. Before long, she is in Chinatown, climbing rickety stairs to the
office of a mysterious Dr. Yang, who can see that there is nothing wrong with
her back but everything wrong with her life. His diagnosis: She has never
followed her own desires. Liberated by means of a dose of potent magical
herbs, the demure Alice is able to cut loose for the first time. Not only is she
empowered to fly over Manhattan like Peter Pan, she also becomes temporarily invisible and spies on her husband making love to one of his office
colleagues. After sorting out her life, Alice Tait finds satisfaction in nunlike

Earliest publicity photo of a bespectacled twenty-six-year-old fledgling comic, who would soon become New York's hottest club act. "A terrific stand-up comic, very charismatic, fast on his feet when it came to improvisation," recalled critic Andrew Sarris. *(Photofest)*

Woody on the Andy Williams television show in 1965. "Elevator music," Woody, dismissive, used to sniff, but television audiences loved him, and his appearances made him a wealthy man. *(Photofest)*

Woody, flanked by Ursula Andress and Raquel Welch at a London movie premiere in the sixties, ogling Queen Elizabeth's bejeweled bosom. *(Archive)*

Louise Lasser leaving Beverly Hills Municipal Court after being charged with possession of cocaine in 1976. Stardom in the television series *Mary Hartman, Mary Hartman* failed to bring happiness. *(Photofest)*

A production still from *Take the Money and Run*, Woody's first feature of his own, about a gloriously incompetent bank robber. The actress is Janet Margolin. *(Photofest)*

Twenty-three-year-old Diane Keaton won the lead in *Play It Again, Sam,* Woody's 1969 Broadway comedy, even though she was too tall and constantly chewed gum. Adored by Woody, who felt superior and once referred to her as "a coatcheck girl," she would be his leading lady throughout the 1970s. *(Photofest)*

Arthur Krim, Woody's Medici prince, who bestowed on him the most gorgeous production deal in the film business. The Hollywood titan was still an eligible bachelor when he escorted Dina Merrill to a United Artists premiere in 1961. *(Photofest)*

Oscar night, 1978. *Annie Hall* won best picture and three other Academy Awards, but Woody was in New York playing clarinet at Michael's Pub. "I'm not interested in an inanimate statuette of a little bald man," he declared. "I like something with long, blond curls." *(Photofest)*

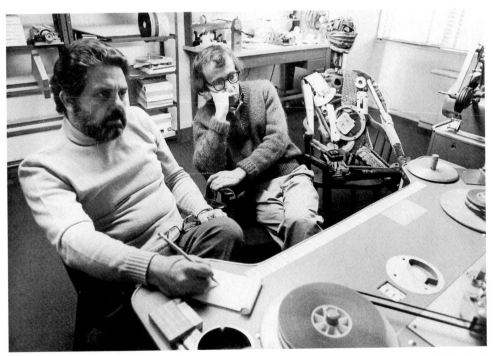

Woody in the editing room with Ralph Rosenblum, film editor par excellence, whose skill helped transform many of Woody's early films into box-office winners. Rosenblum, disgruntled, had a falling-out with Woody and quit. *(Sygma)*

December-May lovers: middle-aged Woody playing opposite sixteen-year-old Mariel Hemingway, as the girlfriend who still did homework, in his 1979 hit, *Manhattan*.

May-December lovers: Mia Farrow, twenty-one, and Frank Sinatra, fifty-one, cutting their wedding cake in 1966. "I finally found a broad I can cheat on," the singer joked to a Las Vegas audience. The marriage lasted sixteen months. *(Archive)*

Mia Farrow at Heathrow Airport in 1977 with four of her six children, including the Korean orphan Soon-Yi in the foreground. After divorcing her second husband, conductor Andre Previn, Mia settled in New York. *(Archive)*

Mia hungered to have Woody's baby. In 1987, pregnant with their son Satchel, she pushes a stroller along Central Park West while Woody carries Dylan. Mia found his preoccupation with the child unusual and excessive. *(Paul Adao)*

America's three premier film directors of the eighties: Francis Ford Coppola, Woody, and Martin Scorsese, who collaborated on the trilogy *New York Stories*. *(Photofest)*

Woody on the set of *Another Woman* with two-year-old Dylan O'Sullivan Farrow. Obsessed, he was determined to adopt her. *(Photofest)*

Caught in the act. Paparazzo Dominick Conde snapped Woody and Soon-Yi Previn holding hands during a Knicks game at Madison Square Garden in January 1990. *(Dominick Conde/Starfile)*

Mia holing up in Bridgewater, Connecticut (here with Satchel and Isaiah), after the breakup with Woody caused a blizzard of headlines the world over. Readers were riveted by the racy details. *(Sygma)*

Fletcher Previn romping about with his sister at their Connecticut home in 1993. Her family in turmoil, Dylan changed her name to Eliza. *(Sygma)*

Battleground: Woody with sister Letty Aronson outside the New York County Courthouse. His suit for custody of Moses, Dylan, and Satchel led to a ferocious six-week war. Letty testified that Woody was an enthusiastic father, who "played games and colored" with his children. *(Sygma)*

Victory press conference: Mia Farrow and attorney Eleanor Alter celebrating after Judge Elliott Wilk denied Woody custody. "Mr. Allen has demonstrated no parenting skills that would qualify him as an adequate custodian for Moses, Dylan, and Satchel." Even so, Mia's family was shattered. *(Sygma)*

Judge Wilk restricted Woody's visits with Satchel. At the Dublin Zoo, father and son stroll hand in hand during a tense reunion in the summer of 1993. Woody could not foresee that contact with Dylan, temporarily prohibited, would never be resumed. *(Archive)*

Soon-Yi and Woody openly affectionate during a 1996 trip to London. In New York, photographers snapped them smooching on Madison Avenue. *(Archive)*

All in the family: Jean Doumanian, Woody's oldest and dearest friend, took over as his producer in 1993. According to an industry insider, "Nobody wants to be involved with him." *(Archive)*

Jaqui Safra, Jean Doumanian's wealthy companion, was believed to be secretly bankrolling Woody's pictures. For years Safra had enjoyed playing bit roles in films such as *Stardust Memories.* *(Photofest)*

Venice, December 24, 1997. Woody and Soon-Yi with Letty Aronson and Venetian mayor Massimo Cacciari, who had married the couple the previous evening. *(Sygma)*

Woody and Soon-Yi showing off their adopted baby daughter, Bechet Dumaine. *(Lawrence Schwartzwald/Liaison Agency)*

celibacy, as she raises her children in a Lower East Side slum and does charitable work for the poor.

Alice, released in December 1990, was a whimsical, fluffy picture, reassuring evidence that Mia and Woody were still everybody's favorite celebrity mom and dad. On location in the Village, they permitted photographers to snap them with Dylan and Satch, on the swings in Abingdon Square Park, in a cozy family atmosphere. The movie almost seemed a throwback to the old days when Woody had presented an adorable Mia in *A Midsummer Night's Sex Comedy,* prompting one reviewer to observe that "he seems to have dedicated this funny valentine to his diminutive sweetheart." It was Mia's last good role from Woody.

••••••••

Rashomon:
"He gets wonderful performances, not necessarily by coaching but by having matched the material to the actor. Since 90 percent of his work is in the writing and casting, there's very little to do when he's ready to shoot. If he doesn't like what you're doing, he usually fires you right away."

—SYDNEY POLLACK

"They [Woody and Robert Altman] have no understanding of actors whatsoever. They're pisspoor as actors' directors. They may be great filmmakers but they have no respect for actors. Individually, each understands zip about acting. Allen knows even less than Altman, which is nothing."

—SAM SHEPARD

"His silences never bothered me. I knew how to play the part and he knew I knew. So let's not sit around and masturbate about acting."

—ELAINE STRITCH

"He spoke to me through an interpreter, as if we were from different countries. [In the recording studio,] I was standing right next to him, and he turned to an assistant and said, 'Tell her to do such and such.' I felt nonexistent. At lunchtime he ordered a tuna fish sandwich. I was not offered so much as a Coke."

—MARILYN MICHAELS

"I always admired Woody. There is no doubt he is one of our very few auteurs with both intelligence and substance. He even has the courage to be both funny and sentimental at times. I would very much like to see his version of the classic Faust legend."

—MAX VON SYDOW

"He would shoot a scene, and if he didn't like it he would rewrite it and reshoot it, again and again. His favorite line—and it was not said with any good humor—was 'I'll see you at the reshoots.' Then he would toddle off to his camper and play his clarinet for hours. Being sensitive, I took it personally and wondered if it was my fault we had to reshoot this stuff. Frankly, I thought—I still think—he's an insufferable little prick. But every time I see *Broadway Danny Rose* I forgive him. I hate him and I love him."

—ACTOR

"He kept telling me, 'Too hammy! No!' But I'm happy he kept badgering me. He took me past the point I thought possible. I wish I could hire him to stand by me in future movies and holler at me, 'That's too phony!' "

—GERALDINE PAGE

"Big names want to work on his films. He does quality work but as a person, he's a spoiled little boy, pampered by the New York critics. Absolute power corrupts absolutely."

—ACTOR

■ ■ ■ ■ ■ ■ ■

The entertainment business treated Woody like royalty. William Hurt, one of Hollywood's leading men, won an Oscar for *Kiss of the Spider Woman* and yet happily accepted union scale to work for Woody. Hurt could scarcely contain his admiration. On the set of *Alice,* he turned to Joe Mantegna and enthused, "Do you believe it? We're actually in a Woody Allen movie!"

If Woody's empty table at Elaine's made more and more people genuflect, others were not so impressed. After *Manhattan,* Meryl Streep took him to task for being "a womanizer, very self-involved," who got "caught up in the jet-set type of life" and thereby trivialized his talent. His ignorance about acting technique never prevented him from imposing line readings. "No theatricality! We don't want any theater!" he snapped at a seasoned stage actress whom he cast in *Radio Days.* "It was frightening," she said. "He had me in tears because I could not satisfy him."

Mostly, however, he came across as the Calvin Coolidge of film directors, famous for cold silences, terse (or nonexistent) instructions, and some of the most unorthodox directing practices in recent memory. Whenever possible, he gave actors only the script pages on which they had lines. In this way, he hoped, the humor would be fresh to audiences. But it made life difficult for actors, who could only guess what the film might be about. An actress in *Manhattan,* denied information about the plot and discouraged from discussing her role with the director, who was sitting off by himself reading Chekhov, found herself in the dark. "After the first day, I called friends from a pay phone," recalled Karen Ludwig. "I said, 'Please come and rescue me. Nobody will talk to me.' " Neither did Woody speak to Kitty Carlisle Hart, chairwoman of the New York Council on the Arts, whom he hired to sing one of the numbers in *Radio Days.* The widow of Moss Hart had not made a movie in fifty years, but she knew Woody socially and included him as a dinner guest at her home. She felt warmly toward him, and assumed he reciprocated. But when she arrived at the Kaufman-Astoria Studios, "suddenly he didn't speak to me. He never said hello, good morning, how do you do. And when it was over, he still didn't say boo." Baffled, she went over and asked why in the world he cast her. "You said you could sing," he replied.

■ ■ ■ ■ ■ ■ ■

Moving Pictures:
ALVY SINGER: A relationship, I think, is—is like a shark, you
　　know. It has to constantly move forward or it dies. And I think
　　what we got on our hands is a dead shark.
　　　　　　　　　　　　　　　　　　　　—Annie Hall, 1977

■ ■ ■ ■ ■ ■ ■

Mia was bewildered. After all their years together, how could he possibly have AIDS? There was a long incubation period, he answered. In the fall of 1991 he went ahead with the test, which proved he was HIV negative. By that time, they were no longer regular lovers. Later he would date the disruption of their sex life to the first trimester of her pregnancy, when Mia stopped sleeping with him. After Satch's birth, she also quit spending weekends at Woody's apartment, which effectively ended their private time together. The sleepovers no longer interested the older children, and the younger ones needed her at home.

Woody was to claim they never slept together again, which Mia called an exaggeration. What neither of them denied, however, was that sex was infrequent. He was unable to perform, according to Mia, but no doubt boredom was a factor. In his screenplay for *Crimes and Misdemeanors,* his hero says that "once the sex goes, it all goes," and jokes about his sexless marriage: "The last time I was inside a woman was when I visited the Statue of Liberty." Audiences, unaware that the humorous lines demeaned Mia, always roared. Ironically, abstinence was unknown to Woody, who had turned to a variety of women over the years, including actresses working in his films. In the 1980s, he became chummy with one in particular who made herself the subject of gossip among his crew and casts ("he was smitten with her") and also was observed in compromising positions at the Kaufman-Astoria studios by one of Mia's children. Aside from romances on the set, neighbors at 930 Fifth Avenue reported seeing mysterious women coming and going from his apartment—"the floozy brigade," one said.

Throughout this period, Woody and Mia remained together, and Woody and his attorneys unsuccessfully continued to work on the adoption problem. Even though she was confronted with HIV tests and gossip about Woody's other women, her life in a mess, Mia convinced herself they would remain a team for the rest of their lives. Her main reason for believing he would never leave was his determination to adopt her children. Would he be so eager if their relationship was not permanent? Mia simply could not conceive of such Byzantine plotting. In an interview that seemed to be scripted by Hallmark greeting cards, she hailed him as "a friend to the older children, the father to the youngest three." He was, she insisted, "absolutely besotted" with all of them. To a member of their circle, the household truly did seem touched with magic. "It was like a fairy-tale family because Mia grew up in Hollywood. A person who grows up in that dazzle isn't going to live a typical, normal, everyday life like everyone else anyway."

Behind the charade of the perfect couple, as the delicate mechanisms of their relationship were quietly rusting, they continued to keep up appearances. Before leaving for work, Woody went over to Mia's and played with Dylan as well as Satch, and in the evening he returned and remained until bedtime. Instead of towing the dead shark out to sea, they went out for dinner once a week. They didn't talk about sex, or love, and there was little touching. Later he was to describe their relationship as "pleasant and convenient. She did her thing and I did mine."

In 1991 he began writing a screenplay about two couples whose marriages have encountered a midlife crisis. Gabe and Judy Roth (Woody and Mia) open the door of their apartment one evening to greet their best friends, Jack and Sally (Sydney Pollack and Judy Davis). "Jack and I are getting a divorce," Sally announces. Gabe and Judy are astonished. Before long, Jack is sleeping with an aerobics instructor half his age, Gabe is in danger of being seduced by one of his students, and everyone's life is in chaos. Woody somehow managed to convince Mia that *Husbands and Wives* was fictional.

*　　　　*　　　　*

Actually, Woody had a *pair* of dead sharks on his hands. At the very time that his pretend-marriage was in trouble, it looked as if his twenty-year association with Arthur Krim, which was undoubtedly the most durable "marriage" of his entire life, was also breaking up. Since its inception, Orion Pictures had been underfinanced, and now the last of the small independent companies was breathing a death rattle. Beginning in 1990, its stock plummeted, and soon Orion owed close to $500 million in long-term debt and had a negative cash flow of $174 million. By the summer of 1991, Woody's eighty-one-year-old patron was attempting to raise $70 million in survival money so that Orion could distribute five finished pictures (including Woody's *Shadows and Fog*) languishing in postproduction limbo. Paradoxically, at the moment Krim was trying to stave off bankruptcy, his company had just collected nineteen Oscar nominations, more than any other studio. *Dances with Wolves* would win Best Picture that year, as would *The Silence of the Lambs* in 1992. In the eighties, Krim released *Amadeus* and *Platoon* (both winning Best Picture Oscars), and *Hannah and Her Sisters* (a strong contender), but these critical and commercial hits were offset by a string of lackluster pictures earning less than $10 million. *September* and *Another Woman* had been financial sinkholes, but Orion's problems went far deeper than Woody's expensive flops. The trouble with Orion, analysts theorized, was a lack of financial resources for marketing their films aggressively. Other critics blamed Krim and his associates for gravitating toward weak stories that were difficult to sell in the first place and then failing to sell them well.

Still, with Woody, Orion had made Hollywood history. Having the right to make films with final cut and without script approval was like a Montessori film school that provided a structured environment and freedom of choice and allowed Woody to experiment as he pleased. So management patiently waited out their auteur's Fellini period, his Bergman period, his Fritz Lang period, all the while hoping he would get back to his Woody Allen period and make funny movies again. It seldom happened. Instead, they got *September* and *Son of September*. According to *Variety*, Woody's eleven pictures cost them in excess of $100 million, and brought in domestic rentals of under $60 million. Including foreign rentals, some of his films managed to break even "but in the fearsome 1990s," wrote editor Peter Bart, " 'breaking even' is not enough." In Bart's opinion, Woody had become "a major drag" who should start thinking about his responsibilities to his friends. "Why isn't Woody out there in Hollywood with his patron, Arthur Krim? Why isn't he rallying around the Orion flag?"

But Woody's money machine had to make do without him. On December 11, 1991, when the company finally filed for Chapter 11 bankruptcy protection, he had already abandoned the dying shark for TriStar, which, along with its sister operation, Columbia, had been acquired by Sony, the powerful Japanese electronics empire.

Dylan's and Satchel's problems were becoming harder to ignore. Two years apart in age, they did everything together because Mia liked to pair her children. By three, however, Satch's development rivaled his sister's. Reported an observer, "In intelligence he was off the board. Practically everything caught his interest, from insects to doll houses." When he and Dylan played dress-up, he begged to wear girl's clothing. "I want to be a girl," he cried. "I'm a girl deer, I'm a girl animal." Eventually, his identification with Snow White and other female story characters began to worry Woody, who blamed Mia for being overprotective. But his own relationship with the little boy, now more involved than before, was also troubled. Satch was a rambunctious child, given to tears, demands, sulks, and temper explosions. On one occasion, Woody reprimanded him by threatening to break one of his legs. In contrast to Mia's contemporary parenting style, Woody behaved according to the standards with which he had been brought up. His blunt approach to discipline sounds as if it might have come from an earlier era, in fact, straight from the mouths of Nettie or Marty.

Later, Mia's lawyers and the media would make much of Woody's supposed inability to take an interest in his son. In some respects, the opposite was true. At Episcopal Nursery School on Park Avenue, where Satch attended preschool, Woody's behavior miffed some of the other parents. "The school had a fast rule: You bring your child and leave," said an Episcopal parent. "If parents hung around, there would be three-year-olds constantly running out into the hall. Well, Woody persuaded Episcopal to make an exception for him. He couldn't detach. What a mess." Disapproval never bothered Woody, who decided the Episcopal parents were aloof and snobbish and transferred Satch to Park Avenue Christian. There he encountered similar problems. "Mr. Allen," said Satch's teacher, "you're upsetting the other parents. You're going to have to break away."

"Satch has no problem breaking away," he replied. "I do." For several hours, until dismissal time, he paced up and down the sidewalk outside the school. "He just adores the boy," a sympathetic mother gushed. "You could see he wanted to be inside the classroom."

As for Dylan, Woody's behavior around her continued to alarm Mia. When she began policing him, he got angry and called her a "spoilsport." She recalled that "he would creep up in the morning and lay beside her bed and wait for her to wake up." He would bury his head in her stomach or crotch. Mia thought it was "excessive." As Dylan grew older, Woody's playfulness seemed to become more ferocious. It upset her. No sooner did Dylan hear his key in the door than she ran away in fear and begged her brothers and sisters to hide her. People who knew the family intimately describe Dylan's nature—intense, emotional, theatrical—as that of a little drama queen. If she enjoyed a story or video, she begged to hear or see it over and over; indeed, wanted to be Bambi or the Little Mermaid. Woody decided that she seemed to have difficulty sometimes distinguishing fantasy from reality, but Mia did not agree with his assessment. At preschool, Dylan, who was unusually shy and clinging, was upset when she was left alone. Even in her second year at Park Avenue Christian, "she carried on when Mia or the baby-sitter attempted to leave," remembered one of the parents. "She had to be pried loose from their necks. On parent-visiting days, Mia and Woody came together, and Mia always held Dylan on her lap."

As tensions escalated, Woody and Mia's life together became a dreary round of arguments about parenting. He thought her close relationship with Satchel was abnormal; she thought the same about him and Dylan. Finally in 1990 both children were evaluated by a clinical psychologist. As Dr. Susan Coates would later testify in court, she understood Mia's concern about Dylan and Woody. "I did not see it as sexual," Coates said, "but I saw it as inappropriately intense because it excluded everybody else" and placed excessive demands on the girl. As a result of the evaluation, Dylan was referred to Dr. Nancy Schultz, a clinical psychologist who helped young children with emotional problems. Dr. Coates herself began working with Woody to modify inappropriate behaviors, which consisted of his putting his face in Dylan's lap, encouraging her to suck his thumb, and constant caressing, among other problems. (After a number of sessions with her, Woody reportedly improved in these areas.) Also around this time, Coates began treating Satch for gender problems. With both tots in therapy, Woody's limo driver was kept busy shuttling them back and forth to their appointments.

■ ■ ■ ■ ■ ■ ■

Moving Pictures:
SANDY BATES: You can make an exception in my case. I'm a
  celebrity.
—*Stardust Memories*, 1980

■ ■ ■ ■ ■ ■ ■

Meanwhile, the adoption case landed in the lap of Renee Roth, a highly experienced, fifty-three-year-old judge who had been first elected to the Surrogate's Court in 1983.

After almost a half-dozen years, Woody's attorney Paul Martin Weltz decided to make an end run around the Family Court, the usual venue for adoption cases. The statute he was up against denied single people the right to separately adopt the same children. As he recalled later, "I didn't want some clerk to say, 'The statute doesn't permit it. Go away.'" Aware that the exception he sought would fare badly there, the tenacious Weltz instead took the case to Surrogate's Court. Woody Allen, he argued, was a person of superior character, intelligence, and financial means. He also was an outstanding parent, more of a father than many natural fathers. He rose before dawn to see his children and returned to tuck them in at night; he paid for their education and attended PTA meetings. Mia submitted affidavits (without reading them, she said later) attesting to his devotion. Given Woody's celebrity, Roth waived the court's requirement for a home study; indeed, she did not find it necessary to perform even a superficial investigation. As a result, she failed to discover that Woody's parenting was marginal. He knew little about the children's lives, and even though he attended PTA meetings, he neither read report cards nor knew the names of their teachers.

Weltz's ploy was successful. On December 17, 1991, two weeks after his fifty-sixth birthday, Woody appeared at Surrogate's Court accompanied by Mia, Dylan, and Moses. In Renee Roth's chambers, a bored Dylan squirmed on Mia's lap and whispered that she wanted to go home. But thirteen-year-old Moses, sitting across the table from his new dad, was grinning from ear to ear. The papers were signed, and so Woody at last became the father of Dylan and Moses.

CHAPTER THIRTEEN

Sidney Kugelmass
Meets His Biographers

Sidney Kugelmass, a middle-aged professor of humanities at the City College of New York (uptown campus), has a depressing dream: He is strolling through a meadow, swinging to and fro a picnic basket packed with luscious goodies that are labeled OPTIONS. Suddenly he looks down and notices the basket has a hole. He is upset to see that some of his options—the best ones, in fact—have disappeared. Describing his dream to Dr. Mandel, Sidney is hoping for sympathy, but the analyst shrugs. Sidney is acting like a big crybaby. All right, so his libido is shriveled, his head bald, his overfed wife, Daphne, a porker. What does he expect at his age?

But all he asked was a bit of pleasure, Sidney argues. Look how hard he slaves at CCNY.

Dr. Mandel refuses to listen. "After all," he grunts, "I'm an analyst, not a magician." Be realistic, he advises.

But realism holds as little attraction for Sidney Kugelmass as for his creator. (In a story written a few months later, Woody reiterated his disdain with masterful brevity: "Cloquet hated reality but realized it was still the only place to get a good steak.") Fantasies of adultery continue to consume Sidney, when a slick Brooklyn magician contacts him about a revolutionary new technology. The Great Persky's magic practice rests on an ingenious literary device: Clients are instructed to climb into a Chinese cabinet with a favorite novel (or short story, play, or poem) and Persky will blast them into the chosen work as though they were astronauts shot into space. Skeptical, Sidney inspects the box, which looks cheap and homemade. Obviously, Persky's practice is far from lucrative. But Sidney finally understands what the magician is offering him—the chance to run amok for only twenty dollars.

Sidney selects *Madame Bovary*, a few pages after Leon's departure and before Emma meets Rodolphe. Persky closes the door of his orbiter, taps three times, and he has liftoff. In a matter of seconds Sidney finds himself touching down in Yonville-l'Abbaye, where fictitious sex with a fictional woman is all he could have hoped for. In the passion of the moment, Sidney invites his paramour to spend a weekend in New York. After checking her into the Plaza and buying her a pair of black velvet slacks by Ralph Lauren, he spares no expense squiring her to Broadway musicals and dinner at Elaine's. When it's time for Emma to go home, however, Persky's cabinet malfunctions and repairs must be made. Emma, tired of watching TV all day, with no regard whatsoever for Sidney's bank account, develops a taste for Dom Perignon and caviar and begins filling in the gaps in her wardrobe. Before long, she has enrolled in an acting class at the Neighborhood Playhouse. But finally Emma is cleared for launch.

Swearing off reckless sexual misbehavior, Sidney is nevertheless tempted to sample a recent best-seller, Philip Roth's *Portnoy's Complaint.* Something goes hideously wrong and Persky keels over and dies. Instead of humping Roth's "Monkey," Sidney finds himself trapped instead in a musty textbook, *Remedial Spanish,* being stalked by the word *tener* (to have)—"a large and hairy irregular verb."

"The Kugelmass Episode," originally published in *The New Yorker,* won the O. Henry Award for best short story of 1978. By 1990, however, as life began to imitate literature more and more, Woody had reached the point of middle-aged angst where he resembled his fictional character, in both his professional and private lives. The needy Sidney Kugelmass is an ordinary middle-aged adolescent seeking a romantic soul mate. Woody Allen, equally in need and trapped in a "joyless, sexless" relationship, is not much wiser. Throughout that spring, he began contemplating his "options."

Years of experience had honed Woody's skills in manipulation of the media. In hundreds of interviews, he funneled the public all the news he wished them to have, which consisted entirely of information that would enhance his screen persona. As a result, there was surprisingly little in the way of independent assessment of his life, no biography, for example. The dozen or so volumes that had been published were largely earnest film criticism by scholars attempting to analyze the work, not the self-mythologizer who created it. Woody viewed biographers as the Ebola plague, dangerous, uncontrollable contagions that might squish his public persona into mousse. Not only did he refuse to cooperate with would-be biographers, but he also sued publishers and authors.

At forty-three, Lee Guthrie, a writer from Louisville, Kentucky, was a newspaper reporter, the author of a biography of Cary Grant, and a mother of three—one of whom would grow up to be film actress Sean Young. In 1977, Guthrie had contracted with Drake Publishers to write about the comedian. In her biography, she quoted titanic chunks of his stand-up material, along with dialogue from film scripts and television specials, and snippets from his *New*

Yorker pieces, all of which she stirred into the manuscript without obtaining or paying for the usual permissions. Woody sued Guthrie and her publisher for copyright infringement, claiming that her unauthorized work unfairly competed with his own plans to write an autobiography. He demanded the defendants recall and destroy all printed copies, as well as search for customers who had purchased the book, and, of course, to cease further publication.

Having crushed the ill-fated Guthrie book, but now feeling more threatened than ever, Woody continued to view biographers as the enemy and himself as a defenseless subject. Approached by Gerald McKnight, a British writer, he rebuffed the would-be biographer with the claim that there was nothing new to report. "You won't get anywhere," one of Woody's employees warned McKnight. "He talks to nobody outside his own tight little circle." On the whole, that proved to be correct, but McKnight managed to uncover several valuable primary sources, including Woody's unsuspecting mother in Florida. Woody, however, took no legal action against McKnight's *Woody Allen: Joking Aside,* possibly because it was only published in England.

Lee Israel, on the other hand, was an experienced American biographer who had written lives of Tallulah Bankhead and Dorothy Kilgallen. She had grown up in Woody's old neighborhood and graduated from Midwood High School in the Class of '57, but having age and birthplace in common with her subject proved of no advantage. By now, Woody's strategy was first to dodge a biographer's letter seeking an interview, then to obstruct the research. His employees, knowing to whom they owed their livelihood but loath to acknowledge his iron control, said the usual things employees say in such situations. They were worried about upsetting him, they claimed, when what worried them was losing their jobs. Even former employees became adept at making excuses ("He feels enough books about him have already been written"). Encountering a stream of nervous people who refused to talk without Woody's consent, Lee Israel had no choice but to return her advance to her publishers.

Another would-be writer was Louise Lasser. Ten years following her divorce, after she made a big splash in the television series *Mary Hartman, Mary Hartman,* her memoirs were sought by Toni Morrison, the novelist who was an editor at Random House. Louise pumped out 2,000 pages of transcribed recollections. Alarmed that his former wife was writing her memoirs, Woody must have discouraged her from writing the book. Still dominated by him, realizing she could never write a truthful account of her own life without including their marriage, Louise reluctantly gave up the project.

The only writers Woody found acceptable were foreigners, especially those who convinced him their sole interest was an academic interpretation of his films. In 1985 the French-born writer Thierry de Navacelle received permission to observe the filming of *Radio Days* and write an insider's diary of the day-to-day shooting. "I was with him for five months," reported de Navacelle, "and he said about five sentences to me, most of them about weather." He was also surprised to notice Woody's "very manipulative" treatment of his employees, for whom he seemed to lack feeling. For example, "he has used the same electrician, the same grips for 10 years, but he never says a word to these people." (Likewise, Woody valued Dennis Kear, his nonintrusive stand-in for a decade, because, Kear believed, "I could fade into the woodwork when not needed.") Before publication of *Woody Allen on Location,* Thierry de Navacelle had to clear the manuscript with Woody. As his account could only be published with Woody's approval, de Navacelle did not feel free to say what he really observed or thought about his subject, and so readers learned nothing significant about the man called Woody Allen.

In the late 1980s, Woody gave his blessing to a handpicked biographer, no doubt hoping to ensure an account of his life that would portray him as a simple, lovable guy—and also to make unnecessary any future books about himself. He felt comfortable with Eric Lax, whom he had known for some fifteen years and with whom he had cooperated on a previous book, *On Being Funny: Woody Allen and Comedy,* published in 1975. Lax had never tilled the messy fields of biography. A native of Canada who grew up in southern California, he had been a Peace Corps volunteer before turning to freelance writing. In his forties, he shared a bachelor apartment with his college roommate Peter Tauber, the same writer who had been Jean Doumanian's nemesis when she worked for *Saturday Night Live.* Sometime later, Lax married the daughter of *New York Times* publisher Arthur Ochs "Punch" Sulzberger.

After making life difficult for previous writers, Woody now proceeded to make life simple for his anointed biographer. "I let him hang around and watch whatever he wanted to watch," Woody said later. "I gave him access to anyone he wanted to talk to." Anyone included Mia, who made herself available for an interview in which she spoke glowingly of Woody as a parent. "I can't imagine a more committed father," she assured Lax.

Instead of chipping at the legends that encrusted his subject's life like so many dripping stalagmites, Lax smoothly repackaged as fact the myths of Woody as an eccentric but lovable and decent little man. Observing Woody and Mia together at social gatherings, he was charmed and reassured by the sight of their holding hands, which he misinterpreted as "a sweetness" that made them more married than most married couples.

Woody Allen: A Biography, which was published by Alfred A. Knopf in 1991, was basically a Woody Allen production. Molly Haskell, writing on the front page of the *New York Times Book Review,* seemed to sense the subject had succeeded in controlling the biographer ("more smoke screen than revelation"), but the film critic (and wife of critic Andrew Sarris) also thought it would be "churlish to nit-pick" in the case of a filmmaker who had given the world so much pleasure. Representing the nitpickers was a reviewer for *Film Quarterly,* who decided that Lax's book offered "a wealth of biographical detail and virtually no critical perspective."

True to form, Woody was unhappy with a biography that could hardly have been more complimentary. He failed to see where Lax had been too soft on him, as some reviewers noted. "I, of course," he said jokingly, "felt that he wasn't complimentary enough."

On page 180 of Eric Lax's biography can be found the briefest of references to the Andre Previn–and–Mia Farrow children, who included the twins, Matthew and Sascha, Fletcher, Lark and Daisy, "both Vietnamese orphan girls, and Soon-Yi, an orphaned Korean girl."

Mia's sixth child, the third whom she adopted while married to Previn, Soon-Yi was born in Seoul, the capital of South Korea and a city that lay in ruins after the devastation of the Korean War. Economic recovery had proceeded slowly. After the war, hardly a tall building was still standing, and millions were left homeless. Even in the late sixties, life remained raw in an agrarian society struggling toward industrialization. There is no way of determining with certainty the year of Soon-Yi's birth, either 1970, 1972, or 1973, depending on whom you listen to. After her affair with Woody became public, she claimed to be twenty-one, born in 1970. But throughout her childhood, Mia always gave her birthdate as 1972 or else cited the results of a bone test indicating she was seven in 1980, so 1973 was also possible. If Mia's figures are correct, she was about four years old at the time of her adoption and as young as seventeen when she became involved with Woody.

If her age was guesswork, so was her history. Mia was told that Soon-Yi's mother had been a prostitute, and, in a society fractured by war, this was a reasonable assumption. Physically abusive, Soon-Yi's mother punished her by forcing her to kneel in a doorway and slamming the door against her head. Eventually, she abandoned the child, and Soon-Yi joined the gangs of lost children who spent their lives in the streets and survived by begging and foraging through garbage cans. By the time she was placed in a Catholic orphanage, dirty and dressed in rags with sores on her lips and a head full of lice, she knew neither her name nor age, nor did she comprehend enough language to answer questions. The people at the orphanage named her Soon-Yee. Had she not found refuge in an institution, she would have undoubtedly become a child prostitute, as did many of Seoul's street children.

A few months later, the foundling was assigned to the Previns for adoption. Complications arose, however, when they discovered U.S. laws limited the number of adoptions of foreign-born children to two by a single family.

Andre and Mia already had their quota. With the help of William Styron and his wife, Rose (who would become Soon-Yi's godmother following the death of Mia's friend Natalie Wood), they personally fought to have Congress pass a bill amending the law, and soon after it was changed, Mia flew to Seoul to bring home her new child.

In adopting infants such as Lark and Daisy, the Previns encountered none of the major difficulties that were associated with children adopted abroad, especially older institutionalized children, who generally had suffered varying degrees of trauma and had trouble adjusting to a new home. Sometimes the children immediately revealed serious problems, which included, in addition to difficulties with speech and language, an inability to laugh or cry, refusal to make eye contact, temper tantrums, and an inability to form emotional bonds. In other cases, however, social and emotional maladjustment did not manifest itself until many years later. When she was first adopted, Soon-Yi stuffed eggshells into her mouth and fled from mirrors. She could only fall asleep on the floor next to her mother's bed. In contrast to her real mother, whom she remembered as "Naughty Mama," Mia became her "Good Mama."

In the blink of an eye, as if going from black-and-white Kansas to Technicolor Oz, little Soon-Yi found herself transplanted from the squalor of Seoul to a life of privilege in which she wanted for nothing. But along with her colossal good fortune, there was also unhappiness and misery because her new parents' marriage was faltering. Lonely and rejected as a woman, Mia found consolation in her children. "Kids are probably the most secure kind of love," she said, "because you know you won't lose them, barring some kind of personality conflict between parent and child." For the first time, but not the last, she reacted to abandonment by adopting an orphan, in this case, Soon-Yi, as a sort of surrogate spouse. "I was in a lot of pain and had no idea what would happen next," she said. Amid the bereavement of a marital breakup, she was also attempting to revive her languishing film career.

Soon-Yi's early life with the Previns was fragmented. Shortly after her arrival in Surrey, England, where the Previns were living, Mia ignored a doctor's warning about the harsh conditions in Egypt, and traveled with Soon-Yi to Cairo, where she was acting in *Death on the Nile*. The following year, Soon-Yi was hauled to the South Pacific island of Bora Bora for *Hurricane*, a twenty-million-dollar disaster epic in which Mia costarred with Jason Robards and Max von Sydow. Shortly thereafter, the Previns separated, with the eldest boys remaining with their father in Surrey and Mia and the four younger children returning to the United States. For several months, they lived on Martha's Vineyard in Massachusetts, before settling permanently in Maureen O'Sullivan's apartment on Central Park West. Within the space of two short years, the peripatetic orphan lived in five countries.

It was not surprising that Soon Yi's impoverished early environment led to what psychologists call "developmental delays." When she was in third grade, tests revealed that she had minor learning disabilities, including trouble in processing information as well as an IQ slightly below average. From grades six to twelve she required tutoring. Her aunt, Tisa Farrow, would refer to her as having "a double-digit IQ. It's not like she's a drooling idiot, but she's very naive and very immature." This picture was neither true nor fair. While not the dim bulb described by her aunt, she did not seem particularly bright compared to the others in the family. "She *was* a little slow," said a family friend, who points out that Soon-Yi received permission to take her S.A.T.'s (Scholastic Aptitude Tests for college entrance) untimed, in a special test situation for learning-disabled students. It took Soon-Yi twice as long—sometimes even longer—as other children to complete her homework, but "she worked damned hard," recalled her sister Daisy.

Soon-Yi never managed to bond with Mia; indeed, she seemed to have trouble empathizing with "Good Mama" in any way, something that her mother preferred to ignore. On the other hand, she was inclined to distrust all people. In her adopted family, sibling rivalry could be intense, and she was reluctant to involve herself with the other children, especially Fletcher, whom she disliked. When he was six, she pushed his head into a toilet, which the family construed as a wish to drown him. Until the age of eight, she seemed closest to Lark, but then her integration into the family seemed to halt. For example, all the children loved music, and despite a lack of talent, dutifully took piano lessons—except Soon-Yi, who told the piano teacher, "I'm the one who's not musical." She always would remain an outsider. Among the brothers and sisters, the least physically attractive, the one with the shyest personality, she was the plain vanilla sister. On an application for camp, in the marital-status blank, she wrote "nun," which elicited teasing from her brothers and sisters. Even at seventeen, she was still pigeonholed as prissy and puritanical, an indication of how seriously they underestimated her ambition. Like the understudy Eve Harrington in *All About Eve,* she was an Anne Baxter to her mother's Bette Davis as she shrewdly studied Mia's life for guidelines on how to navigate the ways of the world. Confident that a woman could win her heart's desire by aggressively pursuing older, successful men, Soon-Yi would soon emulate her mother's behavior.

∎∎∎∎∎∎∎

Rashomon:
"[The children] are very close to Woody, and I'm glad about that. They have a good [father] substitute—he's there for them in important ways. He shares leisure time with them—he takes

them to the park and plays ball with them and takes them around the city. Whenever they want to see him, he's available."

—MIA FARROW

"I had no relationship with him whatsoever. I didn't care either way. I felt that he could be mean to Mom really quietly. He was like that. He could be very nasty."

—LARK PREVIN

"He was never any kind of a father figure to me. I never had any dealings with him."

—SOON-YI PREVIN

"He was a 12-year boyfriend to my mom and then he started going out with my sister. How could he do that?"

—MOSES PREVIN

"He is a stable influence. They [the Farrow children] live in chaotic circumstances."

—LETTY ARONSON

• • • • • • •

Even though Woody got on well with Moses (and Fletcher, too, for a brief time), he had never been interested in Mia's other children. Once or twice, she begged him as a favor to take Soon-Yi for a walk and buy her ice cream, but he had no time. Besides, Soon-Yi made no secret of her dislike for him. "She was someone who didn't like me," he remembered. "I didn't speak to her." To him, she was the shy little creature, the one with the braces whom he paid seventy dollars to baby-sit Satch and Dylan on weekends. She was colorless, bland, and not particularly pretty.

After Satch was born, however, whenever he came up to the apartment to visit Dylan and Satch, she suddenly began asking him questions about basketball, or advice on homework. "She went gaga over him," said Daisy. A friend of the family thought that "growing up in a movie star's family definitely appealed to Soon-Yi. She wanted to be part of the glamour. When she saw a chance, she jumped at it." Of all Mia's children, only Soon-Yi possessed the imagination to see her life as a romantic Hollywood story, with lights, camera, action, which is probably the reason she was more conscious than her siblings of the friction between Woody and their mother. She must have sensed that he was drifting away—out of Mia's life—and that meant out of her own as well. Slowly, Soon-Yi began to register on Woody. Unlike the other children, she listened to him and even laughed at his jokes. He loved the flattery and treated her like a grown-up. She made a point of inviting him to her Sweet Sixteen party and on her next birthday, he invited her and several school chums to a lavish dinner at the Russian Tea Room.

Mia asked him to take Moses and some of her other children to see the Knicks games. Instead of inviting Moses, he asked Soon-Yi because she seemed to be so enthusiastic about basketball. Hungry for attention, she spent one, then two evenings with him at the Garden. A different girl away from her family, she promptly unleashed a stream of complaints about depression and a miserable home life, mostly a long laundry list of grievances against her mother, whom she described bitingly as "no Mother Teresa." The tales she rattled off about Mia, Woody thought, were enough to "curl your teeth." Pouring out her heart, Soon-Yi found a sympathetic audience in Woody, who was willing to listen to her problems with her mother. Apparently he hadn't figured out that a classic pastime of adolescent girls is depicting their mothers as riding on broomsticks.

One evening in January 1990, the New York Knicks were playing the L.A. Lakers at the Garden. On assignment for the *National,* a sports publication, a freelance photographer named Dominick Conde was strolling around fishing for celebrities. Right before halftime, he spotted Woody and Soon-Yi glued together in the seats behind the scorer's table. They were holding hands. Using a long lens, Conde took three shots. "When I came back after halftime," he said, "they were still holding hands, so I shot three more frames." As it turned out, the *National* did not run the photos, which were archived at Star File, Conde's agency, where they remained for the next two years.

Coincidentally, a week or two after Conde photographed Woody and Soon-Yi, another observant Knicks fan happened to notice the couple at a Sacramento game. Seeing Woody stroke Soon-Yi's hair and kiss her cheek, the fan tipped off Cindy Adams, gossip columnist at the *New York Post.* Adams, a product of Andrew Jackson High School in Queens, former Miss New Jersey State Fair, and wife of Catskills comic Joseph Abramowitz aka Joey Adams, was a woman of a certain age who had spent ten years as a professional gossipmonger. By this time she knew a thing or two about the follies of celebrity husbands who got moony over babes half their age. She put in a call to Woody's production office.

"Oh, I know," Woody's secretary told her. "She's an old friend."

Adams laughed. "Yeah? Well, she ain't that old."

Adams ran the item without identifying Soon-Yi. According to Conde, he had no doubt the teenager was Mia's daughter "because I'd been shooting her since she was a little girl." The other person who didn't have to wonder about the identity of Woody's new girlfriend was Mia. Getting wind of the Cindy Adams story, she confronted Woody, who acted as if she were crazy. At first dismissing her suspicions as believing the lies of a gossip columnist, he finally conceded that it was possible he grabbed Soon-Yi's hand for a second as they were elbowing their way into the Garden, as he did when Elaine's was crowded and the restaurateur led him by the hand to his table. When Mia protested Woody's touching Soon-Yi, warning him that "she has a crush on you and she might misinterpret that," he snapped. "Don't be silly." The subject was dropped.

■ ■ ■ ■ ■ ■ ■

Moving Pictures:
Isaac Davis: I'm dating a girl who does homework.
— *Manhattan,* 1979

■ ■ ■ ■ ■ ■ ■

Soon-Yi was beginning her senior year at Marymount, a small all-girl parochial prep school on Fifth Avenue and Eighty-third Street, opposite the Metropolitan Museum of Art. Woody's apartment was only a five-minute walk from the school, and it was easy for her to visit him, wearing her school uniform, on her lunch break. She also figured out a way to see him on weekends. On Saturday mornings, and sometimes Sundays, usually around nine-thirty, she donned miniskirts and slathered on makeup, telling her mother that she was meeting a girlfriend at Bloomingdale's.

What friend? asked Mia, suspiciously glancing at her bare legs.

Nobody special, Soon-Yi said. It was just someone she'd met last summer, who now worked as a salesclerk at Bloomies.

"Well, what do you do when your friend is working?" Mia persisted. "Just stand there all dressed up?"

Mia was determined that her children attend college. Accordingly, Matthew went to Yale, Sascha to Fordham, and Lark attended New York University, where she planned to enter the nursing program. Soon-Yi, however, seemed to have other ideas about her future. She wanted to be an actress, an ambition that seemed possible, if not easily achieved, given her show-business connections. Her fantasies were further fueled in the summer of 1990 when Woody got her extra work in *Scenes from a Mall,* a Disney comedy in which he himself was starring, his first venture outside of Orion since *The Front.* Woody played a wealthy ponytailed lawyer from California who breaks up and gets back together with his wife of sixteen years (Bette Midler) in the Beverly Center, a mall on the west side of Los Angeles. The picture started production there and then moved to Stamford Town Center in Connecticut, and finally to a replica of the Beverly Center mall that had been created at the Kaufman-Astoria Studios in Queens.

Each morning Woody took Soon-Yi to work with him. It was at this time that she began talking about a professional career in modeling and urged him to launch her. Over the opposition of her mother, he had his casting director send her to the Flick modeling agency, which coincidentally represented her cousin, the daughter of Prudence Farrow. But it was doubtful that Soon-Yi could ever have become a model. Not only did she lack the dainty features of a Chinese or Vietnamese woman, but she was also chunky and large-boned, with a head that was not in proportion to her torso. The owner of the modeling agency, Frances Grill, asked Soon-Yi if she had any photographs of herself. "I told her she needed something to be a model, and suggested she get some simple Polaroids." Soon-Yi said she did not have any professional photographs but promised to come back with some pictures. She never returned to the modeling agency. "Of course in person, she wasn't model material at all," Grill said. "She was pretty but not tall enough. But sometimes Polaroids will show that a girl photographs well."

"Soon-Yi had always been rather plain," recalled the family music teacher, Lorrie Pierce. "But suddenly she looked beautiful, like young girls do when they're in love." That spring she graduated from Marymount. "At home on graduation day, she looked as radiant as a bride," Pierce said. In the school yearbook, alongside a recent photo of Soon-Yi, there was a photo of the four-year-old in traditional Korean dress, which had been taken in Seoul at the time of her adoption. Her mother composed a message of congratulations: "A mom couldn't dream of a better daughter. You are a miracle and my pride and joy. I am profoundly grateful for every minute along the way. Congratulations, Bravo and three cheers for our Soon-Yi."

All the Previn and Farrow children had been brought up as ladies and gentlemen. Occasionally, however, they got into mischief. Once Lark and Daisy shoplifted $342 worth of bras, panties, and garter belts from a store in the Danbury Fair Mall. Apprehended by security guards, who observed them mashing lingerie into a shopping bag, they were arrested and charged with fifth-degree larceny, a misdemeanor. In court with their mother, the girls agreed to attend a six-month rehabilitation program in order to erase their arrest records. Another time, Daisy failed to receive her monthly allowance check from Andre Previn and cashed Soon-Yi's check with a forged signature. There were other incidents involving skipping school, jumping subway turnstiles, and sneaking out to late-night parties with boys. Soon-Yi never participated in these adolescent high jinks.

In the fall of 1991, Soon-Yi departed for Drew University, a school in Madison, New Jersey, that Sascha had attended briefly. In academic distinc-

tion, Drew had the reputation for being a haven for debutantes and for placing few intellectual demands on its students. Soon-Yi, unable to make friends
easily, was homesick and frequently phoned Woody for his advice on how to
make college life bearable. "We were both quite unhappy," he later recalled.

■ ■ ■ ■ ■ ■ ■

The March of Time:
A young playwright, Harold Cohen, is dallying with Connie
Chasen, a long-legged blonde actress. But Harold is secretly fascinated by Connie's mother, Emily, for whom he develops lustful
yearnings. Secretly plotting Emily's seduction, he lures her to
Trader Vic's for Mai Tais when he suddenly realizes he is in love
with two women, "a not terribly uncommon problem. That they
happen to be mother and child? All the more challenging!" In
due time, Connie's ardor cools (Harold now seems like a brother),
and he is free to woo and wed the enticing Emily. His family is
incredulous.
   "His girlfriend's mother he's marrying?" shrieks his aunt Tillie
as she falls into a faint.
   Harold's mother reaches for a cyanide capsule. "Fifty-five and
shiksa!"
                                    —WOODY ALLEN, "Retribution," 1980

■ ■ ■ ■ ■ ■ ■

Woody and Soon-Yi became intimate in 1990, if one is to believe the story
she told Mia in the first hours after her mother discovered the Polaroids.
Woody's version was different. He said the sexual relationship began more or
less accidentally when Soon-Yi came home from college for Christmas break
in 1991. "We started talking about following her [graduation] from college,
what would happen, and that was when I put my hand on her," he testified
under oath. It was obvious that if his sexual relations with Soon-Yi could be
established prior to December 17, 1991, his co-adoption of Dylan and Moses
might be reversed. By now there were many people, in addition to Dominick
Conde and untold numbers of Knicks fans at Madison Square Garden, who
had witnessed them together in compromising positions: Lark's boyfriend
noticed Woody caressing Soon-Yi's thigh while riding in Woody's car; Fletcher
caught them in some sort of intimacy in the laundry room; Moses was
shocked to see Woody ducking his head and gazing upward between his sister's bare legs at her crotch. At 930 Fifth Avenue, Woody's neighbors gos-
siped about the frequency of Soon-Yi's visits, and exchanged tart comments
on her appearance. "She was sallow and badly dressed, not at all pretty," one

woman said. "I thought he could surely do better." Other neighbors had lit-tle sympathy for Mia, whom they mocked for acting snooty, and behaving, as some people said, like a "fruitcake."

Jean Doumanian, Woody's friend and confidante, informed *People* maga-zine in 1992 that the romance began soon after Satchel's birth, when Mia was preoccupied with the new baby. In her opinion, Woody's attraction to Mia's daughter seemed perfectly natural precisely because the filmmaker *had* known her since childhood. "She took off her braces and took out her hairpin," Doumanian waxed poetic, "and lo and behold here was this lovely woman. A breath of fresh air, a companion," who was also "charming and intelligent."

While Woody and Mia slept together infrequently in 1990 and 1991, not all sexual contact ceased, Mia later reported. During those two years, Woody Allen had had two mistresses, mother and daughter; one in a public love affair, the other in a secretive one.

Mia seems to have been the only person who wasn't puzzled by Woody and Soon-Yi's increasingly symbiotic relationship. Woody plainly wanted her to know of the infatuation though, even writing a script about middle-aged husbands jettisoning their wives for young women and casting her in the film as one of the rejected women. In retrospect, she seemed to be asleep at the wheel. But then few women can easily conceive of their trusted hus-bands or partners having sexual relationships with the children they have spent years loving and nurturing.

CHAPTER FOURTEEN

The Coiled Cobra

On St. Valentine's Day of 1992, he delivered gifts for the children. As he was leaving Mia's apartment, he went into the kitchen and gave her a red satin box of chocolates and an embroidered heart cushion. She handed him a slender, neatly wrapped box.

Downstairs in the car, he tore off the paper and found a blue Tiffany & Co. box. When he opened the box, however, it was evident the contents had not been purchased at Tiffany's. It was "a very, very chilling Valentine, meticulously worked on, one hesitates to say psychotically worked on," he later said. The ornate Victorian card was a white heart decorated with entwined pink buds and green vines that framed a Brady Bunch family portrait of Mia surrounded by her nine smiling children. Through the hearts of the children she had jabbed steel turkey-roasting skewers. Her own heart was gashed by the tip of a steak knife, whose handle was wrapped in a xerox copy of one of the Polaroids of the nude Soon-Yi. Mia had written next to the photograph: "Once my heart was one and it was yours to keep. My child you used and pierced my heart a hundred times and deep."

A month had passed since that fateful Sunday evening when Woody had photographed Soon-Yi in the nude. The most reasonable explanation is that they were using the Polaroid camera as a sexual accessory, a method similar to ceiling mirrors or erotic videos. In Woody's case, this particular device certainly does not seem remarkable for a man whose livelihood depends on the camera. Of course, rushing off and leaving the photographs on the mantelpiece was exactly akin to scattering a trail of bread crumbs because Mia found them the very next day.

As his limousine swept through Central Park, Woody squirmed in the backseat. It was the knife that terrified him. Not a week earlier, he and Mia had celebrated her forty-seventh birthday with dinner at Rao's, one of her favorite restaurants. As a present, he had given her three expensive leather-bound volumes of Emily Dickinson's poems. Now she was suggesting that she wanted to kill him by driving a stake through his chest. More than bewildering, her queer little gift was "quite frightening," he said later.

Mia's intention, she explained later, was not only to put the fear of God into him, but to make sure he fully understood "the degree of pain he had inflicted on me and my entire family." A month after the discovery of the affair, he failed to appear the least bit repentant and seemed to be treating the incident as an ordinary story about the difficulties of monogamy. He had cheated; he had gotten caught. That Woody could be selfish and self-absorbed should have come as no surprise to Mia, who had known him for twelve years. Still, if she couldn't get him to feel remorse, she at least wanted him to acknowledge—and apologize for—his treachery.

Soon-Yi returned to Drew University. The day that Mia found the pictures, she had collapsed in shame. Like a naughty child caught poaching in her mother's purse, she sobbed, "I'm a bad girl." She threatened to kill herself. In no time, however, her defiance—her sense of specialness—reasserted itself. "The person sleeping with the person is the one with the relationship," she gloated. Those words enraged Mia, who began kicking her. "I just pounced on her," Mia admitted. "She kicked me and I hit her on the side of the face and shoulder." Still clinging to the belief that her daughter's sex with Woody had been nonconsensual, Mia made Soon-Yi promise never to see him again, and to hang up if he ever attempted to phone her. Woody, too, promised Mia that the affair was over. It was not the case. They were "in constant contact," sometimes speaking on the phone five or six times a day.

That winter, Soon-Yi stopped coming home on the weekends and eventually ceased calling her family as well. When her brothers and sisters phoned to see how she was doing, she seemed sullen. Her mother got on the line and began interrogating her about Woody. Had she kept her promise to stay away from him? Soon-Yi's response was to shout, "Stop asking me for things!" and slam down the phone.

Even with their relationship damaged, possibly beyond repair, neither Woody nor Mia seemed sure of whether to separate from each other. For a dozen years, she had been his leading lady, and he was apprehensive about finding a new actress who would possess her charm and ability. Mia, with all her professional eggs in one basket, was caught in an even worse position. Although traumatized by his betrayal, she could not afford to walk away from her employment. She had a family to support. The last thing either wanted was public exposure of their problems.

In February, as he edited *Husbands and Wives*, Woody walled off his emotions and adopted a wait-and-see attitude, but at the same time he pleaded with Mia to give him the photographs. "Let's burn them together," he proposed. But Mia, guarding the Polaroids as closely as the Zapruder film of the

Kennedy assassination, replied that they would remain in her bank vault "for the rest of my life," to serve as a reminder of his betrayal. Lacking Woody's ability to compartmentalize, she redrafted her will to make sure he got custody of none of her children in the event of her death. She also contacted Paul Martin Weltz, the attorney who had overseen Woody's adoptions of Dylan and Moses, to inform him that Woody had deceived her. All the time that he had been clamoring for adoption, he was "screwing one of my kids," she said. Weltz doubted it would be possible to overturn the adoptions and instead suggested a coparenting agreement that would regulate Woody's visitation. Over the next six months, Weltz's negotiations with both parties resulted in an elaborate thirty-page legal settlement outlining their rights and responsibilities toward Dylan, Satch, and Moses. Under the terms of the agreement, Woody was to pay Mia $6,000 a month in child support. He also agreed to one of Mia's primary conditions, that he could not be alone with Dylan and Satch until they were twelve years of age. Curiously, Weltz never got the impression the couple was separating. "I always thought they were trying to put the pieces back together," he remarked later.

During the winter, Woody decided that Mia was having a nervous breakdown. At his insistence, and for the first time in her life, she began seeing a therapist and taking antidepressants and sleeping pills. Nothing helped alleviate her depression, and she felt as if she were walking around in a chemical fog. Her slurred speech made some people assume she was either intoxicated on liquor or high on drugs. One evening when Woody arrived at Elaine's for dinner with Mia at his side, Jean Doumanian noticed that she was groggy and disoriented, "like someone who was out on a doctor's pass for the evening." While visiting his penthouse one afternoon, Mia left a suicide note. Petrified, he dashed to his terrace and leaned over the railing to see if she had jumped to her death. Dutifully relating the incident to her therapist, he suggested hospitalization. "Many times she threatened to kill me, or have me killed," he told friends. "I started getting phone calls all night long, death threats calling me the devil and evil incarnate."

The previous September, Mia had adopted two Vietnamese orphans, both older children. One was a six-year-old boy who became crippled after contracting polio, and the other was an eleven-year-old girl, who, after becoming blind at age eight, was abandoned by her parents. Traveling to Hanoi and meeting the crippled boy, Sanjay, in person, Mia began to doubt the diagnosis. She asked for a further evaluation, which proved inconclusive. When she brought him to New York for tests, she learned he was severely retarded and functioning at an eighteen-month level. Not prepared to care for such a child, whose special needs would draw her attention away from Satch and Dylan, she reluctantly decided to arrange for his transfer to another family.

In the meantime, there remained the blind girl, Nguyen Thi Tam, who had not been able to leave Hanoi with Mia because her papers were still being processed. Although Mia was having second thoughts about taking Tam, she decided that canceling the adoption would be unfair to the girl.

In the case of both these children, Woody had been supportive and had even offered to help pay for Mia's trip to Hanoi. The situation changed after the Polaroids incident, however, and he became intensely suspicious of Mia's motives. Now it seemed clear to him that she was using the children like pacifiers, to bolster her spirits through times of trouble, as she had adopted Soon-Yi and Moses during her painful breakup with Andre Previn. His suspicion was confirmed at the beginning of February—barely three weeks after Mia learned of Woody's affair with Soon-Yi—when Mia agreed to take a sickly month-old African-American infant, whose mother had been addicted to crack. The adoption agency had not found a home for the infant, and he was to be placed shortly in permanent foster care. If Mia wanted him, the staff at the agency said, she had to act immediately. Within days, a bassinet was sitting next to her bed. She named the boy Isaiah Justus Farrow, after Sir Isaiah Berlin, Woody's favorite philosopher. Woody's first reaction was bewilderment. In his opinion, given Mia's depressed mental state, she could not take care of her own children, let alone an ailing infant.

Then, not two weeks after Isaiah appeared, the blind Vietnamese child finally came to join her new family. Malnourished and covered with lice, Tam reacted to her new home with fear, depression, and rage. "She was hard to deal with because she was violent," recalled a member of Mia's household. "She'd scratch and bite and kick and spit. Sometimes we had to physically restrain her." To make matters worse, an openly resentful Satch expressed his feelings toward the newcomer by "throwing things at her across the room and she couldn't see them coming."

In March, Mia arranged for the baptism of the younger children—Soon-Yi, Moses, Dylan, Satchel, Isaiah, and Tam—into the Roman Catholic Church. Over the years religion had played small part in her child-rearing. With such a large family, regular church attendance had proved awkward. She also felt self-conscious attending church. Because she was a movie star, people stared at her. In this time of emotional upheaval, not only did she seek religious comfort for herself, but she also realized that she had neglected to provide her family with a spiritual core.

On March 11, the family gathered at the Church of the Blessed Sacrament, a few blocks from their apartment. It was a joint ceremony with the three children of her close friends Casey and John Pascal. Present were all of Mia's children, with the exception of Matthew, who could not get away from his job. The children wore white shawls over their best dresses and suits, except Soon-Yi, who, unaware of the solemnity of the occasion, had come straight from Drew in her jeans. The children carried lit candles to the altar, where a priest sprinkled their heads with holy water. Afterward, there were refreshments at Mia's apartment for the various godparents, relatives, and neighbors.

Hearing of the baptism after the fact, Woody was given no opportunity to protest. "She was never religious for sixty seconds in all the years I knew her," he said. "And then she suddenly ran out and baptized the kids and told me she had found God. Then twenty-four hours later, she was threatening to stick my eyes out." He was planning to raise Dylan and Satch as humanists and let them choose their own religion when they grew up.

As their relations continued to deteriorate, they began to physically attack each other in public. In Central Park Woody yelled at Mia, and she punched him in the face. On another occasion, after leaving an Irish pub on West Seventy-ninth Street, they began quarreling on the sidewalk. As Woody turned to walk away, Mia, oblivious to passersby, thwacked him hard across the back. A few days after Tam's arrival, they took her for a stroll in Central Park but exchanged sharp words when they returned to the building. As the blind girl clutched helplessly at the sleeve of her new mother's jacket, Mia started to cry. Woody, patting her back, attempted to console her, but Mia, still in tears, dragged Tam into the lobby. A newspaper photographer who had shadowed them up Central Park West caught the quarrel on film. The next day five large photos were plastered across the *New York Daily News* with the soapy headline: REEL-LIFE STARS . . . HAVE REAL-LIFE SCARS.

One of Woody's confidants at this time was Jane Martin, who had worked for him as an assistant nearly as long as Mia had been his leading lady. Hearing about the slapping incidents, Martin was quick to sympathize with her boss. The relationship between the two "wives"—consort/mistress and office majordomo—had always been prickly. Mia, no prima donna, rarely yelled, but she could turn on a dime when somebody made her deeply angry. According to Martin, she would go "berserk screaming crazy," a sight sufficiently chilling that Martin never forgot it. "I've never been chewed out like I was twice by Mia," she recalled. "She can go from zero to 100 miles an hour in one second." Being around her was like "having a huge cobra coiled up in the corner of the room and having to watch it every day so it wouldn't come out."

∎ ∎ ∎ ∎ ∎ ∎

Voice of America:

OPRAH WINFREY: We are certainly empathizing with you but when you saw those pictures of your daughter, legs porno-

> graphically spread, how could you have let him back into your
> life? How could you? What did you tell yourself?"
> MIA: I know. He said he was sorry. I loved him.
> —*Oprah Winfrey Show,* February 11, 1997

■ ■ ■ ■ ■ ■ ■

Shadows and Fog, Woody's twenty-first film and his final picture for Arthur Krim, opened in February 1992. Shot in black and white, with a melancholy score by Kurt Weill, it was a hybrid movie that recycled his 1975 one-act play, *Death,* and paid homage to German Expressionist directors such as Fritz Lang. In a central-European town in the 1920s, Max Kleinman (Woody) is hauled out of bed in the middle of the night to help a posse hunt for a maniacal killer, only to find himself pursued as a suspect. The Kafkaesque clerk meets and falls in love with a circus performer (Mia), a sword swallower who is fleeing from her faithless lover (John Malkovich). To help viewers sit through the cinematic murk, Woody salted his cast with amusing cameos by Jodie Foster, Kathy Bates, Lily Tomlin, John Malkovich, even Madonna as a lusty trapeze artist, although the picture was so dimly lighted that it was difficult for moviegoers to recognize the celebrities. From now on, the director who disdained Hollywood would raid Tinseltown yearly for glamorous stars to pump up his box office. Famous artists appeared on-screen for a moment or two, and in most instances, worked for little salary. Juliet Taylor, with her usual zeal, told Madonna, for instance, that she would enjoy her role that would last two minutes and take only a day to shoot. Although a Woody Allen set was not most actors' idea of fun, the ploy worked. Not only Madonna, but respected actors and actresses were flattered when they were offered a part in a Woody Allen film. A mystified Jay Leno quizzed Kathy Bates on *The Tonight Show* as to why she had made a film about which she knew nothing—it could have been a porno film—and she replied, "Well, you kind of go on blind faith because it's Woody."

Budgeted at $14 million, *Shadows and Fog* received horrible notices. Stanley Kauffmann called the picture "the flip side of creative freedom," an example of "the worst that can happen when a good filmmaker (which Allen has become) gets his unsupervised way." Notwithstanding the presence of Madonna, the film earned an embarrassing $2.7 million, the weakest financially of Allen's films except *September.* The picture was derivative, causing even the usually complimentary French critics to wonder if Woody was not overdoing his imitation of the films of his favorite directors; one reviewer twitted him for lifting wholesale a mother and child scene from Chaplin, to which Woody replied that Chaplin's scene took place in the daytime, his own at night.

A few days before the release of *Shadows and Fog,* no doubt expecting to be panned by critics, Woody discoursed starchily to the *Los Angeles Times* that the reason for being a filmmaker was not to impress audiences or receive glowing reviews—or earn money—but to be innovative. Hopefully, his audiences would paddle along behind as he cruised out of the mainstream. (As usual, hype took precedence over truthfulness because what could be more mainstream than casting Madonna?) For all his confidence, Woody's ambition to navigate the lesser streams had run aground. Depressed and frightened by his problems with Mia, he had developed a full-blown case of writer's block. He was forced to seek the help of a figure out of his past, his old friend Marshall Brickman, who had cowritten three of Woody's biggest hits. Since 1979, when Woody had dropped him, Brickman had written or directed several films, including a big-budget Bette Midler picture, *For the Boys.* If he bore resentment about their past relationship, he kept it to himself.

From his drawer of odds and ends, Woody ransacked material he had dropped from *Annie Hall. Manhattan Murder Mystery* is the story of an East Side couple, Larry and Carol Lipton, who strike up a conversation with their next-door neighbors, a husband and wife. When the wife dies suddenly under suspicious circumstances, the Liptons become amateur sleuths and attempt to solve the mystery with the help of friends (Alan Alda and Angelica Huston).

Despite the turbulence of his life, Woody and Brickman managed to write a comedy-thriller with a few good jokes and a slapdash mystery plot that readers of Nancy Drew could figure out in a minute. Later Woody would guiltily regard *Manhattan Murder Mystery* as a waste of his time and call it a vacation from filmmaking, a pleasurable but "not significant" movie, which was another slap in the face to the faithful Brickman. *Manhattan Murder Mystery* served its purpose, however. Incapable of producing anything creative at this time, Woody relied on work for his emotional salvation.

PMK is a major player in New York's publicity machine. A blue-ribbon public relations giant representing A-list clients such as Robert Redford, Tom Hanks, Michelle Pfeiffer, and Courtney Love, the firm specializes in personal publicity for entertainment celebrities, which includes troubleshooting at a cost of about $3500 a month. Leslee Dart, a co-owner of PMK, had represented Woody since the mid-eighties, replacing his longtime publicist Richard O'Brien. A tall brunette in her late thirties, Dart is a careful, disciplined woman who pays strict attention to her weight, and that meant no sweets, no bread, no pasta, "and no weekend relaxation of the rules."

Among the stable of movie clients handled by PMK are probably a number of stars who have been arrested, divorced, or spent time in psychiatric hospitals. But Leslee Dart had never been required to perform crisis management for Woody Allen. In her eyes, he was a responsible, thoughtful man.

*   *   *

The New York celebrity world inhabited by Woody and Mia is about the size of a Trobriand island. For months there had been whispers of their breakup, including reports of his affair with Australian actress Judy Davis throughout the filming of *Husbands and Wives*. Annoyed, he sent word to columnist Liz Smith, denying that he had ever seen Davis off the set. To squelch rumors, Woody suggested a joint press release to announce there was nothing wrong, but Mia resisted. Privately, Woody didn't believe the public would care about their separation, or his involvement with Soon-Yi. With luck, people would forget in a week.

Unbeknownst to Woody, the media already had the lowdown on the breakup. What's more, it had nailed down the identity of the other woman as well.

On June 10, Richard Johnson, a *New York Daily News* columnist, was the first to break the story. "I reported that Woody and Mia had broken up," recalled Johnson, "but I didn't say why." He was still trying to squeeze further details out of Woody's publicist about the family romance. "But Leslee Dart, the incredible, unbelievable Leslee Dart, denied to me up the yin-yang that Woody was boning Soon-Yi."

Dart pretended to be shocked at Johnson's suggestion. "How can you say such a thing?" she snapped. "That's horrible."

"What's the problem?" Johnson replied. "It isn't his daughter." Nevertheless, for the moment he held back on the story of Woody and Soon-Yi.

Med-O-Lark is a coed camp for children ages eleven to sixteen that is located on a scenic four-mile lake in Washington, Maine, an hour's drive north of Portland. To occupy Soon-Yi over the summer—and to keep her away from Woody—Mia and her former husband, Andre Previn, decided to ship her to camp, where she could earn nine hundred dollars as a counselor and make new friends with youngsters her own age. Mia was familiar with Med-O-Lark because, five years earlier, Matthew Previn had worked there and enjoyed a pleasant summer. While Med-O-Lark offered a variety of outdoor activities such as rock climbing, and rafting on the Penobscot River, it was basically an arts-and-theater camp. Assigned to teach drawing and sketching, Soon-Yi bunked in a cabin with a dozen campers and two other counselors.

A product of Central Park West, and, most recently, Fifth Avenue penthouses and chauffeured limousines, Soon-Yi had not bargained for the camp's rustic ambience. A counselor remembered that she was in a tizzy about mosquitoes and the lack of city amenities. "The first thing she said after getting off the bus was, 'Oh my God, look at all the trees,' " said Hans Weise.

The first time the toilet in her cabin backed up, she said, "We'll have to call a plumber."

"There's a plunger in the bathroom," another counselor replied.

The biggest problem, however, turned out to be the telephone. Half a dozen times a day, a "George Simon" would call the director's office and ask for Soon-Yi. "It was extremely disruptive," said Hans Weise. "This person was phoning when the staff and children were out doing activities. At all hours Soon-Yi would have to be pulled out of her work."

For two weeks, Soon-Yi's art students received increasingly less attention. The camp administrators, tired of operating an answering service, told her to leave.

The party on the spacious lawn at Frog Hollow was for Dylan, who turned seven on July 11. Working in the city, her older brothers and sisters were planning to make a special trip to Connecticut on the bus. Mia warned Woody, whom she had invited reluctantly, about monopolizing Dylan. Lark and Daisy and the twins would be there only a short time because they had to return on the five o'clock bus and everyone wanted to spend time with Dylan. Woody agreed.

By summer, Mia and Woody were behaving like an acrimonious divorced couple. Woody had never enjoyed sleeping at Frog Hollow. Ordinarily he returned to the city on the same day, but this time he decided to stay overnight. Unhappy about having him in such close proximity, Mia told him to check into a motel, or bunk in the guest house on the other side of the pond. He did not listen to her.

On the afternoon of the party, he was unnerved by the sight of Mia, who was clad in her usual summer uniform of white T-shirt and rumpled khaki shorts and appeared poised to erupt like a volcano. Remembering her jokes about poisoning his red wine, he now took the precaution of bringing his own food from New York, usually a large barbecued chicken and a tin of Beluga caviar, which he ate right out of the container. Perhaps because the other guests ignored him, he sarcastically commented on the firecrackers and sparklers brought to the party by Casey and John Pascal, whom he disliked. Soon bored, he disregarded Mia's admonitions about monopolizing Dylan and plopped himself down at his daughter's side. At one point, he put a damper on the activities by dragging Dylan to the pond to play.

After the party was over, Mia angrily pounced on him. He had promised to leave Dylan alone but had done exactly the opposite. Woody did not respond. When it was time to retire, he slept, as usual, in the guest room near the garage. The next morning he was greeted by a note pinned to the door of a nearby bathroom:

CHILD MOLESTER at
BIRTHDAY PARTY!
Molded then abused one sister
Now Focused on Youngest sister
Family disgusted.

Horrified, he quickly ripped down the note and jammed it in his bag. In his opinion, Mia was insane. At that point, said a friend of the actress's, "things had gotten really crazy. There was lots of crying. She didn't hide a whole heck of a lot from the kids."

Med-O-Lark informed Mia that her daughter had been fired because a Mr. Simon "seemed to be her primary focus and definitely detracted from her concentration on being a counselor." Soon-Yi, the camp director wrote Mia, had returned to New York. Confronting "Mr. Simon," Mia demanded that he tell her the whereabouts of her daughter. Woody pleaded ignorance.

Some sixty miles away, in Lawrenceville, New Jersey, Soon-Yi was living in a college dormitory room at Rider, a private liberal arts college that, like Drew, made minimal demands on its students, especially in the summer. Woody had made all the arrangements for her to enroll in the summer session. It was Soon-Yi, however, who had chosen to register for The New South in Literature, Music, and Film, a three-credit course that examined southern culture since World War II, beginning with the spread of New Orleans jazz and ending with the fiction of Flannery O'Connor. Stashed away in rural New Jersey, she waited for the weekends when Woody's chauffeur arrived to drive her back to town.

That July, Soon-Yi abandoned her family. To her sisters and brothers, there remained fleeting memories of her mad giggling on the phone and a few of her personal belongings gathering dust in the girls' bedroom. At the dining table, the space where she had once sat was occupied by Isaiah's high chair. Mia stopped trying to locate her child and turned her attention to still another adoptee in dire need of a family. Some time earlier she had applied for a foster child, Tunisia, a nine-month-old crack-addicted infant, who needed temporary care until her mother recovered from her drug problems. Dylan and Satch were enthusiastic about a new sister until they heard she was only staying with them temporarily. Reluctantly, Mia withdrew the application.

On Tuesday afternoon, August 4, Woody arrived at Frog Hollow to spend the day with Dylan and Satch. Mia and two of the children, Tam and Isaiah, had gone shopping with Casey Pascal. Otherwise, the household was like it was on any other day, swarming with children and baby-sitters: the three

Pascal children being minded by the Pascal sitter, Alison Stickland, and Dylan and Satch in the care of two other sitters, Kristi Groteke and Sophie Berge. For Woody, these visits to Frog Hollow felt rather like a nuclear winter. Satch and Dylan were always excited to see him, but nobody else made him feel welcome. Moses, who would never forgive Woody for sleeping with his sister, deliberately snubbed him by disappearing into the woods for the day. Woody's feeling of entering "a household of enemies" was accentuated by the presence of Kristi Groteke, whom he felt was spying on him. This was the case. She had instructions from Mia to never let Dylan out of her sight. The afternoon passed uneventfully until Mia, who had returned home from shopping, became upset when she discovered that Dylan was not wearing underwear under her white sundress.

That evening Woody and Mia went to a local restaurant for dinner. Mostly their conversation consisted of shop talk about the new picture that was .scheduled to begin principal photography in a few weeks. Returning to the house, he went upstairs to tell Dylan and Satchel a "Little Woody" bedtime story, only to be interrupted by Tam, who began to scream at the sound of his voice. After six months in this country, and despite her enrollment in special-education classes at an excellent public school, she was still having difficulty adjusting to her new life. Her hellish tantrums were so earsplitting that Mia had to turn on the air conditioner to drown out her voice. In a few short months, she had developed a powerful hostility toward Woody, possibly because he seldom acknowledged her or included a toy for her in the shopping bags of gifts he brought for his own kids. "Woody no goody, Woody no goody," she would chant. Woody tried to continue the bedtime story, but Tam wouldn't stop screaming. Later, his nerves frayed from Tam's shrieking, he began upbraiding Mia for compulsively adopting children who were often emotionally or physically damaged. It was having a terrible effect on *his* children, by which he meant Dylan and Satch. Mia told him he could "rot in hell."

As Woody prepared to leave Frog Hollow the next morning, Dylan showed him a well-thumbed toy catalog, in which she had checked off certain items for him to bring when he returned on Saturday. "Daddy, don't forget," she cried as she ran off, her tousled blond curls flying.

"Okay," he replied. "See you Saturday."

Minutes later, after Woody had departed in his black Mercedes sedan, the phone rang. Mia answered it. The caller was Casey Pascal, who sounded apprehensive. Her baby-sitter, returning from Frog Hollow the previous day, had reported that "something very disturbing" had happened. Casey thought that Mia should know about it.

CHAPTER FIFTEEN

What the Heart Wants

While Mia was out shopping, Casey Pascal said, Alison Stickland had walked into the television room looking for one of the Pascal children and noticed Dylan on the sofa. Woody was kneeling beside his daughter with his face buried in her crotch. There was an intimate, unfatherly feeling about the tableau that disturbed Alison, as if she was witnessing something she shouldn't have. The baby-sitter's account deeply disturbed Mia. Hadn't Dr. Coates cautioned Woody about being overly intimate with the child? Her delicate face turned ashen as she suddenly remembered that on that afternoon her daughter was not wearing underpants.

"Did Woody have his face in your lap yesterday?" she asked Dylan, who was sitting on her bed.

Her father was holding her around the waist, Dylan replied. He would not release her, and when she tried to pull away he touched her "privates." Then, he had taken her upstairs to Mia's bedroom, to a crawl space in the closet, and touched her again with his finger. After listening to the child's chilling story, Mia became alarmed. She reached for a videocamera, which she had been using earlier to record Isaiah, and began taping Dylan. For months she had been on red-alert, looking for trouble, "like a pig hunting for truffles," said a person close to the family. She told everyone that Woody was "a sick bastard" who could not be trusted. If he could violate one of her daughters and make disgusting Polaroids, "then anything might happen. I know for a fact Mia didn't make up Dylan's story. She didn't have to. But when something did happen, her reaction was, 'See—I was right.' "

After talking to Dylan, Mia telephoned Eleanor Alter, a New York divorce lawyer she had recently retained as counsel. Alter advised her to take Dylan to the family pediatrician immediately. But Dylan became tongue-tied when she was questioned by Dr. Vadakkekara Kavirajan of New Milford, Connecticut. Prodded, she repeated part of the story but clammed up when the doctor asked where her father touched her. Alone with her mother afterward, as she ate an ice-cream cone, she admitted that speaking to a stranger about those things embarrassed her. The next day, returning to Dr. Kavirajan's, a physical examination revealed no sign of penetration but this time the physician was able to elicit the story Dylan had told to her mother.

That afternoon the pediatrician phoned Mia to say he would be notifying the authorities. Surprised, she tried to dissuade him, but Dr. Kavirajan had already checked with his lawyer. There was no physical evidence that Woody had sexually abused the child, but the law required him to report Dylan's story to the police. Immediately Mia called Dr. Susan Coates, who was treating Satch. If the local pediatrician was going to report the incident, Coates, too, was obligated to contact the New York City Child Welfare Administration and Woody as well. There would be an investigation. Mia burst into tears. Fearing Woody's anger, she begged Coates not to tell him.

Kristi Groteke returned to work after spending her day off in Boston. In describing what had taken place, Mia wanted to know if she observed anything out of the ordinary on Tuesday. Well, said Kristi, she wasn't terribly surprised to hear about Alison Stickland's account. At some point in the afternoon, there was about fifteen or twenty minutes when she couldn't locate Dylan. Or Woody. She had scoured the premises.

■ ■ ■ ■ ■ ■ ■

Moving Pictures:
FIELDING MELLISH: I'm doing a sociological study of perversion. I'm up to child molesting.

—*Bananas*, 1971

■ ■ ■ ■ ■ ■ ■

On the village green of Litchfield, Connecticut, population 8,500, the stone courthouse with its quaint clock tower looked as though it belonged in an Andy Hardy film. In August, the State Attorney for the Litchfield judicial district was on vacation. However, Frank Maco's assistant made a special call to report that a certain Dylan Farrow from Bridgewater was accusing her adopted father, Woody Allen, of sexually abusing her in an attic. Maco laughed. "I figured this was a practical joke," he said later. As it happened, Maco was a fan of Woody's films. His favorite was *Annie Hall*, particularly the scene in which Woody kills a spider "the size of a Buick" in Diane Keaton's bathroom.

Forty-five years old and a veteran prosecutor, Maco was appointed state's attorney for upscale Litchfield County in 1988. His first month on the job he won a conviction in a child sexual-abuse case. Returning from his summer holiday, Frank Maco turned his attention to Woody Allen, and ordered an investigation. At Frog Hollow, crime-squad trucks came barreling down the driveway. The attic was dusted for fingerprints and searched for hair samples. Detectives interviewed Dylan, Mia's other children, and a score of people involved with the family—neighbors, doctors, teachers, and baby-sitters—none of whom seemed to have much regard for Woody. In addition to the police investigation, Maco would go a step further. To determine if a criminal prosecution was warranted, he also asked the Child Sexual Abuse Clinic at Yale–New Haven Hospital—a highly respected group of two social workers and a pediatrician that had investigated 1,500 similar cases—to assess Dylan's claims of abuse.

The New York Child Welfare Administration assigned Dylan Farrow's case to Paul Williams, a thirty-two-year-old Jamaican-born social worker. A skilled investigator with an outstanding record, a quiet, dogged man, Williams had handled more than seven hundred child-abuse cases since he joined the agency in 1987, and was so highly regarded by his superiors that he had been named Caseworker of the Year in 1991. He was now specially selected to handle this high-profile, extremely sensitive case.

Williams's first order of business was to schedule a meeting with Woody, one that Woody promptly canceled. The caseworker made a second appointment. Then a third.

Finally, on August 20, Woody showed up at Lafayette Street. He was accompanied by an attorney. Though Williams did not say so, one of the things he was trying to determine was whether Woody fit the psychological profile of a sex offender. When he questioned him about his visit with Dylan on August 4, Woody looked away with imperial disdain and refused to answer. He was more willing to talk about Satch, and admitted that he had called him a bastard, but said it was only a joke. If a poor relationship existed, it was Mia's fault. At one point, when Williams brought up Soon-Yi, he blandly replied that they had "an adult, healthy relationship."

After a few minutes, Woody abruptly stood up and walked out. He didn't like Paul Williams or his snoopy questions. There was no doubt in his mind that the caseworker was out to get him.

Several days later, one of Williams's superiors informed him of hearing through the grapevine that the charges against Woody Allen were going to be dismissed and the case closed. After all, the filmmaker was one of New York's most distinguished citizens, as symbolic of the city as a wholesome red apple. In full throttle, Williams resolutely ignored the rumor and kept digging anyway. Did Woody Allen, for example, ever have sex with his sister as a teenager? The caseworker's attempt to interview Woody's psychiatrist about this question was quickly foiled by Woody's attorneys. However, in a two-page letter, Dr. Kathryn Prescott stated that she had been treating Woody since 1972, and "there has never been any suggestion that Mr. Allen was suffering from a sexual perversion/deviant sexual behavior." As for engaging in sex with Letty Aronson, Prescott added, there was absolutely no evidence of any such thing. Even bringing up such a bizarre notion, she said, was shocking and disgusting to her patient. From Williams's point of view, however, such inquiries were not ridiculous at all.

When Susan Coates first told Woody about Dylan's accusations, he listened in disbelief. Nothing at all happened, he said. And if he did rest his head on Dylan's lap, it was "a normal paternal thing . . . not in any way sexual." *Attic?* Was she crazy? He was terrified of closed-in places. Besides, there was nothing new about Mia's spreading ugly stories like this. For months she had been making threats. One of her favorites was: "You took my daughter, now I'm going to take yours." Only a few weeks earlier, in the course of a particularly rancorous phone conversation, she warned, "I have something very nasty planned for you." It seemed clear to him that she had acted out of hatred, cooking up the story and coaching Dylan to repeat it on videotape. Fortunately, few people would believe her.

Yet, Woody was worried. Obviously he could not pretend to ignore such a serious charge. In any case, knowing that the matter had been reported to the police propelled him into action. In an effort to take command of the situation, he responded with a preemptive strike, a sort of end run around Mia. That way, he could make public his side of the story, or at least a portion of it, before he could be accused of child molestation or anything else she might dream up.

On the morning of Thursday, August 13, Hal Davis was at his desk in the pressroom on the first floor of the New York County Courthouse. Davis, a reporter for the *New York Post,* who had been covering the courthouse since 1978, received "a call out of the blue" from PMK's Leslee Dart. "This is off the record," Dart announced. "But I have a client who has a case you might be interested in." Without mentioning her client's name, she referred Davis to Harvey Sladkus, a well-known matrimonial attorney.

Minutes later, Davis learned that a sealed motion was filed earlier that morning in Supreme Court by Woody Allen to obtain sole custody of Dylan, Satchel, and Moses Farrow. Once other court reporters began making calls, the story jumped the fence and by noon was hurtling out on the AP wire. Ordinarily, by the end of the day, reporters would have received the computerized printouts of the day's Requests for Judicial Intervention (records of the order to show cause) giving names and the relief being sought. What Dart provided, Davis explained, was "a shortcut."

Like sharks smelling blood in the water, the journalists scrambled for further details. But Dart, climbing to high moral ground, tried to keep them at bay. "Mr. Allen has never discussed his private life in public," she said tersely. "He does not intend to do so now."

Overnight the story gathered momentum. In Bridgewater, the sheriff's car drove up to Mia's front door. When the bell rang, she began screaming because she believed the burly officer had come to take her children away. He was merely trying to serve her legal papers. "Her hysteria and terror were contagious," recalled Kristi Groteke. "There we were, like two chickens without our heads, running from room to room, locking all the doors, and Mia was crying, 'Kristi, don't accept the papers! Don't touch the papers!' "

In the city that Saturday, Fifth Avenue was hot and quiet. Inside his air-conditioned penthouse, Woody kept busy on the phone with his attorneys. In an annoying development, Alan Dershowitz, the prominent Boston lawyer and Harvard Law School professor, was apparently also representing Mia. Dershowitz—who captured national attention when he won an acquittal for Klaus von Bulow, the socialite accused of trying to murder his wife with an insulin injection that had sent her into an irreversible coma—denied he was Mia's attorney. Instead, he described himself as "a kind of mediator" between Mia, for whom he felt pity, and Woody, "a great filmmaker" who unfortunately had acted foolishly by making "a career-destroying decision." Even though a mediator is generally brought in by both sides, in this instance there was no question about Dershowitz's loyalties. As he explained later at the hearing, Mia "needed a defender and an advocate and I reluctantly played that role because I was a great admirer of Woody Allen." Dershowitz demanded unemployment compensation for Mia, suggesting Woody pay her over the next ten years for the loss of her job as his leading lady in thirteen films. The lump sum of $2.5 million was mentioned. Woody decided Dershowitz must be crazy.

Hopes that Woody could keep a low profile were dashed that afternoon when Mia's mother went into battle mode. Unable to contain her fury, Maureen O'Sullivan issued a puzzling statement to the media through her publicist, John Springer. With the precision of a Panzer commander, the eighty-one-year-old actress lobbed faxes into the city's news outlets. Woody was "a desperate and evil man," she wrote. He had injured her family, and she wasn't going to stand for it. When reached by a reporter at her home in Phoenix, she said ominously that the truth "will soon be made public." It was front-page news in the Sunday edition of the *Daily News,* where double banner headlines—BOMBS AWAY and EVIL—bracketed Woody's picture.

On Monday morning, the explosive accusations of child abuse surfaced when the Connecticut State Police confirmed they were conducting an investigation involving Woody Allen and the sexual abuse of his seven-year-old daughter. By that time, PMK was already announcing that Woody had admitted having an affair with Mia's adult daughter, "a lovely, intelligent woman who has and continues to turn my life around in a wonderfully positive way." His only crime was falling in love, which was "real and happily all true." In no way was his affair related to the custody suit charging Mia as an unfit mother. "They are totally separate issues," the statement continued, never making reference to the double police investigations in Connecticut and New York.

Within hours, television crews descended on Woody's building like a horde of marauding Visigoths. The only person who would talk to them was a doorman, who defended Woody as "a very nice guy, a genius, and a great tipper." Woody's problems seemed crystal clear to the doorman. "Mia's just trying to get revenge," he said. Toward evening Woody emerged from the building, his head lowered and his fishing hat pulled down over his glasses. He hopped into his beat-up station wagon and headed over to Michael's Pub. There was a small audience that evening, probably because nobody imagined he would show up. Afterward, he stopped to sign autographs before creeping out the back door.

The next day Woody called a news conference at the Plaza Hotel. Local television stations interrupted regular programming for live coverage. In a room overflowing with reporters and TV cameras, he swept up to the microphone with a businesslike expression on his face. Outfitted in a blue button-down oxford shirt and khaki slacks, he began to read, sonorously, a two-page prepared statement in a style of delivery that combined Hamlet's soliloquy with traces of stand-up comedy. Even though he had always "assiduously avoided publicity," he felt compelled to defend himself because he had absolutely not sexually abused his daughter. It was Mia, a dangerous woman unfit to raise children, who was using the sexual-abuse charge, "a currently popular though heinous card played in all too many child custody cases." Her lawyers were demanding $7 million in exchange for dropping the child-abuse allegations, an offer he of course rejected. While there was nothing funny about the content of his statement, the famous vocal mannerisms invited nervous smiles as reporters seemed unsure how to respond. Completing his prepared text, Woody turned away from the podium without answering questions. As he was heading toward the door, however, he stuttered, "This is my one public appearance in years, and it's all straight lines." The reporters laughed.

After the press conference, Alan Dershowitz denied that Mia had demanded $7 million. The discussions about money were part of negotiations to establish a trust fund for the children. He also pointed out, again correctly, that the child-abuse investigations in Connecticut and New York had not been instigated by Mia, but by Dylan's doctors, acting under state laws. Woody, he suggested, filed his custody suit for one reason: to divert attention from those investigations.

∎∎∎∎∎∎∎

Voice of America, Part One:
Q: What's Woody's latest flick?
A: "Honey, I Bleeped the Kids."
Q: What's his next film?
A: "Close Encounters with a Third Grader."
—*New York Post*, 1992

Voice of America, Part Two:
NEWSWEEK: The question most people are concerned about is Mia Farrow's charge that you sexually molested Dylan. Is this in any sense true?
WOODY ALLEN: Of course not. I'm on record with the most unequivocal denial that you can possibly imagine.
—*Newsweek*, 1992

∎∎∎∎∎∎∎

"The heart wants what it wants," he told *Time*. "There's no logic to those things." It was a paraphrase of Blaise Pascal's maxim, "The heart has its reasons which reason knows nothing of." Most people had not read the maxims of Pascal, but that was another matter. Most people didn't appreciate the maxims of Woody Allen, just as they also rejected his "The Woman I Love" speech as romantic justification for sleeping with Mia's daughter. At the *New York Post*, Cindy Adams reported that mail was running ten to one against "Woodenhead Allen." Readers ranged "from calling him a nerd and a turd to gentler phraseology of bum, scum, crum, and creep. Also pig." To which she added, "And they're the favorable letters." In an interview with *People*, Mia's brother John Farrow, now a boat salesman in Annapolis, Maryland, happily predicted Woody's indictment and ruin. "When all of it comes out, he's going to jail," Farrow chortled. "I'd like to take his little flute and ram it."

According to his friends, Woody was surprised by the public outcry. "He couldn't imagine that other people would react as they did," said Walter Bernstein. His goodness was "self-evident." Above all, Woody was amazed that people actually were taking Mia seriously. He quickly learned that the public was fascinated by his incipient disgrace and that others profited by it.

Hearing the news, Dominick Conde, the photographer who had caught Woody and Soon-Yi holding hands at Madison Square Garden in 1990, checked his agency's files. "Whoa," he whistled, "look what I have." What he had was the only photograph of them together, looking like lovers. According to Conde, it "sold like crazy" all over the world. Soon he bought himself a new apartment.

Over the next several weeks, Woody's problems became the number-one interest of the country, even threatening to overshadow the Republican National Convention. In Houston, evangelical delegates harping on the popular topic of "family values" could not resist casting him as a personification of everything that ailed the country. But the networks slyly sandwiched Woody bulletins between the speeches of Barbara Bush and Marilyn Quayle, as if they were covering an unfolding sensational news story.

Magazines that had been praising Woody's genius for years were suddenly putting his life under a microscope. During the week of August 31, *Time, Newsweek,* and *People* trumpeted the Woody and Mia story across their covers. In endless hours of interviews, Woody tried to explain that he was not Soon-Yi's biological father or a father figure, had never lived in her home, had never been married to her adoptive mother. And yet in a sidebar, *Time* assembled a group of psychiatrists to discuss "What Is Incest?" (Their consensus: Incest might be too strong a word, but Woody and Soon-Yi's relationship is "surely an abuse of power.") No wonder confused readers thought he was sleeping with one of his daughters and had sexually molested a younger one.

Predictably, the Konigsbergs were in shock. Privately mortified, Woody's mother chose not to speak to the press, but Marty Konigsberg had plenty to say, little of it sympathetic toward his son. Mia was "a nice girl" with a conniving mother who "put her up to all this." Still, Woody should not have traded her for Soon-Yi without expecting to "take the heat." Only Letty came forward to defend her brother and accused Mia of adopting children "not for their needs but for hers." What's more, Letty sniped, "she favors her biological children while treating the older adopted kids as servants." Thereafter, Mia would find herself constantly depicted as an unstable woman for wanting a family of eleven, as if the state of mind required to accumulate that number of children was inherently suspicious.

■ ■ ■ ■ ■ ■ ■

Moving Pictures:

STANDARDS AND PRACTICES MAN: Child molestation's a touchy subject.

MICKEY SACHS: Read the papers. Half the country's doing it.

—*Hannah and Her Sisters,* 1986

■ ■ ■ ■ ■ ■ ■

On an impulse, Woody invited Moses to lunch. Woody's motion for temporary support and visitation had resulted in a court ruling: He could see Satch twice a week, with a third person in the room, but not Dylan. However, no restrictions were placed on his meeting with Moses.

To his surprise, the normally sweet-tempered boy had turned against him. In a letter to his father, he lashed out that he never wanted to see Woody again because "I don't consider you my father anymore." Having sex with "his son's sister" was "a horrible, unforgivable, needy, ugly, stupid thing." He hoped that "you get so humiliated that you commit suicide." As for a lunch date, he added, "forget about it."

At the mention of Woody's name, said a family observer, "Moses would get very angry. For months before the scandal ever broke in the papers, he was depressed. He was such a dutiful, good-hearted boy, with total integrity, and now he got hurt big time."

Bridgewater residents were careful to avoid the media. "Mia was going through a bad time," said one local, "and we didn't want to make it worse." However, the Farrow children were constantly running up to the television vans on the road outside Frog Hollow and holding impromptu news conferences to defend the family. Peering solemnly through his glasses, Moses told a newsperson that Woody "has no morals. Everything seems right to him. He says he's in love with Soon-Yi but he's not. He's just using her." Lark and Daisy suddenly showed up in the newsroom of the *New York Post* one morning and asked for news of their sister. "They were nervous," recalled columnist Andrea Peyser. "It was clear their mother had sent them to trade an interview for information. I thought it was mean of Mia to send children to do her dirty work." Sitting down with *Post* reporters, the girls were not shy about putting Soon-Yi on the psychiatric couch. According to Lark's analysis, her sister was "emotionally immature for her age"; Daisy thought the romance was "disgusting."

The sight of Mia's kids denouncing him on CNN and elsewhere embarrassed Woody. The children he had treated royally for the last ten years, whom he had even airlifted to Europe on the Concorde, were suddenly buzzing around the media jackals like a surly Greek chorus. Meanwhile, the person most mortified by the press attention enveloping the children was Andre Previn.

The village of Bedford, New York, a wealthy, exclusive Westchester County community an hour north of the city, is horse country with hundreds of miles of trails winding through the woods. You can still buy a hundred-acre farm and an eighteenth-century house set in a bucolic landscape straight out of *National Velvet*, but Bedford and Bedford Hills and Katonah are also home to so many movie stars that they might be considered Beverly Hills East. Here lived Andre Previn with his wife, Heather, and their eight-year-old son, Lukas, when Previn was not commuting to London for various musical engagements.

Ever since Mia's frantic phone call after finding the Polaroids, he had maintained a calculated distance from Soon-Yi, whom he had scarcely raised. In all likelihood he was counting on Mia, "a remarkable mother," to cope with her customary competence and make sure Woody repaired his "unspeakable breach of trust" by leaving Soon-Yi alone. Beyond that, he was not particularly anxious to talk to the girl and surely did not want the responsibility of her living with his family in Bedford. By now it had been several months since he had spoken to his daughter about Woody Allen or anything else. Therefore, learning that she and Woody were continuing to have sex, he was rendered speechless. As a father, he couldn't find "a colorful enough vocabulary" to express his utter disgust for Woody.

The shameless invasion of privacy that passed for normal in Hollywood continued to repel Previn, who refused to stand for intrusions into his personal life and detested people who flaunted their grievances to the press. In 1970 his affair with Mia generated intense interest from the English paparazzi, who climbed trees outside Previn's Belgravia flat to peek at the couple. He would never forget the "degrading" and "unbelievable" spectacle of the "gutter press corps" nesting in the trees. In a curious way, history was repeating itself. Now it was not only the gutter press but the world's news media roosting in his trees.

Sixty-three and suffering from painful angina, he wanted the whole tawdry investigation to disappear. Instead, the name of Previn, a distinguished conductor and composer, was guaranteeing an automatic laugh on *The Tonight Show.*

As for his youngest daughter, she had become a celebrity in her own right. Television news showed Soon-Yi strutting in and out of Woody's building, looking relaxed and perky, long hair flying, a book bag casually swinging from her shoulder. She appeared resentful that anyone should believe she had been preyed upon. Hinting at her true disposition, she insisted that she made her own choices. "Let's not get hysterical," she declared to *Newsweek.* "I'm not a retarded little underage flower who was raped, molested, and spoiled by some evil stepfather—not by a long shot." Evidently, she clung to the typically juvenile belief that one's parents were incapable of having sex. Except for work and family occasions, she told *Time,* Woody and Mia had "little to do with one another." She also insisted that Mia would have been equally jealous had Woody slept with "another actress or his secretary."

The morning after Woody's press conference at the Plaza, news helicopters began circling the campus at Drew. Later the same day Soon-Yi was located miles away at Rider. Woody instructed her to attend class and say nothing to the media. Nevertheless, Andrea Peyser, the *New York Post* columnist, reached her by phone at her dormitory. Years later Peyser recalled being "stunned by her complete lack of regard for Mia. She hated her like poison. Obviously, she had never bonded with her mother but she seemed to have no feeling for anyone else either. I wondered if she was capable of strong emotions, even for Woody." When Peyser asked about her beau, she broke into a giggling fit and said, "I don't want to talk about it." She told her roommate, however, that she had "a boyfriend," without mentioning his name, therefore making Woody sound like the boy next door.

Soon Rider was transformed into a sideshow. College officials posted a security guard outside Soon-Yi's dorm, corralled reporters behind barricades, and assigned another guard to accompany her to class. Fueling up on Whoppers, delivered by Burger King directly to her dorm room, she spent her time reading Tennessee Williams and making telephone calls to Woody on a pay phone in the hallway. Before her picture appeared in the papers, the school had known nothing about her famous connections. To the surprise of the residence director, Soon-Yi paid no attention to the jumble of cameras, mikes, and reflectors. When the director inquired how she was doing, Soon-Yi smiled and said "she was used to publicity because of her famous parents."

Far from feeling beleaguered, she seemed to be basking in the attention. Her only complaint was that the air-conditioning in her room had broken down.

■ ■ ■ ■ ■ ■ ■

Caught on Tape:

MIA: Now you want little girls to turn you on because you can't get a hard-on with me anymore. That's all it is. You couldn't fuck me anymore so you wanted a little girl.

WOODY: [no response]

MIA: But I know that as people get toward their 60s, it gets harder and harder to get [aroused]. So that's why guys in their late 50s turn to little girls.

WOODY: Why?

MIA: To get sexual stimulation. Something new. Something forbidden. More erotic.

—Excerpt from transcript of a phone conversation,
   ca. August 4–December 31, 1992, taped by Woody Allen
   and subsequently subpoenaed for
   Woody Allen v. Maria Villiers Farrow

■ ■ ■ ■ ■ ■ ■

At long last the summer ended. At the Loews on East Nineteenth Street, the weekend crowd for *Honeymoon in Vegas* slouched in their seats with popcorn and sodas, yawning through a raft of boring previews. When the trailer for *Husbands and Wives* appeared, however, the entire theater snapped to attention. Stern-faced, costumed in frumpy sweater and jeans, Mia asks Woody if he is ever attracted to other women? "Like who?" he replies. The audience shrieked with laughter.

TriStar, stuck with *Husbands and Wives,* was understandably nervous. The film was to open on September 23 in eight theaters, a limited run that could qualify as an art-house opening. But now that art was clearly following life, the studio decided to "go wide" and open five days early in 865 theaters. Despite the free advertising, *Husbands and Wives* did poorly at the box office.

Shortly before the opening of *Husbands and Wives,* Woody began principal photography on *Manhattan Murder Mystery,* the movie he had coauthored with Marshall Brickman. Over the summer, it was obvious that Mia would have to be replaced, and at the last minute Diane Keaton stepped in to play her role. The reunion of Woody and Diane seemed to be an inspired move, resulting in a kind of *Annie Hall Two* that would conjure up the magnificent chemistry of their best work. Unfortunately, nostalgia aside, the idea backfired because audiences found it hard to believe that Annie and Alvy were now middle-aged. Woody looked run-down ("like Rumpelstiltskin" to a discomfited John Simon) and Diane was still pretty but overweight and unquestionably matronly. Together they could pass for a retired couple on Social Security. At the box office, domestic grosses barely topped *Husbands and Wives'* earnings of $10.5 million.

Despite Woody's ability to compartmentalize his life, *Manhattan Murder Mystery* had been made under trying conditions. Shooting on location in Bryant Park, he was booed by bystanders. Off the set, he had only to step out of his building to face a three-ring circus. To the dismay of the co-op board, some of whom remembering from years past his promise to be a model tenant, television trucks and hordes of paparazzi kept vigil.

When summer school ended, Soon-Yi returned to the city and moved in with Woody before it was time to return to Drew for her sophomore year. Adopting a foxhole mentality, the couple tried to stay out of the public eye as much as possible. Because Woody insisted they not be seen together for legal reasons, there were no sightings by the press or fans at Elaine's or his other usual haunts. Like Hansel and Gretel, they passed most of their time playing house in Woody's fortress, the faraway whisper of street traffic swirling below.

In Manhattan, a small group of expensive matrimonial lawyers handle nearly all the high-profile divorce cases of superrich couples. Among this exclusive group is Raoul Lionel Felder, the top family lawyer in the country, and close behind is Eleanor Alter, who was representing Mia. A short, stocky woman of fifty-three, Alter was a partner at Rosenman & Colin, a firm of two hundred lawyers, which charges clients four hundred dollars an hour. In legal circles, the battle-hardened Alter is known as a cold and arrogant person. She has never denied it. "Lots of people will tell you I'm a bitch," she once boasted to the *New York Times*. Even though Woody certainly had the means to hire the most prestigious matrimonial lawyer in the United States, he may have chosen his new lawyer in the same hit-and-miss way that many people pick an attorney, by calling his business lawyer and getting a referral.

Elkan Abramowitz was a respected trial lawyer who specialized in white-collar crime. As he admitted, Woody's case was "a total exception" to his usual activities, which included an antitrust proceeding against the Mafia. In the past, he had also served as special prosecutor in the investigation of a stock transfer involving Mayor David Dinkins. A graduate of New York University School of Law and a partner in Morvillo, Abramowitz, Grand, Jason & Silberberg, Abramowitz was fifty-two, a tall, bearish, silver-haired man with a slight potbelly and an odd gait that suggested his shoes might be pinching. For twenty-five years he had been happily married to a best-selling novelist, Susan Isaacs *(Compromising Positions, Shining Through)*, with whom he had two grown children. They owned a redbrick house in the leafy Long Island suburb of Sands Point, as well as a city apartment on Central Park South.

The first time Abramowitz met Woody, he remarked, "Look, I've only spent three hours with you, but I figure I've known you my whole life." It was not that Woody had suddenly turned into a cuddly person. The astute Abramowitz was merely observing that Woody Allen fans automatically assumed they knew the man, and so it was like representing "somebody who lives next door to everybody."

In legal circles, Woody's choice of a counselor who had never practiced matrimonial law raised a few eyebrows. While Abramowitz was an accomplished lawyer, he was hardly a flamethrower. "Choosing him was a mistake," said Raoul Felder. "He had never played in this playground." An attorney who knew his way around the matrimonial courtrooms, Felder thought that Woody's affair with Soon-Yi would doom his suit for custody of Dylan, Satch, and Moses Farrow. "For all intent and purposes, he has been her father. If this is the case, he'll never be able to visit them much less have custody." For that reason alone, Felder later said that he would have turned down the case. Even at the outset, he considered Woody's case a lost cause.

CHAPTER SIXTEEN

Dirty Laundry

Since August, Woody Allen had been pursued by the television networks for an exclusive interview. "It was a huge story," according to Victoria Gordon, producer of the CBS newsmagazine *60 Minutes.* "Leslee Dart told me Woody wanted to respond in some way and was thinking of writing an op-ed piece for the *New York Times.* Of course I believed he could make the same points more effectively in a television interview." Although Dart preferred *Nightline,* in the end, Woody chose *60 Minutes.* In meetings with Letty Aronson, Gordon and correspondent Steve Kroft nailed down the ground rules: Woody was free to make whatever points he wished, but there would be no deals, no questions off-limits.

As Kroft promised at the start of the program, aired on the Sunday before Thanksgiving of 1992, it would be a "no holds barred" session. Woody claimed that he had no idea how the Polaroids came to be on the mantel. "What about the way Mia discovered the affair?" Kroft asked him. "By finding certain embarrassing pictures."

Woody looked at him in surprise, as if he had not expected Kroft to mention the photographs.

"Yes." In his living room, he sat up straighter in his chair. "What is the question?" he murmured.

After two decades in broadcast journalism, the *60 Minutes* correspondent had perfected his technique. Kroft gazed into Woody's face and said very quietly, "I presume that is not the way you wanted her to find out."

Woody squinted.

"Or did you want her to find out?"

He seemed to be considering the question. "I never really thought about it," he answered. He guessed that he would have told her "eventually."

"He was very organized and had obviously given it a great deal of thought," Kroft recalled. "But there was a total blind spot about the impropriety of his relationship with Soon-Yi. He seemed not to care about what people thought." Instead, he joked about his harrowing problems. "Some of the best material in the interview," Kroft said later, "was cut so as not to offend viewers."

Kroft was completely sympathetic to Woody, who, he said, "had always been a hero of mine. At the time of *Annie Hall,* I thought he was the smartest person in the world." He added that he was not normally "starstruck. But the reading material in his living room, actually everywhere, was heavy stuff. In his bathroom I saw works on Freud, the kind of books you would expect to find in the office of a professor of psychiatry."

As background, Woody supplied *60 Minutes* with visual materials: the dagger-pierced Valentine, the child-molester note, custody affidavits in which Mia swore he was a wonderful father. However, the main point he wanted to get across regarded Mia's parenting. Her adoption of so many children was abnormal behavior, he argued. In addition, she was a poor mother. (Actually, these allegations were shared, to some degree, by a few people who knew Mia and Woody and believed Mia had problems handling so many children. "Her style of mothering was pathological," said one observer, who was not surprised by her "hysterical" reaction to Woody's infidelity, "only its intensity.")

Then Kroft raised the allegations that Woody took Dylan into the attic and touched her. "Is there any truth to that at all?"

Woody deflected the question. "Look, be logical about this. I'm fifty-seven. Isn't it illogical that at the height of a very bitter, acrimonious custody fight, I'm going to drive up to Connecticut, where nobody likes me and I'm in a house full of enemies, and suddenly, on visitation, pick this moment in my life to become a child molester?" He then answered his own question: "It's just incredible. It's so insane!"

Even though *60 Minutes* had earned its stripes as fearless investigators, in this instance the newsmagazine seemed curiously timid. No effort was made to ask tough questions of the subject or shed new light on the story. In fact, Kroft concluded with an exoneration: "Reports we were shown seem to support his contention that he's not a child molester."

■ ■ ■ ■ ■ ■ ■

The Film Critics:
"There was something awful about the Soon-Yi business, but on the other hand something very human, the type of ambivalence that surrounds him and his work."

—JOHN SIMON

"The press depicted him as a dirty old man but nobody considered he might be more of a mentor to Soon-Yi. With Woody Allen, sex is not the point so much as communication."

—ROGER EBERT

■ ■ ■ ■ ■ ■ ■

"I don't care what people say about the age difference. It's just pure jealousy," said Soon-Yi when she returned to Drew after the Thanksgiving break. Rumors that Woody was losing interest in her were instigated by her mother, she informed a reporter, who was furious that Woody had never married her.

Soon-Yi did not appear on *60 Minutes,* to the relief of the producers. "We knew enough about her to think she was not going to be a great interview," said a staff member. On *60 Minutes* Woody had seemed bored when talking about Soon-Yi. When asked if he saw her on weekends, he said, nonchalantly, "Yeah, I see her when she gets off school, when she's off for the holiday or something." "Or something" did not suggest a passionate love affair. In private moments with friends, he displayed more emotion. Of course he was in love with Soon-Yi, a sweet girl who appreciated the things he did for her. But sometimes he thought he had made an error in judgment ("I screwed up"). Some insiders predicted the romance would not endure, especially if Woody was forced to choose between Soon-Yi and getting custody of his children.

Andre and Heather Previn worried that Woody would discard Soon-Yi after he had become bored with her sexually. But for all his sympathy, Andre had no wish to testify in the custody proceeding. His feelings mirrored those of his son Sascha, who one morning confided to Kristi Groteke, with tears in his eyes, "I'm so sick of this whole thing. I wish it would just end." The last thing Andre wanted was to be a spear-carrier in Woody and Mia's drama.

In the summer, Soon-Yi had conducted herself with dignity and composure. But as the spotlight faded, and the loss of her family dawned on her, she seemed less self-assured. Her fame of a few months earlier had taken an unexpected and unpleasant turn. The media wickedly lampooned her in a spate of nasty, disparaging gags that were both sexist and racist. On *Saturday Night Live* she was raunchily impersonated by comedian Rob Schneider; *Mad TV* based an insulting character on her, and she (along with Woody and O. J. Simpson) was the butt of a crude Howard Stern radio skit, "Mandingos Over Broadway."

She was lonely at Drew, where the other students made fun of her behind her back. She had few friends. No one wanted to room with her—or date her—and so she spent every weekend with Woody in New York.

If Soon-Yi felt depressed, her little sister was in far worse shape emotionally. The previous summer, Dylan suddenly began to complain of headaches. In a daze, she lazed in the hammock at Frog Hollow. "If you asked her what was wrong," recalled a visitor, "she'd say she didn't feel well." She also began to wet her bed, something that had not happened since she was three years old. Her father's abrupt and painful removal from her life was wrenching to the child, and yet, under the circumstances, it was impossible for her to directly express any feelings of grief.

Woody saw Satch twice a week, in the presence of a social worker. On the trip to Fifth Avenue, the boy would get nervous, but by the time Woody's driver returned him home to Central Park West two hours later, his mood would have swung 360 degrees. He was extremely fond of toys. Under his arm he would be carrying his latest loot, along with a shoe box full of drawings or a cake he and his father had baked together. Dylan did not like that at all. "Satch and Dylan were very close and so he knew better than to tell her he had a good time," said a member of the household. "If he showed her the cake, she would say right away, 'Put that cake away, I'm not eating it,' just as if she were the divorced woman."

During Christmas week, the Connecticut State Police paid a final visit to Frog Hollow to wrap up loose ends of their investigation. On an earlier visit, Dylan, using anatomically correct male and female dolls that a psychologist employed by the police had shown her, joined the two figures in a simulation of sexual intercourse. This time the investigators decided to quiz her further about it. To Mia's shock, Dylan described a visit to her father's apartment, which Mia calculated to be in the fall of 1991 when she was in Vietnam to adopt Sanjay and Tam. According to Dylan, her father and Soon-Yi were making love on the terrace. The child's description of their intimate behavior was so detailed and so clinical that Mia immediately reported it to Eleanor Alter, who, meanwhile, had successfully subpoenaed Woody's psychiatric records.

■ ■ ■ ■ ■ ■ ■

In His Own Words:
Q: What are sex perverts?
A: Sex perverts are the most wonderful people in the world . . . a
   much maligned majority group.
Q: Have you known many?
A: Just family. Immediate family.

—WOODY ALLEN interview, 1972

■ ■ ■ ■ ■ ■ ■

Acting Justice Phyllis Gangel-Jacob is an expert at dealing with messy legal cases involving the rich and famous. Nevertheless, her assignment in August 1992 to the Allen-Farrow case seemed like a piece of rotten luck for Woody because in legal circles the judge was known as "a man-eater." Donald Trump, after his divorce from his wife, Ivana, declared Gangel-Jacob's court to be "stacked in favor of women." Other disgruntled males—attorneys as well as husbands—complained she was unworthy of sitting on the bench.

In New York Supreme Court, the normal method of processing cases is random assignment by computer. In the Allen-Farrow case, however, a clerk had initially given the case directly to Gangel-Jacob, which aroused the ire of her colleagues, who grumbled that as usual she grabbed all the celebrities. As a result, the case was reassigned to Acting Justice Elliott Wilk. While Wilk was on vacation, Gangel-Jacob continued to handle the preliminary hearing.

For a man of fifty-one, Elliott Wilk was exceptionally fit. He had run in five New York City Marathons and was training for his sixth. Growing up in Queens, the son of an attorney, the justice attended public schools and graduated from New York University Law School in 1966. In private practice, he represented draft protestors during the Vietnam War, and, in the seventies, championed inmates prosecuted for crimes during the Attica prison riot. Now he lived on Central Park West with his wife, Betty Levinson, a specialist in matrimonial and family law who had represented Hedda Nussbaum, the battered wife of convicted child killer Joel Steinberg.

Visitors to Wilk's robing room at 60 Centre Street usually noticed the photograph of the Cuban revolutionary Ernesto "Che" Guevara on the wall. What they did not see was any judicial regalia because the trim, bearded Wilk entered his courtroom in a business suit, even though wearing black robes "would save on cleaning bills," he joked. The backbone of his judicial career had been highly contentious social issues, including child welfare, the homeless, and housing, and not the marital brawls of unmarried movie stars. His admirers spoke of him as a thoughtful jurist with superior intelligence (an I.Q. of 180) and an iconoclastic approach to the bench, a man who "asked sharp questions to cut through the nonsense."

At the same time, the jogging jurist managed to be a controversial figure, a cross between Jimmy Stewart and Abby Hoffman. His critics castigated him for pursuing his own liberal social agenda instead of trying cases. "His reputation for being ultra-liberal is deceptive," according to a divorce attorney who practiced before him. "There's also a defiance of authority, and clearly Woody Allen was a threatening figure to him." Another of New York's premier lawyers called him "a starfucker. In the Allen case, because these were celebrities, there was talk of a video camera in the courtroom. There was no justification. My God, when you have abuse cases you *close* the courtroom. If there had been cameras, those children would have been identified all over the world and their lives ruined, but Wilk and the lawyers would be famous." Both Woody and Mia had in fact tried to close the courtroom to not only TV cameras but also the press and public because the case involved children. Phyllis Gangel-Jacob ruled against the cameras but she did permit press coverage.

Justice Wilk's sympathy for the downtrodden did not end with draft protestors. It was well known in legal circles that he favored women. And mothers.

On January 12, 1993, Wilk held a preliminary hearing to rule on Woody's motion requesting regular visits with all three of his children. In the courtroom that morning, Woody was seated with his lawyers and publicists in a single row on the right side of the room. Camped behind Woody, breathing heavily down his neck, sat eavesdropping *New York Post* reporters. Mia was not present, but Eleanor Alter riffled her folders and informed Justice Wilk that Woody did not deserve additional visitation. For example, she claimed that in a fit of anger he overreacted by grabbing Satch's legs and yelling, "I'm going to break both your fucking legs, you little bastard." Woody listened to her accusation, his face flushed with indignation. Worse than that, Eleanor Alter went on, a grumpy Woody once shoved Dylan's face into a plate of hot spaghetti.

Then Alter dropped a hammer on Woody. Mr. Allen, she announced, had had intercourse with the sister of his children while the little ones were present. Her words sent the *Post* reporters sitting behind Woody scrambling for their notepads. Quoting from an affidavit submitted by Mia, Alter repeated Dylan's account to the Connecticut police: On a visit to their father's apartment, Dylan and Satchel noticed him sitting with Soon-Yi on the terrace and ran out to join them, but they were chased off and told to play. After a while, when Woody and Soon-Yi disappeared into a bedroom, the children tiptoed up to the door and observed them "lying together on top of the covers." Once again, they were shooed away. A short time later, Dylan returned alone and secretly watched her father and sister "complimenting each other and making sounds like snoring," and this time her presence went unnoticed. She saw "Daddy put his penis in Soon-Yi."

In light of Woody's carelessness in disporting himself before the child, Alter told Judge Wilk, "visitation with Dylan is unthinkable." Wilk agreed.

Woody, taken by surprise, looked like a bottle under pressure. As soon as the hearing ended, he stormed down the marble hall to the elevators trailed by a flock of reporters who caught up to him on the steps of the courthouse. With clenched jaw, he cried out, "Great, the wilder the charges the better!" Dylan's story was pure fantasy, "too insane to even think about." He and Soon-Yi never gamboled on his balcony. Likewise, it was "absolutely untrue" that he ever thought of twisting Satch's leg or pushing Dylan into a plate of spaghetti. He was sick of Mia using the children as her mouthpieces to vent her fury against him. "She takes her daughter and makes her say it," he angrily informed the media.

His legal problems had become increasingly time-consuming. Not only was he suing Mia for custody and petitioning to broaden his visitation rights but also fighting her suit, in Surrogate's Court, to invalidate his adoption of Dylan and Moses. In addition, he was threatening a civil suit against Mia, her mother, and her sister for libeling him in a November 1992 article in *Vanity Fair,* "Mia's Story," which painted him as a pervert.

Meanwhile, hanging over his head were the worrisome criminal investigations in Connecticut and New York. He was aware that if charges of sexual misconduct were brought against him, his career as a filmmaker would be finished. He continued to cooperate with the Child Sexual Abuse Clinic at Yale–New Haven Hospital, which had been evaluating Dylan for six months, and he also made sure that Frank Maco's office received affidavits and letters from Dylan's and Satch's therapists, Soon-Yi's psychiatrist, as well as his own doctor, Kathryn Prescott. In contrast to Mia, he even agreed to a take a lie detector test. What more did Maco want?

For several months, Paul Williams at the Child Welfare Administration in New York had worked feverishly to compile a two-hundred-page dossier that documented what he believed to be a cover-up by the city's Human Resources Commission in the Allen-Farrow case, charges that his superiors would vehemently deny. Despite his diligence, Williams was surprised to learn in December that he was being transferred off the Dylan Farrow case. Later on, his superiors would try to portray him as an obsessive malcontent who overstepped his authority and behaved unprofessionally with people he interviewed. Stung by these charges, Williams contended that that was not the reason he had been removed. Rather, it was because he continued to pursue his investigation. In desperation, Williams told, or leaked to, the *New York Observer* that his bosses were acting under pressure from Woody's attorneys and Mayor David Dinkins's office, a claim that was denied. This proved to be a mistake because, before he knew it, he was accused of unethical conduct and fired, although he would be reinstated a few months later. "They played it dirty and ugly," Williams told the media. According to Elkan Abramowitz, the pesky Paul Williams was a clumsy investigator: "He acted in a rude fashion and appeared to be biased against Mr. Allen." But as Williams admitted, "I concluded that abuse did occur and that there was a prima facie cause to commence family-court proceedings against Woody Allen."

Both Paul Williams and Frank Maco were tilling similar ground. Their conclusions about the truth or falsity of Dylan's story would have important consequences for Woody because it raised the specter of his being arrested, prosecuted, and, in a worst-case scenario, convicted and sent to prison. Outwardly, there was no indication that these matters worried Woody, who alternated between periods of going about his business, and continual crises that involved long, paralyzing meetings with attorneys and publicists. By provoking a frenzy of media attention, he had managed to leave himself wide open to the most awful sort of public voyeurism. News of his life had become a business commodity, like pork bellies or soybeans. The most intimate details—his snuffling and snoring during sex, for example—were considered legitimate news to be pawed over by strangers. Granted, he had been dribbling out plenty of details about his private circumstances for thirty years—in fact, ever since he did his first stand-up routines. No comedian was more confessional, or more selective about what he chose to make known. Now he seemed to have little control over what was written about him. In self-defense, he began leaking favorable news about himself to John Miller of Channel 4. Mia's favorite partisan television reporter was Rosanna Scotto of Fox Five, whose children attended school with Dylan. "Let him have *60 Minutes*," Mia said airily. "I have Channel 5 News." Nothing he did seemed to staunch the flow of invective.

The remarkable productivity of his daily life Woody owed to both his own exceptional discipline and the dedication of his personal assistant, Jane Read Martin. At his beck and call for eight years, Martin put up with his moods and whims and performed endless personal chores. No task was too menial. For a measly salary, she worked inhuman hours—seven days a week, often until 10 P.M.—and took only two weeks a year for vacation. In 1990, in her mid-thirties and unmarried, the aide-de-camp had resigned, and although Woody arranged for another assistant, the rapport was never the same because, said a member of his staff, "Jane was very special."

Even though Jane was gone, she and Woody remained fast friends. Not surprisingly, she continued to regard Mia as a reptile slithering in the grass, intent on smearing "an indelible black question mark at the end of Woody's name forever." Out of friendship for her former boss, she provided sympathetic company and also offered to testify in the custody hearing. Grateful for her years of service and touched by her eagerness to stand by him, Woody frequently went out to dinner with Jane, who sometimes brought along her boyfriend, a writer and sometime stand-up comic named Douglas McGrath.

By now, Woody felt comfortable around Doug, a balding, puppyish man of thirty-three. A native of Texas, Doug had graduated from Princeton University, where he performed in Triangle Club musicals, and then obtained a writing job on *Saturday Night Live*. During the eighties, he wrote several unproduced screenplays, articles for *The New Republic,* as well as a single episode of *L.A. Law,* then supported himself as a tutor at a private school for boys. Not only did Woody and Doug establish rapport because he was Jane's steady date, but Woody began to regard him as a trusted insider and part of his extended family. Evenings together were spent talking about jazz and old movies, and trading horror stories about Hollywood. Doug's first produced screenplay, a remake of *Born Yesterday* with Melanie Griffith and Don Johnson, had recently been fried by the critics.

Throughout his long and productive career, Woody insisted that he never ran short of ideas and had no trouble writing, but for the second year in a row he found himself unable to complete a screenplay for a new film. By Christmas of 1992, distracted by staggering legal woes, he was still scrounging around for an idea for a fall project for 1993. Hoping that a collaborator might help rekindle his creative spark, Woody invited the self-effacing Doug to work with him on a screenplay. The neophyte recalled considering the proposition for five seconds before he said yes. It would give him, he remembered thinking, a window that would be "open for about one second" in which people might say, "Hey, who's this guy working with Woody, and what else does he have and what else does he want to do?"

After New Year's, Doug began showing up at Woody's apartment for three or four hours each day to brainstorm ideas for a comedy set in the 1920s. "Whatever we do," Woody told him, "I have to write a part for Dianne Wiest." He had promised the actress a part in his next film. The atmosphere was full of turmoil, McGrath later recalled. Woody, still preoccupied, was frequently on the phone with lawyers. ("Okay, get a detective," McGrath overheard him say.) Mia was as difficult to ignore as a brushfire raging out of control, and practically everything she did upset him. Hearing that Dylan might have to be sedated for a vaginal examination (in an attempt to prove penetration) made him feel ill. And he was livid when he learned that Mia had permitted the British magazine *Hello!* to photograph the children. He called the photos a sickening kind of exploitation.

In the bone-chilling rain, a tide of soggy green hats and wailing bagpipers spilled along Fifth Avenue as thousands of marchers, 160 brass-and-pipe marching bands, and countless beer drinkers clomped along toward Eighty-sixth Street. It was the St. Patrick's Day Parade, one of two annual events (the other was the Puerto Rican Day Parade) that Woody wished he could "sleep through and awaken when they're over." Twenty floors above the parade, Woody received a long-awaited call. After six months, the Child Sexual Abuse Clinic at Yale–New Haven Hospital was ready to issue its report, and the next morning Woody and Mia were summoned to appear in New Haven for the briefing.

The panel attempted to answer two main questions. Was Dylan sexually abused? Was she telling the truth? In the opinion of the experts, the answers to both questions was no. There was no available physical evidence of child abuse and therefore no chance that Woody had molested his daughter. Dylan's account appeared to be the fantasies of an emotionally vulnerable child living in a disturbed family, a response to stress she was unable to handle. The fondling in the attic was "concocted or imagined." The doctor heading the investigation, John Levanthal, who had interviewed Dylan numerous times, called her accounts inconsistent, and he also noted that "those were not minor inconsistencies." Dylan's descriptions had "a rehearsed quality," he said. The story heard on the videotapes, the hospital team believed, was imagined or the result of Mia's coaching, very likely a combination of both. Indeed, as Levanthal later theorized, it was possible that the videotaping had the effect of encouraging fabrication because Dylan enjoyed performing.

According to the sex-abuse experts, "Ms. Farrow has had a very disturbed relationship with Dylan and Satchel." The report also suggested that it was "absolutely critical for the children's emotional health that she be in intensive psychotherapy to address these relationships."

As he listened to the findings, Woody looked immensely relieved. He kept glancing over at the woman he once loved and now could not remember loving, and he was struck by her furious expression. At that moment, he was suddenly aware of how intensely she hated him. All the same, she perplexed him. Any normal mother would be relieved that three experts, two of them women, found her daughter had not been molested. "But so deep is her venom that she actually sees this as a loss," he thought. In any case, "she knows I never molested Dylan."

During the two-hour briefing, Mia verged on collapse. She felt sure that Woody's fame had somehow influenced the panel. Afterward, she made no comment to reporters except to promise numbly that she would "always stand by my children." Late in the afternoon, at home, she nestled on a sofa in her living room and sobbed. Although the panel agreed that Woody too had "disturbed relationships"—mentioning his "boundary problems"—with the children, she was shocked and offended at the suggestion that it was she who needed psychiatric treatment.

For Woody it was Christmas in July because the panel approved of visits with Dylan, even overnight visits at his apartment, and saw no problem with his continuing to see Soon-Yi as well. Outside the hospital, the usually dour Woody wore a triumphant grin on his face. "I think Dylan will be thrilled to see me," he declared to a huddle of reporters.

While the Yale–New Haven Hospital experts concluded that Woody was innocent, the office of the Connecticut State's Attorney was far from convinced. Unbeknownst to Woody, the skeptical Frank Maco was giving scarcely any weight at all to the hospital findings, which constituted only a portion of his investigation. He continued to believe that Woody's behavior with his daughter on August 4 was "grossly inappropriate." In his opinion, there was enough evidence for him to order the actor's arrest.

Back in New York that evening, certain that he had been fully exonerated, Woody kept busy on the phone as he received calls of congratulations from

Diane Keaton and other friends. To share his triumph and record it for posterity, he summoned his favorite reporter, Denis Hamill. Hamill was a columnist at the *New York Daily News;* his prominent brother, Pete, was a *New York Post* columnist and novelist, who had dated Shirley MacLaine and Jacqueline Kennedy; and another brother, Brian, was employed by Woody as official still photographer on his movie sets. The previous summer, sympathetic to Woody's plight, Pete Hamill treated Woody's affair with Soon-Yi as a star-crossed passion out of a Puccini opera. "A pall has fallen on the city and on Woody Allen and upon many people who love him," he wrote in the *Post.* "Love is at the heart of this terrible story, of course; it usually is." In the *Daily News,* using personal details spoon-fed to him by Woody, Denis Hamill reported on the bottles of Xanax and Tofanil in Mia's medicine cabinet, the return of the retarded youngster Sanjay, whom she had found "too burdensome," and the particulars of how she had breast-fed Satchel "until he was 3½ and even had a special harness constructed to do so over Woody's objections."

The night of his return from New Haven, Woody invited Hamill to his apartment. When the reporter asked him how the investigation had affected his career, Woody, sounding giddy, brushed off the question and said that it was only his children, not his career, that interested him. Over the past eight months, he had seen Satch for a total of thirty-six hours. He had not seen Dylan once. The Yale–New Haven team recommended that father and child should be reunited as quickly as possible. Dylan loved and missed him. Child custody laws were so highly prejudiced against men, Woody noted to Hamill, that "the burden of guilt is on you, not on the accusers. This is on me like a tattoo for life. There will always be some people who believe what I was accused of just because I was accused." It was Mia's fault that "my manhood and my fatherhood were being torn apart in front of my eyes."

"Did you pray?" Hamill asked.

In the past, such a question probably would have provoked an arched eyebrow and a sharp one-liner from Woody, an avowed atheist. At the moment, however, he chose not to alienate anybody. "I believe in a superior being but not organized religion," he replied primly.

Two days later, the custody hearing began.

CHAPTER SEVENTEEN

Allen v. Farrow

The New York County Courthouse looms over Foley Square in downtown Manhattan like a picturesque ruin from imperial Rome. Chiseled in large letters above the portico is the inscription: THE TRUE ADMINISTRATION OF JUSTICE IS THE FIRMEST PILLAR OF GOOD GOVERNMENT, an inspirational message from George Washington to the citizens of Gotham. Everything about the massive hexagonal structure promises a square deal for those unlucky enough to wind up there: the steep flight of steps; the fourteen Corinthian columns soaring to a pediment crowned by heroic statues; the magnificent interior rotunda, whose polychrome marble floor is inset with brassy copper medallions representing the signs of the zodiac. On the third floor, Courtroom 341 is a high-ceilinged, wood-paneled room that had looked very impressive in 1927, when the courthouse was built. In 1993, however, the brown walls were peeling, the wooden chairs creaking, and the three large windows covered with yellow paper window shades pulled down to the sills. For three decades, in a multitude of films, Woody had successfully laid claim to Manhattan, particularly to the glamorous Upper East Side. But 60 Centre Street was the private domain of Elliott Wilk.

The custody proceeding of WOODY ALLEN, Petitioner, v. MARIA VILLIERS FARROW, also known as MIA FARROW, Respondent opened unexpectedly on Friday, March 19, 1993. Nothing was supposed to happen for several months, but Judge Wilk did not believe in shilly-shallying. That morning, without warning, he abruptly sent the wheels of justice spinning and announced the hearing would commence after lunch. This suited Woody, who wanted an end to the proceedings. For Mia, it was a devastating blow because she was departing for California to play the wife of Jack Nicholson in *Wolf,* her first acting job since leaving Woody's employ. She was forced to withdraw.

The issues at the heart of *Allen* v. *Farrow* were the following: What are the best interests of the child? What is the competence of the mother? In order for a parent to win sole custody, the burden is on the plaintiff to prove that the change would benefit the child. In addition, terminating Mia's parental rights in regard to Dylan, Moses, and Satchel would mean proving incompetence, abandonment, or behavior damaging to the children's emotional and physical well-being.

On Friday afternoon, Elkan Abramowitz called Woody to the stand. With the good news from New Haven still ringing in his ears, he had every reason to feel confident. Dressed in his usual chinos and casual jacket with unbuttoned shirt, he gazed around with the supreme self-assurance that three decades of movie stardom—and first-class analysis—could provide. On the podium, he seemed to be in a director's chair, as if pondering how to use a drove of extras waiting below for their instructions. As if following one of his scripts, he allowed Abramowitz to lead him through a summary of how the affair with Soon-Yi Previn began a few days after Christmas of 1991, when she was home from college. However, he sounded surprisingly vague about his sexual attraction for the girl. To hear him tell it, the affair was an out-of-body experience. He had felt no particular yearning for Soon-Yi, nor did he have any prior plans to seduce her. Evidently he assumed the sex would be a passing fancy, "a short thing," he said.

Justice Wilk interrupted to ask if he had considered the effect on the other children in the family.

"I felt nobody in the world would have any idea," Woody answered. After all, it was a private matter.

"Wasn't that enough, that you would know you were sleeping with your children's sister?" Wilk wanted to know.

"I didn't see it that way," Woody replied. "I'm sorry." He and Mia, he continued, had not had sex for five years, and their relationship was over. Besides, he reminded the court, he had never lived with her or slept at her apartment, obviously forgetting all his nights at Frog Hollow and the years when she and the kids had slept at his penthouse.

Listening in disbelief, Mia sat only twenty feet from Woody. With her mane of fluffy hair curling in girlish corkscrews and the granny glasses, she had a studious look, as if she had dressed for a day at school: pleated skirt, immaculate starched white blouse, navy blue blazer, sensible flat shoes with black tights. In this courthouse ensemble, which she would wear every single day of the hearing, she gave the illusion of youth and appeared almost as young as any of her teenage daughters, although she was forty-eight and could not quite pull it off. Throughout Woody's testimony, as she heard his references to their "joyless, sexless" years together, his statements about their never having sex since the time of Satch's birth, she sat quivering. During a recess she lit a Marlboro Red and broke into tears. Not only was she a bundle of nerves, but her physical health had been poor for months. Seldom hungry, she subsisted on lunches of sardines or one of her favorite Lindt chocolate bars. (Like Woody, she had a passion for chocolate.) Sometimes she would poke around the refrigerator to find leftovers stored by the housekeeper, Mavis Smith. Spooning rice on a paper plate, she would plop a piece of chicken on top, and eat it cold. As a result of her meager diet, as well as stress, she had become rail-thin.

Taking the stand again, Woody recalled Mia's discovery of the Polaroids and the volcanic rages that followed. She was so crazed with hatred, he said, that she called him "a dozen times a night, raging and screaming into the phone, threatening to kill me." Given her most rabid threat—"You took my daughter and I'm going to take your daughter"—it was hardly surprising that only a few months later she would accuse him of sexually molesting Dylan. Gaining energy, he raised his voice. "It's unfathomable," he said in a rush of words. "It's unconscionable. It's disgusting. It's unappealing. It's not in my history or something I would ever do." After three hours, he was excused, and the hearing adjourned for the weekend. As well-wishers rushed to offer him congratulations, he walked out of the courthouse certain that he would win the custody hearing.

Monday morning, on cross-examination, Eleanor Alter stepped up and asked him an innocuous question: Had he ever dressed Dylan?

"I could have put her socks on." He smiled. "That's always hard work."

"Anything besides socks?"

Woody admitted that he had never changed a diaper or done any of the hard stuff. "Not appreciably, no. I help her on with her jacket, a little bit."

Alter was not done yet. "Satchel?" she asked.

"The same kind of thing, a little bit I help out."

"Moses?"

Woody shook his head. "No, I don't dress Moses."

Still, Alter would not let up. Did he ever bathe Satchel or Dylan? (No.) Ever take the children for a haircut? (No.) Did he know who cuts their hair?

At this point, Woody caught on. "I think Mia cuts their hair," he replied.

In a rising voice, Alter moved on to other topics. She peppered him with questions about report cards and PTA meetings. Did he know the names of friends, teachers, doctors, or pets? Woody, tight-lipped, appeared to be clueless.

Did he know Moses loved baseball? (Perhaps.) And had he taken him to a game? (Probably not.)

Later the media would hail Alter's courtroom cunning, but Raoul Felder, one of her fellow divorce attorneys, dismissed the strategy as "silliness. I don't see how it would impress any judge," insisted Felder. "Men can't remember information like that. I myself couldn't recall answers to those questions. Haircuts have nothing to do with being a good parent."

After Alter had concluded her questioning, Judge Wilk turned to Woody. "The other thing that occurs to me involves your relationship with Soon-Yi," he said quietly. "In the letter that was read from Moses [the "I hope you commit suicide" letter], you refer to her not having had any friends besides you."

"To the best of my knowledge that is correct."

Not for nothing was Wilk known as a judge who "gets into people's heads." Sounding mild-mannered, he continued amicably to ask what would happen to Soon-Yi if Woody broke off the relationship. "I guess the question that I have is, where is her support system?"

Woody shrugged. "Her support system at that time would have been me."

"Well," said Wilk, "it wouldn't have been if she wanted to stay, and you wanted out."

"No." Woody's confidence seemed to wane, and his answers began to sound a bit incoherent. "She would have had the normal support system that she had. Friends. She could have had what she could have gotten from the family. It would not have been an issue."

Wilk cut him off. "I gather it would have been a large issue, because it's not something she could have discussed with her family."

By this time, Woody began to look dazed. He was stuttering and coughing nervously, and sometimes his speech slid into the Brooklyn inflections of Allan Konigsberg. He finally said to Wilk, "My thought was that I would be the one abandoned. I don't see it the other way around."

"Thank you," Wilk said. "You may step down."

Back at the oblong wooden table that Woody and his team of lawyers shared with Mia and her attorneys, Woody seemed subdued. He locked his fingers together and raised them to his lips.

Woody was no match for Eleanor Alter, but questioning by his own attorney, Elkan Abramowitz, proceeded routinely.

Twice the previous year, he told the court, he took Mia to the Carlyle Hotel for sex "because she begged me." On one occasion, when they were in the hotel room, she became abusive and hysterical. "I thought she was going to jump out the window," he said. "Then I realized, mercifully, that the Carlyle's windows are glass walls."

At such moments, Woody was "totally in character," said *Post* reporter Hal Davis. "You remembered that he was after all an actor." Joan Ullman, covering the hearing for *Psychology Today*, thought that he was "very funny. It felt exactly like watching a Woody Allen movie and so naturally everybody laughed."

*   *   *

"Do you have an opinion regarding custody in this case?" Justice Wilk asked Susan Coates, the clinical psychologist who treated Satchel Farrow for two years. Wilk sounded weary. What he wanted was a straight answer about the heart of the matter, the question that was sinking under a pile of fan-magazine details: Who should have custody of the three children?

Coates, in her third day on the stand, was testifying as Woody's witness. She hemmed and hawed and mumbled vague mumbo jumbo to even the simplest question. Apparently she had neglected to take careful notes of her sessions with Satchel. "My feeling," she answered, "is that further evaluation is necessary. I really feel from where I sit now, I wouldn't know what to do."

■ ■ ■ ■ ■ ■ ■

Rashomon:
"It's a classic case of a woman scorned."
—Jane Read Martin McGrath

"His savagery toward women remains primitive. In thirty years, he never got past it. At thirty-five, he was a genius in the sense that he made the whole country respond to his neurotic New York Jew. But pursuing women was his only idea, his one emotion, one perception. He never went anyplace else. He's had a run for his money that is unbelievable."
—Vivian Gornick

"Have I talked to him? Why would I talk to him? I don't know him socially. We're not friends in that sense. I think he's great. We had a good working relationship. Why would I call him? It's just not my business. Why bother him, the poor guy? He's been bothered enough."
—Judy Davis

"I think Mia is a very crazy, vindictive woman. It's not even remotely possible that Woody would have done any of those things. The molestation charge is disgusting."
—Stacey Nelkin

"He's treated like a little god, and little gods don't have to do what everybody else does."
—Leonard Gershe

"When people ask me about Woody and his new girlfriend, I tell them, 'That's the result of a successful analysis.' If you've been in analysis for forty years you can justify anything."

—ELLIOTT MILLS

∎∎∎∎∎∎∎

In the marble corridor outside Courtroom 341, movie fans queued up for one of the few available seats at the afternoon sessions. But with more than eighty of the press corps stuffed into the rows of hard wooden benches with their bags and briefcases, there was little room left over for the curious public. As the trial continued, Woody began hunching over in his seat. He seemed to physically shrink. One reporter described his posture as that of someone trying to "disappear by scrunching up into a small ball." Other members of the press were having second thoughts about him, especially about Mia, whom they once regarded as a frivolous person. "At first people believed Mia to be freaky because she had so many kids," recalled Joan Ullman. "But gradually that changed. She sounded like a wife, or a single mother, somebody you could identify with. Not Woody. I was horrified at the way he behaved with the kids, hanging out at Mia's, staring obsessively at Dylan." Some skeptical female journalists were of the opinion that Mia was no Pollyanna, however. "Her affect was studied," recalled Andrea Peyser, a *New York Post* reporter. "The Catholic schoolgirl outfit, her testimony, everything seemed like acting. It sure played well with the judge though."

The smart money argued Woody was unlikely to win. "Under New York law, he didn't have a case," said Hal Davis. "No evidence suggested Mia was unfit. On the stand, Woody Allen impressed me as a sincere fifty-seven-year-old guy with an emotional age of nineteen. Just your average adolescent male. Nobody with a brain in their head could honestly say he would be a fine parent."

Outside the courtroom, fidgety reporters stood in the halls gossiping. Did Satchel really have a gender disorder? Would he grow up to be gay? They dished about Soon-Yi and cast a Woody-Mia custody movie—Rick Moranis as Woody and Blythe Danner as Mia, with either Gene Wilder or Richard Dreyfuss as Justice Wilk. Hard to cast would be the Soon-Yi role, but the most obvious choice was Lea Salonga, Broadway's Miss Saigon. During the breaks, Woody's sister, Letty Aronson, told *USA Today* that Mia had made so many threatening phone calls to the elderly Konigsbergs that they were forced to change their number. "She eats bullets," huffed Letty. "That's why she's doing this to the children."

*　　　*　　　*

Day after day, a procession of witnesses took the stand to offer theories about Dylan O'Sullivan Farrow. Did her father fondle her? Did she make up the story? Should Judge Wilk let her see her daddy again? Sometimes everybody seemed to forget that the silent and invisible centerpiece of the custody hearing was a seven-year-old who had suffered the devastating loss of a father.

In the six months preceding the court dispute, Mia had driven Dylan nine times to be questioned by psychologists at Yale–New Haven Hospital. At St. Luke's–Roosevelt Hospital in Manhattan, Dylan had become so hysterical when doctors tried to perform a gynecological examination that the procedure was canceled. At times she could not walk on the street without being approached by a photographer or passerby. One morning her mother wrapped her in blankets and carried her out a basement door to escape photographers waiting in front of the building. Dylan's anxiety was also fueled by worries about her mother becoming poverty-stricken. Mia, she thought, would not be able to earn money now that "Woody Allen," as she had begun referring to her father, was no longer starring her in his movies.

While Mia would later insist that Dylan had been spared the details of the trial, this was not the truth. Exposed to her parents bitter hatred of each other for almost two years, she was aware of their battle to retain custody of her. Deeply afraid that she would be forced to leave her mother's home and live with "Woody Allen," she was agitated and depressed.

"Andre is my new daddy," she blurted out wishfully to the doctors in New Haven, following a visit from the famous conductor.

Each morning of the hearing, her mother departed for Foley Square, and she was dropped off at Brearley, the Upper East Side private school where she was in second grade. At school, teachers and classmates heard intimate details of her life on television. A staff member (the second wife of one of Woody's longtime colleagues) took a day off from school to testify that Woody Allen was a fine father, who was sufficiently involved to attend parent-teacher meetings.

As Mia's time and attention were increasingly diverted from her family to the hearing, predictably her children suffered from her absence. The woman seen in news photos, surrounded by smiling, seemingly well-behaved youngsters, was in reality contending with their disturbed reaction. Needy and demanding, her older children were especially rebellious. One evening, Mia came into Daisy and Lark's bedroom to mention a victory she won in court that day. The minute she left, Lark jumped up and shouted to Kristi Groteke, "I can't stand it." She didn't want to hear another word about the trial, she confided to the baby-sitter, which was the reason she spent "so much time out of the house. It's why I hang out with my friends so much."

That winter Dylan O'Sullivan Farrow decided to change her name.

Enchanted by the movie *My Fair Lady*, and Audrey Hepburn as Eliza Doolittle, she selected the name Eliza. Her brother Satch, not to be outdone, changed his name to Harmon.

Custody cases are usually handled in Family Court, where child beatings, wife throttlings, and all manner of domestic free-for-alls are daily fare, and the judges' calendars a mass of motions and pleas, hearings and trials, all waiting to be disposed of speedily. Throughout *Allen* v. *Farrow*, Family Court judges who had been following the case on television could not help making snide remarks about Justice Wilk's handling of the case. As one Bronx judge thought, "Bring on the Woody Allen case. I'll show them how we Family Court judges have to do it. In the middle of the morning, after our fourteenth, fifteenth, or twentieth case, one turns to the court officers and says, 'What's next? The Woody Allen case? OK, let's get them in here. And line up the next three cases, would you?' "

The hearing lasted six and a half weeks. All too often the testimony sounded like reruns of *Lifestyles of the Rich and Famous*. Some thirty witnesses tramped through Courtroom 341: psychiatrists, lawyers, social workers, nannies, tutors, teachers, and maids. Among the minor players was Paul Williams, the formerly suspended, recently reinstated social worker who said flat out that Dylan was telling the truth and the case against her father should not be dropped. Another witness was Letty Aronson, who declared Woody to be an ideal father because he "played games and colored" with his children. For many onlookers, the most mesmerizing testimony came from Jane Martin, Woody's faithful former assistant. Familiar with the daily trivia of Woody and Mia's life, she conjured up in intimate detail the Shangri-la cocoon in which the couple was sealed from the rest of humanity. As she described it, it was a world where men didn't marry their sweethearts but adopted their children, where flunkies and gofers kept life running smoothly, psychotherapists made house calls, and children's allowances were paid by check. Seizing the opportunity to get in a few licks at Mia, she characterized her as a reptilian stepmother who treated her daughter Lark like "a scullery maid" and expected her to cook, tote luggage on trips, and baby-sit the younger children.

In the real world, the case of *Allen* v. *Farrow* concluded quietly at the end of the balmy afternoon of May 4. During closing arguments, Woody sat at the table with his lawyer like a diner who had lost his appetite. For the last time, Alter and Abramowitz enumerated all the ways that the other's client was unfit to be a parent: Alter blasting away at Woody's affair with Soon-Yi as proof that he lacked a moral compass; Abramowitz insisting that Woody had never molested Dylan—he had simply been using the bathroom—and it was her mother's Medea-like wrath that had led her to smear his client, using her children as "soldiers and pawns." To the judge, Abramowitz suggested that Woody would be satisfied with a modified custody arrangement that allowed the children to spend half their time with him. This was noteworthy, not because Woody hoped for nothing less than full custody but because increasingly during the hearing he had not always acted as if he wanted custody at all. When asked by Wilk how he would raise the children should he gain their full custody, he simply said that he would make sure they got a good education. In the event of problems, he would consult with their therapists.

• • • • • • •

Moving Pictures:
RAIN (asking to be kissed): It's magical.
GABE: Why is it that I am hearing $50,000 worth of psychotherapy dialing 911?

—*Husbands and Wives,* 1992

• • • • • • •

Elliott Wilk rendered his decision on the seventh of June, at 10:30 A.M. In a thirty-three-page ruling, he rejected Woody Allen's request for custody of Dylan, Satchel, and Moses because there was no evidence of his parenting ability. Wilk left the children in the care of their mother, who in his opinion was the better parent. As he would say later, he had no faith in Woody's paternal instincts, nor did he "trust his insight." He determined that Woody might have limited visitation with Satch three times a week, for two hours at a time, under the supervision of a third party. He would not force Moses to see Woody and left the choice up to him. As for Dylan, separated from her father for ten months, Wilk had qualms. He refused to grant immediate visiting privileges but did leave open the door for future contact by placing the matter in the hands of professionals. Visitation would be conditioned upon psychological counseling for Dylan. Six months hence, a therapist would determine whether a father-daughter relationship would be harmful to Dylan, at which time Wilk would evaluate the progress of her therapy and review the case. This crucial sentence would be interpreted quite differently by the two sides. Otherwise, Wilk's analysis of the case could not have been more punitive in its view of Woody Allen as a parent.

• • • • • • •

The Public Record:
Mr. Allen has demonstrated no parenting skills that would qualify him as an adequate custodian for Moses, Dylan, and Satchel.

261

His financial contributions to the children's support, his willingness to read to them, to tell them stories, to buy them presents, and to oversee their breakfasts, do not compensate for his absence as a meaningful source of guidance and caring in their lives. These contributions do not excuse his evident lack of familiarity with the most basic details of their day-to-day existences.

He did not bathe his children. He did not dress them, except from time to time, and then only to help them put on their socks and jackets. He knows little of Moses' history, except that he has cerebral palsy; he does not know if he has a doctor. He does not know the name of Dylan and Satchel's pediatrician. He does not know the names of Moses' teachers or about his academic performance. He does not know the name of the children's dentist. He does not know the names of his children's friends. He does not know the names of any of their many pets. He does not know which children shared bedrooms. He attended parent-teacher conferences only when asked to do so by Ms. Farrow.

—Decision, Supreme Court: New York County,
Individual Assignment Part 6, Index No. 68738/92.
Woody Allen, Petitioner, against Maria Villiers Farrow,
also known as Mia Farrow, Respondent

■ ■ ■ ■ ■ ■ ■

Justice Wilk rebuked Woody for being a "self-absorbed, untrustworthy, and insensitive" father, a harsh assessment. But the most damning portion of his decision concerned the critical question of whether or not Dylan had been molested. In spite of the New Haven report, he was not convinced that she had not been sexually abused. In his opinion, the evidence was inconclusive. Even so, he thought it unlikely that Woody could ever be prosecuted and therefore "we will probably never know what occurred on August 4, 1992." Giving Mia nothing more than a slap on the hand, Wilk wrote that her biggest shortcoming was "her continued relationship with Mr. Allen." Finally, Woody was ordered to pay Mia's legal fees for having brought "this frivolous petition."

Not surprisingly, New York's legal community—its judges, matrimonial lawyers, and court reporters—busily rehashed Wilk's ruling. Nobody seemed eager to criticize the performance of Elkan Abramowitz, who'd been dealt a losing hand. In comments after the proceeding, however, some believed Woody might possibly have won with a different judge, even someone like Phyllis Gangel-Jacob, the justice known for her antimale bias. Raoul Felder was of the opinion that Abramowitz "just about lost the case when he got

Wilk." The veteran court reporter Hal Davis thought that any judge who applied the standards for custody would have reached the same conclusion. "Phyllis Gangel-Jacob is more of a wild card because she is supposedly swayed by the celebrity of some cases. She probably would not have written the same scathing decision as Wilk's but would have handed down the same decision. There was no way to find that Mia Farrow was an unfit mother." Another journalist reporting on the trial, Andrea Peyser, did not doubt Mia would get custody but was surprised that Wilk "didn't take into account Mia's complicity in creating that ludicrous arrangement. Exposing her children to Allen for twelve years was indefensible. Why did she allow these horrible things—was she stupid?"

An ecstatic Eleanor Alter called Mia from a phone booth in the courthouse. "We won!" she kept shouting. "You got everything!"

"I'm thrilled I'm going to see my daughter again," said Woody, facing the bank of television cameras. "She has been withheld from me since last August." In defeat, he looked composed. Informed of the decision earlier in the day, he felt devastated because he believed that the facts of the case were overwhelmingly in his favor. It was not that he considered himself the most perfect father in the world but that he regarded Mia a deplorably bad mother, whose consuming need to adopt was an obsession. "People just irresponsibly let her adopt children and no one says, 'Hey, can you really take care of so many children?' " He did not count on getting the wrong judge.

As he began reading the complete text of the decision, however, his shock turned to anger. How dare Elliott Wilk criticize the way he behaved with his kids. He hadn't always been a wonderful parent, but he wasn't so different from a lot of fathers. Besides, he believed that Wilk had never liked him. From the first day Wilk was gaga over Mia, and throughout the entire trial he treated her like a movie star on whom he had a schoolboy crush. It would not have been surprising to hear that he had asked her for an autographed photo. But what most sickened Woody was Wilk's smear about being less certain than the New Haven team that Dylan had not been sexually abused. Suggesting that the true circumstances were unknowable cast a shadow of doubt over the dismissal of the child-abuse charges. In Woody's mind, it was a sly message to the world that he probably was a child molester but there was no way to prove it.

If the decision seemed totally unreasonable to Woody, Elkan Abramowitz viewed it differently. For the media, he was swift to characterize the decision as a major victory. His client had done very well legally because he now could reestablish contact with his daughter, which was the thing he wanted most of all. Wilk's sniping about his deficiencies as a father was offensive but of little importance. The second matter of concern was Woody's reputation, and even though his good name had taken "an enormous hit," Abramowitz admitted, the molestation allegation had been absolutely disproved. "I don't think any one person could do more to prove that this did not happen," he said.

■ ■ ■ ■ ■ ■ ■

The March of Time:
"No one can mistreat Mia; she has developed her own special way of not being taken to the cleaners."
—BETTE DAVIS, 1967

■ ■ ■ ■ ■ ■ ■

That night, Wilk's decision was the leading story on every New York local television news program. Woody did not watch the television coverage. As was his habit every Monday night, he got dressed and prepared for the twenty-block drive to Michael's Pub, where he would not have to speak, only play his clarinet. Afterward, he would come home and go to sleep early. Even though his name was being mentioned on every television and radio show in the nation, he saw no reason to change his routine.

Elkan Abramowitz did not turn on his TV set, either. He and his wife, Susan, were entertaining at their home in suburban Sands Point. Arriving home at seven o'clock, he showered and changed into shorts, then sat down on the screened-in porch to a dinner of grilled salmon, roasted potatoes with rosemary, and cholesterol-free pound cake with berries. There was no talk of the day's events. Finally, a poker-faced Abramowitz brought up the subject to their dinner guest, Alex Witchel, a *New York Times* reporter who was writing a profile of the couple. "Custody went to Mia," he remarked tersely to Witchel. "There will be visitation within six months with Dylan. And the judge encouraged Moses to visit with Woody." Abramowitz was clearly not eager to comment on Wilk's unflattering description of his client.

In the offices of Rosenman & Colin at 575 Madison Avenue, the mood was delirious. During the trial, Eleanor Alter had frequently reminded Mia that she could pick and choose winning cases, and she had agreed to represent her. Later she said that after twenty-eight years in practice and some two thousand divorce cases, Woody's conduct toward Mia and the children remained the most shocking. "Why did he bring a custody proceeding? He never spent a night alone with them, couldn't name one of their friends, nor a pet nor a doctor." In addition to her promise of victory, she had also predicted Woody would be ordered to pay Mia's legal fees, which were estimated in excess of a million dollars.

At noon, wearing jeans and a T-shirt, Mia huddled around a conference table in Alter's office with her lawyer to read the judgment. She gasped when she heard Judge Wilk's low opinion of Woody as a parent. Then, as she and Kristi Groteke, who had accompanied her to the lawyer's office, were eating a lunch of poached salmon and avocado salad they had picked up at a cafeteria downstairs in the building, Alter reminded them that a press conference was about to begin. Rosanna Scotto from *Fox Five News* and Carol Agus from *Newsday* were already waiting in the conference room. Mia sent Kristi back to Mia's apartment to pick up a change of clothes—a skirt and blazer—and her makeup. When it was time to face an armada of cameramen, her hair was fluffed, her makeup flawless. In her moment of triumph, she radiated happiness. "For so many, many months, my family has been living through a nightmare," she said tearfully. "My children have been ripped apart emotionally." Her indirect reference to her children's turmoil, psychological damage which might prove permanent, suggested to some reporters that she had won a Pyrrhic victory. But in her jubilation, she quickly passed over the shadows. "I'm so proud of how they've held themselves together, stood by one another and stood by me."

That night at Mia's apartment, there was no celebration among her children. In the living room, Daisy, Moses, and Kristi Groteke leafed through Fletcher's senior yearbook from Collegiate School, from which he would graduate in two weeks. In the bathroom, eighteen-month-old Isaiah was playfully throwing his toys into the toilet. Dylan and Satch, who had school the next day, went to bed early after watching television. Later, dressed in a slinky black baby-doll dress designed by Betsey Johnson, Mia celebrated at dinner with William Goldman, a screenwriter *(Butch Cassidy and the Sundance Kid)* whom she was dating.

CHAPTER EIGHTEEN

Second Law
of Thermodynamics

Two days after Judge Wilk's decision, Eleanor Alter filed a motion in Surrogate's Court asking Judge Renee Roth to overturn Woody's adoptions of Dylan and Moses, in effect reversing her 1991 decision to permit the adoptions. It was clear Woody had committed fraud, Mia's attorney contended. He was sleeping with Soon-Yi long before the adoptions, "a fact both had freely admitted at first, but that they now denied under oath." In her heart, Mia had no doubt whatsoever that both of them were lying. Judge Wilk's restrictions did not go far enough to suit her or Eleanor Alter, who wanted to sweep Woody completely from the lives of Mia and her children. "He'll hound them as long as he has legal rights," Alter said. "He has the money and the power." Judge Roth was given phone bills showing hundreds of calls between Woody and Soon-Yi in 1990 and 1991. A raft of witnesses swore under oath to seeing the couple together, including the paparazzo Dominick Conde, who submitted a print of his famous hand-holding picture—the Rosetta Stone of Woody's guilt and a key piece of evidence, Alter believed. After hearing all the witnesses, Surrogate Roth seemed reluctant to reverse her earlier position. Sympathetic to Woody, she continued to skirt the issue of fraud and requested additional hearings. Eventually, facing the financial choice of sending her children to college or continuing the warfare, Mia decided to drop the matter.

Although he was loath to admit it publicly, Woody was emotionally drained by the prolonged custody battle. Jean Doumanian suggested that people send him messages of encouragement because he was feeling downcast, convinced that the whole world hated him. Among those who responded was Jean's friend Stephen Silverman, who wrote to reassure Woody that he would be remembered for his work, not for the scandal. Silverman received "a lovely little note thanking me," he recalled.

With others Woody was less courteous. His behavior was nobody's business, he said to a *Rolling Stone* writer, and what people know, "they know tenth hand from tabloid newspapers," he bristled. When he dined at Elaine's, he squeezed past the long smoky bar to his special table, acting as if nothing had happened. Whenever he spoke of the custody case, he described it as "a pain in the ass." Suggestions from the *Rolling Stone* reporter that his audiences might turn against him provoked an outburst. "I don't care," he retorted. If people wanted to see his movies, "fine. If they don't, they won't." People had no notion of what he was really feeling. "I do what I want, and they can take it or leave it."

That summer, far from doing what he wanted, he found himself battling helplessly for crusts. Judge Wilk had given him the right to see Satchel, but this proved easier said than done because Mia made it as difficult as possible. In July, she departed for Ireland with Dylan, Satch, Tam, and Isaiah. She was costarring with Natasha Richardson and Joan Plowright in *Widow's Peak,* a dark comedy of revenge that was being filmed in the green hills of County Wicklow and at Ardmore Film Studios in Bray, about an hour south of Dublin. Knowing Ireland well, Mia looked forward to reunions with her aunts and cousins and a peaceful summer. She no doubt also counted on putting an ocean between Satch and his father. But, as she shortly discovered, she had misjudged Woody's determination. In mid-August, accompanied by Soon-Yi and armed with a court order, he arrived in Ireland to visit his son. News photos taken of them at the Dublin Zoo showed Woody in his fishing hat carrying the pouting five-and-a-half-year-old blond boy, as if Satch were an infant or an invalid. Even after his father bought him ice cream, he continued to look anxious. Because Wilk had forbidden Soon-Yi to be present during the visits, she stayed out of sight.

In Ireland Satch no longer answered to the name of Satchel, or Harmon, or Sean. He wanted to be known as Seamus, but Woody was riled by this rigamarole and refused to cooperate in what he perceived to be another one of Mia's tactics to obliterate his presence in their lives. Mia tried to justify these renamings by maintaining that Satchel's classmates, making fun of the name "Satchel," called him a suitcase. But in truth there was no lack of precedent for the transformations. In addition to Misha/Moses, Daisy, who was originally named Summer Song, received her new name after Mia played Daisy Buchanan in *The Great Gatsby,* and subsequently Summer Song's sister, who was originally called Kym Lark, was renamed Lark. In the Farrow household, even the pets assumed new names, with the dog sometimes being called Maggie and the cat at other times. Woody took comfort from the fact that Satch's and Dylan's new names weren't legal, but he still thought the changes were "the stupidest thing in the world." Obviously, the man who was known to the world as "Woody Allen" had forgotten about reinventing himself at age fifteen when he had changed his name from Allan Konigsberg.

∷∷∷∷∷∷

Moving Pictures:
SALLY: It's the second law of thermodynamics: Sooner or later
everything turns to shit.

—*Husbands and Wives,* 1992

∷∷∷∷∷∷

In the meantime, Frank Maco, the Litchfield County prosecutor, was winding up his fourteen-month investigation. On September 24, 1993, Maco
held a news conference in Wallingford, Connecticut, to announce that he
was dropping the sexual-molestation charges against Woody. Next, in a curious turn of events, and despite all the evidence to the contrary, he added
what seemed almost an afterthought. In his opinion, he said matter-of-factly,
there was no question that Dylan Farrow had been molested. There was per-
suasive evidence to prove his case in court and an arrest warrant for Woody
had been drawn up, but he had decided not to pursue the case in order to
spare Dylan the trauma of a criminal trial. "This was no time for a damn-
the-torpedoes prosecutorial approach," he declared.

Making such a statement—a man is guilty but would not be prosecuted—
was an unusual step. Maco was certainly not obligated to make public his
reasoning. In his defense, however, he said that he felt compelled to explain his
decision to constituents who might assume Woody Allen got preferential
treatment as a celebrity. In fact, like Paul Williams, he genuinely believed
that Woody Allen, celebrity or no celebrity, was guilty. And unlike Elliott
Wilk who, uncertain of the director's guilt, doubted that he could be prosecuted, Frank Maco apparently believed he could be successfully prosecuted.

Understandably, Woody was upset by Maco's branding him a child molester. Although the New Haven group had cleared him of any wrongdoing,
the prosecutor's impromptu postscript left him, in effect, stigmatized as a
pedophile without the benefit of a trial. He believed Maco to be an exhibi-
tionist seeking his fifteen minutes of fame, who knew perfectly well that
Woody was an innocent man but went after him simply because he was a
celebrity. Woody also believed that Maco's disinclination to credit the
Yale–New Haven findings had an insidious ripple effect that must have
influenced Judge Wilk and adversely affected his chance of winning custody
of the children. (Maco had faxed copies of his statement to Wilk and Renee
Roth, who were ruling on both visitation rights and on a motion to annul
the adoptions, a questionable action, in Woody's opinion, and one that had
a prejudicial effect on the case.)

Evidently Frank Maco had touched a nerve because Woody swiftly called a news conference the same day. Losing his customary cool, he characterized Mia and Maco as "a vindictive mother and a cowardly, dishonest, irresponsible state's attorney" whose "cheap scheming reeks of sleaze and deception." For a half hour he let loose in front of a packed house at the Plaza Hotel, coincidentally the same room where he had announced his custody suit the previous summer. Clutching a prepared typed statement, he kept his head down as he delivered a rambling, incoherent speech against Mia and Maco, who "squirm, lie, sweat, and tap-dance" to protect themselves. Maco, he charged, disliked his movies. Or perhaps it was chauvinism that motivated the Litchfield County prosecutor. He was "prejudiced against me because I'm a diehard New Yorker and Ms. Farrow a Connecticut local."

In a bizarre finale, he suddenly lifted his head and stared purposefully into the television cameras. "Because this is being taped, I want to send a message to my little girl," he said. He was sorry to have missed her eighth birthday "but they just wouldn't let me do it." Dylan must not worry, however, because "the dark forces will not prevail." All the "second-rate police," "publicity-hungry prosecutors," the tabloid press, all the "pious or hypocritic or the bigoted" who had rushed to judgment would be punished. "I'm too tough for all of them put together, and I will never abandon you to the Frank Macos of the world." Three weeks later, he filed an ethics complaint with Connecticut's State Criminal Justice Commission, the body that appoints state's attorneys and can also reprimand or dismiss them. He demanded that Maco be disbarred for professional misconduct. Prosecutors are seldom held accountable for their professional conduct, but numerous legal experts agreed that Woody had sufficient cause for grievance. Woody's complaint against Maco failed to bother Eleanor Alter, however, who darkly hinted that "if Woody puts Maco in a position of having to divulge what he has, he won't be happy." As a result of the complaint, the Litchfield County prosecutor was suspended from trying cases. By the time the suit was settled four years later, it had cost the Connecticut taxpayers a quarter of a million dollars to defend Maco against Woody's allegations.

■ ■ ■ ■ ■ ■ ■

Voice of America:
"ar831" [Sean] writes: "Maco struck me from the start as an asshole lawyer in desperate pursuit of publicity at any cost."
"Grifter" [Jesse] replies: "No, no Sean, if a Connecticut prosecutor says something, it must be true. State prosecutors would never tell a lie. If Maco is claiming he has evidence, he must have evidence somewhere. Mind you, it's interesting that he would see allowing a 'confirmed' child molester to run free as better for

society than protecting the state of mind of one girl, but that's his business."

—Newsgroup: alt.showbiz.gossip
Date: 1 Jan 1998
Subject: Woody Allen Is Human Scum

■■■■■■■

Whenever Satch visited Woody at his apartment, Woody always hugged him and told his son how much he loved and missed him. "I love you as much as the stars," he said, and Satchel would answer, "I love you as much as the universe." For all their playfulness, however, the visits caused frustration and heartache. One day the boy confessed, "I'm supposed to say I hate you." Another time he told Woody, "I wish you were dead." He also confided that he was seeing a psychiatrist who was going to ensure that Satch never had to see his father again. Distressed, Woody quickly changed the subject.

During his hours with Satch, his mind compulsively wandered to Dylan and before long he would torture himself by obsessing about where she could be at that moment. Was she swinging in the park? Was she sitting at the kitchen table? "Was she wondering why Satch could see me but not her? How confused could one kid become? And then I would have to refocus on Satchel," he later confided to Denis Hamill for the *New York Daily News*. Passing a playground in Central Park "sent a pang through me," and even the sight of a father and daughter coming toward him flooded him with feelings of "physical pain." He was counting the days until December, when Judge Wilk had hinted at the possibility of a reunion unless, as Wilk said, "it interferes with Dylan's individual treatment or is inconsistent with her welfare." The possibility of something going wrong with the timetable was simply inconceivable to Woody. Nothing would go wrong.

Yet in September, shortly after Maco's press conference, Woody's hopes of seeing his daughter were dashed. With a full three months still to go, Dylan's psychiatrist warned Wilk that resumption of visits would be harmful to the child. Not only did Dylan continue to talk about how "Woody Allen touched my privates," but now she apparently remembered another occasion when her father allegedly touched her genitals one night as she was climbing to the top of a bunk bed. The psychiatrist informed Wilk that were Dylan forced to see Woody in December, she could regress emotionally. He asked for an extension until March of 1994, and Justice Wilk granted his request. But in March when the case came up for review, the therapist once again convinced Wilk that it was not in Dylan's best interest to see her father. This time, Woody demanded the appointment of an independent, court-appointed psychiatrist to review the case, citing Wilk's "pattern of extreme bias."

Despite these setbacks, Woody continued to feel hopeful about seeing Dylan again. In mid-December of 1993, he completed principal photography on *Bullets Over Broadway* and took Soon-Yi to Venice for New Year's Eve, a holiday that he enjoyed tremendously. Otherwise his life was fairly sedate: he worked out on his treadmill, practiced the clarinet, took a walk, came back to the apartment, and tried to do some writing. "I do it seven days a week," he said. "I could never be productive if I didn't have a very regular life." About once every six weeks, he guiltily dined on a prime rib sirloin and hash browns at Sparks Steak House, the East Forty-sixth Street celebrity chophouse whose walls were lined with gilt-frame paintings of the Hudson River School, and the scene of a famous Mafia murder. Woody always made sure to sit in what he called "the nonshooting section."

In light moods, he vented his frustration by making snide remarks about Elliott Wilk. He couldn't really blame him, he told friends, because he was an ordinary guy and Mia could be seductive. Those chiseled cheekbones were awesome. "I went seeking Solomon," he joked, "but I wound up with Roy Bean," the legendary hanging judge who dispensed frontier justice in the Old West. Most of the time, however, he felt sorry for himself and called Wilk an incompetent bungler who was "just not up to the case and made a terrible mess of it." It was Wilk who did not allow him to see his kids, a right not even denied to convicted murderers and drug addicts. Increasingly convinced that Wilk had no intention of ever letting him see Dylan, he did not feel reassured when he read Wilk's comments about him in Cindy Adams's column in the *New York Post*. "I don't trust him," the *Post* quoted Wilk as saying about Woody. "I didn't trust him two years ago, and I don't trust him now. I don't trust his instincts. I don't trust his insights. I don't trust that he does not represent a danger to this child, because the fact that he won't beat him up and throw him out the window does not mean Satchel is safe."* Woody Allen still couldn't figure out how his affair with Soon-Yi might have had "a devastating effect" on her brothers and sisters. The way Wilk saw it, according to the *Post*, Woody Allen had no reason for complaint; he had made a choice about how he wished to manage his life and must accept the consequences. It was Wilk's job to protect two children in danger of suffering further damage.

As the months passed, it became clear to Woody that Wilk was bent on thwarting him, a belief shared by a number of attorneys, even some who had nagging doubts about Woody's innocence. With such "a harsh, punitive decision," one attorney said, it was obvious that Wilk was unreasonably picking

---

*In correspondence with the author, Justice Wilk denied making any comments about the case outside of the courtroom.

on Woody, making him pay "an awful price, beyond the price one should have to pay. Okay, it may be that he is degenerate. But Hitler murdered six million Jews and we're still buying Volkswagens. There comes a point when further punishment becomes unchristian. The worst animal could be rehabilitated."

But Mia's attorney, Eleanor Alter, did not believe that the past could be forgotten. "Whatever hell was created, was created by him," she said, in a near-biblical frame of mind.

Buffeted by as many misfortunes as Job, Woody became increasingly defiant toward life. In fact, he hated Job's defeatist philosophy and regarded him as a blockhead. "They rain all this terrible stuff on him that he doesn't deserve, and then he asks God why." Only Job's wife deserved any respect. "Job's wife had my attitude, which was: Curse God and die. She was the one that had some balls."

He was sick and tired of people talking garbage about his relationship with Soon-Yi. Despite the tenuous beginnings of their liaison (he himself called it "an error in judgment" during the hearing), "a genuine love" had developed between them over the past four years, he said. Moved by her rags-to-riches saga, he saw her as a motherless little girl, who had begun life "starving to death, eating a bar of soap for food and then throwing it up," conveniently forgetting that it was Mia who had rescued her. In his imagination, she must have remained the wretched war orphan whom he could indulge and pamper. It would not be possible for any child to go through what Soon-Yi had gone through—and remain alive—without being profoundly traumatized by the ordeal. The mature Soon-Yi was no fragile Madama Butterfly. She was tough and dominating, a mistress who could be a scold and nag, and if she resembled anyone it was Nettie Konigsberg. Sashaying down Madison Avenue arm in arm with Woody, she generally wore a smile as ferociously triumphant as the explorer Ponce de Leon catching his first glimpse of the island of Puerto Rico.

Now a junior at Drew, she lived in a campus dorm room, but on Friday afternoons Woody's chauffeur ferried her back to 930 Fifth Avenue, where as mistress of the house she felt free to run it as she pleased. The decor was stodgy. The place felt like a mausoleum. To make the apartment more cheerful, as she insisted, Woody agreed to knock down walls and redecorate with country furniture, colorful needlepoint pillows, and antiques. Matching checked sofas were ordered for the living room, and a long oak refectory table for Soon-Yi's computer and textbooks was installed in the blue room, which was the room where Mia had discovered the Polaroids. A small bedroom was redone for Satch and named the "Monster Room." According to Elliott Wilk's rulings, the six-year-old could not sleep at Woody's apartment, take home toys, or see Soon-Yi. Nevertheless, his room contained two eight-foot-tall replicas of space aliens, shelves of *Predator* videos, and toy bins brimming with a jumble of grotesque intergalactic plastic creatures that had been assembled by father and son. An immense rubber spider sprawled across the bed. After the redecoration, discarded furniture was hauled to the basement. Several tenants in the building took the opportunity to recover Woody's castoffs from the trash, dragging tables and chairs to their summer homes or giving the loot to relatives.

Soon-Yi's refurbishing was not confined to the interior of the apartment. The terrace also needed repair. In fact, she could hardly set foot on the decks without sloshing into puddles or stumbling over stained, broken tiles. With his attention focused elsewhere the previous two summers, Woody scarcely noticed a minor problem such as poor drainage on the terrace. He blamed the roofer who five years earlier had replaced and waterproofed both of his roof terraces but, in his opinion, had botched the job. While instigating a lawsuit against Mia Farrow, he had also filed a half-million-dollar action against the roofing firm.

At the same time, he further instructed his lawyers to threaten legal action against a postcard company for poking fun at him with a photomontage card, "Mona Allen," that depicted him as the Mona Lisa.

Soon-Yi never hesitated to speak her mind. Anyone who spent time in the couple's company could not help noting that Soon-Yi was constantly correcting Woody. He, though, seemed willing to make allowances for the "kid who was eating out of garbage pails in Korea," as he liked to call her.

In the privacy of their home, she treated him as a typical teenager might behave with her father—in an affectionate, protective, but often patronizing manner. She thought nothing of mocking what she felt were stuffy friends, his old-fashioned ideas, his outdated taste in hairstyle, clothes, and restaurants. She teased him about the collegiate outfits that he had assembled in the fifties, especially his shapeless hats. Eager to improve his appearance, she plied him with suggestions for making himself over by wearing stylish Armani suits, designer glasses, and adopting a voguish haircut. In general, she was impressed by his enormous fame, but the work that it rested upon seemed not to interest her, and she cheerfully admitted having "never read anything he's written." Nor had she seen many of his films. Woody recommended watching *Annie Hall* with "one of your twitty teenage friends," but she thought it sounded boring. Once she sat through *Interiors* and found it "long and tedious." Her favorite movie, perhaps for obvious reasons, was *Manhattan*. Although she was an opinionated, and often impertinent, young woman, Soon-Yi, according to Jean Doumanian, was good for Woody.

"She's very clear and has a different way of viewing things," Jean noted. "She's very quick to say how she feels."

To some people, Soon-Yi's position as the mistress of a famous man seemed enviable, but it came with a price. She was obliged to live life with a partner who was old enough to be her grandfather, and whose lifelong routines revolved around work and his creative imagination. Entertaining friends at home never interested him. Going away on a weekend was "a punishment." He didn't like parties or rock music. And he didn't even dance. Soon-Yi, however, always liked to be on the go. She loved parties, swimming, dancing, shopping, rock music, and slinky miniskirts. She wore her hair in pigtails, a Pocahontas hairstyle that succeeded in making Woody look like the Ancient Mariner. Dutifully she accompanied him to Knicks games, but soon she was dragging him to Fashion Week collections of her favorite designer, Donatella Versace. It was to please Soon-Yi that Woody could be found in first-class seating next to the runway alongside Whitney Houston and k.d. lang. Sometimes he looked sullen, as he clamped both hands over his ears to block out the throbbing of high-decibel rock.

While they continued to be seen at Elaine's, Woody's favorite luncheonette often took second place to Soon-Yi's choice of restaurants, the new glamorous in-spots patronized by café society. Not long after it opened, Balthazar, the trendy SoHo brasserie, received more than a thousand calls a day. But Soon-Yi and Woody had no trouble getting a reservation—even changing their table because some loud, tequila-drinking stockbrokers at a nearby table made conversation impossible. Other favorite dining spots were the newly reopened Le Cirque 2000 (where Soon-Yi was observed eating with her fingers), Nobu in Tribeca, and a collection of less-elite Upper East Side restaurants, closely guarded secrets such as Asia, Ennio's, and Primola. Without Woody, Soon-Yi was seldom recognized in public. Together, their entrance usually electrified other diners, who stopped eating or talking to gaze spellbound at the famous film director and his young lover.

In the summer of 1994, Woody was furious to learn that Mia Farrow was moving out of the city. New rent laws contained a luxury decontrol provision allowing landlords to deregulate an apartment and charge what the market would bear if a tenant's income exceeded $250,000 a year. The monthly rent of $2,300 on Mia's apartment was in danger of soaring to the full market price of $8,000. When she debated dodging the new rule by putting the lease in her children's name, the building's owners promised to take her to court and "sue her for the rest of her life." Mia felt bad about giving up the apartment that was first rented by her mother in 1963. Maureen O'Sullivan, however, proved far less sentimental. "This used to be a joyous place," she told Mia. "But I think it's depressing now. It's a shrine to the past."

Although some of Mia's neighbors in the same predicament succeeded in negotiating compromises with the owners of the Langham, Mia decided to leave Central Park West for her country home in Connecticut. Whether or not she could afford the new rent, luxury deregulation gave her a faultless excuse for removing Dylan and Satch from proximity to Woody. Her older children were away in college—only Moses had two remaining years of high school—and living at Frog Hollow would be healthier for her younger children. Determined not to be outfoxed, Woody took her to court to prevent the move, but he was unsuccessful and had to drive several hours to Connecticut to see Satch for a mere three-hour visit. Unwelcome at Frog Hollow, he usually wound up taking his son, along with a chaperon, to a movie or to a mall, where they passed the time shopping for toys and eating ice cream.

■ ■ ■ ■ ■ ■ ■

Moving Pictures:
KLEINMAN: I've never paid for sex in my life.
PROSTITUTE: You just think you haven't.
—*Shadows and Fog,* 1992

■ ■ ■ ■ ■ ■ ■

One year after Judge Wilk's decision, the Appellate Division of the Supreme Court unanimously confirmed his ruling. Its harshest criticism was reserved for Woody's involvement with Soon-Yi because, as Justice David Ross wrote, "continuation of the relationship, viewed in the best possible light, shows a distinct absence of judgment. It demonstrates to this court Mr. Allen's tendency to place inappropriate emphasis on his own wants and needs and to minimize and even ignore those of his children." The Appellate Division also upheld Wilk's restrictions on the amount of time Woody could spend with Satch, although two of the five justices dissented because they felt unsupervised visitation for twelve hours a week, plus alternate weekends and holidays, would be more reasonable. As for the famous Polaroid photos, which Woody always argued were nothing but ordinary erotic pictures between two consenting adults, the all-male panel delivered its opinion: "We have viewed the photographs and do not share Mr. Allen's characterization of them." Case closed.

Woody had no intention of giving up Soon-Yi. Their relationship was one of the best—maybe *the* best—of his entire life, he told friends. Besides, he saw no reason why he shouldn't have both his girlfriend and his kids. As he declared earlier, "the heart wants what it wants." Still convinced that he had been the victim of an unjust legal system, he tried to overturn the Appellate Division's ruling. The case went to the State Court of Appeals, New

York's highest court. It was dismissed. There was no other court to which he and his lawyers could mount an appeal. Finally, after three years, the case was over.

The emotional cost of the proceeding proved to be exorbitant, but Woody also paid dearly in dollars. Before the roller-coaster ride even began, he had spent "a couple of million already on seven lawyers, and we're not done yet." Subsequently, his expenses for attorneys and private detectives continued to climb astronomically. Over and above the cost of the hearing and his fight against Mia in Surrogate's Court, there were also the costs of appealing Wilk's ruling, along with his complaints against Frank Maco. And finally, Wilk ordered him to foot the bill for Eleanor Alter, Mia's gilt-edge matrimonial lawyer, an expense that Woody aggressively resisted because, as he initially estimated, her lawyer's fee could run him as much as $300,000. As it turned out, he had gravely underestimated the fee. In 1995 he would be forced to enrich Rosenman & Colin with a cool $1.2 million.

All told, Woody's romance with Soon-Yi set him back upward of $7 million, a king's ransom that would have meant nothing to him had it accomplished his two main goals: clearing his name of the child-molestation charge and winning back his daughter. But for all the energy and time he poured into the struggle, in the end it proved to be money down the drain.

CHAPTER NINETEEN

The Cost of Running Amok

At the Carnegie Deli on Seventh Avenue, where Woody had filmed scenes from *Broadway Danny Rose*, hungry diners could care less about sex scandals involving young women and continued to order the overstuffed, overpriced "Woody Allen" sandwich—"Lotsa corned beef plus lotsa pastrami, $13.45." But on Park Avenue in the peach-colored brick St. Bartholomew's Church, the question of character was bound to count. The rector of St. Bart's had once brightened up his sermons with quotes from Woody's writings, generally a surefire means of drawing delighted chuckles from his Anglican parishioners. One of Reverend William Tully's favorite quips was: "There is no question there is an unseen world. The problem is, how far is it from midtown and how late is it open?" But after Woody's transgressions, Reverend Tully discovered that any reference to Woody Allen was "radioactive because the jokes just didn't play well."

The story that had transfixed the country continued to glow like Chernobyl. On television, *The Simpsons* tagged him a child molester, and the cartoon characters Beavis and Butt-head called their penises "my Woody Allen." More devastating was the continuing contempt of columnist Murray Kempton, the Joe DiMaggio of American journalism, who had attended the custody hearings and in six columns over a period of ten months could find no redeeming qualities in such "a hateful creature." Another harsh critic was the *New York Times* op-ed columnist Maureen Dowd, who compared one of his recent movies to "an infomercial with bad info." In her opinion, it was obviously "a propaganda film, a sentimental exercise in self-promotion," that he had made to rehabilitate his image. Woody bridled at the image of himself as a person in need of rehab. "It's the public that needs rehabilitation, the press," he retorted. Dowd had it backward; he was the real victim. "I'm the one who was suddenly smeared."

Persecuted in his own country, Woody turned to Europe for appreciation. For years he had been one of France's most popular entertainers, a hero in their cultural pantheon. In 1989 he was named a Chevalier de l'Ordre des Arts et des Lettres, even though the French government neglected to inform him of the honor and he only learned of the medal by accident in 1998. Interviewed on French television about *Bullets Over Broadway*, whose subject he summarized as one dealing with compromise and aesthetics, Chevalier Allen said with exasperation, "How do you expect Americans who spend their time watching television, going to church and to shopping malls, to understand this?" The French couldn't figure out why Woody had become a pariah in his own country. "For the French, a man who does not have several loves, several mistresses, is not an interesting man," said a French film producer. "What Woody Allen did is very European and we appreciate his attitude: not being ashamed, and especially not apologizing."

But what Woody did is also very American. Certainly he did not invent the older man–younger woman romance, especially in Hollywood Babylon, possibly the most decadent city in the world, where sexual license has been traditionally enjoyed by male stars ever since its inception. As Woody himself tried to point out, Soon-Yi was as old as Mia Farrow was when she married Frank Sinatra. But the national press, unwilling to make allowances, continued to treat him just as if he had driven up to Soon-Yi's playground in his Mercedes and waved a Snickers bar at her.

■ ■ ■ ■ ■ ■ ■

March of Time:
"Not only is there no God, but try getting a plumber on weekends."

—WOODY ALLEN, 1969

■ ■ ■ ■ ■ ■ ■

On the evening of Tuesday, February 28, 1995, Woody's attorney, Elkan Abramowitz, was invited to dine at the Park Avenue home of Eleanor Alter, who was newly remarried to a psychiatrist. The recent adversaries who had jousted against each other in Elliott Wilk's courtroom were now friends. Promptly at 8:00, they made themselves comfortable in front of the television set and prepared to watch *Love and Betrayal: The Mia Farrow Story*, the first part of a four-hour miniseries. Produced on a low budget and filmed mostly in Toronto, the television movie was cast with look-alike actors and actresses who skillfully impersonated the famous real-life people. Dennis Boutsikaris, a well-regarded but little-known New York stage performer, played Woody, and Mia was portrayed by Patsy Kensit, a British actress who had debuted at age three as Mia's towheaded daughter in *The Great Gatsby*. When he learned of the miniseries, Woody pretended to be surprised that anyone would be interested in filming Mia's life. And the idea of someone playing himself struck him as ludicrous. "I must call Tom Cruise and tell him that there's a job opening," he deadpanned. Despite the joke, his amusement was hollow because the Fox Network production was based largely on a book he had never wanted to be published. The author was a former nanny to Mia's children, who had transformed herself from country hired help into a published author with her own book tour.

In the summer of 1991, Mia had hired the daughter of a Bridgewater neighbor to look after Dylan and Satchel in the country. Kristi Groteke, who lived two miles away, was a pretty, athletic, easygoing young woman of twenty-one, who seemed to fit right in with the family as more of a big sister than an employee. She was attending Manhattan College in Riverdale on a track scholarship and needed one semester to graduate with a B.S. in education. Over the next two years, however, Kristi began spending more and more time helping out in the city, especially when Tam needed extra attention and then during the frantic months when Mia was preoccupied with the custody hearing. As genuine ease and affection grew between employer and employee, Mia came to depend on the loyal Kristi.

During the hearing, Kristi had approached Mia with the idea of using her inside knowledge of the family to write a sympathetic book that would picture Mia as a devoted mother coping with the disintegration of her family. Aware of how much she owed Kristi, Mia gave the project her blessing and cooperated by allowing her to inspect copies of court transcripts and conduct interviews not only with herself but also with Daisy, Lark, and other friends of the family. If Mia had qualms about the project, she did not express them to Kristi. Perhaps she had doubts that a college student with no previous experience as a writer would be capable of completing a book, let alone finding a publisher. There was the possibility that nothing would come of it.

With the help of Marjorie Rosen, a senior writer from *People* magazine, Kristi produced a three-hundred-page book that, despite a tight deadline, was professionally researched, expertly written, and published by Carroll & Graf. In the spring of 1994, the proud author delivered to Mia an advance copy of *Mia and Woody: Love and Betrayal* and expected her approval. But two days before publication, Mia called Kristi in a fury. "Just stop the book!" she yelled. "Stop it!" Kristi, however, was in no position to stop the presses. Besides, she was booked on *Larry King Live*.

As Mia informed Kristi, she objected to the depiction of her marriage to Frank Sinatra as an abusive relationship. But what truly upset her was the speculation that she and her close friends had shared information with Kristi and that now Kristi was making public: Mia's suspicions of a secret affair between Woody and her sister Steffi, after she had discovered photos of Steffi in his apartment; his romance with Diane Keaton's younger sister Robin; and his obsession with one of Mariel Hemingway's sisters. Of course Woody had never made a secret of his fascination with the relationships between sisters, which, as he told the *New York Times,* probably resulted from growing up among a multitude of aunts and female cousins.

Mia never spoke to Kristi again. She had counted on her to be an advocate, "which she was," pointed out coauthor Rosen, "but not in the hysterical way Mia would have liked." When he read the book, Woody was shocked by Kristi's reliance on sealed court transcripts, which were obviously provided by Mia and included confidential details about Satch's therapy and his desire to pretend he was Cinderella. Litigious as usual, he instructed Elkan Abramowitz to stop publication of *Mia and Woody.* In the end, these threats were idle ones because the book contained only what Kristi saw for herself, heard from Mia, or read in the transcripts.

NBC was the first network to consider Kristi's book for a television movie, but it dropped out after network executives decided the story might be too lurid for prime time. The option finally went to Fox, which already had a Woody-Mia movie in development but without the juicy, fly-on-the-wall details Kristi could offer. Mia, full of righteous indignation that any network should profit from her personal miseries, wanted to legally block production of the "biopic." In the end, however, she decided not to sue Fox, however ill-considered their movie, because she already owed a fortune in unpaid legal bills.

Although Kristi Groteke felt that she had been fair in her portrayal of Woody, the Fox movie seemed to demonize him as a whining, neurotic middle-aged man whose main concern in life was the New York Knicks. Dennis Boutsikaris managed to capture the superficial Woody: the bald spot, the glasses, the famous stutter played to the hilt. But the expert portrayal added up to character assassination. Mia's main annoyance with the miniseries seemed to be its emphasis on her talent for attracting powerful men. "Do people say that about Diane Keaton?" she fumed. "She's gone out with some pretty famous people."

As it turned out, neither Mia nor Woody should have worried about the movie's impact on their public images. *Love and Betrayal: The Mia Farrow Story* would be the lowest-rated miniseries in Fox history. "People were really sick of Woody and Mia by then," Marjorie Rosen concluded.

■ ■ ■ ■ ■ ■ ■

Hollywood Vignettes:
"All over Hollywood on Monday mornings, there are people living in their palaces, surrounded by riches that you and I could never imagine, and who look at the weekend grosses, and kvell when their competitors have done poorly. 'Wonderful!' they say.

'Oh, great!' Their only happiness comes from the failures and misfortunes of others."

—Retired Hollywood power broker, 1996

■ ■ ■ ■ ■ ■ ■

When the Woody Allen scandal first broke in the summer of 1992, film pundits began searching for parallel calamities. Of course, the movie industry had never treated its erring comics well. Chaplin was forced to flee the United States after four marriages to teenagers, a paternity suit, and sundry other sins, including an affinity for communism. And in 1921 Roscoe "Fatty" Arbuckle was accused of murdering an actress, whom he supposedly raped with a Coke bottle during a party. The film industry disowned Arbuckle, one of its biggest silent stars. Even though he was acquitted of murder, his life and career were ruined. Attorney Raoul Felder ventured a dramatic prediction. Woody Allen, he said, "can put his career in an envelope and mail it to Roman Polanski." Felder was referring to the Polish-born film director, whose pregnant wife, actress Sharon Tate, was gruesomely murdered by members of the Charles Manson "family." Later, Polanski became a fugitive from American justice after he was convicted of raping a thirteen-year-old and then fleeing the country to avoid a prison sentence.

Among the public, Felder's pithy, widely quoted remark contributed to the mistaken perception that Soon-Yi was underage. But in the picture business, Felder's quip simply called attention to the question uppermost in most film executives' minds: How would Woody's Chappaquiddick affect his gross? Common wisdom had it that his personal problems would have "legs" and interfere with the public's ability to watch his films. Woody laughed off the eulogies because, he said, nobody could prevent him from continuing to write screenplays. On the other hand, racked with self-pity, sometimes he felt like quitting the film industry. "I seriously considered whether I still wanted to entertain, to work hard at whatever gift I had to offer these people," he commented. But these despairing moods never lasted. Movies were his bread and butter, his "therapy." Besides, what would an impassioned workaholic do without activity?

During his years with Arthur Krim, Woody ruled as a nabob of a semi-independent kingdom that was akin to an Italian ministate with its own customs, climate, religion, and history. When his pictures lost money, the Medici financed him anyway, like a beloved old charity. The demise of Orion, however, ushered in the dawn of a new age, in which the kingdom that never deigned to deal with the Hollywood power structure had to grovel for Hollywood money.

Under Woody's three-picture deal, TriStar put up $20 million for *Hus-*

bands and Wives and spent another $5 million to promote it, but the studio lost money with domestic box-office sales of only $10.5 million. *Manhattan Murder Mystery* also failed to cover its cost of $13.5 million. With one film remaining on his contract, the studio quietly pulled out from the arrangement but insisted that it was Woody himself who requested premature release from the contract. "Our deal with Woody was basically finished," said Mike Medavoy. He was backed up by the head of Sony Pictures (TriStar's parent), Jonathan Dolgen, who also emphatically denied that Sony played any part in the breakup. Nevertheless, nobody at TriStar seemed upset to bid Woody farewell, nor did they offer to distribute his future films. For the first time in twenty-five years, he was forced to address an unpleasant reality: Filmmaking is like any other business.

That summer, when it seemed nobody wanted to make movies with Woody anymore, Jean Doumanian was continuing to brood about the media's treatment of her friend. The only way to treat the hogwash printed in newspapers was to "wrap fish in it the next day," she said. In 1991 she had formed her own film production company and released *The Ox*, a Swedish film featuring Max von Sydow that was written and directed by Sven Nykvist. Although *The Ox* received an Oscar nomination for Best Foreign Language Film, it did poorly at the box office and several years later the production company bearing Doumanian's name still lacked a track record. Nevertheless, she was committed to the idea that Woody must continue making films.

Shortly after the release of *Husbands and Wives*, a mysterious new player suddenly appeared on Woody's horizon. Called Sweetland Films, it was a company that would bankroll Jean Doumanian Productions, which in turn would take over the financing of all future Woody Allen pictures. Doumanian declined to publicly identify her backers, except to say Sweetland Films was an independent company of European investors. But Hollywood savants soon concluded that the principal investor in her European consortium was none other than her boyfriend, Jaqui Safra, a wealthy member of a Swiss-Lebanese banking family.

A beefy, swarthy man with a taste for the highlife, Safra owned a glamorous East Side apartment, where he neither lived nor worked, but used exclusively for parties. He was related to Edmond Safra, a principal shareholder in the Republic New York Corporation, a holding company of nationwide commercial and savings banks. Reputed to be something of a dilettante playboy and a self-described "international financier," Safra had been an executive at American Express, as well as executive producer of *The Ox*, and a collector of movie posters. He found it amusing to take an occasional small acting role in Woody's movies: In *Stardust Memories*, he was Sandy Bates's brother-in-law on the stationary bike who keeps having heart attacks, and in *Radio Days,* the diction student with the French accent. More significant, he had been Jean Doumanian's live-in boyfriend for the better part of twenty years, which automatically made him a dear friend of Woody's. Doumanian, terrified of the press ever since the *Saturday Night Live* debacle, did not care to advertise her relationship with Safra. She was always careful to describe her financial sources in terms of euphemisms: private backers, good contacts, and her favorite, a consortium of European investors.

On July 21, 1993, Woody announced that he would be leaving TriStar because Sweetland had offered him a deal he couldn't refuse: a 25 percent larger production budget, a generous director's fee consisting of a cash fee in the low seven figures, and a cut of the profits after Sweetland has recouped its investment. "I love the idea of an isolated, controllable mom-and-pop store for my movies," he said. The news that he was leaving a behemoth such as TriStar for Jean's bodega made people in the movie industry wonder aloud. "Nobody wants to be involved with him," declared a senior studio executive. If his new deal was so wonderful, as another put it, "how come he doesn't have distribution?" An insider who worked on many of Woody's films felt he was becoming "more and more insulated. This linking with his best friend and his sister tells me that." And who was going to distribute the mom-and-pop films, even if pop was Woody Allen? To those in the know, his joining forces with Sweetland had less to do with creative independence than saving face.

Woody's sister, Letty Aronson, who was now a vice president of Sweetland, scoffed at the West Coast cynics. "The story is what the story is," she explained in her best fractured Brooklynese, as if nothing had changed in her brother's life. "Any other story—other than you know of as quoted by representatives of Sony, TriStar, Allen, and Sweetland—is garbage."

If corporate Hollywood didn't buy the story of Sweetland's deal, neither did Woody's uneasy production staff. Remembering Doumanian's calamitous management of *Saturday Night Live,* some wondered if Jean could be trusted anywhere near a film production company. They did not have to wait long to get their answers. According to Doumanian, Sweetland's foreign investors would retain international rights and allow her to sell American rights to whatever distributor she could rustle up. More important, she planned to concentrate on controlling costs. As it turned out, her idea of trimming the production budget was to decree sizable pay cuts for Woody's loyal staff.

Over the next two years Sweetland would be responsible for the exodus of almost the entire production team Woody had assembled since *Annie Hall,* all the familiar names that rolled at the end of each picture. The gentlemanly Robert Greenhut, for example, had produced Woody Allen's films beginning with *The Front* in 1976. "Conceivably," a satisfied Woody said in 1978, "I can see myself working with Greenhut forever." Forever ended in 1995.

Hearing Jean pontificate about cutting fat angered Greenhut. "I put together this great team," he said. "We made twenty movies and they were all very thrifty. For somebody to come in and say we were doing it improperly and we have to pay the editor $1,000 less—that gets my dander up."

Around this time, coproducer Helen Robin departed, likewise associate producer Thomas Reilly and costume designer Jeffrey Kurland, propmasters and sound mixers, boom men and camera operators. "I'd be thrilled if everyone would continue," Woody said. "These are my friends."

But he clearly felt no responsibility for his friends, who were replaced with cheaper help, or with professional number crunchers such as the new producer, Richard Brick, who had been commissioner of the Mayor's Office of Film, Theater, and Broadcasting. Prior to his job as film czar, Brick served an extensive apprenticeship as a production and location manager *(Silkwood, Ragtime)* before producing, in 1991, an independent art film about inner city youths, *Hangin' With the Homeboys.* Brick's new job was to make sure the consortium's money was used for what went on the screen, not for what went into the employees' pockets—or stomachs. One of his first policy changes was to ban free coffee for the crew after lunch. To keep up morale during long, tedious workdays, movie companies have traditionally provided all the free coffee you can drink. When it looked as if the crew might tar and feather him, Brick restored the coffee wagon.

It was not as if Woody had run out of alternatives. He could have retained his staff, very likely at their usual salaries, by alternating personal films with an occasional commercial film, just as Martin Scorsese once in a while would make a *Cape Fear* followed by an *Age of Innocence.* If he had wished to, Woody probably could have made another hit like *Annie Hall.* But he resisted suggestions of compromise. Instead he took the moral high road by involving himself as little as possible in such pedestrian matters as money. Since firing people personally would have been too messy, he left these jobs to Jean and her bean counters. Loyal associates forced to walk the plank preferred to curse her and Letty, "those Sweetland women," rather than hold Woody responsible. "Of course he allowed it," a departed technician admitted. "Because the only thing he cares about is making his movies."

The new emphasis on the bottom line exasperated some ex-staffers because Woody was never known for generosity. "He was cheap," said a former member of his team. "He never picked up a meal tab. There was never a Christmas party or a card or a gift—never!—and he didn't like people to take off holidays because they meant nothing to him. There were no wrap gifts which are standard in the industry. And yet people didn't care about his chintziness because he was so generous in other ways, like credits. He made us feel we were part of something."

Those who remained with Woody and agreed to work for scale, sometimes at half their regular compensation, usually had personal reasons: Either they were nearing retirement age, or they were foreign residents who wanted to continue living in the United States. Circumspect in public, they grumbled among themselves. Unwilling to place the blame on Woody himself, his associates reserved their hostility for Jean Doumanian and Letty Aronson. Jean was smart but abrasive; Letty was known for her temper. While both women were privy to Woody's private life, they had never been involved in his business, and, among his associates, were not considered film professionals. It was assumed that cronyism, not ability, had landed Aronson an executive position at Sweetland. "She belongs in the kitchen with the pots and pans," said someone who had worked with Woody on previous films. "What does she know about running a movie business? Letty would get lost in an elevator." As for Jean, the degree of ill will among his staff was even greater. "She just travels the world on Jaqui's money," one person said.

On location in Europe for *Everyone Says I Love You* in 1995, the stingy behavior of the penny-pinching Sweetland executives antagonized people. In the late afternoons, Aronson and Doumanian would arrive at the location, as one participant reported, "dressed to the teeth and stand around yapping. 'Where are we having dinner tonight? We have to get finished soon.' Every night it was where they were going to eat." Arriving in Paris, they did not hesitate to stay at the Ritz with round-the-clock cars and drivers, while the rest of the crew had to content themselves with the local version of Motel 6, scraping by on a minuscule per diem, "the lowest any American crew has ever got in Europe." It was the same story in Venice, where, recalled a crew member, "we slept at crummy hotels and they were at the Gritti Palace on the Grand Canal."

On the surface, Woody's life returned to normal, and for the first time in several years, his creative energy rebounded. No longer in need of collaborators, he seemed like the legendary Woody of old, who was bursting with ideas for ten writers. As if to prove he had not mailed his career to Roman Polanski, he branched out to tackle new projects in addition to producing his annual feature. One of his cherished whipping boys was television, or "elevator music," as he called it. In the late sixties, when he earned more than a million dollars a year as a comic, a sizable portion of his income had come from television, particularly the hosting of high-rated specials such as *Kraft Music Hall.* But having abandoned stand-up for filmmaking, he had slammed the medium. In the seventies, asked whether television had improved his mind, he replied "a lot"—it raised his level of taste to the point where he no longer watched it. (In reality, he watched sports and old movies.)

By 1994, however, when TV standards had dumbed down to an all-time low, he had a sudden change of heart and decided that "television had improved tremendously." At the urging of Jean Doumanian, her rich boyfriend, and his sister, Letty, Woody agreed to revive *Don't Drink the Water,* his first produced play that he had written when he was thirty-one. Now that he was fifty-eight, he was the correct age to play the father, originally acted by Lou Jacobi, and he also cast Michael J. Fox as the son and one of his favorite actresses, Julie Kavner, as the mother. The rationale for recycling a nearly thirty-year-old work was supplied by Jean Doumanian. "I thought he owes it to his public to give them some quality TV," she told the *Hollywood Reporter.* Woody was in Europe when *Don't Drink the Water* aired on ABC in December 1994. Reviewers noted that he had made no effort to modernize hopelessly stale material, the characters were cartoons, and the depiction of Arab characters was grossly insensitive. A reviewer from *Variety* suggested that he should have left the play in a shoe box under his bed. Apparently viewers agreed because about half of them flipped channels before the teleplay's conclusion. Undeterred, Woody took another plunge into television the following year when he starred with Peter Falk, with even less success, in a remake of Neil Simon's *The Sunshine Boys.*

His safari into "quality" television a mistake, he turned to the legitimate theater. A theatrical producer, Julian Schlossberg, hoped to mount a triple bill of one-act comedies by celebrated playwrights. The three plays he had in mind were by David Mamet, Elaine May, and Woody Allen, but when Schlossberg contacted Woody about *Death Knocks,* he received a chilly response. The short story in play format concerns a middle-aged New York garment manufacturer who challenges Death to a game of gin rummy. A parody of Ingmar Bergman's *The Seventh Seal,* it was written in 1968 for *The New Yorker.* Woody said it was old and dated. Jean Doumanian, intrigued by Schlossberg's trilogy concept, suggested he write a brand-new play.

"If I can think of anything," he promised.

In *Central Park West,* a story of infidelity and May-December sex on the Upper West Side, all the characters have slept with one another: the psychoanalyst, her philandering lawyer husband who has been laying her best friend, the supposed best friend and her husband, and one of the shrink's patients, a beautiful young woman of twenty-one. Under the umbrella title of *Death Defying Acts,* Woody's seventy-minute comedy of New York manners was joined by David Mamet's *An Interview* and Elaine May's *Hotline.* Jean Doumanian was named coproducer, Letty Aronson associate producer, and Michael Blakemore director. A company of talented actors, including the Tony Award–winning Linda Lavin, was assembled, and rehearsals commenced in early January of 1995, followed by a brief tryout in Stamford,

Connecticut. *Death Defying Acts* was scheduled to open at the Variety Arts Theatre on Second Avenue on March 6.

It was a crisp, cold day in the East Village. At John's Italian Restaurant, Michael Blakemore dug into a bowl of pasta dripping with olive oil and punched up with handfuls of pungent chopped garlic and washed the meal down with a carafe of red wine. Returning to the theater, he learned that Woody was waiting out front in his parked car to hand him revisions. Blakemore clambered into the toasty backseat of the Mercedes while Woody frantically flipped through a sheaf of notes. Once inside the car, the director began worrying about his breath. He feared that the aroma of garlic was a tad overpowering. But Woody appeared to be oblivious. Later, during the intermission, Jean Doumanian informed Blakemore that Woody loathed the odor of garlic, whereupon Blakemore could not help feeling a frisson of perverse satisfaction.

Michael Blakemore, a handsome, smooth-voiced man of sixty-six, had recently directed two Broadway hits, *City of Angels* and *Lettice & Lovage*. In England he was known as clever but difficult, his longtime foe being Peter Hall after they had argued over the artistic direction of Britain's National Theatre. In recent years, Blakemore had spent so much time working in New York that he was able to detect fresh scratches on the furniture of his favorite hotel, the Michelangelo.

Evidently Blakemore suspected from the outset that in directing this triple bill of one-act plays, he might be treading into dangerous territory. In his journal, he began jotting down notes that he envisioned as "a very personal account of working with three playwrights who were also directors—a very difficult situation whoever the personalities were." Needless to say, the situation was fraught with more peril when one of the playwrights was reputed to be a world-class neurotic. Still, he was unprepared for outright pathology. Before long, one fact became clear: Woody Allen operated in "manic-depressive cycles." One day he would love the performance, then the next day hate it: "This performance was a great step backward," he chided Blakemore. "That was terrible! *Just terrible!*"

As rehearsals continued, Woody Allen, the perfectionist movie director, was constantly breathing down Blakemore's neck, trying to undermine his authority, warning he was too soft on the actors, pelting him with instructions on how to perform his job. The pace was slow, the blocking precious, Linda Lavin's performance "cutesy," he informed Blakemore. Why didn't he make the actors buckle down? Blakemore, wearing an oatmeal-colored scarf thrown over his canvas jacket, looked the picture of cool confidence. Underneath, he was hissing like a pot ready to boil over as Woody handed him notes that said "just awful." "*Still* shit." Blakemore's favorite scrawl read "PATHTIC [*sic*]." In calm moods, Woody could be lucid, direct, even stimulating. A shadow of a smile would appear on his pale face as he tried to be pleasant. But usually he was in a state of high anxiety. Gazing at him, Blakemore sometimes wondered "which of us was going mad." In his diary he was able to vent his anger, but still found himself arriving at rehearsals in "an icy rage." Had his wife not informed him of a depressing call from their bank manager about their finances, he would have quit the production.

Hostility between the two directors erupted into biological warfare when Blakemore came down with a cold. Having never mastered his terror of germs, Woody deliberately kept his distance lest he be infected by microbial hordes. According to Blakemore, Woody would approach him cautiously holding his overcoat over his nose and mouth "like a nineteenth-century anarchist." What sprang to mind was a character from *The Brothers Karamazov*.

That *Death Defying Acts* ran for more than a year was mainly due to Woody's contribution as well as the popularity of Linda Lavin and then her replacement, Valerie Harper, the popular television star from *The Mary Tyler Moore Show* and *Rhoda*. A year passed before Blakemore unburdened himself in an article, "Death Defying Director," in the June 3, 1996, issue of *The New Yorker*. It was payback time. Although the Englishman took a swipe or two at Elaine May (but none at "absent angel" David Mamet, whom he praised for never showing his face in New York), his target was clearly Woody. The Englishman felt that "not being a New Yorker, I can take liberties that others can't." His liberties involved nailing Woody for being Woody—insecure, controlling as well as out of control, and an unsociable crab. He went after his teeth ("tiny") and his handshake ("minimalist"). In a rare moment of chivalry, Blakemore restrained himself from describing how Soon-Yi bossed Woody, instead calling her, euphemistically, a girl who "knows her own mind" and who bore no resemblance to the mousy creature he had seen on television. When Woody read the piece, the part he resented was his fear of germs. He did not pull his coat up like a spy, he protested. Blakemore had no right to make him sound like a crackpot. "People think God knows what when they meet me," he complained.

Woody's twenty-fourth movie, and his first picture with Jean Doumanian, was *Bullets Over Broadway,* the period comedy written with Doug McGrath during the tumultuous year of the custody battle. The central character is a naively idealistic playwright from Pittsburgh who gives up struggling to write for the theater after his play is rewritten by a hoodlum who happens to have the talent of Eugene O'Neill. Although David Shayne, the playwright in the film, was a typical Woody Allen character, Woody decided he was too old for the role and cast twenty-eight-year-old John Cusack, who stood a strapping six feet two inches and bore no resemblance to Woody offscreen. In an amazing transformation, Cusack pulled off a convincing impersonation of Woody—glasses, twitches, and stammers—as Michael Caine had done subtly in *Hannah and Her Sisters.* Dianne Wiest played Helen Sinclair, a high-strung boozy actress who seduces the young playwright. After appearing in three of Woody's films and winning an Oscar for the flighty sister in *Hannah and Her Sisters,* the forty-five-year-old actress had not worked for him in seven years. Playing motherly types in such films as *Parenthood* and caring for her two adopted daughters, Wiest was now a bit chubby.

After the first day of shooting, Woody telephoned Wiest at home to comment on her performance. "It's terrible!" he exclaimed. Wiest remedied the problem by lowering her normal voice to a growl and by apparently studying Rosalind Russell's performance as Auntie Mame. She won a second Oscar as best supporting actress for her role in the film.

Disrespect from the media notwithstanding, Woody still carried clout in the movie business. In choosing a distributor for *Bullets Over Broadway,* Doumanian took the position that Woody was a Tiffany-quality filmmaker. Distributors interested in licensing the film were asked to submit blind bids and make offers based solely on Woody's name and reputation. If this sounded a bit high and mighty, she explained that in the halcyon days of old, Orion and TriStar approved his projects without question. As it turned out, she got four bids and finally settled on Miramax Films, the upstart releasing company headed by a pair of New Yorkers, Harvey Weinstein and his brother Bob Weinstein. The Weinsteins had set up shop in their hometown because, joked Bob Weinstein, "the Knicks play in New York City. When they move, we'll think about moving." Harvey Weinstein, a mercurial, cigar-chomping wheeler and dealer who is famous throughout the industry for his management-by-screaming style, had no visible patina of class. Woody liked him, however. Miramax, an independent company with a reputation for spotting and making money on specialty and art films such as Steven Soderbergh's *sex, lies, & videotape,* had recently been acquired by the Disney Company for $80 million. Despite recent successes (six Oscar nominations for *The Crying Game*), it wasn't quite yet a player in the eyes of West Coast Hollywood.

In the case of *Bullets Over Broadway,* Weinstein instinctively gobbled up the film sight unseen, not even quibbling over Woody's refusal to do the customary publicity. His instincts were right, because *Bullets Over Broadway* received seven Oscar nominations (in the categories of supporting actor and actress, art direction, costume design, director, and original screenplay). Despite the wrenching events of the past two years, Woody had nonetheless managed to pull out of his hat a stylish film that found favor with mainstream audiences. It was a tribute to his toughness—and an answer to his enemies. An exhilarated Jean Doumanian crowed over the nominations, which she hoped would establish once and for all audience disinterest in Woody's personal shortcomings. "Everybody kind of embraced Woody with that and said, 'We're yours and don't think we'll ever go away,'" she said.

In the fall of 1993, Woody had a chance to thank Jean for her years of loyalty. Dining together at an Italian restaurant, Primola, on Second Avenue, she was eating a piece of *bruscetta* when she choked on the hard Italian bread and started to turn blue. Immediately, Woody leaped up and performed the Heimlich maneuver.

Woody had often wondered about the origins of his adopted daughter. To be so intelligent and charming, he decided, Dylan must have inherited "good genes." It was no coincidence that this ongoing obsession with the child kindled the story for his next movie. In *Mighty Aphrodite*, Lenny Weinrib is a sportswriter with a wife half his age—a cold, neglectful, career-driven gallery owner who wants motherhood but can't quite find time for nine months of inconvenience. When Amanda (Helena Bonham Carter) wants to adopt, Lenny reluctantly agrees. Five years later, the marriage is on the rocks, but their son, Max, has turned out to be bright and funny, so special that Lenny grows obsessive about his birth mother. His quest leads to the door of Linda Ash, aka Judy Cum, a sometime porn actress and full-time hooker, who assumes he's a trick and says: "Hello? Are you my 3 o'clock?"

Mighty Aphrodite (a reference to the Greek goddess of love) ends happily with the prostitute receiving a personality makeover, marrying a nice guy, and having a child. But the point of Woody's narrative—that sometimes the women who put up their babies for adoption are prostitutes—angered adoption agencies. The director of Spence Chapin Adoption Agency noted that adopted children have fantasies about their birth parents, and *Mighty Aphrodite* only "feeds into the message that your birth parent is bad."

By ironic coincidence, the same year that Woody was filming *Mighty Aphrodite*, a Texas paroled convict (larceny, theft, and bail-jumping) claimed that he was Dylan's birth father. The sixty-year-old man insisted that she was born to his common-law wife while both of them were in prison and given up for adoption without his consent. After letters to Mia threatening to "recapture" Dylan and promising "bloodshed" if she was not handed over, the parolee was arrested in Louisiana and returned to prison. Paroled again in 1997, he disabled an electronic monitoring device and disappeared, but not before making similar threatening phone calls to a Hartford newspaper. When asked to comment, Mia swore that Dylan was not the ex-con's child.

Mighty Aphrodite brought Woody his twelfth Oscar nomination—tying Billy Wilder's record—for best original screenplay. He failed to win an Academy Award, but Mira Sorvino took home the supporting actress award for her portrayal of the hooker. Even with the Oscar, the picture bombed at the box office with a gross of $6.7 million, a plunge of $7 million from *Bullets Over Broadway*.

In 1996 the size of Woody's audience continued to melt. He had high hopes for *Everyone Says I Love You,* a retread of the memorable 1938 Kaufmann and Hart comedy *You Can't Take It With You,* which he had adored as a boy when he fantasized about having a lovable, zany family just like the Sycamores in the play. Woody's fictional family were rich liberal Upper East Siders with the mother and father played by Goldie Hawn and Alan Alda. The sudsy musical comedy had a $20 million budget and less of a plot than an average McDonald's commercial. Stars without musical-comedy training were pressured to sing and dance, mostly without success except for Goldie Hawn. Making every effort to please his audience, Woody offered a smorgasbord of golden oldie tunes, attractive performers (including a cameo by Julia Roberts), and luscious picture-postcard photography in Paris and Venice. A number of critics were enchanted by the film. Roger Ebert, for one, predicted "it would take a heart of stone to resist this movie," an opinion that led to a skirmish on *Sneak Previews* when a disgusted Gene Siskel rated the movie two thumbs down. "He's not funny anymore," Siskel declared, and by the way, he added, when was Woody going to grow up?

Ebert was indignant. "Oh, Gene," he fussed.

Filmgoer apathy for *Everyone Says I Love You* was reflected in the box-office revenue that never managed to hit $10 million, in woeful contrast to a dog such as *Beavis and Butt-head Do America,* another new release that took in $20 million during its opening weekend.

■ ■ ■ ■ ■ ■ ■

The Box Office:

Year		Domestic grosses in millions
1986	*Hannah and Her Sisters*	40.1
1987	*Radio Days*	14.7
1987	*September*	0.4
1989	*Crimes and Misdemeanors*	18.0
1990	*Alice*	5.9
1991	*Shadows and Fog*	2.7
1992	*Husbands and Wives*	10.5
1993	*Manhattan Murder Mystery*	11.3
1994	*Bullets Over Broadway*	13.4

1995	*Mighty Aphrodite*	6.7
1996	*Everyone Says I Love You*	9.7
1997	*Deconstructing Harry*	10.6
1998	*Celebrity*	5.0
1999	*Sweet and Lowdown*	N.A.

• • • • • • • •

It was inevitable. The titillating scandal of Woody, Mia, and Soon-Yi retreated into history, to be replaced by fresher Hollywood scandals: the thirteen-year-old boy who alleged he had been molested by Michael Jackson; the black book of Hollywood madam Heidi Fleiss; the breakup of Burt Reynolds and Loni Anderson; the O. J. Simpson and Menendez brothers murder trials.

Those expecting Woody to join Roman Polanski in the gulag of exiled directors were surprised to encounter a Woody on the defensive. The star-makers who had once convinced him of his own genius were long retired from the playing field, but Woody, as seasonally as the birds migrated south, threw himself into a new project every fall and released a new feature in October or December, in time to be considered for the Oscars.

As the market for his films shrank, he felt terrified that his time as an innovative filmmaker had passed, just as the end had come for Francis Ford Coppola, Peter Bogdanovich, Dennis Hopper, and Robert Altman, indeed for most of the brash, young filmmakers of the seventies, except for Martin Scorsese and Steven Spielberg. He was keenly aware he could not continue to make the same kind of film, in which he needed only to be "Woody Allen" to sell tickets. (In fact, there was now a generation of young moviegoers who had never seen *Annie Hall* or *Sleeper,* to whom Woody Allen was a scrawny comedian who couldn't act and who had slept with his girlfriend's daughter.) Obviously, staying au courant, retooling his product, was a matter of economic necessity, reluctant as he was to acknowledge it. Fighting to reclaim his reputation and fatten his grosses, he began to woo a broader range of moviegoers, and that meant playing it safe with fluffy, feel-good stories geared to some of those folks who spent their time visiting shopping malls and seeing Bruce Willis pictures, in short, the mass audience he had derided long ago.

Approaching his sixtieth birthday, he was prepared to forego risky films such as *Interiors, Shadows and Fog,* and the ill-considered Chekhovian *September.* In his eagerness to please his new audience, he visually dazzled them with Busby Berkeley chorus lines of singing and dancing Grouchos, Peter Pan dance numbers filmed in Paris against a background of the Seine, and twenties costume pictures complete with Art Deco sets and antique roadsters. All of his recent comedies were sleek and handsome, but they were also popcorn pictures, distressingly devoid of substance or ideas. Auteur film-making gave way to a new genre, potboiler auteur. In contrast, a film such as *Crimes and Misdemeanors* now seemed as weighty as Bergman's *Seventh Seal.*

More than the cars and costumes, his most conspicuous practice, first seen with *Shadows and Fog,* was to freshen up his pictures with a clever kind of froufrou window dressing that consisted of top stars: Leonardo DiCaprio, Demi Moore, Billy Crystal, Julia Louis-Dreyfus, Kenneth Branagh, Julia Roberts, Goldie Hawn, Kirstie Alley, Robin Williams, Helena Bonham Carter, Elisabeth Shue, Winona Ryder, Ed Norton, and Drew Barrymore, among many others. Since he could not possibly match their customary fees, he had to take potluck and hope to catch them between pictures, or not get them at all. (In this way, for example, he managed to get a week of Robin Williams's time for $10,000 when he was between film roles that paid him millions.)

Nothing worked. His consistently pitiful grosses of recent years utterly mystified him, he said. He could understand why so few people wanted to see an esoteric picture such as *Shadows and Fog,* but why hadn't *Husbands and Wives* and *Manhattan Murder Mystery* taken off? He couldn't figure out what had happened with *Bullets Over Broadway,* which received good notices and seven Oscar nominations (and in which he did not appear). Wanting to believe that the sex scandal had not cost him his audience, he insisted that his films had never been a huge draw in this country, except in a few big cities, and his grosses "were never any good, and they're not good now."

There was a time, in the seventies, when his grosses were quite respectable. In fact, in the years between 1975 and 1979, his films were among the top ten box-office draws. It was not until *Stardust Memories* that his career peaked commercially and began a downward slide. By the nineties, when he received the biggest box-office response of his entire career, it was for something else—his personal, offscreen drama, which, ironically, played to packed houses in big cities and small.

CHAPTER TWENTY

Getting Even

Year after year, to regain his children, Woody had feverishly poured money and hope into the stew of lawsuits he had kept simmering on the back burner, a kettle that by now had almost burned dry. At the end of 1995, his weekly visits with Satch were suspended after Satch claimed his father physically abused him, an episode Woody vehemently denied. The boy told his therapist that he "hated and feared" his father and was not looking forward to any more visits. Furthermore, the therapist reported to Elliott Wilk, the child "suffered from nightmares and stomach aches."

As defeat followed defeat, it seemed as if Woody could do nothing right against his foes. His efforts to remove Elliott Wilk from the case on the grounds of bias had failed, and even his determination to punish Frank Maco came to naught. After four years, the Connecticut Grievance Committee dismissed his ethics complaint against the prosecutor. Although Maco's actions were sharply criticized on the grounds of insensitivity, he was neither dismissed nor disbarred. At the Litchfield Inn, he celebrated with a lunch of softshell crabs and returned to his job. Although these reverses would have discouraged even the most bullheaded person, they had no effect whatsoever on Woody, who, in the spring of 1996, redoubled his fight for more liberal visitation rights and again confronted Elliott Wilk. As if the previous three years never existed, Woody pushed to see Dylan and Satch on alternate weekends without a chaperon and in the presence of Soon-Yi. This repetitive petition was a mistake, not merely because he had lost every previous round, but also because he seemed oblivious to the true situation: Neither Dylan nor Satch had any desire to see him.

In his reply, a testy Wilk said that his making such a request only confirmed how "little understanding or empathy" he had with respect to his children. Again the judge vetoed any contact with eleven-year-old Dylan, her emotional state being still "too fragile and unsettled." The very thought of seeing him made her hysterical and she told her therapist she did not want to lay eyes on Woody Allen ever again because of his "boyfriend-girlfriend relationship" with her sister. Both Satch and Moses, now an eighteen-year-old college student, despised him. The verdict was unanimous: Everyone in the family hated him. In the same decision, however, Wilk said he would permit resumption of supervised visitation with Satchel for a test period of four weeks at the office of his therapist, at which time he would reassess the situation. Smarting, Woody was not about to agree to such restrictive terms. Instead, his legal options exhausted, he dreamed out loud about taking revenge on Elliott Wilk—perhaps by filming a documentary about the judge that he would call *An Error in Judgment*.

It looked as if the bloody custody battle was finally over. The war, however, continued.

On a Friday night in late February 1996, Woody arrived at Teterboro Airport in New Jersey to board a private jet that would take him to Paris and fourteen other cities, a grand total of twenty-three days of mostly one-night stands. Accompanying him was Soon-Yi, Letty, and Jean Doumanian with her dog, a silver-gray, sixty-pound slobbering weimaraner named Jasmine that he trusted would stay as far from him as possible. As soon as the seat-belt sign went off, a documentary filmmaker and a crew of three went into action.

His last experience on the road was the stand-up circuit in the seventies, a dismal memory because the monotony of the work practically killed him. The idea of a backbreaking musical road tour, one that paraded his lack of natural musical skill before large audiences in a different city every day, sounded like the last thing he needed. On the contrary, he certainly did not need the money or the aggravation. Usually he warned people he was a "terrible" clarinetist, like Jack Benny on the violin, an amateur who was tolerated by the public and music critics alike because he was a celebrity. But what he needed at the moment was more spectacular ammunition in his continuing public-relations skirmishes with Mia. Like so many of his projects lately, the concert tour was conceived by the head of his brain trust, Jean Doumanian, who was impressed by the enthusiasm of European visitors to Michael's Pub, and decided that Woody and his band should star in a quality music documentary. The *Citizen Kane* of this genre was a rock documentary, *Don't Look Back*, D. A. Pennebaker's transfixing backstage classic that followed a baby-faced twenty-three-year-old Bob Dylan on his 1965 tour of England. Anyone who saw the film never forgot the unobtrusive camera capturing Dylan rushed by screaming fans, Dylan teasing reporters backstage, Dylan bantering with Donovan in his hotel suite, always refusing to suffer fools gladly. In Jean's view, an updated *Don't Look Back* might be just what the spin doctor ordered to emphasize Woody's charismatic side. The crucial question was, Who would get behind the camera?

Recently Doumanian had seen a documentary chronicling the life of comics artist Robert Crumb (creator of Fritz the Cat), which was produced by a talented San Francisco filmmaker, Terry Zwigoff, who spent six years studying the counterculture illustrator. The result was an extraordinary film that scooped up a cluster of awards and earned more than $3 million. Doumanian thought that *Crumb* was "an incredible piece of work and I knew he would be right for this." Learning that Zwigoff had filmed the life of blues musician Howard Armstrong (*Louie Bluie,* 1985) and also collected old jazz and blues recordings clinched it in her mind. Zwigoff and Allen would be a perfect match.

Everyone was pleased when Terry Zwigoff said he was interested in making the film. Of course, from Zwigoff's viewpoint, an authorized film would mean loss of independence, but a budget in the neighborhood of $500,000 would make it financially worth his while. Tempted, he cautioned Woody that he "wouldn't take it easy on him," and Woody replied that was precisely what made *Crumb* so special. Only a few weeks before the concert tour was scheduled to begin, Zwigoff, perhaps realizing that he was not going to retain final approval after all, bowed out. Making no secret of his unhappiness, he complained to *Entertainment Weekly,* "They were like, 'Who do you think you are, Orson Welles?'" Insiders speculated that the problem was Jean Doumanian, who evidently was not shy about boasting that Woody didn't get final cut on her projects—"I do." (Zwigoff denied that he left over the issue of final cut, citing personal reasons.) Undaunted, Doumanian quickly hand-picked a replacement for Zwigoff.

Winner of two Academy Awards, Barbara Kopple had been the darling of the documentary film business for almost two decades. Although she possessed a self-effacing manner and a pretty, baby-doll face, she was, in fact, a fearless, highly manipulative filmmaker who had made several outstanding documentaries: one, about the labor struggles of Kentucky coal miners (*Harlan County, U.S.A.*); the other, about Minnesota meatpacking plant strikers (*American Dream*). Some thought her greatest film was *Fallen Champ: The Untold Story of Mike Tyson,* a 1993 television documentary. From the beginning of her career, by presenting herself as a breathless, helpless little girl, an affect not unlike Mia Farrow's, Kopple learned how to get what she wanted, and that included bursting into tears if the occasion demanded it. Now in her fifties, she still wore her coal-black hair long and straight with a center part, a resolutely seventies hairstyle reminiscent of the one worn by the actress Valerie Bertinelli.

In early February, Kopple visited Woody at his apartment to discuss the project, and for a half hour they made small talk about everything but the film and the tour. Finally, Kopple recalled, "30 minutes went by and I knew I had to say something." Out of desperation, she asked if he was looking forward to the tour.

"No," he groaned. "I have too much to do here." Besides, the thought of visiting all those cities depressed him. It was at that moment, Kopple said, she decided to make the film. Avoiding the issue of final cut, she asked instead for "total access," which included the right to take her camera anywhere she liked to record his private moments offstage. "I told Woody I wouldn't do it any other way," she said. In fact, she had fallen in love with her subject.

Woody slipped out of a white terry-cloth robe and tiptoed to the edge of a private swimming pool in Milan's regal Principe de Savoia. He was followed by Soon-Yi, who was wearing a matching robe over a black-and-white bikini. In his light blue swim trunks, he tumbled into the water and paddled a few laps before announcing he was tired of swimming and was going to get out of the pool to read the *International Herald Tribune*. Soon-Yi raised an eyebrow.

"Just one more time," he told her uncertainly.

"A few more times," she coaxed. Sometimes she spoke to him as if he were a recalcitrant patient who refused to take his medicine.

Throughout the entire three weeks of the tour, Woody remained hooked up to a wireless mike sixteen hours a day. Often he did not know when the camera was rolling, so he stayed in character. Incredibly, not once did Kopple manage to catch him with his guard down, which made the documentary sound scripted and led a film critic at *Newsweek* to later call it "the only Woody Allen film not directed by Allen." Soon-Yi, in what amounted to her screen debut, was obviously struggling to overcome her self-consciousness and sounded a bit tense. She did, however, firmly dispel her aunt's insinuation that she was stupid. Rounding out the supporting cast was Letty, taking a dizzy Diane Keaton role ("He's a rock star!") and doing her best to hog every frame.

Although tickets for the concerts sold out in three or four hours, critics were not always kind. His playing provoked malice and mirth from the British press, with one paper writing that "while he is a better clarinetist than Naomi Campbell is a novelist, he would be well advised not to give up his day job." It did not take long for Woody to feel claustrophobic, and he soon tired of slogging through the dirty ice and slush of a European winter, hopping from airports to marble-lobbied hotels to theaters where heavy-jowled men made speeches and rich dowagers offered autograph books. As the air began leaking out of the touring balloon, he fretted constantly. Would the hotel laundry send back his underwear with holes? Would he fall prey to a crazed gondolier and get his throat cut? Could he rent the hotel room next door in order to have a bathroom separate from Soon-Yi?

With little to do all day but shop, get massages, and eat at three-star Michelin restaurants, Soon-Yi busied herself with improving Woody's manners. She was concerned about the way he treated his musicians, who, except for Eddy Davis, one of New York's leading jazz banjo players, were not the Michael's Pub regulars. For the tour, he invited a select group of six competent professionals from his 1993 recording, "The Bunk Project," all of whom eclipsed Woody in their musical skills but also made his playing sound better. In Europe Woody ignored the band. He never went out of his way to speak with them, had difficulty recalling all their names, and only communicated through Davis. Unlike Woody and his entourage, who toured by private jet and limousine, the band traveled on commercial airlines and by vans, and stayed at separate but ordinary hotels. Soon-Yi felt sorry for them.

"You should let them all know they're very good," she told Woody.

Why? he said perversely. He had never been chummy with his sidemen at Michael's Pub.

Soon-Yi didn't mince words. "Because it's nice to hear," she retorted, reminding him that he looked like "a crazy" when he was in a room with the entire group and spoke only to Davis. He ignored her suggestion. While the pickup band wore professional black outfits, he and Eddy Davis emerged in rumpled, grungy clothing. Personal contact with audiences discomfited him, although eventually he took to throwing them air kisses from a safe distance. More often, standing at hotel windows, he hid behind curtains and peeked out at the crowds, as if he were a Russian czar. Cut off not only from fans but also from talking to the local artists, he was surrounded by his protective coterie of women—Kopple, Soon-Yi, Letty, and Jean, all of whom continually gave him advice. At times, he seemed to be thoroughly manipulated by his handlers, who played on his need to be coddled and adored. "He needs people to help him make decisions," Kopple decided.

Dissatisfied with the eleven hours of film she had shot, Kopple later staged a Konigsberg family get-together at Marty and Nettie's East Side high-rise. Mentally alert at the age of ninety-seven, Marty was deaf but still had a full head of snow-white hair and ninety-one-year-old Nettie looked like an older, more animated version of Woody. Both of them seemed to be decidedly indifferent to their son and treated him as if he were a nonentity. As he was seated at the dining table, which was next to the china cabinet containing his Academy Award statuettes, Woody turned to his father and showed him his latest medals and awards. Marty picked up one of the plaques. "Look at this engraving," he remarked expertly. Jewelry engraving had been one of his various professions before retirement. From behind the camera Kopple's breathy voice could be heard faintly prodding Nettie. Had she ever imagined her son's fame? With no further prompting, Nettie confided in a raspy voice that she had always known "the kid" had "a terrific brain" as well as a flair for tap dancing, sports, and music, "but never pursued them." She would have preferred him to be a pharmacist. Woody knew this harangue by heart, and cut her off with the reminder that she used to beat him every day with her hand or a strap. It was a miracle he never grew up to be a drug addict, he told her. Or a criminal.

"I'm sorry," she interrupted, "but you were brought up in a household that knew right from wrong. Don't think for a minute that you are what you are all by yourself."

"You think you're a big shot," Marty piped in.

Woody rolled his eyes and changed the subject to "Asian girls." Evidently Letty's son Christopher was also seeing "an Asian girl." Nettie frowned. "Personally I don't think it's right," she croaked. Taking a politically incorrect stance, she warned "that's why the Jews someday will be extinct and that's very bad." Soon-Yi, looking unperturbed, began to laugh. Intent on having the last word, Nettie turned to Kopple and said she always hoped he would "fall in love with a nice Jewish girl," obviously forgetting about his two former wives, both of whom are Jewish.

As Woody stood up to leave, he smiled weakly. "Truly the lunch from hell," he murmured.

In the spring of 1998, Barbara Kopple's road movie was released by Fine Line Films as a 104-minute feature, *Wild Man Blues,* the title of a famous Jelly Roll Morton–Louis Armstrong collaboration. As usual, Woody was pessimistic about the film's reception. Documentary audiences tended to be limited, especially audiences for pictures about New Orleans jazz. "No one," he predicted, "will be interested in this film." He was not taking into account Kopple, who was regarded in the industry as a famous documentarian, as well as a woman who relentlessly sought attention.

When Kopple had edited the film to three and a half hours, she invited Woody and Soon-Yi to her East Village film studio to view it. According to Kopple, they huddled silent and bemused, occasionally giggling or breaking into shrieks of laughter. At the end, Woody stood up and said politely, "Very entertaining."

"Thank you, but that's you," Kopple replied.

"No, no, no," he said, "that's *you.*"

Although he brought up several technical questions involving the editing, Kopple later gave the impression that she resisted his professional advice and told him, "Well, the burden is on me."

"Yes, it is," agreed Woody as he headed for the elevator. Considering everything that he had riding on the film, including Sweetland's half-million-dollar investment, this response sounds suspicious. From the beginning, the premise of the documentary was to restore his image. Despite the sticky question of final cut, the balance of power between Allen and Kopple was never in doubt. On the other hand, Woody wanted everyone to believe he had cut Kopple loose to make her own film, once again demonstrating his extraordinary ability to manipulate the public.

When Stanley Kauffmann saw *Wild Man Blues,* he was amazed because it was "the best performance Woody's ever done on film. You see him involved in something he cares about and doing it well. The last scene ridiculing both his parents and himself—the son who never made good with the father—is an Arthur Miller situation. Even if its purpose was to get sympathy it shows him as a human being, not as a star." Most reviewers, however, panned Woody's vanity feature. Going straight to the heart of the matter, the *Village Voice* reviewed the press kit, and other publications followed suit by calling Woody's advertisement for himself "a blatant attempt to clean up his scandal-tainted image," a slick corporate film "inseparable from p.r. spin." Since it was obviously not a concert film—Kopple repeatedly truncated the musical interludes—critics instead reported on Woody's offstage life with Soon-Yi, who, wrote Roger Ebert, "seems more like the adult in the partnership," a combination of wife, mother, and manager.

For all its billing as a music documentary, *Wild Man Blues* was not about jazz but personal relationships, an *Annie Hall* for the nineties. It was about Alvy Singer in middle age, no longer worrying about why Annie left him because now he has a twenty-eight- (or twenty-five- or twenty-six-) year-old Asian woman, who has turned out to be the woman of his dreams. Soon-Yi impressed Kopple as a strong, mature woman, highly opinionated, who was also living a fairy-tale romance. "She's able to be her own person, she's able to have anything she wants!" Kopple said, adding that "to find someone you can have fun with, who's a soul mate, who speaks truthfully to you, not just telling you the things you want to hear, that's rare and wonderful." Ironically, Woody succeeded in mesmerizing Kopple, who chose to ignore the fact that Soon-Yi was the daughter of the mother of Woody's three children and the sister of these children. Aside from one remark of Woody's about "the notorious Soon-Yi Previn," the film contained no allusions to the scandal or his children. Most strikingly, there was no mention of Mia, which film writer Bill Luhr likened to "telling the story of O.J. without mentioning Nicole." Not only did Kopple accept the relationship with Soon-Yi as normal, she lost her critical perspective and became a part of her subject's insulated world. In Kopple's eyes, Woody and Soon-Yi were living a Cinderella love story. Another filmmaker might have regarded them differently.

■ ■ ■ ■ ■ ■ ■

In His Own Words:
ERICA JONG: Does Soon-Yi miss her mother?
WOODY: Not at all.

—*Marie Claire,* 1998

■ ■ ■ ■ ■ ■ ■

Several years before meeting Mia, Woody imagined the character of an estranged wife who takes revenge on her husband with a memoir that graphically exposes why their marriage went haywire. In *Manhattan,* consoling himself with seventeen-year-old Tracy, Isaac Davis muses about how Jill is going to ridicule his "disgusting little moments" and how her book will surely become a best-seller. Naturally, Jill hates him but she's also a bisexual feminist who left him for a woman, which explains everything. An older and wiser Woody might have guessed that Mia, if she ever got her hands on a ghostwriter, would tear his heart out in print.

In the fall of 1992, barely three months after Woody sued for custody, Mia announced she was going to write her autobiography. Unlike many celebrities who use professional writers as collaborators, Mia promised that she would write the book herself. For all of her hysteria about the custody action and the bombardments of the media, she managed to pull herself together and write a book proposal, consisting of a dozen or so pages about her childhood in Hollywood, which her literary agent submitted to editors at Putnam, Warner Books, and Simon & Schuster. It was eventually sold to Doubleday for an advance reported to be $3 million. The acquiring editor was Nan Talese, a sympathetic partisan of Mia's during the custody hearing. (Another Doubleday editor who had deluged Mia with phone calls and letters urging her to write a memoir was Jacqueline Onassis.) In terms of celebrity advances, Mia's was respectable but not extraordinary, especially when it was compared to the spectacular sums commanded by Whoopi Goldberg ($6 million), Paul Reiser ($5.6 million), and Marlon Brando ($5 million). Mia's high-powered literary agent was Lynn Nesbit, with whom Mia had a close, personal relationship. Lynn happened to be the mother of Matthew Previn's girlfriend, Priscilla Gilman, whom he had met as an undergraduate at Yale and whom Mia regarded as one of her own daughters. In her literary endeavors, Mia was fortunate to enjoy both the emotional support and literary guidance of two powerhouses in publishing.

At the time of the book deal in 1992, Mia promised that her memoirs would cover her entire life: her movie-star family, her childhood ambition to be a pediatrician in Africa, the marriages to Sinatra and Previn, her acquaintance with such icons as Salvador Dalí and the Beatles. Three years later, however, she was declaring that a portion of the book, perhaps no more than a single chapter, would speak about her dispute with Woody. Instead, she said during an interview, she would focus her thoughts on religion and philosophy: "What is the meaning of things? And who are people anyway? And what to make of what you're given." The idea that she planned to hold forth in her book on weighty philosophical issues sounded unrealistic when the obvious reason for the book—and its large advance—was to dot the *i*'s and cross the *t*'s on her broken relationship with Woody. Did readers really want to hear about the existential Mia, even if she was married to Frank Sinatra? Their main interest was the Woody Wars. As it transpired, once she had obtained a book contract, Mia found little time for writing. After the custody trial, she needed to earn money as an actress. Following *Widow's Peak,* she did *Miami Rhapsody,* in which she played a middle-aged wife whose secret liaisons shocked her children when they discovered them. Her next picture, *Reckless,* was about a happily married housewife who, discovering her husband has hired a hit man to murder her, escapes a violent death by crawling out a window clad in a flannel nightgown. It was a story that no doubt appealed to Mia because of its parallels with her own life. Then, to her dismay, Mia, like most middle-aged screen actresses, found that scripts were scarce.

The vast amount of her time was spent in raising her children. By now, she had adopted three more children, who were physically disabled in one way or another and demanding far greater amounts of attention than other children. As a companion for Isaiah, she took in another African-American baby, whose mother was addicted to crack, and named her Kaeli-Shea, and a few months later she adopted a six-year-old paraplegic from India, who had been abandoned in a Calcutta train station. She gave him the name Thaddeus and bought him a small red wheelchair. Finally, in 1995, she adopted another blind Vietnamese orphan, a three-year-old whom she named Frankie-Minh for Frank Sinatra. Frankie-Minh, Mia decided, would be her last child. She was fifty, the mother of fourteen children, and soon to become a grand-mother.

Her older children no longer lived at home. Although Mia always wore a smiling, serene Hallmark face for the media, the truth was different, and the emotional bloodbath of the custody hearing, along with her two-year depression, had scarred the family. For some of her kids, survival meant flight. The first to leave home was Fletcher, who spent two years at a prep school in Hamburg, Germany. Returning to the United States at the age of twenty-two, he enrolled as a freshmen at Connecticut College, where roommates in his triple dormitory room remembered him as a friendly young man who dreamed of becoming a film director and one summer wangled an internship with Tom Hanks. After graduating from Yale University, Matthew Previn obtained his law degree at Georgetown University in Washington, D.C., graduated cum laude, and began working as a law clerk for a federal court judge. His twin brother, Sascha, graduated from Fordham University, then left for Colorado with his girlfriend, Carrie Englander, shortly after the custody hearing. Returning to New York in 1995, Sascha married Carrie and worked as an accountant with a media buying company.

In the case of Mia's girls, Soon-Yi was the only one to complete college.

After Drew, she enrolled in graduate school at Columbia University's Teachers College, studying for a degree in childhood education. Lark, after two years at New York University, abandoned her plans to become a pediatric nurse and married Christopher McKinzie, a Brooklyn construction worker and furniture mover. Her sister Daisy spent one semester at Wheaton College in Massachusetts before dropping out of school and then she moved to Brooklyn and married the brother of Lark's husband. Both girls soon became pregnant. In contrast to their ambitious sister Soon-Yi, who was reportedly well maintained with a million-dollar trust fund from Woody, Lark and Daisy had obviously taken altogether different directions. In 1997, after giving birth to a second daughter, Lark developed serious medical problems.

In the years following the acrimonious end of her relationship with Woody, Mia insisted she had no plans to remarry, but soon she was seen with a number of well-known actors, writers, and directors. Aware that her judgment about men had been "very limited, very flawed indeed," she admitted that it was a fault that "has had catastrophic consequences. I think I'm much shrewder now. I hope I am."

In 1995 she began dating Philip Roth, one of America's premier novelists whose prolific output—some twenty works of fiction and nonfiction— rivaled Woody's output in film. Roth was Mia's neighbor in Connecticut and had recently gone through a divorce. His wife of eighteen years was the celebrated English actress Claire Bloom. In his 1990 novel, *Deception,* one of the characters was a whining, middle-aged English actress named Claire, until the real Claire Bloom insisted he create another name for the character, but it was hardly the first instance of his cannibalizing the lives of people he knew for his fiction. In 1987, after a painful knee operation, Roth had encountered problems with the hypnotic drugs Halcion and Xanax and had experienced severe depression. Six years later, he suffered a complete breakdown and entered Silver Hill, a psychiatric hospital in New Canaan, Connecticut. When he was released from the hospital, Roth served his wife with divorce papers in which he accused her of inhumane treatment. What Claire Bloom shared in common with Mia Farrow, besides a talent for acting, was a maddening passivity in her relationships with men.

Philip Roth was exactly the type of man whom Mia usually found appealing: Like Andre Previn, he was a cerebral Jew, a man some years her senior who exuded superior intelligence, charm, and wit. Like Woody, Roth's life centered around his work. Both Woody and Previn were small men, physically the opposite of Roth, who was six feet one with piercing black eyes and sultry dark looks. But Mia Farrow and Philip Roth had something in common: They both despised Woody Allen.

*   *   *

Born within two years of each other, Woody Allen and Philip Roth came from the same postwar generation of middle-class Jewish males with high IQs and perpetually tormented libidos, who were eager to escape their parents' orbits and revel in the new sexual revolution that was taking place in the 1960s. As it happened, their writing embraced some of the same subject material. One of Roth's targets in his novel *Portnoy's Complaint* was the leading character's overpossessive mother, Sophie. Like Roth's uninhibited heroes, Woody's Alvy Singer and his other fictional characters doted on blond gentiles—his Harold Cohen in "Retribution" achieving an ultimate fantasy by indulging his sexual appetites with a mother and daughter. Apart from their creative similarities, neither Roth nor Woody were personally able to sustain mature relationships with women. Finally, their names would become synonymous with the term "self-hating Jew," not only because they are uncomfortable with their Jewishness but also because they find humor in Jewish paranoia and neuroses.

For all these ironic parallels, however, there was no professional or personal sympathy between them. In the seventies, Woody said, deadpan, that he couldn't relate to Roth's characters because "I have never had that obsession with Gentile women." Roth "always detested Woody," reported a friend of Claire Bloom's, "because of the sentimentality and the vulgarity. The thing about Philip is that he has exquisite taste because he knows when he is being vulgar." Over the years, the novelist's increasing animosity toward Woody was further fueled by his suspicion that the filmmaker had pickpocketed some of his ideas. In 1972, for instance, the year Roth published his novel *The Breast,* Woody made *Everything You Always Wanted to Know About Sex,* which contained a memorable scene showing a giant breast that escapes from a sex researcher's laboratory and terrorizes the countryside until it is lured into an X-cup bra. When Woody's affair with Soon-Yi became public, Roth was said to be disgusted by the revelation. His scorn amused friends of Claire Bloom's because evidently Roth, like Woody, had also developed a taste for teenage girls. Although Bloom had no idea that he behaved as he had at the time, she later discovered that Roth had propositioned her daughter's best friend, a girl who had been practically a daughter to her.

When Woody learned about Mia and Roth's relationship, he must have seen it as an opportunity to exact a double revenge. In 1988 he chose to cast Claire Bloom as the deceived wife in *Crimes and Misdemeanors,* and then, aware that she was separated from Roth and in need of money, he hired her for a second time as the hero's mother-in-law in *Mighty Aphrodite.* Then he wrote a screenplay about a renowned novelist and academic who freely plunders for his fiction the lives of people close to him, before suffering writer's block and teetering on the edge of a crack-up. "A nasty, shallow, superficial, sexually obsessed" man was how Woody happily described his protagonist, Harry Block. Undoubtedly, he must have hoped that moviegoers would never think to connect Harry Block with Philip Roth. Everyone would assume that in the film Woody was slyly mocking himself, donning a reverse hair shirt and justifying his mistreatment of Mia. In a final embellishment to his private joke, he cast Richard Benjamin as one of the performers playing Harry Block. The hero in the film versions of both *Portnoy's Complaint* and *Goodbye, Columbus,* Benjamin had seldom worked in recent years.

On a muggy summer night in 1996, Woody brought his touring band to the 92nd Street Y in New York. The concert was sold out and for the first time in memory the Y attracted scalpers. The crowds streaming into the hall that July evening were predominantly middle-aged suburbanites, the hard-core fans who had not missed one of his movies since *What's New, Pussycat?* and had even liked *Stardust Memories.* Nostalgic, they were hungry for the old Woody magic. They were disappointed, however, by the sight of the real man who had brought them so many funny, unforgettable moments. Collapsed on a chair with his pale white arms dangling from the short sleeves of a blue shirt, his eyes staring limply into his lap, he ignored the audience, who enthusiastically applauded him. As they filed out of the auditorium, some of them expressed concern about his health.

"Doesn't he look like a cadaver?" a fiftyish man said to his wife.

"No, he doesn't look like a cadaver," she replied. "He looks like he ought to be on life support."

At sixty, Woody's skin had the waxy, white pallor of a solitary-confinement inmate. Although he would not admit it to anyone, his daily strolls on the treadmill hardly counted as exercise, since he seldom got beyond 2.6 miles per hour, which was barely enough to work up a sweat.

Always worried about his health, Woody had a separate doctor for practically every part of his anatomy. Arriving for a consultation with a new specialist that year, he looked fearful and morose, so uncomfortable among the other patients in the reception area that the nurse quickly ushered him into an examining room. In an attempt to cheer him, she chuckled, "We even use clean needles here," a joke that he failed to appreciate. His movie character's reputation as an intractable hypochondriac was based on reality. For many years, he had kept a thermometer at Mia's apartment and also carried with him, in his pants pocket, a silver pillbox that contained Compazine, Librium, Excedrin, Zantac, and a couple of Donnazyme tablets. Not that he had often needed to use the pills—he disliked even taking an aspirin—but knowing he was prepared for any mental or physical emergency made him feel safer.

∎∎∎∎∎∎

Caught on Tape:
"I don't spend two seconds thinking about him if I can help it, and most of the time I can."
—MIA FARROW, *20/20*, 1997

∎∎∎∎∎∎

"Very quickly I learned that this man had no respect for everything I hold sacred—not for my family, not for my soul, not for my God or my goals."

In June of 1996, Mia was a featured speaker at the annual American Book-sellers Association convention in Chicago, along with John Grisham and other blockbuster authors. Her speech was a message to booksellers that Doubleday intended to hustle the title with a major promotional campaign. In spite of her schoolgirl uniform that consisted of a flouncy skirt, Peter Pan blouse, and black tights—the same kind of costume she had worn during the court hearing—there was no doubt that Mia was going straight for the jugular. She told the booksellers that she had been forced to write about herself after suffering "shouting distortions and loud lies and real-life pain, terrible pain."

Despite the hyperbole, it is doubtful she was the sole author of her memoir; in fact, it most likely benefited from the extensive editorial assistance of several people, including writer and family friend Rock Brynner, the son of Yul Brynner; Nan Talese, known to be an exceptionally hands-on editor; and Philip Roth, whose brilliant literary talent had no doubt helped to shape the final product.

∎∎∎∎∎∎

Moving Pictures:
SANDY BATES: You can't control life. It doesn't wind up perfectly. Only—only art you can control. Art and masturbation. Two areas in which I am an absolute expert.
—*Stardust Memories*, 1980

∎∎∎∎∎∎

Ordinarily, Woody's publicity machine treated the media as an interference with the filmmaker's artistic schedule. As a result, some journalists referred to the imperious Leslee Dart as "that woman" if they were feeling kind and other unprintable names if they weren't so inclined. Once a photographer for a major newspaper called Dart with a request to take Woody's picture to accompany an interview scheduled to appear in the publication. He could have five minutes, Dart told the photographer, adding that someone would tell him where to set up his equipment. When he suggested a more creative camera angle, she became peevish. "We don't care about creative," she said.

In recent years, PMK had rewritten the rules of celebrity journalism to the dismay of magazine and newspaper editors, who were being forced to bow to public relations firms' demands or do without the star profiles that sold their publications. More and more, it was common practice for publicists to make their clients available for interviews in exchange for control over the finished profile. Not only did they expect to select the writer and photographer, they also dictated what questions could be asked or what sources could be interviewed, and in addition insisted on quotation and layout approval and the right to read the story in advance of publication. By negotiating the terms of an interview, a celebrity could completely control his public image. As Mia's book was expected to stir up the dust, PMK began a vigorous campaign to trivialize her revelations.

Damage control got under way in the fall of 1996 when Woody and PMK negotiated a profile by *The New Yorker* that was to be written by John Lahr, the magazine's senior drama critic. During a weeklong series of interviews, he trailed after the director from his "book-lined and flower-filled Fifth Avenue penthouse" to his handsome Park Avenue screening room "wall-papered in olive-green brushed velvet" to "the high-ceilinged elegance" of Michael's Pub, which was now relocated in the Parker Meridien hotel.

Woody speaking of himself, however, sounded like a homespun journey into the land of "let's pretend." Seizing the opportunity to reinvent himself once again, he even tried to do the impossible and remake his physical appearance. All his adult life he had stood five feet five and a half, five feet six if he stood up very straight, but in his new incarnation, as other men his age were losing height, he had gained inches and now claimed to be five feet seven. Working hard to present himself as white-bread, coupled with eagerness to spin an *It's a Wonderful Life* tale, he sounded as if he were a happy-go-lucky New York George Bailey, who was fortunate to be surrounded by a circle of loyal employees, business colleagues, and ex-mistresses. Woody's preapproved sources—his agent Sam Cohn, Diane Keaton, and Dianne Wiest—delivered testimonials to his talent and generous friendship. Evidently Lahr was not permitted to ask Woody embarrassing questions, because his stormy relationship with Mia and his children were glossed over. Displaying no emotional attachment to her children, he discounted any parental role in Mia's household, even dismissing their own twelve-year relationship as one of no particular importance. "It was comfortable and very distant, I mean, very distant, uh, you know, in every way." Talking about his romance with Soon-Yi, a union that was repugnant to many people, he described it as "genuine." The profile was titled

"The Imperfectionist," even though John Lahr, as had Eric Lax, described few imperfections in his subject.

Besides John Lahr, Woody granted interviews to other journalists during those months. For *Newsday*, he made an effort to debunk some of the so-called myths about himself. It was not true that he hated Hollywood, he declared. His twenty-year absence from the Oscars was no more than a coincidence because the Academy insisted on holding its awards on Mondays, when he had a prior commitment to Michael's Pub. On the subject of his discarded women, he claimed to be "close friends with Louise Lasser, my second wife, and even friends with my first wife who doesn't live anywhere near me." This was undoubtedly news to Harlene, who had had no contact of any kind with Woody after taking him to court in 1967.

Not only *The New Yorker* and *Newsday* but a number of other publications refrained from asking Woody embarrassing questions and promoted his Capraesque fantasies. This was not always the case. Throughout the eighties, he had been regularly interviewed—at least once a year—by Roger Ebert. While there was no bigger fan of Woody's, Ebert possessed the courage to contradict him. "Many times," Woody once told him, as a prelude to a morose harangue on the futility of life, "I've gone to sleep at night, and thought it wouldn't bother me for a second if I didn't wake up in the morning."

"This is all so depressing," Ebert interrupted.

With calculated timing, Doubleday slipped Mia Farrow's memoir, *What Falls Away*, into the bookstores on February 5, 1997, despite the fact that Barnes & Noble had told customers inquiring about the book that it was not due to be published for months. To avoid news leaks and any possibility of legal action, there were none of the usual advance reading copies. At the Doubleday warehouse, shipping cartons bore no author identification, only an 800 number to report cases of tampering. On the eve of publication, Nan Talese and her husband, Gay, hosted a gala book party for Mia at their East Side town house. Among the 140 A-list celebrities in attendance were Margaret Atwood, Lauren Bacall, Walter Cronkite, Kurt Vonnegut, and Dominick Dunne. Mia, arriving on the arm of Stephen Sondheim, was also accompanied by five of her children—Sascha, Fletcher, Daisy, Lark, and Moses. Posing months earlier for the jacket photo, she had twisted her long blond hair into a braid and looped it over one shoulder. Now evidently hoping to be taken seriously as a member of the literary community, she replaced her Shirley Temple ringlets with a short nineties bob. Her youthful bloom—she looked in her thirties—raised suspicions among some of her female contemporaries, who were in their fifties. "There was so much collagen in her face that she had a beatific look," said one skeptical observer.

What Falls Away, which borrowed its title from a verse in Theodore Roethke's poem "The Waking," was dedicated to "my mother and my children who have stood by me, and to those grandchildren and great-grandchildren whom I may never meet." The book's central metaphor, on which Mia strung all the sorrows of a lifetime, was that as a child stricken with polio, she had become an unwitting carrier of a contagious disease. Infantile paralysis had made her fear that she had endangered those she loved most. Years later, her liaison with Woody had exposed her family to another deadly infection. Roughly half of the narrative concerned her years with the film director, who was depicted as both a killer disease and a tyrant, only a little to the left of Stalin. The rest of the narrative concerned her Hollywood childhood, her father, and her early career as a film and television star. Despite her efforts to sanitize her marriage to Frank Sinatra, it was clear that Mia's men had much in common. Like Woody, Sinatra had been unable to break up with her directly, and had dispatched his lawyer to do his dirty work. For Mia, however, the passage of time had blurred his betrayal. (Upon hearing of Sinatra's death the following year, Mia would tell the press that he was "the first love of my life.") Barely mentioned in passing was the publicity-hating Andre Previn, who presumably instructed her not to write about their marriage or his personal life. In an appendix, Mia reprinted in its entirety Justice Elliott Wilk's excoriating decision in the child-custody hearing.

What Falls Away earned respectable sales and mixed reviews. The *New York Times Book Review*, for instance, assigned it to Kathryn Harrison, a novelist who could be expected to sympathize with Mia's problems. Harrison's controversial new book, *The Kiss*, about her consensual four-year affair with her father, had made her the new incest expert on the literary scene, but she lacked any pity for Mia, a martyr whom she characterized as a compulsive adopter of children, who was waging a holy war to "solicit sympathy in the court of public opinion." In Britain, reviewers unanimously rejected "a pathologically indiscreet book" from a celebrity "most famous for her impressive collection of men and children." The London *Sunday Times* ran Mia's jacket photo with a snide caption: "Should a 50-year-old really have a pigtail?" Nevertheless her book succeeded in further damaging Woody's reputation because it provided considerable ammunition to his enemies. Once again it became open season on Woody Allen. On his late-night show, Jay Leno never seemed to tire of Woody jokes, including the one about a new cocktail called The Woody Allen: "Mix Old Grandad with a Shirley Temple your wife ordered." But not everyone was laughing. Bill Maher, the prosecutorial host of *Politically Incorrect*, devoted an entire show to *What Falls Away*, in which he pilloried Woody as a "white O. J. Simpson."

A fixture on the talk-show circuit that spring, Mia rambled endlessly about herself and Soon-Yi, whose face, in photos and video clips, flashed on the television screen as Mia reiterated the details of her betrayal. Not surprisingly, whenever she talked about her daughter she omitted details that did not fit her script. Repeatedly describing the incriminating Polaroids, she failed to mention that the same young woman was now an industrious graduate student at Columbia University. In those months, Soon-Yi was doing her student-teaching semester at Spence, an elite private school for girls, where she taught reading to third-graders. Her students did not realize her fame until one of them happened to spot her on television.

"Ms. Previn," a girl teased, "do you have a boyfriend?"

"Yeah," Soon-Yi retorted. "Tom Cruise. Let's get back to reading." After class, the girls fluttered around her desk. Wasn't Tom Cruise married?

"Period's over," she scolded.

Soon-Yi was popular with both her students and the staff. "She's going to be a fine teacher," said a school official. Some parents and alumnae, however, thought that because of her notoriety she was a poor role model for young girls.

When she was interviewed by both Barbara Walters and Katie Couric, Mia made it clear that she was not extending any olive branches to Soon-Yi. She also told Oprah Winfrey that nobody in the family had heard from her in five years. There was no doubt in Mia's mind that Soon-Yi was a victim at the beginning but "now she's responsible for continuing the affair." She no longer had any desire to see Soon-Yi, she said.

As best he could, Woody tried to ignore *What Falls Away.* "Not interested in that whole thing," he insisted. "I know what happened, and I know what she thinks. It's history." His only sadness was that "I don't get to see my kids— whom I love." Dylan, whom he had not seen for five years, was a twelve-year-old, no longer the dimpled little girl who had so enchanted him. Mia was strict about sheltering her daughter from the public eye, and when camera crews from the Oprah Winfrey and Barbara Walters television shows descended on Frog Hollow for interviews, Eliza O'Sullivan Farrow, as she was now called, always was away visiting a friend. However, when Mia appeared on *The Tonight Show,* during a commercial break, Dylan was seen backstage in the green room munching potato chips with her mother and Satchel. This rare glimpse of Woody's kids revealed Dylan to be a gawky preadolescent girl, while Satch was still blond and adorable, a nine-year-old boy who resembled his mother. Then, Dylan smiled self-consciously and Satchel stared wearily as both children stopped eating their chips and reluctantly faced the camera. Being the children of Woody Allen would never be easy.

CHAPTER TWENTY-ONE

"Help"

On December 19, 1997, Seamus (aka Satchel) O'Sullivan Farrow turned ten years old. Even though Woody continued to have visitation rights, he had not seen him in two years. The meetings were suspended by mutual agreement, he said. Sometimes he told people that he had stopped the visits for Satch's sake, or that Mia had so thoroughly poisoned the child's mind against him that he became anxious whenever he saw his father. Whatever the reason for the estrangement, there was no doubt that he had lost his son's love. For five years, his all-consuming obsession—to obtain parental visiting rights with Dylan and Satchel—had been stymied until it seemed he had journeyed far beyond the boundaries of common sense. Although he had successfully defended himself against the charges of child molestation, all the lawsuits and appeals and petitions to Elliott Wilk came to nothing. Gradually, as months passed without seeing Satch, he must have decided that his son was also a lost cause. Several days after Satch's birthday he took a step that effectively ensured he would be shut out of the boy's life, at least as long as Justice Wilk had anything to say about it.

Two days before Christmas, he married Soon-Yi.

◼◼◼◼◼◼◼

The March of Time:
"As far as I'm concerned, there is no age difference between Frank and me. There is nothing wrong with an older man marrying a younger woman if they are in love."
—MIA FARROW
(after marrying Frank Sinatra)

"Love is pretty strong. So you don't fight what feels good."
—MIA FARROW (after marrying her friend
Dory Previn's husband, Andre)

◼◼◼◼◼◼◼

Bride and groom left the Hotel Gritti Palace in their street clothes to avoid attracting the attention of passing Venetians. Woody, who was bundled in overcoat, tweed cap, and muffler, looked as casual as though he were cruising down Madison Avenue to his office, and Soon-Yi, under her long camel-colored coat, was wearing a sweater and skirt. Had she desired to wear a bridal gown to her wedding, she would have been overruled by her husband, and if she wanted an elegant occasion, he would not wish that, either. Offici-ating at the twilight ceremony at the Palazzo Cavalli, near the Rialto Bridge, was the city's mayor, who helped to orchestrate a secret wedding that required careful planning and a certain amount of subterfuge. The short, businesslike ceremony was witnessed by only three invited guests, Woody's sister, Letty, her husband, Sidney, and one of their children. Afterward, a blustery wind was blowing off the Grand Canal as the wedding party cele-brated the occasion at Harry's Bar, famous since Ernest Hemingway and the twenties and by far the city's grandest restaurant, where they dined on pasta with truffles, scampi, and *crêpes á la crème.*

On Christmas Day, the couple flew by private jet to Paris. An icy drizzle was falling as they checked into the Ritz for a combination honeymoon and publicity junket for the French release of *Deconstructing Harry.* In his favorite city, Woody's mood brightened and he appeared relaxed. Ambushed by a mob of photographers outside the hotel, he donned a cheerful smile and obligingly planted affectionate kisses on his new wife's cheek. In his atro-ciously accented French, he said that he was "very, very happy to be in Paris," and other platitudes parroting the script of a television commercial *("J'aime la France")* he made recently to promote French tourism. After praising the city, he impatiently mumbled to Soon-Yi, "Can we go to lunch now?" and ducked into a waiting limousine.

Five days later, he and Soon-Yi returned to New York. Their first public appearance took place at the Café Carlyle on Madison Avenue a few blocks from his apartment and the supper club where his band now played. In the past, Soon-Yi had absented herself from the weekly Monday shows, but that evening she was obviously eager to take her place in the celebrity spotlight as Mrs. Woody Allen. In a pink cashmere sweater, she conspicuously held court at one of the tiny ringside tables as she sipped Evian water and showed off her wedding ring. Her husband's solo of "Sweet Georgia Brown" stirred her to vigorous applause, but it was another number, Frank Sinatra's sentimental ballad "September," about age and youth, that made her misty-eyed. "This really is quite lovely," she said.

Earlier that day, Soon-Yi's mother, who had been Sinatra's third wife, had attended the introduction on Ellis Island of a commemorative postage stamp on immigration. Seated with their mother and holding American flags were Seamus and Eliza, Isaiah, Kaeli-Shea, and Mia's three foreign-born children—Tam, Thaddeus, and Frankie-Minh, the five-year-old blind Vietnamese orphan whom Mia had named after Sinatra. Following the ceremony, a television reporter buttonholing Mia for a reaction to the marriage received a frosty look. Then she looked away without a reply. But in London, the news had prompted an angry response from Soon-Yi's father. As angry as he could possibly be, Andre Previn (who received an honorary knighthood in 1996) told the *Daily Telegraph*: "I'll tell you what I think of Woody Allen. I think he is the worst human being on the planet. I think he is the worst human being I have ever heard of, read of, or been able to imagine."

In the weeks that followed, Woody and Soon-Yi continued to celebrate their marriage. After a Knicks game they joined Jean Doumanian and her ex-husband, John, at Elaine's. Elaine Kaufman plunked herself down at their table and then organized impromptu toasts by George Plimpton, Michelle Phillips, and other celebrities who happened to be dining at the restaurant. The porcine restaurateur said that she had known all along that the couple would marry because "happiness is just a girl called Soon-Yi."

Beyond Elaine's, the marriage failed to fly with the public. On the contrary, it stimulated fifty-seven varieties of incest and pedophilia jokes. In comparison to the sick, racist jokes that were posted on the Internet ("What do Woody Allen and Kodak Film have in common?"), the gags of late-night television monologists sounded tame. Jay Leno cracked that Soon-Yi married her father, which made Woody his own son-in-law: "He's 62 and she's 27—sounds like halftime at a Clippers game," he joked. David Letterman kidded that he knew of "few pleasures in life greater than having your ex-girlfriend as your mother-in-law."

With a straight face, Leslee Dart swore to the press that Woody did not ask Soon-Yi to sign a prenuptial agreement, which elicited shrieks of laughter in some quarters and a professional snicker from lawyer Raoul Felder. If that was truly the case, he smiled, "he needs a psychiatrist more than an attorney." Those persons least surprised by the nuptials were Mia's friends, some of whom had been expecting the couple to wed. "She's his ball and chain. If he betrays her—or if she leaves him, which is unlikely because she has no family—she has a good three- or four-million-dollar book in her. He can't cut her loose," said one of Mia's confidants. That viewpoint pretty much echoed Felder's prediction of their future life together. He compared them to "the Duke and Duchess of Windsor. They're basically trapped with each other, and they'll forever be drifting through time."

■ ■ ■ ■ ■ ■

Voice of America:
Q: What did Michael Jackson say to Woody Allen?
A: Swap you a ten for two fives.
—Internet One-Liners, January 23, 1998

■ ■ ■ ■ ■ ■

In his sixties, Woody seemed determined to overhaul his life. Apart from a third marriage, he took other surprising measures. After thirty-six years in psychotherapy, the world's oldest living analysand kicked the habit of a lifetime and terminated treatment. Like brushing his teeth twice a day, analysis was part of his personal regimen and had helped an unfocused, floundering twenty-four-year-old to thrive and exploit his extraordinary gifts to their fullest. The habit of withholding praise remained strong, however, because he seemed reluctant to offer any endorsements of the analytic profession. To be sure, psychotherapy could be helpful "to get past a little crisis" but long-term treatment was not "user-friendly," he said. "People expect a really dramatic result, but legitimate growth is not that dramatic." In an interview in London with *Radio Times,* he confided to Andrew Duncan that his marriage to Soon-Yi had made therapy unnecessary. "Did you need it in the first place?" Duncan asked. "Probably not," Woody replied. Friends heard a different story, however. In a burst of candor, he admitted quitting analysis after his most recent therapist complained about his tendency to hold back feelings.

Still, nobody in America had done more to popularize psychotherapy than Woody Allen. He cheerfully had spent a fortune on analysts, even though he loved to complain about their exorbitant fees—unlike the old days of therapy, when, he once wrote, you could be treated by Freud himself and he would also press your pants. In *Annie Hall,* Alvy Singer swore that after fifteen years he was giving his doctor "one more year and then I'm goin' to Lourdes." And in *Hannah and Her Sisters,* Mickey Sachs's analyst supposedly became frustrated over his patient's lack of progress. "The guy finally put in a salad bar," said Mickey. In reality, Woody's shrinks earned so much from him they had no need of salad bars; most likely they were able to take early retirement.

Meanwhile, perhaps the most dramatic changes were taking place in his career. In 1992, when the sex scandal and custody battle had adversely affected his box office, falling profits seemed a temporary response to a barrage of unusually negative publicity. According to Woody, the scandal was "a neutral factor," which sold newspapers but had nothing to do with him. "It's come and it's gone. It was nothing either way. It didn't help me. It didn't hurt me." The truth was the opposite. By the end of the nineties, the scandal continued to hurt him, and professionally he was basically treading water.

Desperate for a hit, he began to robotically recycle and cannibalize his old movies while competing in an increasingly sex-oriented film marketplace. Being regarded by a new generation of filmmakers as a dusty old museum piece petrified him. ("He didn't need a scandal to bring him down," believes Andrew Sarris. "Comedy is definitely a young man's racket, and when you get older, you lose the capacity to make people laugh. Some of his recent films have been unfunny.") Beginning with *Mighty Aphrodite* in 1995 and continuing through *Deconstructing Harry* and *Celebrity*, he made a series of films that are best described as his Hooker-Fellatio Trilogy. These three pictures present a parade of female characters who are whores (professional or amateur), nymphomaniacs, or psychotics. The roles (played by Mira Sorvino, Hazelle Goodman, Bebe Neuwirth, Judy Davis, Julia Louis-Dreyfus) appeared to have been the creation of an embittered, misogynistic writer consumed by primitive hatred of the female sex and fixated on the kind of passive sex that permits no conversation. As Harry Block remarks, hookers are wonderful because you needn't discuss Proust.

Deconstructing Harry turned out to be Woody's most controversial film since *Stardust Memories*, primarily owing to the number of film critics and moviegoers it managed to offend. The unpleasant Harry Block was an older version of Sandy Bates, on his hundredth god-awful relationship and his third shrink, a man who still expected the women he mistreated to love him because he was an artist. In the *New York Times*, Molly Haskell described the picture as "one long diatribe against women, wives, and Jews." Female audiences in particular tended to recoil from Woody's new screen persona, namely the horny senior citizen who becomes involved with pretty young women played by Elisabeth Shue and Julia Roberts. A disgusted *Los Angeles Times* columnist wondered how many people would want to see Joan Rivers write, direct, and star in movie after movie in which she indulged in sexual liaisons with sexy young men? "Joan in a heavy make-out session with Johnny Depp? Joan lounging in bed, basking in the afterglow with Leonardo DiCaprio?" the writer mused. But Woody, on screen and off, preferred his women very young.

Equally jolting to filmgoers was a new dirty-talking Woody, whose Harry Block declares: "Beth Kramer's an aggressive, tight-ass, busybody cunt, and it's none of her fucking business how I speak to my son." This extraordinary departure from his neurotic but engaging screen persona was calculated to draw a younger, hipper generation of moviegoers, who, in Jean Doumanian's words, finally "got a film out of Woody they can identify with." That remained to be seen, but some of the younger critics did praise Woody's nerve. "Here's a guy who had been blasted in the press for sexual deviancy," said Neil Rosen.

"Instead of defending himself, he said 'Look, I pay hookers, I'm everything they said I was.' He's not an idiot, he knew parallels would be drawn between Harry and himself. But he didn't back away. That was very courageous."

Woody's next picture, his twenty-eighth, was *Celebrity,* about the cult of celebrity and the public's obsession with famous people, a subject with which he could identify. Like his biggest moneymaker, *Manhattan,* it was filmed in black and white, this time by Sven Nykvist, who had last worked for Woody on *Crimes and Misdemeanors,* and featured an all-star cast with Leonardo DiCaprio, Judy Davis, Winona Ryder, and Melanie Griffith. Woody's anti-hero is Lee Simon, a lecherous freelance journalist who suffers a mid-thirties crisis, divorces his wife (Davis), and embarks on a quest for life's meaning and a book contract. This time Woody stayed behind the camera and assigned his character to young British actor-director Kenneth Branagh, who is best known for his stellar Shakespearean roles. Rather than creating a character, Branagh did a Woody Allen impersonation, nervous stutters and all, and the director seemed unable to stop him. He recalled taking Branagh aside. "You know," he said, "it seems to me you're doing me."

"Don't worry," Branagh replied.

Eventually, Woody recalled, "I just sort of threw in the towel." For some moviegoers, it seemed appropriate that *Celebrity* began and ended with a plane writing the single word *HELP* across the Manhattan skyline.

Miramax Films elected to market *Celebrity* as an all-star vehicle. In ads, Woody's name appeared in small type, as if the Weinsteins wanted the public not to be aware of his participation. Woody expressed wry amusement. "They're probably ashamed of me," he said. As with most of Woody's pictures, *Celebrity* had a few flashes of sublime hilarity, but was otherwise a clunky, painfully thin film, a twenty-minute screenplay strung out to two hours. Stanley Kauffmann imagined Woody switching on his word processor and pecking along "hoping that the tapping would lead somewhere. It didn't, but he discovered that he had enough pages for a film anyway." (In reality, Woody still writes on his antique Olympia typewriter.) Dismal reviews lamented *Celebrity*'s lack of wit and inspiration; despite a glittering cast, especially Leonardo DiCaprio, and aggressive marketing by Miramax, profits would be disappointing.

■ ■ ■ ■ ■ ■ ■

The March of Time:
"I grew up with Woody. I got old with Woody. He's getting on, not so much making films but simply being in the chase."
—ANDREW SARRIS, 1998

■ ■ ■ ■ ■ ■ ■

It had been five years since Sweetland Films took charge of Woody's business. To wring a profit from his movies, Jean Doumanian pledged to cut fat, not muscle, but the numbers did not move in the right direction, and finally there was nothing left but skin and bones. Despite the Los Alamos–type secrecy that surrounded his productions, news leaked out in the spring of 1998 that he had lost virtually every member of his remaining creative team. Those who decamped, presumably unwilling to accept substantial pay reductions, included Sandy Morse, Woody's film editor for twenty-two years; cinematographer Carlo Di Palma; and the set photographer, Brian Hamill. They were replaced by less-expensive personnel. Even the A-list stars who had once happily appeared in Woody's films for cut rates would in the future be working for half of their customary $10,000 a week fee. The only two of Woody's regulars exempt from the pay cuts were his casting director, Juliet Taylor, and Santo Loquasto, the production designer.

A *New York Times* article about Woody's financial predicament contained chilly quotes from some of his former associates, who privately blamed the troubles on his affair with Soon-Yi. After the scandal, one of them said off the record, his value was "diluted" and "people weren't knocking down the doors to do business with him." Woody ridiculed the article. "Completely irresponsible journalism," he fumed, adding that it was a hatchet job cooked up by a reporter with "an agenda" to give the impression he was using minor-league people. "But of course that's absurd. We're using top people."

Increasingly, he seemed insulated from reality, and when unpleasant events intruded, he fell back on denial. With costs averaging $18 to $20 million per feature (and profits in the neighborhood of $6 to $10 million), his pictures regularly lost money, but he pretended not to care. "In today's American film market," he declared stubbornly to *Newsweek*'s Jack Kroll, "if my films don't make a profit, I know I'm doing something right." Although the exact amount of his compensation was a secret, he continued to take home millions of dollars for each film. He was no spendthrift. "I don't have a boat," he told Kroll. "I don't have a country house. I don't go on elaborate vacations." He was "rich cumulatively because I've done so many films over the years."

The disintegration of his professional circle continued when he parted company with Sam Cohn, his agent for more than thirty years. In a business of quickie professional marriages, his defection seemed the worst sort of betrayal. "Working with Woody is like holding a puppy," remarked a disgusted film executive. "It's warm and nice, but you know if you hold on too long he's going to piss all over you." Encouraged by Jean, Letty, and Soon-Yi, his personal think tank, he transferred his representation to John Burnham, Diane Keaton's agent at the William Morris Agency in Los Angeles, whom he hoped would effectively rebuild his business image in Hollywood and find him more acting jobs in mainstream pictures.

In fact, Woody's recent successes have come from plying his trade as an actor. In 1998 he took the lead in *Antz,* the story of a heroic misfit ant, which was the first animated feature from the Dreamworks studio of Jeffrey Katzenberg and Steven Spielberg. *Antz* was an attempt to do a computer cartoon version of *Sleeper,* Woody's 1973 hit about a totalitarian society in the twenty-first century. In *Antz,* Sharon Stone is the voice of the slightly woolly-brained character once played by Diane Keaton, and Woody is Z, a nervous worker ant who has a personality disorder: he thinks too much. The middle child in a family of five million insects, Z's life is spent toiling in an ant colony in the middle of Central Park. Like Miles Monroe in *Sleeper,* Z resists regimentation. On the shrink's couch, he complains of feeling insignificant, but his psychiatrist reminds him that he is. As a disembodied voice, Woody was completely endearing. Unlike his own pictures in recent years, *Antz* was clever entertainment, which raked in $16.8 million at the box office on opening weekend, more than one of his own films usually earned in several years.

If he had finally discovered the secret door back into public favor, it was sad but predictable. Time and again, for many in the netherworld of film auteurs, their declining years were spent in precisely such endeavors. For instance, Orson Welles, who was forced to scrounge for work after failing to obtain funding for his film projects, was cursed with having to narrate *Bugs Bunny Superstar,* and Buster Keaton in his later years made Alka-Seltzer television commercials. That modern audiences liked Woody better as a bug than as a human being on the screen must have given even Woody Allen pause for reflection.

Victim of an Irregular Verb

In writing about a living figure, there is no way to spin out an ending to the story. When exactly will the subject draw his final breath? Will he leave in a rush or float away? What, if any, secrets will a death certificate or an autopsy report spew forth as a mischievous finale? And of course, in the case of a long-distance runner such as Woody, whose life continues to pour out, there may be surprises yet to come.

Even so, most of his dreams of adulation and honor came true long ago, although not his striving for a series of serious films that would rank alongside those of the great masters. If his goals fell short by his own yardstick, judging by any other measurement he succeeded far beyond any reasonable expectation. "Who else has written, acted in, and directed his own films over such a length of time?" said Vincent Canby. "In any discipline, that kind of longevity would be mind-boggling. He has dominated the second half of the twentieth century."

In all possible ways his everyday life approximated his celluloid world, which practically never guaranteed a happy ending. There was always what the philosophers call "the grit in the oyster." In both worlds, he played by his own rules. Having never learned the art of accommodation, he felt no need to please, compromise, collaborate, or regret. "Guilt," says one of his characters in *Bullets Over Broadway,* "is petty bourgeois crap. An artist creates his own moral universe." All the admirable qualities that have won him a unique place in American filmmaking—all his daring, toughness, perfectionism, and fierce artistic independence—have been strangely misapplied in his personal life.

By following the logic of his heart, Woody paid heavily. The cost of pleasure, marriage or no marriage, added up to millions in legal fees, the loss of his children, and abandonment by his audience, altogether a remarkable price, but he seems not to care. Just as Charlie Chaplin would never be forgiven his transgressions with un-American politics and underage girls, the public's memories of the sex scandal and accusations of child molestation stubbornly cling like barnacles to Woody's reputation. "There are some things people never forget," muses Andrew Sarris. "After forty years, we still associate the name of Charles Van Doren with the scandal of the quiz show contestants. I don't think Woody's scandal will ever go away either. It has cost him his primary audience. Women in particular abandoned him. The technical definition of incest doesn't matter so much as the fact that he meddled with the family, and you can't do that. In films like *Manhattan,* he set himself up as a moral paragon, but all that came tumbling down. People decided he was a hypocrite." A contrarian view is offered by Roger Ebert, who contends that "it was the kind of escalating situation people go through during a messy divorce. There was no evidence that he was guilty of the charges. I don't think people think about it now. Life goes on."

Among film critics—the ubiquitous Greek chorus who for a living has followed Woody's artistic progress over two or three decades—his legacy continues to be debated. The critics have themselves grown old and faded— and in some cases, considerably more mellow. John Simon, after sticking pins in Woody all those years, now asks, "How can you debate whether the Eiffel Tower adds to or detracts from Paris? He's part of the landscape, and we would be poorer without him. His productivity is admirable. Quantity can be impressive because it proves he has energy, ideas, creative spirit. Some people have done their best work in their seventies or eighties. On the other hand, you can outstay your welcome in any field."

Another detractor who admits that he still arrives at Woody's screenings with a sense of anticipation is Stanley Kauffmann. "He's written some of the funniest lines I know of in films. He's not a major artist but a notable and unique figure who will be remembered by the history books as an object of study and scrutiny." Kauffmann thinks Woody's films have sociological interest. "Like Jules Feiffer, he dramatized modern urban Jewish neuroses. One of the reasons for his critical success is that people recognize his contribution to America's understanding of itself. That's an achievement. Probably the future will think more highly of him than we do."

Twenty floors beneath Woody's penthouse, a ribbon of night traffic on Fifth Avenue spiraled slowly toward midtown. A half-mile distant on the western edge of Central Park gleamed the tiny white lights of the apartment houses along Central Park West: the Dakota, the San Remo, the Beresford. From his windows Woody could pick out the Langham, to which he once rushed each morning at dawn. No longer did he heed the ghostly Langham, long abandoned by his loved ones, who were carried away on tides of tears and hatred.

Eight hard years had passed since Mia Farrow beheld the photographs of her daughter on his mantelpiece. On that mild January afternoon in 1992, the long love affair between Woody and Mia—and his adoring public, for that matter—came to an end. Now he went about his business quietly making a picture of his own each year and, every so often, films for other directors. You would think he'd have left the tempestuous years behind him. Not so. For one thing, he has scripted a life meant to be played in the limelight. And don't forget his infinite capacity for pulling rabbits out of hats.

One sunny Saturday in the spring of 1999, a clump of four or five paparazzi were gathered, without much enthusiasm, outside the Giorgio Armani boutique at Sixty-fifth Street and Madison Avenue waiting for Jerry Seinfeld to leave the store with his girlfriend, Jessica Sklar. Nothing much was happening. Seinfeld and Sklar were not that hot anymore. It was shaping up to be a lazy, routine, boring afternoon, remembered Lawrence Schwartzwald. "We were standing there when all of a sudden—*boom!*—there were Woody and Soon-Yi coming up the block from Park Avenue. They were coming straight at us, and they were pushing this stroller. *What the hell! Look there! Oh, my God!* Everybody started shooting." The previous year, when Soon-Yi looked to have "a little belly," Woody had assured the paparazzi that his wife was not pregnant, and so now the excited photographers swarmed around and began peppering the couple with questions.

"Is the baby yours?" asked Schwartzwald, one of Woody's favorite paparazzo, whose shots appear regularly in the *New York Post*.

With the Saturday shoppers coming and going, as the cameras clicked away all at once, Soon-Yi paid no attention to the question. Somewhat reluctantly, Woody finally acknowledged it was indeed their child.

"How old is it?"

"I can't tell you that," Woody replied.

Looking at the baby, Schwartzwald judged it to be "about six weeks or two months old and one hundred percent Asian. There was not one bump on the kid's nose that came from Woody Allen. Then it dawned on me that it was adopted." Walking alongside the stroller, he asked Woody for the child's name.

"I'll tell you later," Woody said. But when Schwartzwald handed him a business card and pencil, he printed, "BECHET DUMAINE," and in parentheses, he added, "GIRL." Trailed by the paparazzi, Woody and Soon-Yi kept walking until they reached Fifth Avenue, then headed north to their apartment.

On Sunday morning, Schwartzwald's photo ran on the front page of the *Post.* By then the media had figured out that the name Bechet was a tribute to Woody's idol, Sidney Bechet. As for Dumaine, it turned out to be the name of a street in New Orleans.

In the eighteen months since his marriage, Woody appeared to have achieved a degree of serenity. "About nine or ten years ago," recalled Larry Schwartzwald, "he used to look terrified all the time, nervous, twitching, as if he were suffering a perpetual anxiety attack. He never made eye contact. Shaking hands with him was like touching a dead, cold fish. But all that has changed in the last year or so. He's settled. He jokes. He seems happy."

A few months later, Woody sold his penthouse for $14 million. He bought a $17-million, five-story townhouse on East Ninety-second Street, where there would be more room to raise a child.

One thing that he had never made secret was his desire to have a family with Soon-Yi. But why they preferred adoption over the natural method is a mystery. Does she—or he—suffer fertility problems? Was she trying to re-create her own beginnings?

And what about the Farrow-Allen offspring, who had taken their places in Woody's story as outtakes, like unused footage trimmed but not forgotten? "I went as far as I could go, every legal channel," he said in 1998. Comforting friends assure him that his kids, Satch, Dylan, even Moses, will someday seek him out. He is not so sure. In fact, he has lost all hope of ever seeing them again.

At the same time, though, his imagination occasionally runs wild, as when he fancied the possibility of resuming a friendship with Mia. "It's not my personality to continue a feud. So if I got a phone call tomorrow saying, 'Let's have a drink and talk things over,' well, I'd be there in a shot. It would be nice." He has a better chance of being struck by a meteoroid.

Such a fantasia ignores the rancor on both sides. Mia has said she can't imagine trusting men again. "When I introduce them to my children, what do I say: 'Don't diddle with the daughters'?"

Just as the passage of forty years never deterred Woody from continuing to insult Harlene in his films, his need to even the score with Mia still burns white-hot. At every opportunity, he brands her unfit to raise children. In an interview with Erica Jong for a women's fashion magazine, he savagely undermined Mia's reputation as "a supermother. You just can't provide correct parental attention to thirteen or fourteen kids." He then tendered the eccentric notion that his former lover quarantined her children "in a cultish compound in Connecticut where going out has always been discouraged," thereby conjuring up gruesome images of a Jim Jonesian jungle outpost. Had he wished to go into detail, he hinted darkly, "there are many horrible things I could say." Although the horrible things are left to the imagination, his charges immediately created an almost Pavlovian response from Mia. Shortly thereafter, she invited *Inside Edition,* a television tabloid show, to tour Frog Hollow, ostensibly to prove to the public that her current household of seven children bore no resemblance to a cult.

Woody's adoption of little Bechet chilled Mia. "I don't know how the courts permitted this," she declared. "Especially in light of a judge not allowing Mr. Allen to see his own children. I guess if you have enough celebrity, you can snow anybody." In case anyone had forgotten, she added that "I have a son [Satchel] whose sister is married to his father." Some of Mia's children, she went on to report, were in therapy and "some are on antidepressants." The person she faulted for all of these fractured lives is "an old pedophile," which was why she felt "frightened" for Bechet Dumaine Allen.

Woody, who is now sixty-four, appears older than his age. The person who had always been eternally boyish for the camera looks tired and somewhat crumpled. He seems oblivious to his physical changes, however. "I'm very compartmentalized," he remarked edgily. "For better or for worse, even during all that chaos I was able to just snap it off. It's a survival mechanism." Who could say that life cracked him? Who could ever deny that he has outlasted the twists and turnings of experience? On his face, for all to read, are the scars that prove it.

■ ■ ■ ■ ■ ■ ■

Moving Pictures:
PROFESSOR LEVY: But we define ourselves by the choices we have
   made.
                                       —*Crimes and Misdemeanors,* 1988

■ ■ ■ ■ ■ ■ ■

POSTSCRIPT

Harlene Susan Rosen Allen lived in Woodstock, New York, for many years. Insofar as is known, she did not remarry. After winning her lawsuit, she steered clear of her ex-husband and those who wished to pump her for information about him. In 1982 a British writer, Gerald McKnight, tried to win her trust, but she got cold feet at the last minute and refused to meet with him. "We were happy together," she told him on the telephone. "I don't want any scandal." A decade later, another British journalist, Tim Carroll, tracked down Harlene to nearby Phoenicia, New York. Driving up to her house, he glimpsed "a small woman with a shawl wrapped over her head going inside. When I knocked on the door, a muffled voice asked, 'Who is it?' I said that I was calling to see Harlene Allen."

"No such person lives here," she answered.

Fanatical about her privacy, Harlene left Phoenicia without giving a forwarding address.

Louise Lasser lives on the Upper East Side of Manhattan with her Yorkshire terrier. After becoming a popular television star during the seventies in *Mary Hartman, Mary Hartman,* she fell victim to depression, obesity, and cocaine addiction and virtually disappeared from public view. In 1998 she made one of her rare forays into movies in the Todd Solandz film *Happiness.* Although she has little contact with her ex-husband, she continues to care about him "and always will," she said. Like Harlene Allen, she has never remarried after her divorce from Woody.

Diane Keaton's career thrived in the late nineties with several successful films: *The First Wives Club,* with Goldie Hawn and Bette Midler; and *Marvin's Room,* for which she received a Best Actress Oscar nomination. She has never married, but in 1996, at the age of fifty, she adopted a baby girl whom she named Dexter Dean. They live in a 1926 Mediterranean-style hacienda in Beverly Hills.

Jean Doumanian still handles Woody's films but no longer depends solely on them for her livelihood. Operating from a luxurious office on East Fifty-seventh Street, which occupies the entire twenty-second floor, she recently produced a number of other pictures including David Mamet's thriller *The Spanish Prisoner,* and *Just Looking,* the directorial debut of *Seinfeld*'s Jason Alexander. She is also part-owner of the Crazy Carrot, a health-food restaurant on Second Avenue.

Jane Read Martin and **Douglas McGrath** are married and the parents of a son. Jane became associate producer of the Joan Rivers television show and also wrote several children's picture books. Doug, who received an Oscar nomination as coscreenwriter for *Bullets Over Broadway,* wrote and directed *Emma* (1996), which was based on the novel by Jane Austen and starred Gwyneth Paltrow.

Stacey Nelkin became a film actress and appeared in such classics as *Halloween 3—Season of the Witch,* as well as *Bullets Over Broadway.* During the custody hearing, she publicly defended her affair with Woody as "mature," adding that he had taught her "a lot about music and film." Now forty, she lives in Los Angeles.

Nancy Jo Sales is a contributing editor for *New York* magazine and specializes in investigative reporting about crime, street gangs, and literary figures. In 1993, while a researcher at *People,* she published a nostalgic account, "Woody and Me," about her preadolescent crush on the filmmaker and reprinted several of his letters. Still reverent about Woody, she could not help wondering "if I could possibly have had some lasting effect on him, as he so affected me." Nancy Jo is now thirty-four and lives in the Gramercy Park area of Manhattan.

Andre Previn was honored with a lifetime achievement award by the John F. Kennedy Center for the Performing Arts. The conductor of five symphony orchestras during his life, he recently composed an opera that was based on Tennessee Williams's *A Streetcar Named Desire.* His fourth wife, Heather, filed for divorce after seventeen years of marriage, amid reports, in the *Boston Herald,* of his relations with a bassoonist in the Pittsburgh Symphony. Previn remains close to Mia Farrow but has no contact with Soon-Yi. "That is a closed chapter," he says.

Arthur Krim suffered a stroke after the demise of Orion Pictures. He died in 1994 at the age of eighty-four.

Nick Apollo Forte has spent the years since *Broadway Danny Rose* as a fisherman and lounge entertainer. Occasionally, he does a "Broadway Danny Rose" night at Manhattan clubs. "What happened to Nick Apollo Forte," he reported, "is that he never did another movie. When they put the movie in *TV Guide* now, it's just Woody Allen and Mia Farrow, never a mention of Nick Apollo Forte. So what did he contribute? How come Nick Apollo Forte never gets another movie job?"

Pauline Kael retired from film criticism in 1991, after twenty-three years at *The New Yorker*. At the age of eighty, she suffers from Parkinson's disease and lives a reclusive life in Great Barrington, Massachusetts.

Ralph Rosenblum turned to television directing after falling out with Woody. He also taught at Columbia University's graduate film school and coauthored a book *(When the Shooting Stops . . . the Cutting Begins)* about his life in film editing. After the sixty-nine-year-old Rosenblum died of heart failure in 1995, Woody sent a letter of condolence to his widow, Davida, but did not attend the memorial service.

Marshall Brickman remains a loyal supporter who believes Woody received "a bad judgment" in the custody case. After their last collaboration, *Manhattan Murder Mystery* in 1993, Brickman next cowrote the screenplay for *Intersection*, a 1994 feature film starring Richard Gere and Sharon Stone. He works out of a studio on Central Park South, but lives on Central Park West, as well as in the Hamptons.

Vincent Canby shifted to theater reviewing in 1993, after a quarter of a century as the *New York Times*'s chief film critic. Since *Husbands and Wives*, the last Allen picture he reviewed, his opinions of the filmmaker have varied. He "wasn't crazy" about *Manhattan Murder Mystery*; "adored" *Bullets Over Broadway*; and "hardly remembers the plot" of *Mighty Aphrodite*, he says.

Justice Elliott Wilk's other prominent trials involved squatters on New York's Lower East Side; civil assault *(Mitch Green* v. *Mike Tyson)*; and medical malpractice (the Libby Zion case).

Elaine Kaufman's restaurant was featured in two recent Woody Allen pictures, *Everyone Says I Love You* and *Celebrity*. In 1998 Kaufman made headlines when she was arrested for assaulting a customer whom she had noticed nursing a gin and tonic at the bar.

THE CAREER OF WOODY ALLEN

FILMS

What's New, Pussycat? (Famous Artists/UA, 1965)
Director: Clive Donner
Screenplay: Woody Allen
Woody Allen (Victor Shakapopolis), Peter O'Toole, Peter Sellers

What's Up, Tiger Lily? [Originally *Kagi No Kagi*] (American International Pictures, 1966)
Director: Senkichi Taniguchi
Screenplay and dubbing: Woody Allen, Len Maxwell, Louise Lasser, Mickey Rose

Casino Royale (Famous Artists/Columbia, 1967)
Directors: John Huston, Ken Hughes, Val Guest, Robert Parrish, Joseph McGrath
Screenplay: Wolf Mankowitz, John Law, Michael Sayers, from the novel by Ian Fleming
Woody Allen (Jimmy Bond), Peter Sellers, David Niven, Ursula Andress, Orson Welles, Jacqueline Bisset, Jean-Paul Belmondo, William Holden

Don't Drink the Water (Avco Embassy, 1969)
Director: Howard Morris
Screenplay: R. S. Allen and Harvey Bullock, from Woody Allen's play
Jackie Gleason, Estelle Parsons, Ted Bessel, Joan Delaney

Take the Money and Run (Palomar Pictures, 1969)
Director: Woody Allen
Screenplay: Woody Allen and Mickey Rose
Woody Allen (Virgil Starkwell), Janet Margolin, Louise Lasser, Jackson Beck

Bananas (United Artists, 1971)
Director: Woody Allen

Screenplay: Woody Allen and Mickey Rose
Woody Allen (Fielding Mellish), Louise Lasser, Howard Cosell

Play It Again, Sam (Paramount Pictures, 1972)
Director: Herbert Ross
Screenplay: Woody Allen from his play
Woody Allen (Allan Felix), Diane Keaton, Tony Roberts, Jerry Lacy

Everything You Always Wanted to Know About Sex (But Were Afraid to Ask)
  (United Artists, 1972)
Director: Woody Allen
Screenplay: Woody Allen from the book by Dr. David Reuben
Woody Allen (Fool, Fabrizio, Victor, Cowardly Sperm), Lou Jacobi, Gene
  Wilder, Lynn Redgrave, Tony Randall, John Carradine, Burt Reynolds,
  Louise Lasser

Sleeper (United Artists, 1973)
Director: Woody Allen
Screenplay: Woody Allen and Marshall Brickman
Woody Allen (Miles Monroe), Diane Keaton

Love and Death (United Artists, 1975)
Writer-director: Woody Allen
Woody Allen (Boris), Diane Keaton, Jessica Harper, James Tolkan

The Front (Columbia, 1976)
Director: Martin Ritt
Screenplay: Walter Bernstein
Woody Allen (Howard Prince), Zero Mostel, Michael Murphy, Andrea Marcov-
  icci, Herschel Bernardi

Annie Hall (United Artists, 1977)
Director: Woody Allen
Screenplay: Woody Allen and Marshall Brickman
Woody Allen (Alvy Singer), Diane Keaton, Tony Roberts, Carol Kane, Paul
  Simon, Shelley Duval, Janet Margolin, Colleen Dewhurst, Christopher
  Walken, Sigourney Weaver

Interiors (United Artists, 1978)
Writer-director: Woody Allen
Marybeth Hurt, Diane Keaton, Kristen Griffith, E. G. Marshall, Geraldine Page,
  Maureen Stapleton, Sam Waterston

Manhattan (United Artists, 1979)
Director: Woody Allen
Screenplay: Woody Allen and Marshall Brickman
Woody Allen (Isaac Davis), Diane Keaton, Michael Murphy, Mariel Heming-
  way, Wallace Shawn, Meryl Streep, Karen Ludwig, Tisa Farrow

Stardust Memories (United Artists, 1980)
Writer-director: Woody Allen
Woody Allen (Sandy Bates), Charlotte Rampling, Jessica Harper, Marie-
  Christine Barrault, Tony Roberts, Daniel Stern, Sharon Stone, Louise Lasser

A Midsummer Night's Sex Comedy (Orion Pictures, 1982)
Writer-director: Woody Allen
Woody Allen (Andrew Hobbes), Mia Farrow, Jose Ferrer, Julie Hagerty, Tony
  Roberts, Mary Steenburgen

Zelig (Orion Pictures, 1983)
Writer-director: Woody Allen
Woody Allen (Leonard Zelig), Mia Farrow, with Susan Sontag, Saul Bellow, Irving Howe, Bricktop, Dr. Bruno Bettelheim, and Professor John Morton Blum
  as themselves

Broadway Danny Rose (Orion Pictures, 1984)
Writer-director: Woody Allen
Woody Allen (Danny Rose), Mia Farrow, Nick Apollo Forte, with Milton Berle,
  Howard Cosell, and Joe Franklin as themselves

The Purple Rose of Cairo (Orion Pictures, 1985)
Writer-director: Woody Allen
Mia Farrow, Jeff Daniels, Danny Aiello, Stephanie Farrow, Ed Herrmann, Van
  Johnson, Dianne Wiest, Zoe Caldwell

Hannah and Her Sisters (Orion Pictures, 1986)
Writer-director: Woody Allen
Woody Allen (Mickey), Mia Farrow, Michael Caine, Maureen O'Sullivan, Lloyd
  Nolan, Dianne Wiest, Barbara Hershey, Max von Sydow, Carrie Fisher, Sam
  Waterston, Julie Kavner

Radio Days (Orion Pictures, 1987)
Writer-director: Woody Allen
Woody Allen (narrator), Julie Kavner, Wallace Shawn, Mia Farrow, Dianne
  Wiest, Diane Keaton, Danny Aiello, Jeff Daniels, Judith Malina, Kitty
  Carlisle Hart, Josh Mostel, Seth Green

King Lear (Cannon Films, 1987)
Writer-director: Jean-Luc Godard
Woody Allen (Mr. Alien), Burgess Meredith, Peter Sellers, Molly Ringwald, Norman Mailer

September (Orion Pictures, 1987)
Writer-director: Woody Allen
Mia Farrow, Elaine Stritch, Dianne Wiest, Jack Warden, Denholm Elliott, Sam Waterston

Another Woman (Orion Pictures, 1988)
Writer-director: Woody Allen
Gena Rowlands, Ian Holm, Mia Farrow, Blythe Danner, Gene Hackman, Betty Buckley, John Houseman, Sandy Dennis, Martha Plimpton

"Oedipus Wrecks" (from *New York Stories*) (Touchstone Pictures, 1989)
Writer-director: Woody Allen
Woody Allen (Sheldon Mills), Mia Farrow, Julie Kavner, Mae Questel, George Schindler

Crimes and Misdemeanors (Orion Pictures, 1989)
Writer-director: Woody Allen
Woody Allen (Cliff Stern), Martin Landau, Alan Alda, Mia Farrow, Anjelica Huston, Sam Waterston, Jerry Ohrbach, Joanna Gleason, Claire Bloom

Alice (Orion Pictures, 1990)
Writer-director: Woody Allen
Mia Farrow, William Hurt, Joe Mantegna, Alec Baldwin, Judy Davis, Bernadette Peters, Cybill Shepherd, Keye Luke, Blythe Danner, Gwen Verdon, Julie Kavner

Scenes from a Mall (Touchstone Pictures, 1991)
Director: Paul Mazursky
Screenplay: Paul Mazursky and Roger L. Simon
Woody Allen (Nick Fifer), Bette Midler, Bill Irwin

Shadows and Fog (Orion Pictures, 1992)
Writer-director: Woody Allen
Woody Allen (Kleinmann), Mia Farrow, John Cusack, John Malkovich, Madonna, Donald Pleasance, Kathy Bates, Jodie Foster, Lily Tomlin, Kate Nelligan, Julie Kavner, Wallace Shawn

Husbands and Wives (Columbia-TriStar, 1992)
Writer-director: Woody Allen
Woody Allen (Gabe Roth), Mia Farrow, Juliette Lewis, Sidney Pollack, Judy Davis, Liam Neeson, Lysette Anthony, Blythe Danner, Benno Schmidt, Jeffrey Kurland

Manhattan Murder Mystery (Columbia-TriStar, 1993)
Director: Woody Allen
Screenplay: Woody Allen and Marshall Brickman
Woody Allen (Larry Lipton), Diane Keaton, Alan Alda, Anjelica Huston, Jerry Adler

Bullets Over Broadway (Jean Doumanian/Sweetland/Miramax, 1994)
Director: Woody Allen
Screenplay: Woody Allen and Douglas McGrath
John Cusack, Dianne Wiest, Jack Warden, Chazz Palminteri, Jennifer Tilly, Rob Reiner, Mary-Louise Parker, Jim Broadbent, Tracey Ullman

Mighty Aphrodite (Jean Doumanian/Sweetland/Miramax, 1995)
Writer-director: Woody Allen
Woody Allen (Lenny), Helena Bonham Carter, Mira Sorvino, Michael Rappaport, F. Murray Abraham, Olympia Dukakis, Claire Bloom, Jack Warden, Jeffrey Kurland

Everyone Says I Love You (Jean Doumanian/Sweetland/Miramax, 1996)
Writer-director: Woody Allen
Woody Allen (Joe), Goldie Hawn, Alan Alda, Drew Barrymore, Natasha Lyonne, Edward Norton, Julia Roberts, Tim Roth

Deconstructing Harry (Jean Doumanian/Sweetland/Fine Line Features, 1997)
Writer-director: Woody Allen
Woody Allen (Harry Block), Judy Davis, Kirstie Alley, Billy Crystal, Hazelle Goodman, Demi Moore, Elizabeth Shue, Robin Williams, Mariel Hemingway, Richard Benjamin, Julia Louis-Dreyfus, Eric Bogosian, Bob Balaban, Julie Kavner, Amy Irving, Stanley Tucci

Wild Man Blues (documentary) (Jean Doumanian/Sweetland/Fine Line Features, 1998)
Director: Barbara Kopple
Woody Allen, Soon-Yi Previn, Letty Aronson, Eddy Davis, and others as themselves

Antz (Dreamworks Pictures, 1998)
Directors: Eric Darnell and Tim Johnson
Screenplay: Todd Alcott, Chris Weitz, and Paul Weitz
Woody Allen (Z), Sharon Stone, Dan Aykroyd, Danny Glover, Jane Curtin, Anne Bancroft, Gene Hackman, Jennifer Lopez, Sylvester Stallone, Christopher Walken, John Mahoney

The Imposters (Fox Searchlight, 1998)
Writer-director: Stanley Tucci
Woody Allen (theater director, uncredited), Oliver Platt, Stanley Tucci, Lili Taylor

Celebrity (Sweetland/Miramax, 1998)
Writer-director: Woody Allen
Kenneth Branagh, Judy Davis, Leonardo DiCaprio, Melanie Griffith, Joe Mantegna, Winona Ryder, Gretchen Mol, Charlize Theron, Bebe Neuwirth

Sweet and Lowdown (Sweetland/Sony Pictures Classics, 1999)
Writer-director: Woody Allen
Sean Penn, Uma Thurman

Picking Up the Pieces (1999)
Director: Alfonso Arau
Woody Allen, Sharon Stone, Cheech Marin, Fran Drescher, David Schwimmer

"Woody Allen Spring Project '99" (Jean Doumanian/Sweetland, 2000)
Writer-director: Woody Allen
Woody Allen, Hugh Grant, Jon Lovitz, Tracey Ullman

STAGE PLAYS

From A to Z (opened April 20, 1960, Plymouth Theater, New York)
Director: Christopher Hewett
Musical revue including two Woody Allen sketches, "Hit Parade" and "Psychological Warfare"
Cast: Hermione Gingold and others
Performances: 21

Don't Drink the Water (opened November 17, 1966, Morosco Theater, New York)
Director: Stanley Prager
Cast: Lou Jacobi, Key Medford, Anita Gillette, Tony Roberts
Performances: 598

Play It Again, Sam (opened February 12, 1969, Broadhurst Theater, New York)
Director: Woody Allen
Cast: Woody Allen, Diane Keaton, Jerry Lacy, Tony Roberts
Performances: 453

(opened September 11, 1969, Globe Theatre, London)
Director: Joseph Hardy
Cast: Dudley Moore, Patricia Brake, Bill Kerr
Performances: 355

The Floating Light Bulb (opened April 27, 1981, Vivian Beaumont Theater, New York)
Director: Ulu Grosbard
Cast: Brian Backer, Beatrice Arthur, Danny Aiello, Jack Weston
Performances: 65

(opened May 17, 1990, Nuffield Theatre, Southampton, England)
Director: Patrick Sandford
Cast: Gian Sammarco, Paul Russell, Sylvia Syms, Sam Douglas, Lee Montagu
Performances: 25

Central Park West (opened March 6, 1995, Variety Arts Theater, New York)
Death Defying Acts was a trio of one-act plays: *Hotline* by Elaine May, *An Interview* by David Mamet, and Woody's *Central Park West*.
Director: Michael Blakemore
Cast: Linda Lavin, Debra Monk, Gerry Becker, Paul Guilfoyle, and Tari T. Signor
Performances: 343

RECORD ALBUMS

Woody Allen's stand-up routines were recorded on three albums:

Woody Allen (Colpix, 1964)
Woody Allen, Volume 2 (Colpix, 1965)
The Third Woody Allen Album (Capitol, 1968)

Previously recorded material later appeared on two compilation albums:

Woody Allen: The Night Club Years, 1964–1968 (United Artists, 1976)
Woody Allen Standup Comic, 1964–1968 (Casablanca Records, 1978)

At present, the routines are available on a CD:

Woody Allen, The Nightclub Years 1964–68 (EMI, 1990)

PUBLISHED PLAYS AND SCREENPLAYS

Don't Drink the Water (Random House, 1967)

Play It Again, Sam (Samuel French, 1969)

Woody Allen's Play It Again, Sam (Grosset & Dunlap, 1972)

Four Films of Woody Allen, including *Annie Hall* (cowritten with Marshall Brickman), *Interiors, Manhattan* (cowritten with Marshall Brickman), and *Stardust Memories* (Random House, 1982)

The Floating Light Bulb (Random House, 1982)

Hannah and Her Sisters (Random House, 1987)

Three Films of Woody Allen, including *Zelig, Broadway Danny Rose,* and *The Purple Rose of Cairo* (Vintage Books, 1987)

BOOKS

Getting Even (Random House, 1971; Vintage Books, 1978)

Without Feathers (Random House, 1975; Warner Books, 1976)

Side Effects (Random House, 1975; Ballantine Books, 1981)

The Illustrated Woody Allen Reader, Linda Sunshine, ed. (Knopf, 1993)

NOTES

This book was written without the cooperation of Woody Allen. Scores of individuals who have known him throughout his life agreed to be interviewed. But such is the influence of the subject—and the controversy that has surrounded him—that other informed sources hesitated to talk candidly about his virtues and failings. Those people who preferred to speak off the record are designated as "confidential sources."

In addition to my own interviews, both on and off the record, the book is also based on a voluminous collection of previous published interviews given by Woody Allen over a period of thirty-six years.

Court transcripts from the *Allen* v. *Farrow* custody hearing are sealed, as is customary when minor children are involved. Therefore, I have had to rely on contemporary reports that were previously published in the *New York Times, Chicago Tribune, New York Post, New York News-day,* and *New York Daily News,* as well as Kristi Groteke's memoir, *Mia and Woody: Love and Betrayal.* Quotations from the trial testimony are identified in the notes as "*Allen* v. *Farrow,* court testimony."

Some figures have been adjusted for inflation. Calculations of current dollars are based on the Bureau of Labor Statistics' *Consumer Price Index 1913–1998.*

PREFACE: *Grapes of Wrath*

13 "so I don't get depressed": *Newsweek,* 7/20/98.
15 "It took me": Mia Farrow, *What Falls Away,* Doubleday, 1997, p. 274.
15 "I found the pictures!": Ibid.
15 "Totally traumatized": *20/20,* 2/7/97.
15 "She always looked": Confidential source.
15 "Woody's been fucking": Farrow, *What Falls Away,* p. 274.
15 "Twenty minutes after": Confidential source.
15 "lay back": *Allen* v. *Farrow,* court testimony.
16 "graphic, erotic pictures": *Newsweek,* 8/31/ 92.
16 "a tepid little affair": Farrow, *What Falls Away,* p. 275.
16 "a meltdown of my very core": Ibid., p. 285.
16 "beside herself": *Allen* v. *Farrow,* court testimony.
16 "chatting with": Ibid.
17 "I must think": *Everything You Always Wanted to Know About Sex (But Were Afraid to Ask),* unpublished screenplay.
17 "A thousand grilled cheese": *Bananas,* unpublished screenplay.
17 "we're just good friends": *New York Times,* 6/20/75.
18 "Woody Allen, c'est moi":*New York Times,* 1/7/73.
18 "where he's coming": Richard Schickel, *Schickel on Film,* William Morrow, 1989, p. 271.
18 "To you I'm an atheist": Woody Allen, *Four Films of Woody Allen (Annie Hall, Interiors, Manhattan* and *Stardust Memories),* Random House, 1982, p. 334.

19 "What is that your business?!" Ibid., p. 5.
19 "one of the good guys": Walter Bernstein interview with MM.
19 "the most original": *New York* magazine, 4/25/88.

21 "Chapter One": Allen, *Four Films of Woody Allen,* p. 181.
21 "something wonderful": *Gentleman's Quarterly,* 2/86.
24 "She gets up": *The Realist,* 4/65.
25 "high-stepper": Eric Lax, *Woody Allen: A Biography,* Knopf, 1991, p. 13.
25 "they came from": Jack Victor interview with MM.
25 "My mother": *Playboy,* 5/67.
26 "The depressing thing": "Mechanical Objects," Monologue (Capitol, 1968).
26 "there all the time": *The New Yorker,* 12/9/96.
27 "His one regret": Woody Allen, *Getting Even,* Random House, 1971, jacket.
27 "His mother": Jack Freed interview with MM.
27 "Did you hit": Lax, *Woody Allen,* p. 18.
28 "Mia's mother": *Chicago Tribune,* 1/26/86.
28 "I remember": Lax, *Woody Allen,* p. 18.

29 "My God": Woody Allen, *Three Films of Woody Allen,* Vintage Books, 1987, p. 351.
29 "a total, total joy": Stig Bjorkman, *Woody Allen on Woody Allen,* Grove Press, 1993, p. 149.
30 "into the ugly light": Lax, *Woody Allen,* p. 27.
30 "cousins and uncles": *New York Post,* 12/22/63.
30 The house still stands. The current owners of 1144 East Fifteenth Street, Esther and Levi Kramer, purchased the house in 1993 and are aware of living in Woody Allen's boyhood home. During Woody's last year of high school, the Konigsbergs moved to the corner of Fifteenth and K, into the Ethan Allen apartments with Nettie's parents, and Woody slept on an army cot. According to a resident on Woody's old block, the Ethan Allen has become "the scourge of the neighborhood," a run-down building known for its drug users and welfare families.
31 "One day": Jack Freed interview.
31 "He was a wild kid": Doris Freed Shaffer interview with MM.
31 "But lots of kids": Jack Freed interview.
31 "real prose": *Newsweek,* 4/28/78.
31 "nothing of value": *New York World Journal Tribune,* 3/18/66.
32 "My parents didn't get divorced": Woody Allen, *Play It Again, Sam,* Samuel French, 1969, p. 35.
32 "They were the oddest": Jack Victor interview.
33 "When we came home": Jack Freed interview.
33 "Marty was": Elliott Mills interview with MM.
33 "I wish you were": Jack Victor interview.
33 "was always doing": *New York Sunday News,* 6/11/67.
33 "He's never let": *Chicago Tribune,* 1/26/86.
34 "I'm going to cut": Jack Victor interview.
34 "Don't waste time!": *Chicago Sun-Times,* 12/19/90.
34 "Prussian discipline": Ralph Rosenblum and Robert Karen, *When the Shooting Stops . . . the Cutting Begins,* DaCapo, 1979, p. 241.
34 "His mother was extremely naggy": Jack Victor interview.
34 "He was small": Elliott Mills interview.

34 "to meander": *New York Times Book Review,* 12/2/84.
35 "I'd eat in the cellar": *Newsweek,* 4/24/78.
35 "pessimistic, depressed": *University Review,* 11/72.
35 "I have memories": *New York Times,* 1/19/86.
35 "there wasn't an enemy": *Cosmopolitan,* 9/74.
35 "not a day": *Chicago Sun-Times,* 2/2/86.
35 "seductive": *Chicago Sun-Times,* 12/19/90.
36 "everything dissatisfied me": *New York Times,* 11/3/63.
36 "very depressed": Jack Victor interview.
36 "he was full": Elliott Mills interview.
36 "It was just something": *New York Times,* 1/19/86.
36 "It was a golden age": Elliott Mills interview.
36 "exchange of intimate": Jack Victor interview.
37 "I'd come home": *Jazz Times,* 9/96.
37 "Sidney Bechet live": Ibid.
37 "born with the real": Ibid.
37 "nor did I care": *New York Times Book Review,* 9/18/88.
38 "drove me crazy": Jack Victor interview.
38 "Roses are red": *New York Times,* 11/29/98.
38 "was the kind of school": Alan Lapidus interview with MM.
38 "He was bright": Gladys Bernstein interview with MM.
38 "emotionally disturbed": *New York Sunday News,* 2/2/64.
39 "getting up": *New York* magazine, 10/17/94.
39 "He appeared": Jack Victor interview.
39 "This typewriter": *Chicago Sun-Times,* 10/8/89.
39 "It was an ongoing": Elliott Mills interview.
39 "Enclosed are": Lax, *Woody Allen,* p. 68.
40 "Woody Allen figured": *New York Post,* 11/25/52.
40 "Knowing a sucker": *New York Post,* 8/12/72.
40 "It's the fallen women": Reprinted Ibid.
40 "in a column": *Newsweek,* 4/24/78.
40 "carrot-topped senior": Midwood *Argus,* 2/27/53, quoted in Gerald McKnight, *Woody Allen: Joking Aside,* London: W. H. Allen, 1983, p. 41.
40 "When Bryna Goldstein": Alan Lapidus interview.
40 "There were dozens": Eddie Jaffe interview with MM.
41 "my life began": *Rolling Stone,* 4/9/87.
41 "I would get on": *Paris Review,* Fall 1995.
41 "a terrible, terrible": "Final Cut" on *CBS Eye on People,* 12/97.
41 "Don't get off": *Rolling Stone,* 4/9/87.
41 "couldn't care less": Ibid.
42 "all strange": Eric Lax, *On Being Funny, Woody Allen and Comedy,* Charterhouse, 1975, p. 41.
42 "I was given": *Playboy,* 6/67.
43 "like getting paid": "Final Cut" on *CBS Eye on People,* 12/97.
43 "I don't know what": *Time Out New York,* 12/4–12/11, 1997.

CHAPTER 3: *Stand-Up*

45 "as romantic": Jack Victor interview.
46 "In those days": Jimmy Moore interview with MM.
46 "a continual awareness": *New York Times,* 9/22/67.
47 "He was a very timid": Buddy Hackett interview with MM.
47 "we'd be standing": Pat Boone interview with MM.

47 "a playpen": Larry Gelbert quoted in transcript of Museum of Broadcasting seminar, 10/2/84.

47 "that rotten little kid": Abe Burrows, *Honest Abe,* Little Brown, 1980, p. 347.

47 "never communicated anything": Mel Brooks interview with MM.

48 "People joked": Mary Rodgers interview with MM.

48 "confident of what": Jane and Gordon Connell interview with MM.

48 "George S. Kaufmanesque": Martha LoMonaco interview with MM.

48 "always had a cold": Mary Rodgers interview.

48 "Hansel and Gretel": Jane Connell interview.

48 "All you do": Phil Berger, *The Last Laugh,* Ballantine Books, 1975, p. 110.

48 "didn't show her feelings": McKnight, *Woody Allen,* p. 66.

48 "a blind alley": Larry Wilde, *The Great Comedians Talk About Comedy,* Citadel Press, 1968, p. 17.

48 "to earn a living": Ibid.

48 "making me sick": Tim Carroll, *Woody and His Women,* Little Brown, 1993, p. 88.

49 "There have been very few": *Media and Methods,* 12/77.

50 "a child doing show-and tell": *The New Yorker,* 12/9/96.

50 "It was unspeakably": *Seventeen,* 5/66.

50 "We *smelled*": *Cosmopolitan,* 9/74.

51 "zero": Berger, *The Last Laugh,* p. 109.

51 "a Godforsaken": *New York Times Magazine,* 11/3/63.

51 "he was going to choke": Berger, *The Last Laugh,* p. 109.

51 "stoically go through": Ibid.

51 "dogs with high-pitched ears": *Time,* 7/3/72.

52 "He got sick": Elliott Mills interview.

52 "known something": Carroll, *Woody and His Women,* p. 104.

53 "that was the nice thing": Ibid., p. 105.

53 "Whenever I got off": *Newsweek,* 5/3/76.

53 "I'll never forgive her": Carroll, *Woody and His Women,* p. 116.

53 "the smartest of all": Jack Victor interview.

53 "It was only when": *Newsweek,* 4/24/78.

53 "I never set out": *New York Sunday News,* 2/2/64.

54 "The simple fundamentals": *New York Times Magazine,* 11/3/63.

54 "an exaggerated version": Jack Victor interview.

54 "Gradually, the character": *New York World-Telegram & Sun,* 11/7/63.

55 "Not only did they": "Down South," Monologue (Capitol, 1968).

55 "I was hunting": "The Moose," Monologue (Colpix, 1965).

56 "It must have been 1963": Helen Gurley Brown interview with MM.

57 "a Chaplin-esque victim": *New York Times,* 11/5/62.

57 "by far my most satisfying": Rogers E. M. Whitaker and Tony Hiss, *All Aboard with E. M. Frimbo,* Kodansha, 1997.

57 "seem normal to me": *New York Times Magazine,* 11/3/63.

57 "Leaving when she did": Jack Victor interview.

57 "really a great experience": *New York Daily News,* 2/2/64.

57 "a weird woman": All Harlene one-liners cited in *Harlene Allen (aka Konigsberg)* v. *National Broadcasting Co.,* NY SupCt, Index No. 5376/67.

58 "the jokes were funny": Jack Victor interview.

58 "Why don't you": Carroll, *Woody and His Women,* p. 94.

CHAPTER 4: *What's New, Pussycat?*

59 "I go up on stage": *University Review,* 11/72.

59 "a wallflower": *Newsday,* 7/10/64.

60 "What the hell": Ibid.
60 "what my wife": *Coliseum,* 2/16/67.
60 "If her husband": "Private Life," Monologue (Colpix, 1964).
60 "Attitudes like yours": Lax, *Woody Allen,* p. 189.
60 "respond nastily": *Dick Cavett Show,* 10/4/77.
61 "for six, seven months": *Crawdaddy,* 12/73.
61 "Don't do that": Ibid.
61 "a Greek widow": Confidential source.
61 "That is *soo* funny": Stephen Silverman interview with MM.
61 "a wonderful side": Laurie Zaks interview with MM.
62 "To know Woody": Peter Tauber interview with MM.
62 "closest friend": *Rolling Stone,* 9/16/93.
62 "the person you want": *New York Times,* 6/1/98.
62 "He's very lucky": Stephen Silverman interview.
62 "Would you accept": "Question and Answer Session," Monologue (Capitol, 1968).
63 "just the throw of the dice": *Spin,* 1/98.
63 "the struggles": Diane Jacobs, . . . *But We Need the Eggs: The Magic of Woody Allen,* St. Martin's Press, 1982, p. 3.
63 "do something": *University Review,* 11/72.
64 "I hate rock": *Cosmopolitan,* 9/74.
64 "Do you know": *New York Post,* 8/19/72.
64 On a wintry night: In *Premiere* magazine, 1/92, Warren Beatty recalled that he was Feldman's companion at the Blue Angel. According to Eric Lax, Feldman was with Beatty's sister, Shirley MacLaine.
65 "a ride I couldn't": *Holiday,* 5/69.
66 "Not very much": *What's New, Pussycat?,* unpublished screenplay.
66 "They just killed it": *Cinema,* Winter 1972–1973.
66 "fuck off": Lax, *Woody Allen,* p. 215.
66 "It would only bother": *New York Morning Telegraph,* 6/28/65.
66 "unless I had complete": *Cinema,* Winter 1972–1973.
66 "a shrieking, reeking": *New York Herald Tribune,* 6/23/65.
66 "It was a delightful": Judith Crist interview with MM.
66 "probably reads hilariously": *The New Republic,* 7/10/65.
67 "a more tasteful sex comedy": *Village Voice,* 7/8/65.
67 "a terrific stand-up": Andrew Sarris interview with MM.
67 "one of the funniest movies": *Village Voice,* 12/8/66.
67 "a handbook": *Media and Methods,* 12/77.
67 "He was very loyal": Carroll, *Woody and His Women,* p. 66.
68 "WOODY ALLEN at various": *Harlene Allen (aka Konigsberg)* v. *National Broadcasting Co.*
68 "If I were to close": *The New Yorker,* 12/9/96.
68 "Many things about him": Mia Farrow interview with *Hello!* magazine, quoted in *Philadelphia Inquirer,* 10/29/92.
68 "Every day I raced": *New York* magazine, 4/5/93.
68 "He's dependable": *Newsweek,* 4/24/78.
68 "Life is difficult": Ibid.
69 "We both decided": *New York Post,* 11/15/80.
70 "we went down": *New York Daily News,* 3/18/67.
70 "Whose party is this?": *New York Post,* 11/18/67.
70 "he keeps shooting": Ibid.
70 "I'm bringing 500 mice": Ibid.
70 "crazy as a loon": Lax, *Woody Allen,* p. 170.
71 "finicky and touchy": *New York Times,* 9/22/68.
71 "Hiya, Louise": Carroll, *Woody and His Women,* p. 126.

71 "the story and staging": *Variety,* 10/5/66.
71 "a terrible play": *Media and Methods,* 12/77.
72 "every 20 minutes": *New York Times,* 10/19/80.
72 "She was once a nobody": Norma Lee Clark, *Lady Jane,* Fawcett, 1984, jacket copy.
72 "This is a good piece": *Chicago Tribune,* 9/24/78.
72 "hallowed ground": *Paris Review,* Fall 1995.
72 "obvious he could write": Roger Angell interview with MM.
72 "The insults and exaggeration": Roger Angell to Woody Allen, 9/29/65.
73 "This is very funny": Roger Angell interview.
73 "In many ways": Roger Angell interview.
73 "Mr. Shawn is delighted": Roger Angell to Woody Allen, 4/26/66.
73 "regarded Woody as a gift": Roger Angell interview.
73 Publication in *The New Yorker:* Woody's sixty comic literary pieces from *The New Yorker, The New Republic, The Kenyon Review,* and other magazines are collected in three volumes: *Getting Even* (1971), *Without Feathers* (1975), and *Side Effects* (1980).
74 "Shall we begin?": "The Whore of Mensa," *The New Yorker,* 12/16/74, reprinted in *Without Feathers.*
74 "When he turned somber": Roger Angell interview.
74 "little souffles": *The New Yorker,* 12/9/96.
74 "guys like S. J. Perelman": *Saturday Review,* 6/86.
75 "Sorry to let you down": Roger Angell to Woody Allen, 7/10/79.
75 "almost every sentence": Roger Angell to Woody Allen, 12/16/76.
75 "I kid my ex-wife": "What's New, Pussycat?" Monologue (Colpix, 1965).
75 "while holding me": *Harlene Allen (aka Konigsberg) v. National Broadcasting Co.*
75 "So you thought": *New York World Journal Tribune,* 3/21/67.
76 "statements attributing to me": *Harlene Allen v. National Broadcasting Co.*
76 "settle for half": *New York Post,* 5/19/71.
77 "But I'm not a comedian": William F. Buckley, Jr., interview with MM.
77 "For God's sake": Groucho Marx to Woody Allen, 3/22/67.

CHAPTER 5: *The "Coatcheck Girl"*

79 "hadn't seen a woman": *Dick Cavett Show,* 9/69.
79 "The way I look at it": Press release, Palomar Pictures, 1969.
79 "Can you come": Bjorkman, *Woody Allen on Woody Allen,* p. 20.
79 "That's the worst problem": *Cosmopolitan,* 9/74.
80 "a great honor": Jerry Lewis quotation relayed to MM by Joe Stabile.
80 "Woody, I spend": Shawn Levy, *King of Comedy. The Life and Art of Jerry Lewis.* St. Martin's Press, 1997, p. 340.
80 "Please put $50,000": *Take the Money and Run,* unpublished screenplay.
80 "I'm sorry": *The Realist,* 4/65.
80 "In prison the psychiatrist": Ibid.
81 "I don't like": *New York Times,* 1/2/98.
81 "little personal, honest films": Peter Biskind, *Easy Riders, Raging Bulls,* Simon & Schuster, 1998, p. 75.
81 "the master of coitus interruptus": *Take One,* 12/73.
82 "a bad case": *The New Republic,* 1/19/98.
82 "a frantic amateur": *The New Republic,* 10/4/93.
82 "very unusual": Rosenblum and Karen, *When the Shooting Stops,* pp. 242–244.
82 "He asked to see": Davida Rosenblum interview with MM.
83 "one of the most": Rosenblum and Karen, *When the Shooting Stops,* p. 246.
83 "didn't matter too much": Ibid., p. 248.
83 "a silly symphony": *Newsweek,* 8/25/69.

83 "the cinematic equivalent": *New York Times,* 8/19/69.
83 "more of a personal kick": Jacobs, . . . *But We Need the Eggs,* p. 51.
84 "the results ought to be": *Newsweek,* 8/25/69.
84 "It was like being": *Rolling Stone,* 6/30/77.
84 "She was a Broadway star": *Time,* 9/26/77.
85 "Oh, God": *Vanity Fair,* 11/95.
85 "I'd seen him on television": *Rolling Stone,* 6/3/77.
85 "very charming": Ibid.
85 "the Sandy Dennis Prize": *National Review,* 10/13/78.
85 "She was the type": *Rolling Stone,* 6/3/77.
85 "When I first met her": *Time,* 9/26/77.
86 "a coatcheck girl": *New York Times,* 8/15/93.
86 "It was the easiest job": Bjorkman, *Woody Allen on Woody Allen,* p. 48.
87 "What's happening": Carroll, *Woody and His Women,* p. 132.
87 "good time": Ibid., p.134.
87 "protest against": *Family Circle,* 8/74.
87 "That's Diane's drawer": Carroll, *Woody and His Women,* p. 147.
88 "ten blocks": *Holiday,* 5/69.
88 "grave reservations": Confidential source.
89 "Are you Woody Allen?": Confidential source.
89 "fantasies and inner life": *Architectural Digest,* 11–12/72.
89 "I don't understand": McKnight, *Woody Allen,* p. 125.
90 "The inequality of my relationship": *New York Daily News,* 12/26/97.
90 "a trace of intellectualism": *Time,* 4/30/79.
90 "a real hayseed": *McCall's,* 11/79.

CHAPTER 6: *The Medici*

92 "Who's she looking for": *Bananas,* unpublished screenplay, 1971.
92 "Arthur was very much": Eric Pleskow interview with MM.
92 "when he is good": *New York Times,* 4/29/71.
93 "the rocks of his acting": *The New Republic,* 5/22/71.
93 "on-the-job training": Stanley Kauffmann interview with MM.
93 "That wasn't the point": Confidential source.
93 "Arthur was not a self-made man": Judy Feiffer interview with MM.
93 "Woody was the emotional son": Confidential source.
94 "a nice, simple": *Chicago Tribune Magazine,* 5/15/77.
94 "I have absolute control": *Cinema,* Winter 1972–1973.
94 "Had there been no Arthur": Steven Bach interview with MM.
94 "sui generis": Stanley Kauffmann interview.
94 "Sometimes I felt like": Eric Pleskow interview.
94 "He knew how": Steven Bach interview.
94 "carte blanche": Confidential source.
94 "an intelligent young man": Eric Pleskow interview.
95 "humor, charm": Dr. David Reuben, e-mail, 10/8/96.
95 "It's hard to believe": *Sleeper,* unpublished manuscript.
96 "I'm taller": *New York Times,* 7/3/77.
97 "tension pervaded": Rosenblum and Karen, *When the Shooting Stops,* p. 260.
97 "informally between shows": Vincent Canby interview with MM.
98 "a limply, good-natured": *The New Yorker,* 10/4/69.
98 "a beautiful little piece": *The New Yorker,* 12/31/73.
98 "beyond belief": Andrew Sarris interview.
99 "like a setter's ears": *The New Yorker,* 2/2/74.

99 "a touch of the surreal": Ved Mehta, *Remembering Mr. Shawn's New Yorker,* Overlook Press, 1998, p. 283.
99 "two dreadful little boys": Vincent Canby interview.
99 "He's made his lunacy work": Walter Bernstein interview.
99 "one emotionally charged moment": *Cosmopolitan,* 9/74.
100 "Underneath": Confidential source.
100 "I'm disciplined": *Esquire,* 5/77.
100 "If he took three": Vincent Canby interview.
100 "What happened": Eric Pleskow interview. Elements of the discarded mystery wound up in the first cut of *Annie Hall* and later as the plot of *Manhattan Murder Mystery.*
101 "Krim was one": Steven Bach interview.
101 "an exceptional animal": Eric Pleskow interview.
101 "going for the character": *New York* magazine, 7/16/75.
101 "most shapely": *The New Yorker,* 6/16/75.
101 "Woody's War and Peace": *New York Times,* 6/11/75.
101 "in the right place": *The New Republic,* 7/12/75.
102 "What about the kid?": Walter Bernstein interview.
102 "expresses me politically": *Rolling Stone,* 7/1/76.
102 "never disrespectful": Andrea Marcovicci interview with MM.
103 "Woody is never deliberately": Walter Bernstein interview.
103 "Shut up, out there": Andrea Marcovicci interview.
103 "Woody shrinks": Walter Bernstein interview.
103 "because they are trying": *The New Republic,* 10/2/76.
103 "for fun": *New York Times,* 6/4/84.
103 "Come on, Woody": *Chicago Sun-Times,* 10/22/78.
104 "Put it this way": *New York Times,* 10/19/80.
104 "a very stylish person": Karen Roston interview with MM.
104 "as if she had just read": Confidential source.
104 "the kind of person": Confidential source.
105 "boys": Willie Morris, *New York Days,* Little Brown, 1993, p. 259.

CHAPTER 7: *"A Picture About Me"*

107 "I'm becoming more attractive": *New York Times,* 12/1/75.
107 "I don't even have my teeth filled": Ibid.
107 "the worst thing that could happen": *The New Yorker,* 2/4/74.
108 "It was a picture": Rosenblum and Karen, *When the Shooting Stops,* p. 283.
108 "The first draft": Ibid., p. 274.
109 "White is very cleansing": *Rolling Stone,* 6/30/77.
109 "She was abysmal": Stanley Kauffmann interview.
109 "Oh, well, la-de-dah": Allen, *Four Films of Woody Allen,* p. 31.
110 "the largest appetite": *Newsweek,* 2/15/82.
110 "an untitled and chaotic": Rosenblum and Karen, *When the Shooting Stops,* p. 273.
110 "running off": Ibid., p. 281.
110 "The thing was supposedly": Ibid., p. 275.
110 "kept cutting": Ibid., p. 281.
111 "I would but I need the eggs": Allen, *Four Films of Woody Allen,* p. 105.
111 "basically stupid": *Chicago Tribune,* quoted in Jonathan Moor, *Diane Keaton, the Story of the Real Annie Hall,* St. Martin's Press, 1989, p. 58.
111 "walked over to the window": Rosenblum and Karen, *When the Shooting Stops,* p. 289.
111 "Listen, I have Woody": Eric Pleskow interview.
111 "a catchy title": Ibid.
112 "he actually did have": Confidential source.

112 "No, it was a boring": *Toronto Star,* 4/9/77.
112 "He figured people": Confidential source.
112 "There was accuracy": Stanley Kauffmann interview.
112 "technically pushes": *The New Yorker,* 4/25/77.
112 "everything we never wanted": *New York* magazine, 5/2/77.
113 "I'm obsessed with looks": John Simon interview with MM.
113 "just junk their lives": *Take One,* 11/78.
113 "a subtle first course": *Redbook,* 10/76.
113 "I expected to find him": Vivian Gornick interview with MM.
114 "Tell me": *Village Voice,* 1/5/76.
114 "When you do comedy": *Newsweek,* 4/24/78.
115 "I'm sure they were all set": Eric Pleskow interview.
115 "Woody needed to get": Steven Bach interview.
115 "The *Interiors* script": Confidential source.
115 "I think they sent me": Davida Rosenblum interview.
115 "the real meat": *Esquire,* 5/77.
115 "a series of great films": *New York Daily News,* 6/12/81.
116 "You want to do mankind": Allen, *Four Films of Woody Allen,* p. 367.
116 "That's my mother": Carroll, *Woody and His Women,* p. 188.
116 "a New York woman": *Chicago Sun-Times,* 9/10/78.
116 "I was very intimidated": *Take One,* 11/78.
117 " 'What's the big deal?' ": Maureen Stapleton interview with MM.
117 " 'Albeck,' reported Steven Bach": Steven Bach, *Final Cut, Dreams and Disaster in the Making of Heaven's Gate,* William Morrow, 1985, p. 110.
117 "It's not going to make": *Take One,* 11/78.
117 "What man in his forties": *The New Yorker,* 10/27/80.
118 "Woody Allen's beautiful new": *New York Post,* 1/19/77.
118 "extremely sophisticated": *New York Post,* 1/7/93.
119 "Hard to believe": *New York* magazine, 4/5/93.
120 "if you're really the age": *New York Times Magazine,* 4/22/79.
120 "not completely a disaster": Walter Bernstein interview.
120 "It was the first time": Delta Willis interview with MM.
120 "My dear Mr. Allen": Dorothy Herrmann, *S. J. Perelman, A Life,* Putnam's, 1986, p. 289.
121 "I thought it was a joke": Delta Willis interview.
121 "The whole concept": *Los Angeles Herald-Examiner,* 4/3/78.
121 "If it were a special occasion": *Newsweek,* 4/17/ 78.
122 "I turned my phone": *Chicago Tribune,* 9/24/78.

CHAPTER 8: *Vanity Fair*

123 "You've got to be kidding": *Ladies' Home Journal,* 7/78.
123 "a million messages": *Chicago Tribune,* 9/24/78.
123 "No joy?": *Newsweek,* 4/24/78.
123 "United Artists had said": 50th Annual Academy Awards, ABC-TV, 4/4/78.
123 "no idea": *Ladies' Home Journal,* 7/78.
123 "What do you want to do": *Esquire,* 4/87.
124 "He hit his high point": Elliott Mills interview.
124 "Everybody is entitled": Neil Rosen interview with MM.
124 "America's Ingmar Bergman": *New York Times,* 4/24/77.
124 "helped ruin Allen": *National Review,* 3/27/87.
124 "John has no sense of humor": Vincent Canby interview.
125 "I didn't like the picture": Ibid.
125 "a giant step forward": *The New Yorker,* 8/7/78.

125 "a handbook of art-film mannerisms": *The New Yorker,* 9/25/78.
125 "a tour of the Ingmar Bergman Room": *The New Republic,* 5/19/79.
125 the "disaster": *National Review,* 9/29/78 and 10/13/78.
125 "tough on everyone": John Simon interview.
126 "charitable": Bjorkman, *Woody Allen on Woody Allen,* p. 95.
126 "that sad, miserable movie": Roger Angell interview.
126 "a bore": Steven Bach interview.
126 "Why don't you give her": Rosenblum and Karen, *When the Shooting Stops,* p. 269.
126 "By the time": Ibid., p. 265.
127 "we've never shared": Ibid., 264.
127 "What do you do": Allen, *Four Films of Woody Allen,* p. 193.
127 "the thing that always seemed": *New York Post,* 1/7/93.
128 "So I'm off": *In Style,* 1/98.
128 "if this is it": *Chicago Sun-Times,* 2/2/86.
128 "terrifying to me": *Rolling Stone,* 9/6/93.
128 "I'm dying!": Woody Allen, *Hannah and Her Sisters,* Vintage, 1987, p. 67.
129 "break out in a rash": *New York Times,* 5/8/79.
129 "lots of people": Andrew Sarris interview.
129 " 'Hey,' Hope drawled": Stephen M. Silverman, *Public Spectacles,* Dutton, 1981, p. 93.
129 "Hey, it's an honor": Bob Hope interview with MM, conducted by Sue Terry.
129 "a *near* genius": *New York Times,* 5/8/79.
129 "Have you ever heard": Silverman, *Public Spectacles,* p. 97.
129 "pure, unambiguous pleasure": Bach, *Final Cut,* p. 223.
129 "all the reasons": Ibid., p. 225.
130 "the only truly great": *Village Voice,* 4/30/79.
130 "not the only one": Andrew Sarris interview.
130 "it almost makes you forget": *New York Times,* 4/20/79.
130 "What kind of girls": *New York Post,* 8/19/72.
131 "a prisoner": *Esquire,* 5/77.
131 "no place to hide": Ibid.
131 "an inconvenience": *University Review,* 1/72.
131 "He was full of contradictions": Eric Pleskow interview.
132 "Love you": Vivian Gornick interview.
132 "a fear of being shot": *Seventeen,* 5/66.
132 "who went to art houses": Judith Crist interview with MM.
133 "It's about malaise": *Los Angeles Times,* 2/15/81.
133 "Directors can get": *Modern Maturity,* 3–4/98.
134 "a small forsaken animal": *Life,* 5/5/67.
135 "one of America's major": *New York Times Magazine,* 4/22/79.
136 "a hard ticket": Helen Gurley Brown interview.
136 "Earl 'the Pearl' ": Roger Angell interview.
136 "everywhere in beautiful jars": Andrea Marcovicci interview.
136 "the best": Andy Warhol, *The Andy Warhol Diaries,* Pat Hackett ed., Warner Books, 1989, p. 252.
136 "Mia gets what she wants": *McCall's,* 5/67.
137 "would kill me": *Village Voice,* 12/3/79.
137 "it's no accomplishment": *People,* 10/4/76.
138 "I've never had a marriage": *Chicago Tribune,* 6/1/81.

CHAPTER 9: *Beware of Young Girls*

139 "an almighty temper": Farrow, *What Falls Away,* p. 27.
139 "I didn't know": *Playbill,* 5/80.

140 "The dog": *Interview* magazine, 4/94.
141 "There were four sisters": *Life,* 5/ 29/70.
142 "pretty girl": Farrow, *What Falls Away,* p. 86.
143 "You're not dating": "Mia Farrow: A Life of Drama," A&E, 3/12/98.
143 "a nice man": Gannett News Service, 9/27/87.
143 "The groom, his retreating hairline": Earl Wilson, *Sinatra,* Macmillan, 1976, p. 223.
143 "Well, you see": Kitty Kelley, *His Way: The Unauthorized Biography of Frank Sinatra,* Bantam, 1986, p. 364.
143 "with all the powers": *Mirabella,* 3–4/97.
143 "Frank soaks": Kelley, *His Way,* p. 364.
143 "could be so charming": *New York Times,* 5/8/94.
144 "You have to understand": *Esquire,* 3/96.
144 "Sending Rudin": Roman Polanski, *Roman by Polanski,* William Morrow, 1984, p. 274.
144 "When you look": *Cosmopolitan,* 1/70.
144 "She was a real sad": *New York Daily News Magazine,* 10/15/89.
144 "gentle and flighty": John Phillips, *Papa John,* Doubleday, 1986, p. 204.
145 "I'll get you down": Ibid., p. 204.
145 "No dogs or Jews": Helen Drees Ruttencutter, *Previn,* St. Martin's Press, 1985, p. 36.
145 "Esther Williams days": Ibid., p. 38.
145 "a pretty house": Andre Previn, *No Minor Chords: My Days in Hollywood,* Doubleday, 1991, p. 137.
145 "the British Leonard Bernstein": Martin Bookspan and Ross Yockey. *Andre Previn: A Biography,* Doubleday, 1981, p. 209.
145 "There was nothing appealing": Confidential source.
146 "she were still wrapped": Dory Previn, *Bog-Trotter, An Autobiography with Lyrics,* Doubleday, 1980, p. 52.
146 "Well, that's interesting": Bookspan and Yockey, *Andre Previn,* p. 221.
147 "Dory was not OK": Confidential source.
147 "I started to say": *Photoplay,* 11/71.
147 "as many as I could": Ruttencutter, *Previn,* p. 30.
147 "a lot of problems": *Photoplay,* 11/71.
148 "just 'one of the Farrows' ": Kelley, *His Way,* p. 343.
149 "I believed": *Mirabella,* 3–4/97.

CHAPTER 10: *Woody in Love*

151 "Your future husband": Farrow, *What Falls Away,* p. 197.
152 "zero interest": Ibid., p. 195.
152 "I would like to have": *Allen* v. *Farrow,* court testimony.
152 "She never met a baby": Lorrie Pierce interview with MM.
153 "the perfect vegetable terrine": *New York Review of Books,* 8/16/79.
153 "it leaves my mind": Joan Didion to MM, 3/22/97.
153 "or else it piles up": *The New Yorker,* 2/4/74.
153 "accused me of things": *Chicago Tribune,* 5/31/81.
153 "marvelous": *New York Times,* 9/28/80.
154 "the neurotic's version": *The New Yorker,* 10/27/80.
154 "What a shame": Roy Blount, Jr., "Books: Lustily Vigilant," *The Atlantic,* 12/94.
154 "the way in which he put down": Andrew Sarris interview.
154 "the most mean-spirited": *Village Voice,* 10/1–7/80.
154 "existential sniveler": *National Review,* 12/28/80.
154 "I didn't see myself": Judith Crist interview.
154 "what we have here": *Saturday Review,* 12/80.
154 "the best I ever did": *Esquire,* 4/87.

155 "a lot of flack": *Paris Review,* Fall 1995.
155 "So many people": Jacobs, . . . *But We Need the Eggs: The Magic of Woody Allen,* p. 147.
155 "I'm a spartan": *Dick Cavett Show,* 10/4/77.
155 "What Mr. Allen says": *New York Times Magazine,* 10/19/80.
156 "She'd make us watch": Quoted in Frank Sanello, *Eddie Murphy: The Life and Times of a Comic on the Edge,* Birch Lane, 1997, p. 29.
156 "Studio 8H": Laurie Zaks interview.
156 "Where are you from?": Peter Tauber interview.
157 "She pissed off": Laurie Zaks interview.
157 "Anyone who replaced": Karen Roston interview.
157 "The first time I ever saw": *Radio Days,* unpublished screenplay.
157 "The Couple of the Year": *New York Daily News,* 9/16/80.
158 "May I be your Daisy?": Robert Evans, *The Kid Stays in the Picture,* Hyperion, 1994, p. 251.
158 "It was an impossible": Steven Bach interview.
158 "Arthur is like a *father*": Bach, *Final Cut,* p. 113.
158 "It was perfectly clear": Steven Bach interview.
159 "the price he paid": *New York Times,* 7/18/83.
160 "a bon-bon": Bjorkman, *Woody Allen on Woody Allen,* p. 132.
160 "the way I want it to be": *Chicago Sun-Times,* 7/11/82.
160 "is almost a ventriloquist": Andrew Sarris interview.
160 "a rank amateur": *New York Times,* 1/22/84.
160 "It's hard work": Farrow, *What Falls Away,* p. 202.
161 "easily his best-directed": *The New Republic,* 8/16–23/82.
161 "a sense of control": Stanley Kauffmann interview.
161 "Watching Woody": *Chicago Tribune,* 7/16/82.
161 "Little sex and less comedy": *National Review,* 9/17/82.
161 "tableaux that suggest": *The New Yorker,* 7/26/82.
162 "Therefore his sickness": Allen, *Three Films of Woody Allen,* p. 126.
162 "foolish": Saul Bellow to MM, 8/20/96.
162 "Next question": Carl Rollyson e-mail to MM, 5/27/98.
162 "we New York critics": Andrew Sarris interview.
163 "a brilliant cinematic collage": *Newsweek,* 7/18/83.
163 "utterly alone and lost": *The New Yorker,* 8/8/83.
163 "Say he's incredible": Patrice Chaplin, *Hidden Star, Oona O'Neill Chaplin: A Memoir,* Trafalgar Square, 1996, p. 186.

CHAPTER 11: *Pushing the Baby Cart*

165 "You've got to realize": *Chicago Sun-Times,* 7/11/82.
166 "I expected to walk": Lorrie Pierce interview.
166 "The pets, the cat": *Allen* v. *Farrow,* court testimony.
166 "cooing, cuddling": *New York Daily News,* 3/2/83.
167 "The drain is in the middle": Farrow, *What Falls Away,* p. 206.
168 "a gun under the bed": *Chicago Sun-Times,* 2/2/86.
168 "I hated it": *Movieline,* 1/8/87.
168 "I walked around": *Chicago Sun-Times,* 7/11/82.
170 "So we started tracking": *New York Daily News,* 4/17/84.
170 "they just went bananas": Nick Apollo Forte phone conversation with MM.
171 "a perfectionist": *Los Angeles Times,* 2/1/84.
171 "just couldn't get it": Bjorkman, *Woody Allen on Woody Allen,* p.147.
172 "she would be sued": Thierry de Navacelle, *Woody Allen on Location,* William Morrow, 1987, p. 188.

173 "in no remote way": Bjorkman, *Woody Allen on Woody Allen,* p. 148.
173 "there was just no part": *New York Times,* 2/24/85.
174 "one of the best movies": *Time,* 3/4/85.
174 "This is the first": *The New Yorker,* 3/25/85.
174 "I say a purple rose": *National Review,* 5/3/85.
174 "lit up the room": Bjorkman, *Woody Allen on Woody Allen,* p. 151.
174 "If you ask her": *New York Times,* 2/24/85.
174 "more interesting in other things": Andrew Sarris interview.
174 "love letters": Vincent Canby interview.
175 "And that was my life": *Interview* magazine, 4/94.
175 "Would you like to have children?": *Playboy,* 5/67.
175 "Mia has a talent": *New York Daily News Magazine,* 10/15/89.
176 "simply used passive-aggressive": Confidential source.
176 "I had no pronounced feeling": *Allen* v. *Farrow,* court testimony.
176 "I got a great thrill": *Allen* v. *Farrow,* court testimony.
176 But there was a problem: New York State has since modified its adoption laws. In 1995, the State Court of Appeals ruled on two cases: one in which a man was denied permission to adopt the biological child of his live-in partner and the other involving a lesbian couple. One of the women had been inseminated and had given birth, but the lower courts prohibited the adoption of the child by her partner. In both of these cases, the appeals court decided the second partner had the right to adopt the child of a person to whom he or she was not married. In the intervening years, however, there have been few second-parent adoptions, mostly by gay couples.
177 "a workable compromise": *Allen* v. *Farrow,* court testimony.
177 "She's a wonderful woman": Woody Allen, *Hannah and Her Sisters,* p. 106.
178 "a boozy old flirt": *New York Times,* 2/2/86.
179 "the apartment was chaotic": Jean Reynolds interview with MM.
180 "never had five minutes": *New York Times,* 3/26/86.
180 "a very wonderful person": *Louisville Courier Post,* 9/29/87.
180 "the great American film": *Village Voice,* 2/11/86.
180 "only authentic auteur" and "the urban poet": *New York Times,* 2/7/86 and 2/9/86.
180 "Woody Allen has found": *The New Yorker,* 3/9/87.
181 "What's left for Woody": *National Review,* 3/27/87.
181 "I think this may be": *Chicago Tribune,* 1/26/86.
181 "the Chicago morons": Farrow, *What Falls Away,* p. 222.
181 "If I had my way": *Chicago Tribune,* 1/26/86.
182 "a happy man": Ibid.

CHAPTER 12: Dead Sharks

183 "By you?": Lax, *Woody Allen,* p. 182.
183 "a second-rate actress": *Vanity Fair,* 11/92.
183 "a grand plan": *Time,* 8/31/92.
183 "just hated him": Kristi Groteke and Marjorie Rosen, *Mia and Woody: Love and Betrayal,* Carroll & Graf, 1994, p. 161.
183 "so of course Woody": *Newsweek,* 5/11/87.
183 "I don't think this relationship": *Allen* v. *Farrow,* court testimony.
184 "I hope it's a she": *New York Times,* 11/14/87.
184 "I love Dylan": *Movieline,* 1/8/88.
184 "not my idea of a fun Saturday": *60 Minutes,* 11/22/92.
185 "It's a healthy thing": *New York Times,* 7/18/83.
185 "He's a magpie": Walter Bernstein interview.
185 "I was numb": Eric Pleskow interview.

186 "This would make a great setting": *New York Times,* 12/6/87.
186 "that doesn't suggest anything": Ibid.
186 "We couldn't get copacetic": Ibid.
186 "Montana?": *The New Yorker,* 12/9/96.
187 "We were well into it": Elaine Stritch interview with MM.
187 "What is this": *National Review,* 3/4/88.
187 "as acute an author": *Chicago Sun-Times,* 12/18/87.
187 "that many people in America": Roger Ebert interview with MM.
187 "profoundly derivative": *The New Yorker,* 1/25/88.
187 "Allen's little Max von Sydow": *Washington Post,* 3/11/88.
188 "a pathetic, desperately imitative": *The New Republic,* 11/21/88.
188 "An homage is a plagiarism": *The New Yorker,* 10/31/88.
188 "Each person": *Paris Review,* Fall 1995.
188 "It was like a father": Lorrie Pierce interview.
189 "She was cute": Confidential source.
189 "played on the camera": George Schindler interview with MM.
189 "Look at that": Lorrie Pierce interview.
189 "She's a child": *Newsday,* 11/18/92.
189 "You look at her": *Allen* v. *Farrow,* court testimony.
190 "If there was a roomful": *New York* magazine, 9/21/92.
190 "wired": Lorrie Pierce interview.
191 "There is no justice": *National Review,* 12/8/89.
193 "he seems to have dedicated": *Washington Post,* 1/25/91.
193 "He gets wonderful performances": Sydney Pollack interview with MM.
193 "They [Woody and Robert Altman]": *Esquire,* 11/88.
193 "His silences": Elaine Stritch interview.
193 "He spoke to me": Marilyn Michaels interview with MM.
193 "I always admired": Max von Sydow to MM, 9/11/96.
194 "He would shoot": Confidential source.
194 "He kept telling me": *Newsweek,* 4/24/78.
194 "Big names": Confidential source.
194 "Do you believe it": Douglas Brode, *The Films of Woody Allen,* Carol Publishing, 1992, p. 279.
194 "a womanizer": *Ladies' Home Journal,* 3/80.
194 "No theatricality": Confidential source.
195 "After the first day": Karen Ludwig interview with MM.
195 "suddenly he didn't speak": Kitty Carlisle Hart interview with MM.
195 "A relationship I think": Allen, *Four Films of Woody Allen,* p. 93.
196 "The last time": Woody Allen, *The Illustrated Woody Allen Reader,* Linda Sunshine, ed., Knopf, 1993, p. 116.
196 "he was smitten": Confidential source.
196 "the floozy brigade": Confidential source.
196 "a friend to the older children": *New York Daily News Magazine,* 10/15/89.
196 "It was like a fairy tale": Confidential source.
196 "pleasant and convenient": *60 Minutes,* 11/22/92.
196 "Jack and I": *Husbands and Wives,* unpublished screenplay.
197 "but in the fearsome": *Variety,* 2/18/91.
198 "In intelligence": Lorrie Pierce interview.
198 "I want to be a girl": *Allen* v. *Farrow,* court testimony.
198 "The school had a fast rule": Confidential source.
198 "Mr. Allen, you're upsetting": *Newsday,* 8/15/92.
198 "spoilsport": *Allen* v. *Farrow,* court testimony, 3/26/93.
199 "he would creep up": *Allen* v. *Farrow,* court testimony.

199 "she carried on": Confidential source.

199 "I did not see it as sexual": *Allen* v. *Farrow,* court testimony. Also Wilk Decision.

199 "You can make an exception": Allen, *Four Films of Woody Allen,* p. 374.

200 "I didn't want some clerk": *Vanity Fair,* 11/92.

CHAPTER 13: *Sidney Kugelmass Meets His Biographers*

201 " 'After all,' he grunts": Allen, "The Kugelmass Episode," *The New Yorker,* 5/2/77, reprinted in *Side Effects,* Ballantine, 1980, p. 62.

201 "Cloquet hated reality": Allen, "The Condemned," *The New Yorker,* 11/21/77, reprinted in *Side Effects,* p. 13.

202 "a large and hairy": Ibid., p. 78.

202 "joyless, sexless": *Allen* v. *Farrow,* court testimony.

203 "You won't get anywhere": McKnight, *Woody Allen: Joking Aside,* p. 11.

204 "I was with him": *Chicago Tribune,* 5/24/87.

204 "I could fade": Dennis Kear interview with MM.

204 "I let him hang around": *Los Angeles Times,* 3/15/92.

204 "I can't imagine": Lax, *Woody Allen,* p. 182.

205 "churlish to nit-pick": *New York Times Book Review,* 5/12/91.

205 "a wealth of biographical detail": *Film Quarterly,* Fall 92.

205 "I, of course, felt": *Los Angeles Times,* 3/15/92.

205 "both Vietnamese orphan girls": Lax, *Woody Allen,* p. 180.

206 "Kids are probably": *Photoplay,* 11/71.

206 "I was in a lot": *Interview* magazine, 4/94.

207 "a double-digit IQ": *Newsweek,* 8/31/92.

207 "She *was* a little slow": Confidential source.

207 "she worked damned hard": Groteke and Rosen, *Mia and Woody,* p. 161.

207 "I'm the one": Lorrie Pierce interview.

207 "[The children] are very close": *McCall's,* 5/85.

208 "I had no relationship": Groteke and Rosen, *Mia and Woody,* p. 161.

208 "He was never": *Newsweek,* 8/31/92.

208 "He was a 12-year boyfriend": Ibid.

208 "He is a stable influence": *New York* magazine, 9/21/92.

208 "She was someone": *Allen* v. *Farrow,* court testimony.

208 "She went gaga": Groteke and Rosen, *Mia and Woody,* p.161.

208 "growing up": Confidential source.

209 "curl your teeth": *Allen* v. *Farrow,* court testimony.

209 "When I came back": Dominick Conde interview with MM.

209 "Oh I know": *New York Post,* 2/8/90.

210 "she has a crush": *Allen* v. *Farrow,* court testimony.

210 "I'm dating a girl": Allen, *Four Films of Woody Allen,* p. 185.

210 "Well what do you do": *Allen* v. *Farrow,* court testimony.

211 "I told her she needed": Frances Grill interview with MM.

211 "Soon-Yi had always been rather plain": Lorrie Pierce interview.

211 "A mom couldn't dream": *Newsweek,* 8/31/92.

212 "We were both": *Allen* v. *Farrow,* court testimony.

212 "a not terribly uncommon problem": "Retribution," *The Kenyon Review,* Summer 1980, reprinted in *Side Effects,* 1980.

212 "We started talking": *Allen* v. *Farrow,* court testimony.

212 "She was sallow": Confidential source.

213 "She took off her braces": *New York Daily News,* 8/24/92.

213 "charming and intelligent": *People,* 9/7/92.

CHAPTER 14: *The Coiled Cobra*

215 "a very, very chilling": *60 Minutes,* 11/22/92.
215 "Once my heart was one": *Newsday,* 11/18/92.
215 "quite frightening": *60 Minutes,* 11/22/92.
216 "the degree of pain": *Allen* v. *Farrow,* court testimony.
216 "I'm a bad girl": Farrow, *What Falls Away,* p. 284.
216 "The person sleeping": *Allen* v. *Farrow,* court testimony.
216 "I just pounced": Ibid.
216 "in constant contact": Ibid.
216 "Stop asking me": Farrow, *What Falls Away,* p. 293.
216 "Let's burn them": Ibid., p. 295.
217 "screwing one of my kids": Ibid., p. 282.
217 "I always thought": *New York* magazine, 9/21/92.
217 "like someone who was out": *New York Daily News,* 8/24/92.
217 "Many times she threatened": *60 Minutes,* 11/22/92.
218 "She was hard": Confidential source.
218 "She was never religious": *60 Minutes,* 11/22/92.
219 "REEL-LIFE STARS": *New York Daily News,* 3/10/92.
219 "berserk screaming crazy": *Vanity Fair,* 11/92.
219 "We are certainly empathizing": *Oprah Winfrey Show,* 2/11/97.
220 "Well, you kind of go": *The Tonight Show,* 12/17/91.
220 "the flip side": *The New Republic,* 4/20/92.
221 "not significant": Bjorkman, *Woody Allen on Woody Allen,* p. 192.
221 "and no weekend relaxation": *New York Post,* 8/15/96.
222 "I reported that Woody": Richard Johnson interview with MM.
222 "The first thing she said": Hans Weise interview with MM.
224 "things had gotten really crazy": Confidential source.
224 "seemed to be her primary": *Allen* v. *Farrow,* decision.
225 "a household of enemies": *60 Minutes,* 11/22/92.
225 "Woody no goody": Groteke and Rosen, *Mia and Woody,* p. 193.
225 "rot in hell": *Newsday,* 11/18/92.
225 "Daddy, don't forget": *Esquire,* 10/94.
225 "something very disturbing": "Mia Farrow: A Life of Drama," A&E, 3/12/98.

CHAPTER 15: *What the Heart Wants*

227 "Did Woody have his face": Farrow, *What Falls Away,* p. 299.
227 "like a pig": Confidential source.
228 "I'm doing a sociological study": *Bananas,* unpublished screenplay.
228 "I figured": *Hartford Courant,* 3/31/96.
228 investigation: According to *What Falls Away,* p. 307, the police found hair samples in Mia Farrow's attic that were microscopically similar to Woody's.
229 "an adult, healthy relationship": *Newsday,* 4/20/93.
229 "there has never been any suggestion": *Allen* v. *Farrow,* court testimony.
230 "a normal paternal thing": Ibid.
230 "You took my daughter": *60 Minutes,* 11/22/92.
230 "a call out of the blue": Hal Davis interview with MM; also *New York* magazine, 9/21/92.
231 "Mr. Allen has never": *New York Post,* 8/14/92.
231 "Her hysteria and terror": Groteke and Rosen, *Mia and Woody,* p. 143.
231 "a kind of mediator": *Newsday,* 4/17/93.
231 "needed a defender": *Newsday,* 4/18/93. In 1986, when the Klaus von Bulow story was being filmed *(Reversal of Fortune),* Alan Dershowitz wanted Woody to play his own char-

acter. Woody, amused and flattered, replied, "Well, I'm a comedian and it sounds like it would be fun. But I don't know if I could do it justice—no pun intended." (*The National Law Journal*, 7/21/86) Dershowitz was portrayed by Ron Silver.

231 "a desperate and evil man": *New York Daily News,* 8/16/92.
232 "a lovely, intelligent": *New York Post,* 8/18/92.
232 "a very nice guy": *Newsday,* 8/18/92.
232 "assiduously avoided publicity": *New York Times,* 8/19/92.
233 "What's Woody's latest flick?": *New York Post,* 8/20/92.
233 "The question most people": *Newsweek,* 8/31/92.
233 "The heart wants": *Time,* 8/31/92.
233 "The heart has its reasons": Blaise Pascal, *Pensees*—iv. 277.
233 "Woodenhead Allen": *New York Post,* 8/28/92.
233 "When all of it": *People,* 9/7/92.
233 "He couldn't imagine": Walter Bernstein interview.
234 " 'Whoa,' he whistled": Dominick Conde interview.
234 No wonder confused readers: Many people continued to lump Woody's behavior with Joey Buttafuoco's, contributing to the impression that Woody, too, had sex with an underage girl. According to New York state law, the age of consent is seventeen. Amy Fisher had been sixteen when she first had sex with Buttafuoco, and therefore was plainly a victim of statutory rape, for which Buttafuoco would serve six months in prison. Soon-Yi, over eighteen, was legally a consenting adult. Still, these differences were swept under the rug. Probably confusion rose from the fact that nobody was 100 percent certain about her age, not even Soon-Yi.
234 "a nice girl": *New York Post,* 8/26/92.
234 "not for their needs": *Time,* 8/31/92.
234 "Child molestation's a touchy subject": Allen, *Hannah and Her Sisters,* p. 30.
235 "I don't consider you": *Allen* v. *Farrow,* trial exhibit.
235 "Moses would get very angry": Confidential source.
235 "Mia was going": Confidential source.
235 "has no morals": 1992 television news clip, aired on the *Oprah Winfrey Show,* 2/11/97.
235 "They were nervous": Andrea Peyser interview with MM.
236 "a remarkable mother": *New York Post,* 8/20/92.
236 "degrading" and "unbelievable": Bookspan and Yockey, *Andre Previn: A Biography,* p. 252–253.
236 "Let's not get hysterical": *Newsweek,* 9/31/92.
236 "little to do": *Time,* 8/31/92.
237 "stunned": Andrea Peyser interview.
237 "I don't want to talk": *New York Post,* 8/20/92.
237 "she was used to publicity": *Newsday,* 8/25/92.
237 "Now you want little girls": *Allen* v. *Farrow,* trial exhibit.
239 "Lots of people": *New York Times,* 8/16/95.
239 "Look, I've only spent": *New York Times,* 12/20/92.
239 "Choosing him": Raoul Felder interview with MM.
239 "For all intent": *New York Post,* 8/18/92.

241 "It was a huge story": Victoria Gordon conversation with MM.
241 "What about the way": *60 Minutes,* 11/22/92.
241 "He was very organized": Steven Kroft interview with MM.
242 "Her style of mothering": Confidential source.
242 "There was something awful": John Simon interview.
242 "The press depicted": Roger Ebert interview.

243 "I don't care": *New York Post*, 12/4/92.
243 "We knew enough": Confidential source.
243 "I screwed up": *Allen* v. *Farrow*, court testimony.
243 "I'm so sick": Groteke and Rosen, *Mia and Woody*, p. 223.
243 "If you asked her": Confidential source.
244 "Satch and Dylan": Confidential source.
244 "What are sex perverts?": *New York Times*, 8/6/72.
244 "stacked in favor": *New York Post*, 2/19/97.
245 "would save on cleaning": *New York Law Journal*, 5/4/93.
245 "asked sharp questions": Ibid.
245 "His reputation": Confidential source.
245 "a starfucker": Confidential source.
246 "I'm going to break": *New York Post*, 1/13/93.
246 "lying together": *Allen* v. *Farrow*, affidavit.
246 "Great, the wilder": *Chicago Tribune*, 3/24/93.
247 "They played it dirty": *New York Post*, 11/6/95.
247 "He acted in a rude fashion": *New York Times*, 2/11/93.
247 "I concluded that abuse": Farrow, *What Falls Away*, p. 311.
248 "Let him have *60 Minutes*": *New York Daily News*, 3/21/93.
248 "Jane was very special": Confidential source.
248 "an indelible black": *Vanity Fair*, 11/92.
249 "open for about one second": *New York Times*, 8/25/96.
249 "Whatever we do": Douglas McGrath interviewed by Neil Rosen, New School for Social Research, 12/8/97.
249 "sleep through and awaken": *Chicago Tribune*, 1/26/86.
249 "concocted or imagined": Report, Child Sexual Abuse Clinic, Yale–New Haven Hospital, quoted in *New York Times*, 5/4/93.
250 "Ms. Farrow has had a very disturbed": Ibid., quoted in *Newsday*, 3/19/93.
250 "But so deep": *New York Daily News*, 3/21/93.
250 "always stand by": *Chicago Tribune*, 3/19/93.
250 "I think Dylan": Ibid.
250 "grossly inappropriate": *Hartford Courant*, 12/7/96.
251 "A pall has fallen": *New York Post*, 8/21/92.
251 "too burdensome": *New York Daily News*, 8/24/92.
251 "the burden of guilt": *New York Daily News*, 3/21/93.

CHAPTER 17: *Allen* v. *Farrow*

254 "a short thing": *Allen* v. *Farrow*, court testimony.
255 "I could have put her socks": *Allen* v. *Farrow*, court testimony.
255 "silliness": Raoul Felder interview.
256 "gets into people's heads": *Newsday*, 3/24/93.
256 "because she begged me": *Allen* v. *Farrow*, court testimony.
256 "totally in character": Hal Davis interview.
256 "very funny": Joan Ullman interview with MM.
257 "Do you have an opinion": *Allen* v. *Farrow*, court testimony.
257 "It's a classic case": *Vanity Fair*, 11/92.
257 "His savagery toward women": Vivian Gornick interview.
257 "Have I talked": *Newsday*, 9/16/92.
257 "I think Mia": *New York Post*, 1/7/93.
257 "He's treated": *Vanity Fair*, 11/92.
258 "When people ask me": Elliott Mills interview.
258 "disappear by scrunching": *New York Times*, 3/25/93.

258 "At first people believed": Joan Ullman interview.
258 "Her affect was studied": Andrea Peyser interview.
258 "Under New York law": Hal Davis interview.
258 "She eats bullets": *USA Today,* 4/20/93.
259 "Andre is my new daddy": Groteke and Rosen, *Mia and Woody,* p. 194.
259 "I can't stand it": Ibid., p. 231.
260 "bring on the Woody": Richard Ross, *A Day in Part 15,* Four Walls Eight Windows Press, 1997, p. 75.
260 "played games and colored": *Allen* v. *Farrow,* court testimony.
260 "a scullery maid": *Allen* v. *Farrow,* court testimony.
261 "soldiers and pawns": *Allen* v. *Farrow,* court testimony.
261 "It's magical": *Husbands and Wives,* unpublished screenplay.
261 "trust his insight": *New York Post,* 3/14/95.
261 "Mr. Allen has demonstrated": Decision, Supreme Court: New York County, Individual Assignment Part 6, Index No. 68738/92. Woody Allen, Petitioner, against Maria Villiers Farrow, also known as Mia Farrow, Respondent.
262 "self-absorbed, untrustworthy": Ibid.
262 "just about lost the case": Raoul Felder interview.
263 "Phyllis Gangel-Jacob": Hal Davis interview.
263 "didn't take into account": Andrea Peyser interview.
263 "We won!": *New York Times,* 6/8/93.
263 "I'm thrilled": Ibid.
263 "People just irresponsibly": *Esquire,* 10/94.
264 "an enormous hit": *New York Times,* 6/8/93.
264 "No one can mistreat Mia": *McCall's,* 5/67.
264 "Custody went to Mia": *New York Times,* 6/16/93.
264 "Why did he bring": *New York Times,* 8/16/95.
265 "For so many, many months": *New York Times,* 6/8/93.

CHAPTER 18: *Second Law of Thermodynamics*

267 "a fact both had freely": Farrow, *What Falls Away,* p. 330.
267 "He'll hound them": *New York Post,* 6/9/93.
267 "a lovely little note": Stephen Silverman interview.
268 "they know tenth hand": *Rolling Stone,* 9/93.
268 "the stupidest thing": *Esquire,* 10/94.
269 "It's the second law": *Husbands and Wives,* unpublished screenplay.
269 "This was no time": *New York Times,* 9/25/93.
270 "a vindictive mother": Ibid.
270 "Because this is being taped": Press conference transcript, quoted in Groteke and Rosen, *Mia and Woody,* p. 263.
270 "if Woody puts Maco": *New York Times,* 10/14/93.
271 "I love you": *Woody Allen, Petitioner-Appellant v. Maria Villiers Farrow, Respondent,* Supreme Court, Appellant Div., 611 N.Y.S. 2d 859 (A.D. Dept. 1994).
271 "I'm supposed to say": Ibid.
271 "Was she wondering": *New York Daily News,* 3/21/93.
271 "it interferes with Dylan's individual treatment": Decision, Supreme Court: New York County, Individual Assignment Part 6, Index No. 68738/92. Woody Allen, Petitioner, against Maria Villiers Farrow, also known as Mia Farrow, Respondent.
271 "Woody Allen touched": Groteke and Rosen, *Mia and Woody,* p. 253.
271 "pattern of extreme bias": *New York Post,* 8/26/97.
272 "I do it seven days": *New York Times,* 1/2/98.
272 "the nonshooting section": *Esquire,* 10/94.

272 "I went seeking Solomon": *New York* magazine, 10/17/94.

272 "just not up to the case": London *Times*, 2/15/97.

272 "I don't trust him": *New York Post*, 3/13/95.

272 "a harsh, punitive decision": Confidential source.

273 "Whatever hell was created": *New York Times*, 11/2/95.

273 "They rain all this": *Spin*, 1/98.

273 "a genuine love": *The New Yorker*, 12/9/96.

274 "kid who was eating": *Wild Man Blues*, documentary, 1998.

274 "never read anything": *New York Times*, 4/19/98.

274 "long and tedious": Ibid.

275 "She's very clear": Ibid.

275 "a punishment": *Wild Man Blues*.

275 "sue her for the rest": *New York Daily News*, 3/7/96.

275 "This used to be a joyous place": *New York Times*, 5/8/94.

276 "I've never paid": *Shadows and Fog*, unpublished screenplay.

276 "continuation of the relationship": *Woody Allen, Petitioner-Appellant v. Maria Villiers Farrow, Respondent,* Supreme Court, Appellant Div., 611 N.Y.S. 2d 859 (A.D. Dept. 1994).

277 "a couple of million": *New York Daily News*, 3/21/93.

CHAPTER 19: *The Cost of Running Amok*

279 "There is no question": "Examining Psychic Phenomena," *The New Yorker*, 10/7/72, reprinted in *Without Feathers*, Random House, 1975, p. 7.

279 "radioactive because the jokes": William Tully conversation with MM.

279 "my Woody Allen": Groteke and Rosen, *Mia and Woody*, p. 244.

279 "a hateful creature": *Newsday*, 3/24/93.

279 "an infomercial": *New York Times*, 10/1/95.

279 "It's the public": *Newsday*, 12/1/96.

279 "I'm the one": *New York Times*, 11/2/95.

280 "How do you expect": *San Francisco Examiner*, 2/6/95.

280 "For the French": *Hollywood Reporter*, 1/20/98.

280 "Not only is there no God": Allen, "My Philosophy," *The New Yorker*, 12/27/69, reprinted in *Getting Even*, p. 31.

280 "I must call Tom Cruise": *Esquire*, 10/94.

281 "Just stop the book!": *Minneapolis Star Tribune*, 4/25/94.

282 his fascination with sisters: *New York Times*, 1/19/86.

282 "which she was": Marjorie Rosen interview with MM.

282 "Do people say that": *W*, 12/95.

282 "People were really sick": Marjorie Rosen interview.

282 "All over Hollywood": Confidential source.

283 "can put his career in an envelope": *Time*, 8/31/92.

283 "I seriously considered": *New York Times*, 11/2/95.

283 "therapy": *Philadelphia Inquirer*, 12/21/97.

284 "Our deal with Woody": *Newsday*, 7/26/93.

284 "wrap fish in it": *Hollywood Reporter*, 9/23/94.

285 "I love the idea": *Rolling Stone*, 9/93.

285 "Nobody wants to be involved": *Los Angeles Times*, 7/28/93.

285 "The story is": Ibid.

285 "Conceivably I can see myself": *Take One*, 11/78.

286 "I'd be thrilled": *New York Times*, 6/1/98.

286 "Of course he allowed it": Confidential source.

286 "He was cheap": Confidential source.

287 "She belongs in the kitchen": Confidential source.

287 "dressed to the teeth": Ibid.
287 "elevator music": *Rolling Stone,* 4/9/87.
288 "television had improved": *Newsday,* 7/18/94.
288 "I thought he owes": *Hollywood Reporter,* 9/23/24.
288 "If I can think": *Playbill,* 4/95.
289 "a very personal account": Michael Blakemore conversation with MM.
289 "manic-depressive cycles": *The New Yorker,* 6/3/96.
290 "not being a New Yorker": Michael Blakemore conversation.
290 "People think God knows what": *Newsday,* 12/1/96.
291 "It's terrible!": *The New Yorker,* 12/9/96.
291 "the Knicks play": *New York* magazine, 4/6/98.
292 "Everybody kind of embraced": *New York Times,* 10/1/95.
292 "good genes": *New York Daily News,* 10/20/95.
292 "Hello?": *Mighty Aphrodite,* unpublished screenplay.
292 "feeds into the message": *All Things Considered,* National Public Radio, 10/27/95.
292 "recapture" . . . "bloodshed": *Hartford Courant,* 6/6/97.
293 "it would take a heart": *Chicago Sun-Times,* 4/22/98.
293 "He's not funny": *Sneak Previews,* 12/8/96.
295 "were never any good": *Newsday,* 12/1/96.

CHAPTER 20: *Getting Even*

297 "hated and feared": *New York Daily News,* 12/6/96.
297 "little understanding": *New York Post,* 12/6/96.
297 "terrible": *London Evening Standard,* 3/12/96.
299 "an incredible piece of work": *Los Angeles Times,* 11/19/95.
299 "wouldn't take it easy": *Entertainment Weekly,* 2/23/96.
299 "30 minutes went by": *New York Times,* 4/19/98.
300 "Just one more time": *Wild Man Blues,* documentary, 1998.
300 "the only Woody Allen film": *Newsweek,* 4/13/98.
300 "while he is a better clarinetist": *London Independent,* 3/19/96.
301 "You should let them all know": *Wild Man Blues,* documentary, 1998.
301 "He needs people": *Newsday,* 8/29/97.
301 "Look at this engraving": *Wild Man Blues,* documentary, 1998.
302 "No one will be interested": *Vanity Fair,* 4/98.
302 "Very entertaining": *The Guardian,* 5/7/98.
303 "the best performance": Stanley Kauffmann interview.
303 "a blatant attempt": *New York Post,* 4/17/98.
303 "seems more like the adult": *Chicago Sun-Times,* 5/15/98.
303 "She's able to be": *The Guardian,* 5/7/98.
303 "telling the story of O.J.": William Luhr conversation with MM.
303 "Does Soon-Yi miss": *Marie Claire,* 12/98.
304 "What is the meaning": *New York Post,* 12/13/95.
306 "very limited, very flawed": *Mirabella,* 3/4/97.
307 "I have never had that obsession": *Rolling Stone,* 7/1/76.
307 "always detested Woody": *New York* magazine, 10/21/96.
308 "A nasty shallow": *The New Yorker,* 12/9/96.
308 "Doesn't he look like a cadaver": Personal observation, audience conversation, 92nd Street Y, 7/25/96.
308 "We even use": Confidential source.
309 "I don't spend": *20/20,* 2/7/97.
309 "Very quickly I learned": Speech delivered at American Booksellers Association convention, 6/96.

309 "shouting distortions": Ibid.
309 "You can't control life": Allen, *Four Films of Woody Allen,* p. 335.
310 "We don't care": Confidential source.
310 "book-lined and flower-filled": *The New Yorker,* 12/9/96.
310 "It was comfortable": Ibid.
311 "close friends with Louise": *Newsday,* 12/1/96.
311 "Many times": *Chicago Sun-Times,* 2/2/86.
311 "There was so much collagen": Confidential source.
312 "the first love": *New York Post,* 5/16/98.
312 "solicit sympathy": *New York Times Book Review,* 2/23/97.
312 "a pathologically indiscreet": London *Sunday Telegraph,* 2/16/97.
312 "Should a 50-year-old": London *Sunday Times,* 2/16/97.
312 "Mix Old Grandad": *The Tonight Show,* 3/17/97.
312 "white O. J. Simpson": *Politically Incorrect,* 7/97.
313 "Ms. Previn, do you have": *The New Yorker,* 5/19/97.
313 "now she's responsible": *The Oprah Winfrey Show,* 2/11/97.
313 "Not interested": *New York Daily News,* 10/5/97.

CHAPTER 21: *"Help"*

315 "As far as I'm concerned": *McCall's,* 5/67.
315 "Love is pretty strong": *Photoplay,* 11/71.
316 "very, very happy": *New York Post,* 12/26/97.
316 "This really is quite": *New York Post,* 1/6/98.
317 "I'll tell you": *London Daily Telegraph,* reprinted in *Vanity Fair,* 12/98.
317 "happiness is just a girl": *New York Daily News,* 12/25/97.
317 "He's 62": *The Tonight Show,* 12/30/97.
317 "few pleasures": *The Late Show with David Letterman,* 12/29/97.
317 "he needs a psychiatrist": *New York Post,* 12/25/97.
317 "She's his ball": Confidential source.
317 "the Duke and Duchess": *New York Times,* 12/25/97.
318 "to get past a little crisis": *Time Out,* 12/4–11/97.
318 "Did you need it": Andrew Duncan interview with MM.
318 "one more year": Allen, *Four Films of Woody Allen,* p. 36.
318 "The guy finally": Allen, *The Illustrated Woody Allen Reader,* p. 124.
318 "a neutral factor": *New York Observer,* 11/30/98.
319 "He didn't need a scandal": Andrew Sarris interview.
319 "one long diatribe": *New York Times,* 2/8/98.
319 "Joan in a heavy make-out": *Los Angeles Times,* 12/14/97.
319 "Beth Kramer's": *Deconstructing Harry,* unpublished screenplay.
319 "got a film": *New York Times,* 12/14/97.
319 "Here's a guy": Neil Rosen interview.
320 "You know": *New York Daily News,* 11/15/98.
320 "They're probably ashamed": *New York Observer,* 11/30/98.
320 "I grew up with Woody": Andrew Sarris interview.
321 "diluted": *New York Times,* 6/1/98.
321 "Completely irresponsible": *Indie* magazine, 9–10/98.
321 "In today's American": *Newsweek,* 7/20/98.
321 "Working with Woody": *New York Post,* 7/2/98.

EPILOGUE: *Victim of an Irregular Verb*

323   "Who else has written": Vincent Canby interview.
323   "Guilt is petty": *Bullets Over Broadway,* unpublished screenplay.
323   "There are some things": Andrew Sarris interview.
324   "it was the kind of escalating": Roger Ebert interview.
324   "How can you debate": John Simon interview.
324   "He's written": Stanley Kauffmann interview.
325   "We were standing": Lawrence Schwartzwald interview with MM.
326   "I went as far": *New York Daily News,* 11/15/98.
326   "It's not my personality": Ibid.
326   "When I introduce them": London *Sunday Times,* 7/25/99.
326   "a supermother": *Marie Claire,* 12/98.
326   "I don't know how": *Atlanta Journal-Constitution,* 5/10/99.
327   "I have a son": *New York Post,* 5/11/99.
327   "an old pedophile": Ibid.
327   "I'm very compartmentalized": *Staten Island Advance,* 12/29/97.
327   "But we define ourselves": Allen, *The Illustrated Woody Allen Reader,* p. 198.

POSTSCRIPT

329   "We were happy": McKnight, *Woody Allen: Joking Aside,* p. 104.
329   "a small woman": Tim Carroll interview with MM.
329   "and always will": *New York Post,* 3/5/97.
330   "a lot about music": *New York Post,* 1/7/93.
330   "if I could possibly": *New York* magazine, 4/4/93.
330   "That is a closed chapter": *Vanity Fair,* 9/98.
331   "What happened": Nick Apollo Forte phone conversation with MM.
331   "a bad judgment": *Los Angeles Times,* 6/12/93.
331   "wasn't crazy": Vincent Canby interview.

ACKNOWLEDGMENTS

The biographer who decides to write about a person who is still alive cannot help fantasizing. Might not the subject be willing to answer a few elementary questions about his life and work? Or, at the very least, contribute an entertaining family anecdote? If not, there are bound to be plenty of friends and colleagues with meaningful experiences to relate. And should all else fail, the biographer may even glimpse the subject in a smiling pose at a social event or chatting on late-night television with Charlie Rose.

In reality, living subjects by no means welcome the idea of a stranger, uninvited, rooting around in their personal affairs. Accustomed to a hard-won position in the driver's seat, they are more likely to rebuff offers to reminisce. Instead, they warn friends and relatives not to talk. They fire off churlish letters to the *New York Times Book Review.* They phone their attorneys with complaints of victimization, and sometimes, in desperation, they appoint an official biographer. Having spent their professional lives trying to attract attention, they suddenly wish to be left alone.

As I soon realized, however, the live subject's lack of enthusiasm is not a handicap but a blessing. Writing anyone's life story is laborious enough without having to relate to the subject too. Therefore, foremost among the many people to whom I am indebted is Woody Allen himself. Mr. Allen's disapproval compelled me to dig harder and deeper to unearth minutiae from his sixty-four years, particularly to seek out people who had direct knowledge of him but had never been interviewed before. This book would have been shorter had he decided to "help" me.

The names of those who chose to discuss with me the part they personally played in Woody Allen's story are listed in the notes. They allowed me countless hours of their time over lunches, in their homes and offices, or talking on the phone.

I regret that I can give no more than a mention to others who were equally generous in sharing their recollections: Bella Abzug, Conrad Bain, Bruce Baron, Marty Bregman, Mel Bourne, Barbara Boyle, Stan Cardinet, Tim Carroll, Irene Copeland, Prudence Crowther, Marion Dougherty, Daren Firestone, Al Franken, Harriet Garber, Baylis Glascock, Hazel Greenberg, Stuart Hample, Margo Howard, Bill Irwin, Coleman Jacoby, Dennis Kear, Norberto Kerner, Ruth Kravette, John Kuney, Ruth Last, Martha LoMonaco, Judith Malina, Ernest Mitler, Julius Moshinsky, Joshua Peck, Marvin Peisner, Anthony Picciano, Dorothy Rabinoff, Leah Reisman, Amelia Rollyson, Jeanne Safer, Naomi Diamond Sachs, Steve Sands, Barbara Shack, Stephen Spignesi, Jules Spodek, and Jeff Weingrad.

For various types of research and tips, I must thank Louise Bernikow, Myron Brenton, Marlene Coburn, Don DeLillo, Clyde Gilmour, Amy Goldberger, John Haber, Don Harrell, Tony Hiss, Jeff Hoffman, Ted Klein, Herb Leibowitz, Michael Martinez, Angela Miller, Patricia Parmalee, Matthew Ross, Roselle Salzano, Victor Sidhu, Brian Skene, Richard Stern, Sue Terry, Pamela Turner, Philip Turner, Ben Yagoda, and Susan Yankowitz.

In gathering nearly four decades' worth of clippings, I received assistance from Liz Campochiaro, Mary Epifanio, Peggy Sprague, and Nelson Winters. Both Charles Stecy and Bob Borgen gave me access to their excellent clipping collections stretching back to the 1960s.

For genealogical research, I relied on the expertise of Laurie Thompson.

Acknowledgments

I am indebted to the talented professionals associated with many institutions and archives: Julio Hernandez-Delgado at Hunter College Library Archives, Wendy Keys and Rosemary Hawkins of the Film Society of Lincoln Center, Paul Kerr at BBC-TV, Rachel Gottlieb at the *Hartford Courant,* Kendall Crilly at Yale University Music Library, Wendy Shay at the National Museum of American History, Margaret Sherry from Princeton University Library, Charles Silver at the Museum of Modern Art Film Library, Harold Miller at the State Historical Society of Wisconsin, the staffs of the New York Public Library Rare Book and Manuscript Library and the Billy Rose Theatre Collection at Lincoln Center and the Academy of Motion Picture Arts and Sciences, Karen Mix at Boston University Mugar Memorial Library, the staff of the Robert F. Wagner Labor Archives at New York University, Jonathan Rosenthal of the Museum of Television & Radio, Michael Shulman at Sygma Photo News, Ron and Howard Mandelbaum at Photofest, Larry Schwartz at Archive Photos, Rosa Di Salvo at Liaison, and Ken Podsada at Star File.

In the last several years I have spoken at length to many individuals about Woody Allen. I would like to single out for special gratitude the editor Carol Southern, who initially offered me encouragement to write this book over breakfast one morning at Sarabeth's Kitchen in the fall of 1995.

Throughout my research, one of the people who gave most freely of her time was Carole Chazin, the documentary filmmaker. Thanks as well to my old friends Janet Gardner and Minda Novek, who also taught me a great deal about documentaries.

As always, my good friends and colleagues at the New York University Biography Seminar provided unwavering interest and support, in particular Barbara Foster, Diane Jacobs, Brenda Wineapple, Kenneth Silverman, Nancy Dougherty, Judith Hennessee, Sydney Stern, Ann Waldron, Judy Feiffer, Amanda Vaill, and William Luhr.

For friendship and wise counsel when the road seemed endless, I have again depended on Dorothy Herrmann, Carole Klein, Lisa Paddock, and Carl Rollyson.

In London I was skillfully represented by Bill Hamilton, Andrew Nurnberg, and Anna Chodakowska, who worked hard on behalf of this project.

To my American and British editors, deepest thanks for guiding my work. At Scribner, Jane Rosenman was a patient and caring editor whose enthusiasm for the project was invaluable throughout and whose sage judgment helped to refine the material. At Weidenfeld & Nicolson, Ion Trewin was enormously helpful as a witty and astute sounding board. Thanks, also, to his resourceful assistant Rachel Leyshon.

I have the good fortune to have as my literary agent Lois Wallace, whose friendship and support over the years have meant so much to me, and whose perceptive criticism never dulls. Her contributions to this book—apart from her eagerness to accompany me on field trips to Michael's Pub and the Café Carlyle—are on every page.

Most of all I thank my daughter Alison Sprague, who was always there when I needed her, and whose observations as a youthful Woody Allen fan added immeasurably to my understanding.

INDEX

Index

Index

Index

Index

LINCC

Plant City